The New Arab Revolt

COUNCIL on
FOREIGN
RELATIONS

The Council on Foreign Relations (CFR) is an independent, nonpartisan membership organization, think tank, and publisher dedicated to being a resource for its members, government officials, business executives, journalists, educators and students, civic and religious leaders, and other interested citizens in order to help them better understand the world and the foreign policy choices facing the United States and other countries. Founded in 1921, CFR carries out its mission by maintaining a diverse membership, with special programs to promote interest and develop expertise in the next generation of foreign policy leaders; convening meetings at its headquarters in New York and in Washington, DC, and other cities where senior government officials, members of Congress, global leaders, and prominent thinkers come together with CFR members to discuss and debate major international issues; supporting a Studies Program that fosters independent research, enabling CFR scholars to produce articles, reports, and books and hold roundtables that analyze foreign policy issues and make concrete policy recommendations; publishing *Foreign Affairs*, the preeminent journal on international affairs and U.S. foreign policy; sponsoring Independent Task Forces that produce reports with both findings and policy prescriptions on the most important foreign policy topics; and providing up-to-date information and analysis about world events and American foreign policy on its website, www.cfr.org.

The Council on Foreign Relations takes no institutional positions on policy issues and has no affiliation with the U.S. government. All views expressed in its publications and on its website are the sole responsibility of the author or authors.

For further information about CFR or this publication, please write to the Council on Foreign Relations, 58 East 68th Street, New York, NY 10065, or call Communications at 212.434.9888. Visit CFR's website, www.cfr.org.

Contents

THE CRACKS SPREAD

INTERVENTION IN LIBYA

DOCUMENTS

Contents

The Middle East and North Africa

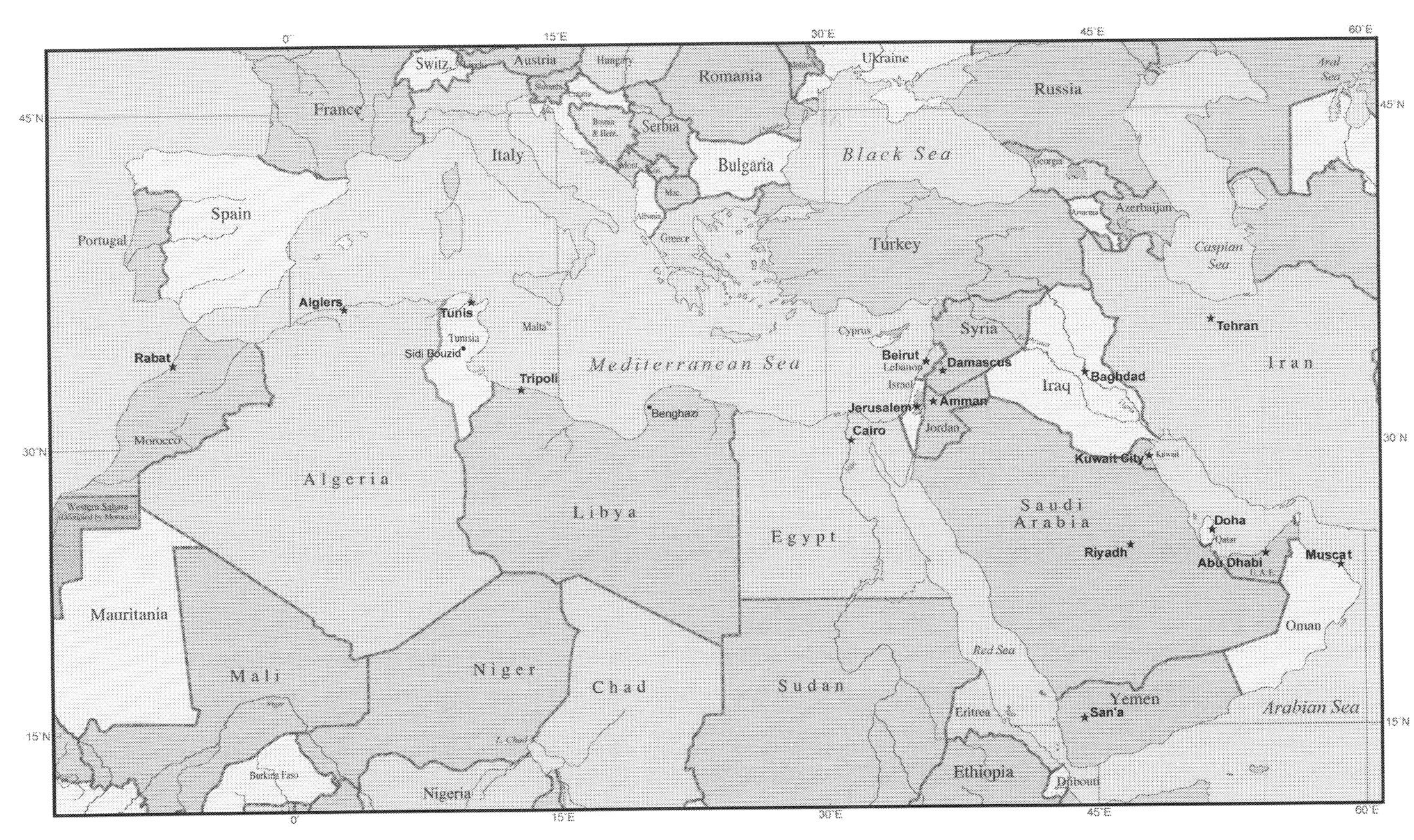

Introduction

Gideon Rose

In late April 1974, a group of young military officers in Portugal launched a coup against Marcello Caetano, their country's aging dictator. Within days, the old regime was gone, and after eighteen months of political turmoil, Portugal was on its way to freedom. Thus began what scholars came to call "the third wave" of global democratization—an extraordinary movement that galvanized the political development of region after region. In the decades that followed, dozens of countries with all kinds of authoritarian political systems—monarchies, oligarchies, military dictatorships, one-party regimes—shifted into the democratic camp. As most of the world was transformed, however, one area remained frozen in time: the Arab Middle East.

While other countries surged forward (and sometimes backward again), the Arab world stuck to its guns—quite literally, as regimes from North Africa to the Persian Gulf used all the tools at their disposal, including force, to suppress discontent and cling to power. They were so successful, in fact, that eventually their very obduracy became the story, and a generation of scholarship emerged to explain the phenomenon of "authoritarian persistence" in the region. Revolutionary idealism curdled into brutal cynicism; economic development stalled; hopeful republics turned into family kleptocracies. Year after year, decade after decade, a lot happened in the Middle East, but little changed.

Until now.

On December 17, 2010, a policewoman confiscated the unlicensed vegetable cart of a twenty-six-year-old street vendor, Mohamed Bouazizi, in the small Tunisian city of Sidi Bouzid. Humiliated by his abuse and exasperated by his inability to get redress, Bouazizi went to a local government building, doused himself with gasoline, and lit himself on fire. Setting off a combustible mixture of economic despair, social frustration, and political yearning throughout the region, in the weeks and months afterward the flames consumed not only Bouazizi—who died on January 4, 2011—but the regimes of Tunisian president Zine El Abidine Ben Ali, Egyptian president Hosni Mubarak, and quite likely others to come.

Why did this happen? Why now? What does it mean, and what comes next? Nobody really knows, of course. The smart money, such as it was, didn't think Tunisia was on the verge of an eruption, didn't think the upheaval would spread from Tunisia to Egypt, didn't think the shocks would reverberate around the Middle East. The old regimes themselves were taken aback by the force and speed of the uprisings, and even traditional opposition parties were behind the curve, often remaining hesitant well after newer popular protest movements sprang up and seized the moment—with the help of social media and communications technologies that proved to be a new and powerful political tool.

We at *Foreign Affairs* and the Council on Foreign Relations have been following the "new Arab revolt" along with everyone else, trying to provide not simply news or opinions but true intellectual context. Looking over the remarkable output we produced in recent months, we decided it was worth gathering and preserving the highlights of it in one place—not so much a first draft of history, but rather a first draft of historiography, of the serious attempt to understand the extraordinary events unfolding before our eyes.

The first section of the book, "The Past as Prologue," sets the stage by describing the Middle East's regional order prior to the upheavals. Fouad Ajami's 1995 article "The Sorrows of Egypt" paints an indelible portrait of the Mubarak regime in all its Brezhnevite torpor, showing just what regional publics would rise up against a decade and a half later. Martin Indyk's 2002 article "Back to the Bazaar" explains the cold-blooded calculation behind Washington's acceptance and even support of such a state of affairs—because the existing regional order did a passable job at serving American interests, at least in the short to medium term. Bernard Lewis's 2005 article "Freedom and Justice in the Modern Middle East," written during a brief moment a few years ago when it seemed as if the authoritarian order was crumbling, debunks the notion that tyranny is somehow the natural state of affairs in the Arab world—a concept that brings to mind George W. Bush's classic line about "the soft bigotry of low expectations." And Steven A. Cook's 2009 essay on Mubarak's succession, together with his postscript a year later on Mohammed El Baradei's presidential candidacy, shows an Egypt still trapped in political amber with no immediate prospects of release.

The second section, "The Ice Breaks Up," explores the events in the first two critical upheavals. Michele Penner Angrist's piece, written just after Ben Ali's ouster in mid-January 2011, analyzes what happened in Tunisia and why. That is followed by a series of articles on Egypt, from an all-star lineup of regional experts, that look at every aspect of the situation there from the role of the military and the Muslim Brotherhood to the dynamics of constitutional reform and the implications for Cairo's relations with Washington and Jerusalem. The section closes with a detailed analysis of the Egyptian case by Dina Shehata and a provocative comparison of two "black swans," Egypt's turmoil and the recent global financial crisis, by Nassim Nicholas Taleb and Mark Blyth.

The third section, "The Cracks Spread," details the effects of the Tunisian and Egyptian uprisings on the region at large. In country after country, the storyline of the spring went from "It can't happen here" to "Can it happen here?" to "It's happening here!" Yet the crisis played out differently in different cases, gaining lasting traction in some but not others. The section includes pieces on Algeria, Bahrain, Iran, Iraq, Jordan, Morocco, Palestine, Saudi Arabia, Syria, and Yemen, along with some region-wide discussions of food prices, demography, and women's rights. Sometimes we ran articles that made contrasting arguments and predictions—about regime stability in Syria, say—and rather than quietly disappear the ones that look bad in retrospect, we have included them here not only for the sake of intellectual honesty but also to give readers a sense of how events played out, and were perceived, in real time.

The fourth section, "Intervention in Libya," looks at the debate over policy toward one country in particular. Until early March, the Obama administration had watched the unfolding regional crisis as raptly as everybody else. Aside from some last-minute diplomatic interventions to speed Mubarak out the door, Washington played a largely passive and reactive role, allowing local actors substantial autonomy to shape their own destinies. Libya proved to be a special case, however. When the rebellion against Muammar al-Qaddafi's regime faltered and Qaddafi's forces regained momentum, the Obama administration decided to join France and Britain in a military operation to stave off a rebel defeat (and the massacres that some believed would follow). Sanctified by both the United Nations and the Arab League, Operation Odyssey Dawn quickly (and perhaps unintentionally) became a test case for a new doctrine of humanitarian intervention, one that promised limited results for a limited investment. As of this writing in mid-April, the intervention had achieved its initial goal of preventing possible reprisals against helpless civilians in rebel strongholds, but at the price of a military stalemate and de facto partition of Libya. How the operation will end and what history will make of it remains to be seen, but here we include a generous sampling of our coverage of the decision to intervene and the early stages of the conflict.

The fifth section, "What it Means and What Comes Next," steps back and tries to put the spring's chaotic happenings in some sort of perspective. Lisa Anderson explains what the Tunisian, Egyptian, and Libyan cases had in common and where they diverged. Jack Goldstone asks what sort of revolutions these uprisings actually were and what implications the answer has for what the future holds. Michael Doran looks to the demise of the British-sponsored regional order in the 1950s for contemporary lessons and argues that in the months and years ahead Iran might try to play Gamal Abdel Nasser's role and galvanize opposition to Washington and the West. And Shadi Hamid and Daniel Byman assess the impact of the upheavals on Islamist political parties and terrorism, respectively.

A sixth and final section of the book, meanwhile, presents a selection of some important documents relevant to the new Arab revolt, from statements by President Obama and Secretary of State Hillary Clinton to speeches from several of the rulers in trouble.

Bismarck once said that the task of the statesman was "to hear God's footsteps marching through history and to try and catch on to His coattails as He marches past." Divine or not, something has been on the move in the Arab world this spring, and we at *Foreign Affairs* and the Council on Foreign Relations have been tracking its progress and trying to clutch its garment as it passes. We hope you find these records of our attempts worth reading.

The Past as Prologue

The Sorrows of Egypt

A Tale of Two Men

Fouad Ajami

FOREIGN AFFAIRS, SEPTEMBER/OCTOBER 1995

A generation after that day of October 6, 1981, when Anwar al-Sadat was struck down, a strange bond has been forged between Sadat and his assassin, Khalid Istanbuli. A place has been made in the country's narrative for both men. The history of Egypt, her very identity, is fluid enough to claim the wily ruler who swallowed his pride to deal with Israel and the United States, and also the assassin appalled by the cultural price paid in the bargain. In a sense, Sadat and Istanbuli are twins, their lives and deeds one great tale of the country's enduring dilemmas and her resilience amid great troubles, about the kind of political men Egypt's history brought forth when her revolutionary experiment of the 1950s and 1960s ran aground.

It is not hard for Egyptians to recognize much of themselves and their recent history in Istanbuli, the young lieutenant who proclaimed with pride that he had shot the pharaoh. He was in every way a son of the Free Officer Revolution of Gamal Abdel Nasser, of July 23, 1952, when Egypt cast aside her kings and set out on a new, nonaligned path. Istanbuli was born in 1957, a year after the Suez Crisis, during what seemed to be a moment

FOUAD AJAMI is Majid Khadduri Professor of Middle Eastern Studies at the School of Advanced International Studies, Johns Hopkins University.

of promise in the life of Egypt. He was named after Nasser's oldest son. His father was a lawyer in a public-sector company that was a product of the new, expanding government. He was ten years old when calamity struck Egypt in the Six Day War, and the Nasser revolution was shown to be full of sound and fury and illusion. The country had been through a whirlwind and Istanbuli's life mirrored the gains and the setbacks.

He had not been particularly religious; he had attended a Christian missionary school in his town in Middle Egypt. Political Islam entered his life late in the hour, not so long before he was to commit his dramatic deed of tyrannicide. An older brother of his, a religious activist, had been picked up in a massive wave of arrests that Sadat ordered in September 1981. All sorts of political men and women had been hauled off to prison: noted men and women of the elite, from the law, journalism, the universities, former ministers, Muslims and Copts alike. The wave of arrests had been a desperate throw of the dice by Sadat and it had backfired. It broke the moral contract between Sadat and his country. In taking revenge, Istanbuli did what normal society could not do for itself. "Khalid," an admiring author wrote in tribute to the assassin, "I spoke and you did, I wished, and others wished, and you fulfilled our wishes."

But Sadat too has a place, and an increasingly special one, in the country's memory. Sadat, it is true, had died a loner's death. Presumably victorious in October 1973 in the war against Israel, he was yet judged a lesser figure than his predecessor, who was defeated in 1967. But a certain measure of vindication has come Sadat's way: he had broken with Arab radicalism, and the years were to show that Arab radicalism's harvest had been ruin and bankruptcy. He had opted for peace with Israel; the Palestinians and other Arabs, so many of them shouting treason and betrayal, had followed in his footsteps. The crafty ruler, to his fingertips a wily man of the countryside with a peasant's instinctive shrewdness and wisdom, was able to see before it was evident to others that the Soviet Union was no match for American power.

It has not been lost on his people that Sadat had foreseen American primacy and had placed his bets on American power, making the sort of accommodation with America that his proud predecessor would have never been able to pull off. Then there is of course the gift he bequeathed his country: the liberation of the land that his legendary predecessor had lost in 1967. Indeed, ten days after Istanbuli was put to death with four of his fellow conspirators on April 15, 1982, Israel returned the Sinai Peninsula to Egyptian sovereignty.[1]

This tension in the psyche and politics of Egypt will persist: between Sadat's world, with its temptations and its window on modernity, and Istanbuli's world, with its rigors and its furious determination to keep the West at bay. A fissure has opened, right in the heart of Egypt's traditionally stoic and reliable middle class. A wing of this class has defected to theocratic politics. The rest are disaffected and demoralized. There is no resolution in sight for this dilemma.

But we misconstrue Egypt's reality and the nature of its malady if we see it as another Islamic domino destined to fall, if we

---

[1]Sadat's legacy was given its due in a recent work of fiction by Naguib Mahfouz, *Before the Throne*. In the novella, the country's rulers, from the time of King Mina to Sadat, appear before a panel of judges drawn from their own ranks. The court is presided over by Osiris, chief deity in the Egyptian pantheon, and his wife, Isis. Sadat's rendition shows him as a simple Egyptian who held deep within himself the spirit of patriotism. Akhenaton greets him as a kindred spirit who opted for peace in his time as Akhenaton had done. Amenhotep III sees in Sadat his own love of glory and splendor but pities him because Sadat ruled during a time of poverty. Only Nasser audits Sadat harshly, rails against his shameful peace with Israel, his betrayal of the poor, the rampant corruption of his regime, the breach of faith with the revolution of 1952. The final words, though, belong to Isis and Osiris. Isis welcomes Sadat as a faithful son of the land of Egypt who restored Egypt's independence; Osiris grants him a place of honor among the immortals.

lean too hard on the fight between the regime and the Islamicist challengers. For all the prophecies of doom and the obituaries written of the Egyptian state, the custodians of political power have ridden out many storms. This is a country with a remarkable record of political stability. Only two regimes have governed modern Egypt over the last two centuries: the dynasty of the Albanian-born Muhammad Ali, the soldier of fortune, who emerged in the aftermath of the chaos unleashed by Napoleon Bonaparte's invasion of the country in 1798, and the Free Officer regime of Nasser and Sadat and their inheritors. The sorrow of Egypt is made of entirely different material: the steady decline of its public life, the inability of an autocratic regime and of the middle class from which this regime issues to rid the country of its dependence on foreign handouts, to transmit to the vast underclass the skills needed for the economic competition of nations, to take the country beyond its endless alternation between false glory and self-pity.

THE THEOCRATIC CHALLENGE

We must not exaggerate the strength of the theocratic challenge or the magnitude of the middle class' defection. In our fixation on the Iranian Revolution—the armed imam chasing Caesar out of power—we have looked for it everywhere and grafted its themes and outcomes onto societies possessed of vastly different traditions and temperaments. There never was a chance that Sheikh Omar Abdel Rahman, the blind Egyptian preaching fire and brimstone in Brooklyn, would return to his land, Khomeini-like, to banish the secular powers and inherit the realm. Even the men who gunned down Sadat were under no illusions about their own power in the face of the state. No fools, these men knew the weight of the state, the strength of all they were hurling themselves against. They sought only the punishment of "the tyrant," sparing the lives of his lieutenants

(Hosni Mubarak included), who stood inches away on the reviewing stand. Sadat's inheritors, the assassins hoped, would be humbled by what they had seen; they would refrain from playing with fire and from the kinds of violations Sadat (and his wife Jihan) had committed against the mores of the land.

Nor should we project Algeria's descent into hell onto Egypt. Look at Algeria with its terror and counterterror: armed Islamic groups campaigning against all perceived Francophiles, secularists, and emancipated women, reprisals by the state and its "eradicationists" who pass off their violence as the defense of modernity itself, state-sponsored killer squads, the ninjas with their ski masks. This politics of zeal and cruelty, so reminiscent of Argentina and Chile in the 1970s, is alien to the temperament of Egypt. The chasm between the Francophiles and the Arabo-Islamicists at the root of the terror in Algeria has no parallel in the experience and the life of Egypt. Contempt for the government there is aplenty in Egypt today, but the political and cultural continuity of the place has not ruptured. No great windfall was squandered by the Egyptian elite the way the nomenklatura in Algeria blew the oil revenue of the last three decades. Most important, unlike the shallow roots of the Algerian state—a postcolonial entity that rose in the 1960s—central authority in Egypt reaches back millennia.

The recent troubles began in 1992 when a small war broke out between the state and the Gamaat Islamiyya, the Islamic groups, as the loosely organized underground of the forces of political Islam call themselves. The armed bands treated the country to a season of wrath and troubles. But the state fought back; it showed little mercy toward the insurgents. It pushed their challenge to remote, marginal parts of the country, provincial towns in Middle and Upper Egypt, the country's poorest areas. There, beyond the modernity of Cairo and Alexandria, away from the glare of publicity, the running war between the police and the Islamicists degenerated into the timeless politics of vengeance and vendettas, an endless cycle of killings and reprisals. The campaign of terror against foreign tourists, the targeting of men of letters, the killing in the summer of 1992 of Farag Foda, a brave secularist commentator, the attempt on the life of the venerated and aging Naguib Mahfouz two years later—all played into the hands of the state. Men of the regime were also targeted by the insurgents. In 1993 there were three separate attempts, over the space of some six months, on the lives of the minister of information, the minister of the interior, and the prime minister.

Thus faced with a relentless campaign of subversion, the regime responded by showing no mercy. The state apparatus was given a green light to root out armed Islamic groups and to do it without the kinds of protections and restraints a society of laws honors and expects. The governors and police officers dispatched to Middle and Upper Egypt, the hotbeds of religious strife, have invariably been men known for their willingness to use force. Massive searches and arrests have been routine there, as they have been, when deemed necessary, in the poorer and more radicalized parts of Cairo. The military tribunals were swift. Nearly 70 death sentences were decreed and carried out.

Tough police work was one side of the response to the terror of the Islamicists; the other was a discernible retreat on the part of the regime from secular politics and culture. Historically the agent of social change, the one great instrument for transforming this old land and pushing it along, the state now seems to have slipped into a cynical bargain with some devoted enemies of the secular idea. It granted these preachers and activists cultural space as long as the more strictly political domain (the police power of the regime, its hegemony over defense and foreign affairs) was left to it.

The custodians of the state drew a line between the legitimate and moderate Islamic groups and the armed Islamicists. While the regime hunted down the latter, it made its peace with the former. A regime anxious for religious credentials of its own and for religious cover bent with the wind. Preachers and religious activists drawn from the ranks of the old Muslim Brotherhood, an organization now sanitized and made respectable in comparison with the younger, more uncompromising members of the Gamaat, were given access to the airwaves and the print media and became icons of popular culture. They dabbled in incendiary material, these respectable sorts, careful to stay on the proper side of the line. They advocated an Islamic state but said they would seek it through legitimate means. They branded as heretics and apostates noted secular figures in politics and culture. (One such influential preacher, Sheikh Muhammad Ghazali, a figure of the original Muslim Brotherhood and its clone, so branded all believers in Western law.) They hounded the Copts and made no secret of their view that the best the Copts, a community of no less than six million people, could hope for in a would-be Islamic state was the protected but diminished status of a subordinate community.[2] To all this the state turned a blind eye.

The country's leading center of Islamic learning and jurisprudence, al-Azhar University, has been given greater leeway and authority than it has possessed at any time this century. Where al-Azhar had been on the defensive during the Nasser years as an institution that had to be modernized and reformed, it now speaks with self-confidence on the social and cultural issues of the day. A wide swath of the country's cultural life is now open

[2]The demographic weight of the Copts is one of the great riddles of Egypt. "We count everything in Egypt: cups, shoes. The only thing we don't count are the Copts. They have been two million since 1945. No one has died; no one has been born," political historian Rifaat Said observed. The political Islamicists prefer a low estimate of two million Copts. The number was given to me by Adel Hussein, a noted figure in the Islamic political movement. Other estimates run as high as ten million.

to the authorities of al-Azhar. The theological alternative has seeped into the educational curriculum. Until the state caught on a year or two ago and set out to reclaim some of this lost ground, whole schools had been ceded to the Islamicists. There the advocates of political Islam, their apparent zeal and devotion a marked contrast to the abdication all around, had gone to work, weaning the young from the dominant symbols and outlook of the secular political order. In schools captured by the Islamicists the national anthem and the Egyptian flag were banned for they were, to the religious radicals, the symbols of an un-Islamic state. "Political Islam had been checked in its bid for power," the shrewd analyst and observer Tahseen Basheer said, "but the Islamization of society has gained ground."

It did not come on the cheap, this victory of the state over the political Islamicists. The country feels trapped, cheated, and shortchanged in the battle between an inept, authoritarian state and a theocratic fringe. The tough response of the state did its work, but important segments of the population in the intellectual, political, and business classes drew back in horror at the tactics. Some of the very men and women sheltered by the regime against the fury of the Islamicists were taken aback by the number of executions ordered and the speed with which they were carried out. "Mubarak orders the executions but loses no sleep over them," a prominent figure of the opposition said to me. It has come down to this because the regime has little else in its bag. It is no consolation to Egyptians that they have been spared the terror visited on less fortunate places like Syria or Iraq or the Sudan. This is a country where lawyers and the rule of law had an early footing, a society with a rich syndicalist tradition and associational life and an independent judiciary with pride in its legacy. The terror had given Mubarak a splendid alibi and an escape from the demands put forth by segments of the middle class and its organizations in the professional syndicates—the lawyers, the engineers, and the journalists—for a measure of political participation. Mubarak had done order's work; it had become easy for him to wave off the tangled issues of economic and political reform.

ET IN ARCADIA EGO

At the heart of Egyptian life there lies a terrible sense of disappointment. The pride of modern Egypt has been far greater than its accomplishments. The dismal results are all around: the poverty of the underclass, the bleak political landscape that allows an ordinary officer to monopolize political power and diminish all would-be rivals in civil society, the sinking of the country into sectarian strife between Muslim and Copt, the dreary state of its cultural and educational life.

A country of 60 million people, the weekly magazine *al-Mussawar* recently revealed, now produces a mere 375 books a year. Contrast this with Israel's 4,000 titles, as the magazine did, and it is easy to understand the laments heard all around. *Al-Ahram*, the country's leading daily—launched in 1876 and possessed of a distinguished history—is unreadable. There is no trace of investigative journalism or thoughtful analysis on its pages, only the banal utterances of political power. No less a figure than the great novelist Naguib Mahfouz, a product of the ancien régime (he was born in 1911), has spoken with sorrow and resignation about this state of affairs. "Egypt's culture is declining fast," he wrote. "The state of education in our country is in crisis. Classrooms are more like warehouses to cram children in for a few hours than places of education. The arts and literature are barely taught in these institutions, which are run more like army barracks than places where cultural awareness and appreciation can be nurtured." In more apocalyptic terms, the commentator Karim Alrawi warned that the modernizing imperative that has dominated and driven Egypt since the early 1800s after its encounter with Europe is being reversed.

It is out of this disappointment that a powerful wave of nostalgia has emerged for the liberal interlude in Egyptian politics (the 1920s through the revolution of 1952), for its vibrant political life, for the lively press of the time, for the elite culture with its literati and artists, for its outspoken, emancipated women who had carved a place for themselves in the country's politics, culture, and journalism. Some of this is the standard nostalgia of a crowded, burdened society for a time of lost innocence and splendor; some, though, is the legitimate expression of discontent over the mediocrity of public life. Egypt produced better, freer cinema in the 1930s than it does today. Its leading intellectual figures were giants who slugged out the great issues of the day and gave Egyptian and Arabic letters a moment of undisputed brilliance. When the critic and writer Louis Awad, a Copt, a prolific and independent man of letters born in 1915, died in 1990, an age seemed to come to a close. The Egypt of the military has produced no peers for Awad and Mahfouz and their likes.

Curiosity about this bourgeois past and about its contemporary relevance led me to the home of Fuad Pasha Serageddin, a nearly legendary figure of that era, born in 1908, a man of the ancien régime, who was the boy wonder of his time, rising to become a minister at age 32. On the eve of the Free Officer revolt, he was the ancien régime's largest landholder: he was secretary-general of the Wafd Party, the repository of bourgeois Egyptian nationalism from 1919 until the military revolt of 1952. The Free Officer regime had imprisoned and then exiled him; he had returned in the 1970s when Sadat opened up the life of the country; in no time his political party, under its revered old name, the Wafd, became a force to reckon with. It was in many ways a natural home for the professionals and the Copts and the men and women of private industry and commerce. Sadat had derided the Pasha, had called him Louis XVI, but the figure from the prerevolutionary past made a place for himself in the new political order.

The Pasha—the country knows him by no other name—lives in a palace in Garden City, one of Cairo's neighborhoods that still has patches of what the city was in more quaint and less crowded times a half-century ago: villas once grand but now shabby and covered with dust, homes with gardens where the great bourgeois families once lived secure in their sense of place and order. The Pasha's palace, built by his father in 1929, speaks of bygone splendor. Dark and decaying inside, with the threadbare furniture of the era, it has the grand entrance and the marble columns of its time. The staff and servants, too, old and bent by the years, must have been with the Pasha's household since better times.

A scent of old Egypt, the Egypt of the grand tour, the country celebrated by Lawrence Durrell in his *Alexandria Quartet*, blows in with the Pasha when he enters the reception room. He has spanned decades and worlds of Egypt's contemporary history. Nostalgia and a scathing judgment of the military regime drive the Pasha's vision. He ridicules the government-controlled press; he now reads *al-Ahram*, he says, for the obituaries of his old friends; there is nothing else to read in the subservient press. He has a jaundiced view of the American role in Egypt. The Americans, he believes, feel quite comfortable with authoritarianism. The American fear of a fundamentalist takeover, he observes, plays into the hands of Mubarak's regime.

The Pasha's world, the world of his Wafd Party, has deep roots in this conservative land. But after a moment of genuine enthusiasm, the Wafd lost much of its lure. A bargain it made to contest the parliamentary elections back in 1984 in alliance with the Muslim Brotherhood seemed like a betrayal of the party's secular heritage. The Pasha's age was another handicap. The memories his presence evoked were increasingly his alone. He reintroduced into the political world a measure of courage in the face of the state and launched a daily paper infinitely better than the official organs of the regime, but Egypt's troubles seemed beyond his scope. Sixteen million people have been added to the population since Mubarak came to power in 1981. This increase alone is more than the combined total populations of Jordan, Israel, Lebanon, and the Palestinians of the West Bank and Gaza. The facts of Egypt's poverty and need are so well known that one hardly need state them. One set of figures reveals the trouble: 400,000 people enter the job market every year; 75 percent of the new entrants are unemployed; 90 percent of these people have intermediate or higher education diplomas. That is why some of Mubarak's critics concede the burden the regime has to carry. The task of keeping the place afloat and intact is like plowing the sea. This crowded land has gone beyond that pleasant bourgeois age and its houses with gardens.

THE PAST IS ANOTHER COUNTRY

In one of the country's best recent works of fiction, *War in the Land of Egypt*, Yusuf al-Qaid, a novelist of the younger generation, expresses the sense of siege and failure among his contemporaries:

> Every generation has a particular fate, and our fate, we the sons of Egypt, is that our ambitions were greater than our possibilities. We stepped forward but we found no ground underneath us; we lifted our heads to touch the clouds and the sky disappeared from above us. And at the very moment we divined the truth of our time our leader [Nasser] deserted us with his death right when we needed him. Let us look carefully at our land and our country. It is a strange place, at once dangerous and safe, hard and accommodating, harmonious and full of envy, satiated and hungry. The age of wars has ended; in Egypt today it is the age of words, and because words feed off one another the land of Egypt will only know the reign of words.

This is a jaded country that has known many false starts and faded dawns. Modern Egyptian history telescopes easily: from the time Napoleon Bonaparte's armada turned up off the coast of Alexandria in the summer of 1798, Egypt's history has in the main been its Sisyphean quest for modernity and national power. The ease with which the modern artillery of the French shredded the Mamluk soldiers who had conquered and possessed Egypt was the great dividing line in Egypt's history and the great spur of its political class. A quintessential romantic who knew texts and understood the power of memory, Bonaparte evoked Egypt's former splendor and greatness: "The first town we shall come to was built by Alexander. At every step we shall meet with grand recollections worthy of exciting the emulation of Frenchmen," he told his soldiers. From Cairo, in a later dispatch, the great conqueror noted a paradox: "Egypt is richer than any country in the world in corn, rice, vegetables, and cattle. But the people are in a state of utter backwardness."

The paradox the outsider saw may have been the self-serving justification of a commander who had happened onto a foreign adventure that had gone badly for him and was seeking a way out. But it would be fair to say that this paradox has engaged Egyptians over the last two centuries. Egypt has thrashed about in every direction, flirted with ideologies of all kinds—liberal ways, Marxism, fascist movements, Islamic utopias—but the urge for national progress, and the grief at being so near and yet so far, have defined the Egyptian experience in the modern world.

Dreams of national power and deliverance have visited Egypt no less than four times in its recent history, and they all ended in frustration. Muhammad Ali (who ruled 1805–1848) made a bid of his own, a classic case of revolution from above, but he overreached and ran afoul of his nominal Ottoman masters and of Pax Britannica; his attempt to build a powerful state and a national manufacturing base came to naught. His descendant, the vainglorious Ismael Pasha (who ruled 1863–1879) gave it another try when cotton was king and a windfall came Egypt's way. Ismael built boulevards, railways, and an opera house; he declared on one occasion, "My country is now in Europe; it is no longer in Africa." But Ismael's dream ended in bankruptcy and ruin and led to the British conquest of Egypt in 1882.

The liberals of the 1920s and 1930s had their moment, flirted with a native capitalist path and parliamentary politics of sorts. But theirs was a fragile liberalism, prone to corruption, outflanked by collectivist ideologies (it was here in this period, in 1928 that the Muslim Brotherhood was formed), a liberalism in the shadow of an occupying foreign power. Then came Nasser's bid, perhaps Egypt's most heartbreaking moment of false promise: import substitution, pan-Arabism, a place in the nonaligned world, a national army that looked imposing and fierce before the whole edifice of Nasserism came crashing down.

Egyptians who know this narrative by heart see all these bids as brushes with success. This is part of the country's self-image. To rule Egypt is to rule against the background of these expectations and disappointments. Pity the air force officer who now presides over a country groaning under the weight of its numbers, scrambling to pay for its food imports, reconciling its claims to greatness with the fact of its dependence on American power and largess. Egyptians are not blind to what has befallen their country. They can see the booming lands in Asia, countries that were once poorer than Egypt, digging out of the poverty of the past. No way out has materialized for Egypt. The dreams of liberal reform, the hopes for revolution from above, the socialist bid of Nasser all withered away. The country drifts. No Lee Kuan Yew has risen here to make the place orderly and efficient even at a price in political and cultural freedom. The economy remains a hybrid. It combines a wild form of laissez-faire capitalism for the sharks and fat cats who raid the place with subsidies for the poorer classes. There is endless talk of economic reform. But the state has chosen the path of least resistance and stays with the status quo. The push for privatization that raised the share of the private sector from 23 percent of industrial output in 1974 to 30 percent a decade later has stalled. Four decades of positioning the country for foreign assistance from the Soviet Union, the Arab oil states, and the United States have done terrible damage to Egypt. A political economy and a mentality of dependence have set in.

THE GENDARME

Chroniclers of the Mubarak regime may look back at his rule as ten good years followed by lean years of trouble and drift.[3] By his own early accounts and self-portrayal an ordinary man with no claims to greatness, Mubarak appeared to heed the fate of his predecessor. A cautious man, he drew back from the precipice, stitching back together as best he knew how the fault line between the state and the mainstream opposition. He rebuilt bridges to the Arab world burned by Sadat; he gave every indication that the fling with America and the West that had carried Sadat away would be reined in, that a sense of proportion and restraint would be restored to Egyptian politics. He presented himself as a man with clean hands who would put an end to the crony capitalism and economic pillage of the Sadat era.

But Mubarak was no great reformer bent on remaking the political landscape. To begin with, he labored against the background of an adverse set of changes in the economic domain. The 1980s proved to be a difficult decade for Egypt's economy. The rate of annual growth plummeted; in 1989–90 the economy grew a mere 2 percent, less than the growth in the population. Egypt dropped from the World Bank's group of lower-middle-income countries to its lower-income category; inflation rose

[3]There is material here for the immortals in Mahfouz's fictional court to pronounce on Mubarak when his turn comes.

and the real income of industrial workers eroded. A regime unable to reverse this decline fell back on its powers of coercion when the Gamaat took on the state.

In retrospect, the choice that mattered was made by Mubarak with his coronation for a third term in 1993. A modest man (a civil servant with the rank of president, a retired army general of Mubarak's generation described him to me) had become president for life. Mubarak had broken a pledge that he would limit himself to two terms in office. Though outsiders may have a romantic view of Egyptians as patient fellaheen tilling the soil under an eternal sky, in veritable awe of their rulers, in fact a strong sense of skepticism and a keen eye for the foibles of rulers pervade Egyptian political culture. No one had the means to contest Mubarak's verdict; a brave soul or two quibbled about the decision. An open letter was sent to Mubarak by Basheer, one of the country's most thoughtful and temperate public figures, questioning the wisdom of the decision. Autocracy prevailed, but a healthy measure of the regime's legitimacy seemed to vanish overnight.

That keen eye for the ruler's foibles now saw all Mubarak's defects. He had hung around too long. An inarticulate man, he had done it without bonding with the country. The national elections he presided over became increasingly fraudulent and transparent. Worse still, Mubarak ran afoul of his country's sense of propriety by refusing to designate a successor or help develop a process of orderly succession. His two predecessors, much larger historic figures with far greater claims to political legitimacy, their personal histories deeply intertwined with their country's, never dared go that far. Supreme in the political domain, Nasser always ruled with a designated successor in place. And Sadat had chosen Mubarak in homage to generational change. Mubarak had no claim to inheritance when Sadat picked him from a large officer corps; it was Sadat's will that made him. In contrast, Mubarak rules alone: the glory (what little of it there has been of late) and the burdens are his. He stands sentry against the armed Islamicists, but the expectations of the 1980s—modernizing the polity, giving it freer institutions, taking it beyond the power of the army—have been betrayed. At heart he is a gendarme determined to keep intact the ruler's imperative. Is it any wonder that those rescued from the wrath and the reign of virtue promised by the Islamicists have no affection for the forces of order and feel no great sense of deliverance?

The defects of a political system without an orderly succession in place and reliant on the armed forces as a last arbiter were laid bare last June when Mubarak, in Addis Ababa to attend a meeting of the Organization of African Unity, escaped unhurt from an armed attack on his motorcade. He rushed back home full of fury against the Sudanese whom he accused of masterminding the attempt on his life; he was eager, as well, to tell of his cool under fire, the man of the armed forces who had known greater dangers. The play of things was given away in the scripted celebrations of Mubarak's safety. The men of the religious establishment hailed Mubarak as a just ruler who kept the faith. The military officers renewed their pledge of allegiance and warned that they were there to ward off the dangers to the regime. The minister for municipalities said that the crowds from the provinces who had wanted to come to Cairo would have covered the "face of the sun." The one obvious lesson that was not drawn, the danger that went unexamined and unstated, was the vacuum, the uncertainty, that would have been left behind had Mubarak been struck down in Ethiopia. Egyptians were no doubt relieved to have Mubarak back: that is not the kind of tragedy they would want for him or for themselves. But no staged celebrations and no display of bravado on the Egypt-Sudan frontier could hide the stalemate of the Egyptian political order.

PAN-ARABISM REDUX

A pan-Arab wind, a pan-Arab temptation, has lately emerged in Egypt. It is the return of an old consolation that brought Egypt failure and bitterness. From her pundits and intellectuals can now be heard a warmed-over version of the pan-Arab arguments of the 1960s, a disquiet over the country's place in the region. And for all the vast aid the United States has poured into Egypt over the last two decades, there is in the air as well a curious free-floating hostility to American ideals and interests, a conviction that the United States wishes Egypt permanent dependency and helplessness, a reflexive tendency to take up, against America's wishes, the cause of renegade states like Libya and Iraq, a belief that the United States is somehow engaged with Israel in an attempt to diminish and hem in the power and influence of Egypt. The peace with Israel, we know, stands, but it is unclaimed and disowned by the professional and intellectual class in the country, the pharaoh's peace, concluded by Sadat a generation ago and kept to a minimum by his inheritors.

This new version of pan-Arabism, we are told, would be pragmatic whereas the old movement led by Nasser was romantic and loud and strident. Egypt would lead other Arabs, she would help defend the security of the Persian Gulf states (against Iran) and set the terms of accommodation with Israel, but she would do all this without shrillness, without triggering a new ideological war in the Arab world. She would use her skills and her vast bureaucratic apparatus to balance the power of Israel.

In truth, the pan-Arabism that the Egyptian state (and the intellectual class) wishes to revive is a mirage. Egypt's primacy in Arab politics is a thing of the past. Arabs have gone their own separate ways. Egypt was the last to proclaim the pan-Arab idea, the first to desert it. If Egypt succumbs again to that temptation as a way of getting out of its troubles, the detour will end in futility. To borrow an old expression, pan-Arabism will have visited twice: the first time as tragedy, the second as farce. Egypt cannot set the terms or the pace of the accommodation in the Fertile Crescent between Israel and each of its neighbors. These terms will be decided by the protagonists. The irony was not lost on the Jordanians when the Egyptians began to deride them for their forthcoming peace with Israel. It was under Egyptian command during those fateful six days in 1967 that Jordan lost the West Bank and east Jerusalem. Jordan then had to wait on the sidelines for an entire generation after the Camp David accords as Egypt garnered the wages of peace and the vast American aid that came with it.

Egypt cannot render services that are no longer in demand: her doomed and quixotic campaign, waged earlier this year, against the extension of the Nonproliferation Treaty and the attempt to hold the treaty hostage to new controls over Israel's nuclear capabilities offers a cautionary tale. The campaign rolled together Egypt's panic about its place in the region, the need to demonstrate some distance from American power, and the desire to reassert Egypt's primacy in Arab politics. The regime threw everything it had into the fight. For months it was high drama: Egypt against the elements. But it was to no avail. There were no Arab riders anxious to join the Egyptian posse. The passion had gone out of that old fight.

Nor is there a special assignment for Egypt in securing the sea-lanes of the Persian Gulf or defending the Arabian Peninsula. To balance the two potential revisionist states, Iran and Iraq, the conservative states of the gulf will rely on American power and protection. This is an assignment for an imperial power; it is now America's, as it had been Britain's. In that kind of work Egypt has a minor role, as it did in Desert Storm, providing an Arab cover for American power. There could be gains for Egypt here, but they are at best marginal ones.

Egyptians who know their country so well have a way of reciting its troubles, then insisting that the old resilient country shall prevail. As an outsider who has followed the twists of the country's history and who approaches the place with nothing but awe for its civility amid great troubles, I suspect they are right. The country is too wise, too knowing, too tolerant to succumb to a reign of theocratic zeal. Competing truths, whole civilizations have been assimilated and brokered here; it is hard to see Cairo, possessed of the culture that comes to great, knowing cities turning its back on all that. The danger here is not that of sudden, cataclysmic upheaval, but of the steady descent into deeper levels of pauperization, of the lapse of the country's best into apathy and despair, of Egypt falling yet again through the trap door of its history of disappointment.

Some two decades ago, in the aftermath of the October war of 1973, the influential journalist Mohamed Heikal, Nasser's main publicist, set out to explain to Henry Kissinger that Egypt was more than a state on the banks of the Nile, that it was an idea and a historical movement. Yet that is all that remains. Both the Mediterranean temptation of Egypt being a piece of Europe and the pan-Arab illusion have run aground. To rule Egypt today is to rule a burdened state on the banks of the Nile and to rule it without the great consolations and escapes of the past.

Back to the Bazaar

Martin Indyk

FOREIGN AFFAIRS, JANUARY/FEBRUARY 2002

THE POST-GULF WAR BARGAIN

A decade ago, the United States faced a defining moment in the Middle East. It had just deployed overwhelming force to liberate Kuwait and destroy Iraq's offensive capabilities. The outcome of the Gulf War, combined with the collapse of the Soviet Union, had left the United States in an unprecedented position of dominance in the region. Washington was debating what to do with this newfound and unchallenged influence. With the rapid collapse of the Taliban regime in Afghanistan, the United States finds itself again at a crucial point of decision in the Middle East. But this time it has had little opportunity to ponder what to do. As Washington scrambles to define a policy for "phase two" of the campaign against terror, policy-makers should look back to how the United States fared the last time it had such an opening.

At the end of the Gulf War, some idealists argued that it was time to spread democracy to a part of the world that knew little of it. They suggested starting with Iraq, using U.S. military might to topple Saddam Hussein and install a democratic regime, as

MARTIN INDYK is Senior Fellow at the Brookings Institution. He served as Special Assistant to the President and Senior Director for Near East and South Asia on the staff of the National Security Council in 1993–95, as Assistant Secretary of State for Near East Affairs in 1997–2000, and as U.S. Ambassador to Israel in 1995–97 and 2000–2001.

had been done in Germany and Japan after World War II. And they questioned the wisdom of reinstalling the emir in liberated Kuwait, advocating instead that the United States should bring democracy to the sheikhdoms of the Persian Gulf.

These ideas got short shrift at the time. President George H.W. Bush strongly preferred the regional status quo, and America's Arab allies, determined to return to business as usual, were quick to reinforce his instinct. The Saudi rulers, for example, had come to understand how dangerous talk of democracy was for their own grip on power when Saudi women spontaneously expressed their desire for greater freedom by doing the hitherto unthinkable: driving themselves up and down the streets of Riyadh.

Even while the Iraq crisis was raging, these Arab allies had anticipated the idealistic U.S. impulses and had found a way to deflect them. They extracted from the president and his secretary of state, James Baker, a promise that after the war the United States would focus on solving the Arab-Israeli conflict. Sure enough, Washington obliged, leaving them alone to reestablish the old order in their troubled societies.

In October 1991, the Bush administration successfully used America's newfound regional dominance to convene the Madrid Middle East Peace Conference, which—for the first time in history—launched direct peace negotiations between Israel and all its Arab neighbors. And in June 1992, sensing the change in the local environment, Israelis went to the polls and delivered a mandate to Yitzhak Rabin to pursue peace. Thus, when President Bill Clinton assumed office in January 1993, he inherited an ongoing peace process, one that held out the promise of agreements on all fronts in short order.

Nevertheless, the new Democratic administration had come to Washington eager to promote democracy abroad. So the officials responsible for the task—particularly Morton Halperin on the staff of the National Security Council and John Shattuck in the State Department's Bureau of Democracy, Human Rights, and Labor—asked why the Middle East should be exempt. But those with responsibility for the Middle East (myself included) put forward a more powerful argument in favor of focusing on peacemaking rather than democratization.

Our case was straightforward. There was a window of opportunity to negotiate a comprehensive peace in the Middle East. If the negotiations were successful, that outcome would have a profound effect on the region, as leaders would no longer be able to use the excuse of conflict with Israel to delay political and economic reforms at home. Once peace was established, moreover, resources previously devoted to war could be freed up for reform. In the meantime, the United States could not afford the destabilizing impact that pressure for reform would generate in deeply traditional and repressed societies. Pushing hard for political change might not only disrupt the effort to promote peace but could also work against vital U.S. interests: stability in the oil-rich Persian Gulf and in strategically critical Egypt. The United States should therefore focus its energies on peacemaking, while containing the radical opponents of peace (Iraq, Iran, and Libya) and leaving friendly Arab regimes to deal with their internal problems as they saw fit. This argument prevailed, and on its basis the Clinton administration fashioned a bargain with America's Arab allies that held, more or less, until September 11, 2001. Moderate Arab states would provide the U.S. military with access to bases and facilities to help contain the "rogues" and would support Washington's efforts to resolve the Arab-Israeli conflict; in return, Washington would not exert significant pressure for domestic change.

A MARRIAGE OF CONVENIENCE

The United States did not ignore political reform entirely; it just tinkered with it on the margins. The Clinton administration supported the right of women to vote in Qatar, Oman, and Kuwait (in the case of Kuwait, legislation granting that right was defeated by Islamic fundamentalists). It urged the Algerian regime, which was battling Islamist militants, to open some political space for its people and engage Islamist fundamentalists in dialogue (much to the chagrin of the French, who were more directly affected by instability in Algeria). It supported successful efforts by the kings of Morocco and Jordan to co-opt their political oppositions into government and parliament. And it made a significant effort to support democratic reforms in Yemen in the hope that, over time, change there might spur similar reforms in the rest of the Arabian Peninsula. But when it came to the mainstays of U.S. interest in the Arab world, Egypt and Saudi Arabia, Washington left well enough alone.

The administration was particularly worried that the Algerian malady might spread to Egypt. President Hosni Mubarak's government had become, to use Shakespeare's words, "weary, stale, flat, and unprofitable"—except, of course, for those lucky enough to be associated with it. Mubarak was confronting a particularly vicious form of Islamist militancy, promoted by the Gamayat Islamiya and the Egyptian Islamic Jihad, which were using murder and assassination to try to bring down the regime. In these circumstances, Washington decided to stand by Mubarak while he brutally suppressed his extremist opponents. There were occasional expressions of concern at human rights abuses cautiously documented by the State Department, but the Egyptians were far more sensitive to even this mild criticism than the administration expected them to be.

A high-level initiative, led by Vice President Al Gore, tried to get Mubarak to reform, privatize, and deregulate the Egyptian economy, in the belief that successful liberalization and modernization would have a profound demonstration effect on the rest of the Arab world and help Mubarak meet the basic needs of his people. But the Gore-Mubarak Commission was very much a partnership in which the United States provided encouragement but let the Egyptians dictate the pace.

In the Saudi case, the Clinton administration indulged Riyadh's penchant for buying off trouble as long as the regime also paid its huge arms bills, purchased Boeing aircraft, kept the price of oil within reasonable bounds, and allowed the United States to use Saudi air bases to enforce the southern no-fly zone over Iraq and launch occasional military strikes to contain Saddam Hussein.

Under pressure from Congress, the State Department occasionally and delicately raised concerns about religious freedom. But it never mentioned the "D" word. It watched the Saudi regime lock up or deport its opposition. When 19 American soldiers were killed in the terrorist bombing of the Khobar Towers in 1996, the United States accommodated the Saudis by moving the bulk of U.S. forces out into the desert, where they would be unseen and less easily targeted. (Typical of the bargain, the Saudis paid the bill for the move.) The administration tussled with the Saudi government to get access to the perpetrators, but the attempt succeeded only after the Saudis had reached a modus vivendi with the Iranian government and were confident that the trail of evidence would not be adequate to justify U.S. retaliation against Tehran. And perhaps most significant, in retrospect, the administration tolerated Saudi Arabia's relationship with the Taliban regime in Afghanistan, hoping that the United States could use Saudi influence to get the Taliban to expel Osama bin Laden.

Overall, the policy toward Egypt and Saudi Arabia seemed successful. Mubarak overcame the threat of Islamist extremism and stabilized his regime. His government was able to show modest achievements from the U.S.-sponsored economic reform. Although the United States had some tense moments with the Saudis, the relationship served the interests of both sides. Despite occasional protestations to the contrary for the benefit of their respective publics, both the Egyptian and the Saudi regimes were comfortable with the containment of Saddam Hussein and willing to assist the United States quietly in its use of force to maintain that containment. Both balked when it came to providing support for an effort to remove him, but since the United States had little confidence in that endeavor itself, their demurrals did not pose a significant problem.

The disillusionment, to the extent there was any, came from the failure of both Egypt and Saudi Arabia to play any significantly helpful role in the Arab-Israeli peace process, which the United States had launched partly at their behest. The Saudis provided modest financial assistance to the Palestinians but otherwise kept their distance; the Egyptians were usually prepared to endorse Palestinian Authority leader Yasir Arafat's decisions but rarely prepared to press him, and Cairo occasionally even opposed Washington's efforts, especially when it came to promoting Israel's regional integration. At the critical moment in November 2000 when Clinton put forward U.S. parameters for resolving the Israeli-Palestinian conflict, both the Saudis and the Egyptians privately signaled their acquiescence but failed to provide any demonstrable support for the deal.

In spite of these shortcomings, however, Washington, Cairo, and Riyadh had a workable deal. Their bargain worked because they had a common interest in maintaining the stability of the status quo.

THE PROBLEMS UNDER THE RUG

And then came September 11—a direct attack on the United States killing around 3,000 people, a day of infamy that should have changed everything. Americans have started to ask questions: How was it that the leaders of al Qaeda, the organization that perpetrated the attacks, were a Saudi and an Egyptian? And why did so many of the hijackers come from Saudi Arabia and

Egypt, America's two closest Arab allies? If the United States is going to uproot the terrorists, as President George W. Bush insists, does it not also need to, in the words of one U.S. official, "dry up" the Egyptian and Saudi "swamps" that bred them?

These questions are indicative of the new understanding Americans are developing of what happened while their government was busy taking Egyptian and Saudi advice and focusing on peacemaking in the Middle East. The effective suppression of the Islamist opposition in Egypt and Saudi Arabia forced the extremists first to seek refuge and then to set up operations outside the region, in Africa, Asia, Europe, and the United States. The al Qaeda network established by bin Laden (a Saudi) and his associate Ayman al-Zawahiri (an Egyptian) wanted to overthrow the Saudi and Egyptian regimes, but with U.S. support these governments had become hardened targets. So al Qaeda made a strategic decision to strike at their patron, the more powerful but also more vulnerable United States.

The Saudis had protected themselves by co-opting and accommodating the Islamist extremists in their midst, a move they felt was necessary in the uncertain aftermath of the Gulf War. Since Saddam Hussein remained in power, weakened but still capable of lashing out and intent on revenge, the Saudis could not afford to send their American protector packing. Instead, they found a way to provide the United States with the access it needed to protect Saudi Arabia while keeping the American profile as low as possible. They were not oblivious to the bonanza that a U.S. military presence in the Islamic holy land created for their internal critics. And once Crown Prince Abdullah assumed the regency in 1996, the ruling family set about the determined business of buying off its opposition.

One mainstay of Abdullah's policy was rapprochement with Iran, which required burying any connection between the Khobar bombing and Ayatollah Khomeini's regime. Less noticed by the administration, because it seemed less important to

U.S. interests, was a new development in the partnership that had long existed between the House of Saud and the Wahhabi religious sect, which practiced a puritanical and intolerant form of Islam. This partnership had already resulted in the ceding of control over social, religious, and educational affairs to the Wahhabis in return for the burnishing of the Islamic legitimacy of the royal family. The vulnerabilities exposed by the Gulf War, however, created a greater need for shoring up Wahhabi support. The regime accordingly financed the export of Wahhabism through the building of hundreds of mosques and madrassas (religious schools) abroad. The activity was particularly intense in areas affected by the collapse of the Soviet Union—the Balkans, Central Asia, Afghanistan, and Pakistan—where the Saudis engaged in competition with Iranian mullahs for the hearts and minds of local Muslim populations. A public-private partnership was also created in which rich Saudi families would help to fund the enterprise.

While Saudi export of Wahhabism was proceeding apace, the charitable organizations established to funnel the money were being subverted for other purposes. It is now clear that bin Laden, despite being stripped of his Saudi citizenship, was able to take advantage of this system to raise funds and establish his network. Saudi-backed institutions such as the International Islamic Relief Organization, the Muslim World League, and the Muwafaq Foundation were used as covers for financing al Qaeda's nefarious activities. And the Sunni fundamentalist Taliban regime in Afghanistan, providers of sanctuary to bin Laden and his cohort, also found itself the direct and indirect beneficiary of Saudi largess.

Egypt pursued a different but in the end equally damaging route. With its much larger population and with far fewer resources for purchasing the allegiance of its disaffected, the Mubarak government confronted its violent and ruthless Islamist opposition with brute force. The resulting conflict cost more than 1,200 lives between 1992 and 1997. Given the terrorist tactics of the Islamist militants, the regime's response appeared the only answer. Along the way, however, Cairo also suppressed legitimate dissent, effectively reducing the already limited space allowed for civil society. The incarceration of Saad Edin Ibrahim, a distinguished Egyptian sociologist who criticized the regime for election irregularities, is a celebrated case in point. The regime also tried to introduce a law placing all nongovernmental organizations under strict government control. Having defeated its opponents through incarceration or exile, moreover, and having deflected the United States by insisting it focus on Arab-Israeli peacemaking, the Mubarak government also succeeded in deflecting criticism away from itself. An anti-American consensus was created between Islamist fundamentalists on the right, who regarded Americans as infidels; pan-Arab nationalists on the left, who viewed Americans as imperialists; and the regime itself, which found it convenient for the Egyptian intellectual class to criticize the United States and Israel rather than its own government's shortcomings.

In retrospect, the September 11 attacks and the hatred they revealed toward America in the Islamic world can be seen as the logical consequence of these trends. The question now, therefore, is not whether the United States needs to renegotiate the bargain it struck in the 1990s with the governments of Egypt and Saudi Arabia; the death of so many Americans demands such a reappraisal. Instead we should look to a new deal. What new bargain can and should be struck with Arab allies with whom the United States shares common strategic interests but whose policies are compromising U.S. national security?

A POSTNUPTIAL AGREEMENT?

America's Arab allies have been quick to register their requirements for participating in the coalition against terrorism: no

Israeli participation, no attacks on any Arab country (including Iraq), and a new initiative to solve the Israeli-Palestinian problem. By and large the Bush administration has been responsive to these requirements. Israel's participation—providing quiet intelligence cooperation, training for special forces, and advice on homeland defense—has been as low-key as the Arabs' own. Washington's hot contest over whether to use this crisis as justification for launching a war against Iraq is apt to be deferred until business in Afghanistan is successfully concluded. And, succumbing to intense pressure from Saudi Arabia and Egypt, the president has overcome his skepticism and allowed Secretary of State Colin Powell to launch a new initiative to stop the violence of the renewed Palestinian intifada, the necessary precursor to a more robust effort to resolve the Palestinian problem.

The United States, however, has been slower to determine and register its own needs. The short-term requirement is clear enough: overt support for the war on terror. This demand is not yet an issue of military backing. The war in Afghanistan has required only low-profile intelligence, logistical, and communications support from U.S. partners in the Middle East, which the Egyptians and the Saudis have been willing to provide. The crunch will come later, if the United States decides to go after Saddam, since that effort cannot succeed without access to Saudi and Egyptian facilities. America's Arab allies are prepared to provide tacit support for a war in Afghanistan but are no longer willing to provide active military support for a war against an Arab country. Indeed, absent clear evidence of Iraqi involvement in the September 11 or anthrax attacks, if Washington judges a war on Iraq as necessary to the new bargain, there is unlikely to be any deal at all.

Yet if Egypt and Saudi Arabia will not back a U.S. military campaign to remove Saddam from power, Washington should at least insist that they actively join in the effort to shut down

Middle Eastern safe havens for terrorists. As the United States turns its focus to other states that allow terrorists to operate from their territory, it will need its Arab friends to make clear to Iran, Iraq, Syria, and Lebanon that they will be on their own in the Arab world and the international community if they continue to provide succor for terrorists. In the 1990s, Saudi Arabia was able to convince Iran to end its support for terrorism and subversion in the Arabian Peninsula; it should now use the same powers of persuasion on all the state sponsors of terrorism in its neighborhood. Many of those governments will argue that terrorism is justified because it is aimed at Israelis. But President Bush answered that argument decisively when he addressed the U.N. General Assembly in November, asserting that "no national aspiration, no remembered wrong can ever justify the deliberate murder of the innocent." At a time when America's Arab friends are expecting the United States to promote Arab-Israeli peace, the United States will need them to actively oppose the Middle Eastern terrorism that has done so much in the past to impede its attainment.

Drying up the sources of funding for al Qaeda is also an urgent priority. The United States must insist that Saudi Arabia undertake a complete overhaul of public and private Saudi funding for charitable organizations and institute new regulations for monitoring the flow of funds.

One of the most important requirements will come in the battle for the hearts and minds of Muslims around the world. Here Washington needs the Egyptian and Saudi governments, as the most influential players in the Arab and Islamic worlds, to take the lead in legitimizing its assertion that it is not at war with Islam. The United States also needs its Arab allies to make the case to their own people and to Muslims everywhere that U.S. objectives are justified because the terrorists have defamed Islam and done great damage to the Islamic cause. Washington has to persuade Cairo and Riyadh to lead public opinion through a sustained campaign in their government-controlled media and their government-funded mosques. These governments' essential silence in these matters to date conveys the impression that they are afraid of public opinion. Yet the prevailing calm in their streets, in the face of an intense U.S. bombing campaign in Afghanistan, indicates that the Egyptian and Saudi regimes have less to fear than they imagined. They should at least start to encourage those thin, small voices in their media that are holding a mirror to their own societies rather than joining the default chorus that avoids responsibility by blaming the United States.

Calming the situation in the West Bank and Gaza will also help to remove the excuse that the Egyptian and Saudi governments use to avoid taking stands in defense of the United States. Powell's initiative, launched on November 19, presented the right mix: one part broad vision of an eventual two-state solution, and four parts specific steps involving stopping the violence, arresting terrorists, ending the Palestinian incitement, and ceasing settlement activity. Dispatching envoys to the region to sustain the initiative, as Washington has done, is also the only effective way to test whether September 11 has changed the calculations of Chairman Arafat and Israeli Prime Minister Ariel Sharon enough to end the intifada and resume meaningful negotiations.

But now that the United States has allowed Saudi Arabia and Egypt to make their bids for a new bargain, this time Washington must be much more insistent that these governments reciprocate. They must partner U.S. efforts to resolve the Palestinian problem. It is unacceptable that at a time when Washington is insisting that the Palestinian Authority end its anti-Israel incitement campaign, Cairo and Riyadh should do nothing to counter the vitriolic antisemitism in their media and the shameful efforts to legitimize terrorist attacks against civilians because they happen to be Israelis. It is also unacceptable, given the genesis of this new U.S. initiative, that the Saudi and Egyptian governments should sit on the sidelines while the United States tries to broker an agreement. They will need to be public advocates of fair and reasonable compromises on the critical issues of Jerusalem and refugees. And, in the Saudi case, Washington should not heed Riyadh's insistence on Israeli and U.S. recognition of a Palestinian state unless the Saudis are willing to reciprocate by extending their own recognition to Israel.

LET'S MAKE A DEAL

The longer-term U.S. requirements for a new bargain are even more problematic. If the United States is to "dry up the swamp" that generated the al Qaeda terrorist phenomenon, it is going to have to confront the dilemma of political change in the Arab world. In the past, recognizing that the dynamics of change in traditional societies could be deeply destabilizing, Washington posed the choice as one "between corruption and chaos." It opted to back corrupt governments because it feared that the alternative would be worse for vital U.S. interests. In the case of Iran, the United States backed the shah for fear of the alternative. In the end it got the alternative anyway. The theocratic regime of ayatollahs that replaced the shah was far worse, and U.S. support for the shah contributed to the profound anti-American manifestations of the Iranian Revolution. It was the worst of all worlds.

In the Egyptian and Saudi cases the dilemma has now been exacerbated. The United States backed their regimes and they begat al Qaeda. But insisting on political reform in Cairo and Riyadh could help bin Laden achieve his ultimate objective: toppling these regimes even after he has gone. That outcome would be the ultimate irony. Whatever the shortcomings of these regimes, fundamentalist alternatives are bound to be worse for the Egyptian and Saudi people, as they were for Iran and Afghanistan. And revolution in Saudi Arabia and Egypt could have a devastating impact on vital U.S. interests in the Middle East. Yet if they do not change their ways, over time these regimes could fall anyway, and in the meantime their failings may continue to generate unacceptable threats to U.S. national security.

The way out is to develop a middle path, working with the Egyptian and Saudi governments to promote political and economic reform—even if doing so requires them to loosen some controls and take some risks. They have to be persuaded that opening political space for the encouragement of civil society in their countries can help to legitimize their regimes rather than destabilize them. The Saudis and the Egyptians will also need to be encouraged to develop a more tolerant model of Islam, one more reconciled to modernity, as an alternative to the hatred and xenophobia now propagated through school and mosque. And they will have to be prodded into undertaking economic reforms that can provide meaningful employment and the hope of a better future for their young people, who now make up the majority in these countries.

All of this, of course, is much easier said than done. U.S. efforts to promote such an agenda would have met opposition even during easier times; in the midst of an Islamist confrontation with the United States, the resistance will be stiffer yet. On the other hand, success in the war against al Qaeda and the Taliban will open a window of opportunity just as did success against Iraq during the Gulf War a decade ago. When this window opens, the United States will need to seize the moment and put its demands on the table, so it should be formulating them now. In this regard, one question to examine is whether Islamic states that have embarked on political and economic reform can provide models for others to emulate. Jordan, for example, is a weak, resource-poor buffer state. Yet its ruling

Hashemites have found a way to bring Islamic fundamentalists into the mainstream of political life even as the government vigorously pursues terrorist cells within the country's borders, and to promote economic reform while maintaining their peace treaty with Israel. Similarly, Morocco's leadership has brought its political opposition into the government while embarking on social and economic reforms.

America's Egyptian and Saudi interlocutors will come to the postwar bargaining table with counter-demands. Just as they did after the Gulf War, they will do their best to deflect the United States by focusing attention on solving the Palestinian problem. The United States has its own reasons for making this issue a priority, but this time around pursuing Arab-Israeli peace needs to be part of the bargain and not a substitute for it. And in return, Washington will need Cairo and Riyadh to act as full partners in the peacemaking effort.

But beyond that, the United States will have to persuade the Egyptian and Saudi governments to attend to its short-term needs in the continuing war on terrorism and to begin working on their own long-term need to address more effectively their people's basic requirements for greater political and economic progress. Persuading Arab leaders to stop financing terrorism, promote tolerance in their societies, and cooperate with the United States in shutting down terrorist safe havens in the Middle East are conditions that Washington must insist on—the failure to do so will have a direct impact on U.S. national security. Persuading them to undertake difficult political and economic reforms, however, could have a direct impact on their own security, which would make them more resistant to U.S. arguments.

Nevertheless, the United States can no longer afford to desist from this longer-term task. At a minimum, America's Arab friends must know that political and economic reform will be an integral part of the ongoing U.S. agenda with them—a constant issue in diplomatic exchanges, a subject for congressional scrutiny, and a component of U.S. assistance programs. Even if they start paying attention to these issues only to get Washington off their backs, they will create openings for the growth of civil society in their countries.

Merely listing the parameters of such a new deal with the leaders of the Arab world suggests how difficult and daunting the task of negotiating it will be. The main reason even to try, in fact, is simply because the United States has few alternatives. If it allows another return to business as usual, as it did after the Gulf War, it will sow the seeds of its own destruction in the Middle East—and that of its regional allies as well.

Freedom and Justice in the Modern Middle East

Bernard Lewis

FOREIGN AFFAIRS, MAY/JUNE 2005

CHANGING PERCEPTIONS

For Muslims as for others, history is important, but they approach it with a special concern and awareness. The career of the Prophet Muhammad, the creation and expansion of the Islamic community and state, and the formulation and elaboration of the holy law of Islam are events in history, known from historical memory or record and narrated and debated by historians since early times. In the Islamic Middle East, one may still find passionate arguments, even bitter feuds, about events that occurred centuries or sometimes millennia ago—about what happened, its significance, and its current relevance. This historical awareness has acquired new dimensions in the modern period, as Muslims—particularly those in the Middle East—have suffered new experiences that have transformed their vision of themselves and the world and reshaped the language in which they discuss it.

BERNARD LEWIS is Cleveland E. Dodge Professor Emeritus of Near Eastern Studies at Princeton University. This essay is adapted from a lecture given on April 29, 2004, as part of the Robert J. Pelosky, Jr., Distinguished Speaker Series at the Elliott School of International Affairs, George Washington University.

In 1798, the French Revolution arrived in Egypt in the form of a small expeditionary force commanded by a young general called Napoleon Bonaparte. The force invaded, conquered, and ruled Egypt without difficulty for several years. General Bonaparte proudly announced that he had come "in the name of the French Republic, founded on the principles of liberty and equality." This was, of course, published in French and also in Arabic translation. Bonaparte brought his Arabic translators with him, a precaution that some later visitors to the region seem to have overlooked.

The reference to equality was no problem: Egyptians, like other Muslims, understood it very well. Equality among believers was a basic principle of Islam from its foundation in the seventh century, in marked contrast to both the caste system of India to the east and the privileged aristocracies of the Christian world to the west. Islam really did insist on equality and achieved a high measure of success in enforcing it. Obviously, the facts of life created inequalities—primarily social and economic, sometimes also ethnic and racial—but these were in defiance of Islamic principles and never reached the levels of the Western world. Three exceptions to the Islamic rule of equality were enshrined in the holy law: the inferiority of slaves, women, and unbelievers. But these exceptions were not so remarkable; for a long time in the United States, in practice if not in principle, only white male Protestants were "born free and equal." The record would seem to indicate that as late as the nineteenth or even the early twentieth century, a poor man of humble origins had a better chance of rising to the top in the Muslim Middle East than anywhere in Christendom, including post-revolutionary France and the United States.

Equality, then, was a well-understood principle, but what about the other word Bonaparte mentioned—"liberty," or freedom? This term caused some puzzlement among the Egyptians. In Arabic usage at that time and for some time after, the word "freedom"—*hurriyya*—was in no sense a political term. It was a legal term. One was free if one was not a slave. To be liberated, or freed, meant to be manumitted, and in the Islamic world, unlike in the Western world, "slavery" and "freedom" were not until recently used as metaphors for bad and good government.

The puzzlement continued until a very remarkable Egyptian scholar found the answer. Sheikh Rifa'a Rafi' al-Tahtawi was a professor at the still unmodernized al-Azhar University of the early nineteenth century. The ruler of Egypt had decided it was time to try and catch up with the West, and in 1826 he sent a first mission of 44 Egyptian students to Paris. Sheikh Tahtawi accompanied them and stayed in Paris until 1831. He was what might be called a chaplain, there to look after the students' spiritual welfare and to see that they did not go astray—no mean task in Paris at that time.

During his stay, he seems to have learned more than any of his wards, and he wrote a truly fascinating book giving his impressions of post-revolutionary France. The book was published in Cairo in Arabic in 1834 and in a Turkish translation in 1839. It remained for decades the only description of a modern European country available to the Middle Eastern Muslim reader. Sheikh Tahtawi devotes a chapter to French government, and in it he mentions how the French kept talking about freedom. He obviously at first shared the general perplexity about what the status of not being a slave had to do with politics. And then he understood and explained. "When the French talk about freedom," he says, "what they mean is what we Muslims call justice." And that was exactly right. Just as the French, and more generally Westerners, thought of good government and bad government as freedom and slavery, so Muslims conceived of them as justice and injustice. These contrasting perceptions help shed light on the political debate that began in the Muslim world with the 1798 French expedition and that has been going on ever since, in a remarkable variety of forms.

JUSTICE FOR ALL

As Sheikh Tahtawi rightly said, the traditional Islamic ideal of good government is expressed in the term "justice." This is represented by several different words in Arabic and other Islamic languages. The most usual, *adl*, means "justice according to the law" (with "law" defined as God's law, the sharia, as revealed to the Prophet and to the Muslim community). But what is the converse of justice? What is a regime that does not meet the standards of justice? If a ruler is to qualify as just, as defined in the traditional Islamic system of rules and ideas, he must meet two requirements: he must have acquired power rightfully, and he must exercise it rightfully. In other words, he must be neither a usurper nor a tyrant. It is of course possible to be either one without the other, although the normal experience was to be both at the same time.

The Islamic notion of justice is well documented and goes back to the time of the Prophet. The life of the Prophet Muhammad, as related in his biography and reflected in revelation and tradition, falls into two main phases. In the first phase he is still living in his native town of Mecca and opposing its regime. He is preaching a new religion, a new doctrine that challenges the pagan oligarchy that rules Mecca. The verses in the Koran, and also relevant passages in the prophetic traditions and biography, dating from the Meccan period, carry a message of opposition—of rebellion, one might even say of revolution, against the existing order.

Then comes the famous migration, the *hijra* from Mecca to Medina, where Muhammad becomes a wielder, not a victim, of authority. Muhammad, during his lifetime, becomes a head of state and does what heads of state do. He promulgates and enforces laws, he raises taxes, he makes war, he makes peace; in a word, he governs. The political tradition, the political maxims, and the political guidance of this period do not focus on how to resist or oppose the government, as in the Meccan period, but on how to conduct government. So from the very beginning of Muslim scripture, jurisprudence, and political culture, there have been two distinct traditions: one, dating from the Meccan period, might be called activist; the other, dating from the Medina period, quietist.

The Koran, for example, makes it clear that there is a duty of obedience: "Obey God, obey the Prophet, obey those who hold authority over you." And this is elaborated in a number of sayings attributed to Muhammad. But there are also sayings that put strict limits on the duty of obedience. Two dicta attributed to the Prophet and universally accepted as authentic are indicative. One says, "there is no obedience in sin"; in other words, if the ruler orders something contrary to the divine law, not only is there no duty of obedience, but there is a duty of disobedience. This is more than the right of revolution that appears in Western political thought. It is a duty of revolution, or at least of disobedience and opposition to authority. The other pronouncement, "do not obey a creature against his creator," again clearly limits the authority of the ruler, whatever form of ruler that may be.

These two traditions, the one quietist and the other activist, continue right through the recorded history of Islamic states and Islamic political thought and practice. Muslims have been interested from the very beginning in the problems of politics and government: the acquisition and exercise of power, succession, legitimacy, and—especially relevant here—the limits of authority.

All this is well recorded in a rich and varied literature on politics. There is the theological literature; the legal literature, which could be called the constitutional law of Islam; the practical literature—handbooks written by civil servants for civil servants on how to conduct the day-to-day business of government; and, of course, there is the philosophical literature, which draws heavily on the ancient Greeks, whose work was elaborated in translations and adaptations, creating distinctly Islamic versions of Plato's *Republic* and Aristotle's *Politics*.

In the course of time, the quietist, or authoritarian, trend grew stronger, and it became more difficult to maintain those limitations on the autocracy of the ruler that had been prescribed by holy scripture and holy law. And so the literature places increasing stress on the need for order. A word used very frequently in the discussions is *fitna*, an Arabic term that can be translated as "sedition," "disorder," "disturbance," and even "anarchy" in certain contexts. The point is made again and again, with obvious anguish and urgency: tyranny is better than anarchy. Some writers even go so far as to say that an hour—or even a moment—of anarchy is worse than a hundred years of tyranny. That is one point of view—but not the only one. In some times and places within the Muslim world, it has been dominant; in other times and places, it has been emphatically rejected.

THEORY VERSUS HISTORY

The Islamic tradition insists very strongly on two points concerning the conduct of government by the ruler. One is the need for consultation. This is explicitly recommended in the Koran. It is also mentioned very frequently in the traditions of the Prophet. The converse is despotism; in Arabic *istibdad*, "despotism" is a technical term with very negative connotations. It is regarded as something evil and sinful, and to accuse a ruler of *istibdad* is practically a call to depose him.

With whom should the ruler consult? In practice, with certain established interests in society. In the earliest times, consulting with the tribal chiefs was important, and it remains so in some places—for example, in Saudi Arabia and in parts of Iraq (but less so in urbanized countries such as Egypt or Syria).

Rulers also consulted with the countryside's rural gentry, a very powerful group, and with various groups in the city: the bazaar merchants, the scribes (the nonreligious literate classes, mainly civil servants), the religious hierarchy, and the military establishment, including long-established regimental groups such as the janissaries of the Ottoman Empire. The importance of these groups was, first of all, that they did have real power. They could and sometimes did make trouble for the ruler, even deposing him. Also, the groups' leaders—tribal chiefs, country notables, religious leaders, heads of guilds, or commanders of the armed forces—were not nominated by the ruler, but came from within the groups.

Consultation is a central part of the traditional Islamic order, but it is not the only element that can check the ruler's authority. The traditional system of Islamic government is both consensual and contractual. The manuals of holy law generally assert that the new caliph—the head of the Islamic community and state—is to be "chosen." The Arabic term used is sometimes translated as "elected," but it does not connote a general or even sectional election. Rather, it refers to a small group of suitable, competent people choosing the ruler's successor. In principle, hereditary succession is rejected by the juristic tradition. Yet in practice, succession was always hereditary, except when broken by insurrection or civil war; it was—and in most places still is—common for a ruler, royal or otherwise, to designate his successor.

But the element of consent is still important. In theory, at times even in practice, the ruler's power—both gaining it and maintaining it—depends on the consent of the ruled. The basis of the ruler's authority is described in the classical texts by the Arabic word *bay'a*, a term usually translated as "homage," as in the subjects paying homage to their new ruler. But a more accurate translation of *bay'a*—which comes from a verb meaning "to buy and to sell"—would be "deal," in other words, a contract between the ruler and the ruled in which both have obligations.

Some critics may point out that regardless of theory, in reality a pattern of arbitrary, tyrannical, despotic government marks the entire Middle East and other parts of the Islamic world. Some go further, saying, "That is how Muslims are, that is how Muslims have always been, and there is nothing the West can do about it." That is a misreading of history. One has to look back a little way to see how Middle Eastern government arrived at its current state.

The change took place in two phases. Phase one began with Bonaparte's incursion and continued through the nineteenth and twentieth centuries when Middle Eastern rulers, painfully aware of the need to catch up with the modern world, tried to modernize their societies, beginning with their governments. These transformations were mostly carried out not by imperialist rulers, who tended to be cautiously conservative, but by local rulers—the sultans of Turkey, the pashas and khedives of Egypt, the shahs of Persia—with the best of intentions but with disastrous results.

Modernizing meant introducing Western systems of communication, warfare, and rule, inevitably including the tools of domination and repression. The authority of the state vastly increased with the adoption of instruments of control, surveillance, and enforcement far beyond the capabilities of earlier leaders, so that by the end of the twentieth century any tin-pot ruler of a petty state or even of a quasi state had vastly greater powers than were ever enjoyed by the mighty caliphs and sultans of the past.

But perhaps an even worse result of modernization was the abrogation of the intermediate powers in society—the landed gentry, the city merchants, the tribal chiefs, and others—which in the traditional order had effectively limited the authority of the state. These intermediate powers were gradually weakened and mostly eliminated, so that on the one hand the state was getting stronger and more pervasive, and on the other hand the limitations and controls were being whittled away.

This process is described and characterized by one of the best nineteenth-century writers on the Middle East, the British naval officer Adolphus Slade, who was attached as an adviser to the Turkish fleet and spent much of his professional life there. He vividly portrays this process of change. He discusses what he calls the old nobility, primarily the landed gentry and the city bourgeoisie, and the new nobility, those who are part of the state and derive their authority from the ruler, not from their own people. "The old nobility lived on their estates," he concludes. "The state is the estate of the new nobility." This is a profound truth and, in the light of subsequent and current developments, a remarkably prescient formulation.

The second stage of political upheaval in the Middle East can be dated with precision. In 1940, the government of France surrendered to Nazi Germany. A new collaborationist government was formed and established in a watering place called Vichy, and General Charles de Gaulle moved to London and set up a Free French committee. The French empire was beyond the reach of the Germans at that point, and the governors of the French colonies and dependencies were free to decide: they could stay with Vichy or rally to de Gaulle. Vichy was the choice of most of them, and in particular the rulers of the French-mandated territory of Syria-Lebanon, in the heart of the Arab East. This meant that Syria-Lebanon was wide open to the Nazis, who moved in and made it the main base of their propaganda and activity in the Arab world.

It was at that time that the ideological foundations of what later became the Baath Party were laid, with the adaptation of Nazi ideas and methods to the Middle Eastern situation. The nascent party's ideology emphasized pan-Arabism, nationalism, and a form of socialism. The party was not officially founded until April 1947, but memoirs of the time and other sources show that the Nazi interlude is where it began. From Syria, the Germans and the proto-Baathists also set up a pro-Nazi regime in Iraq, led by the famous, and notorious, Rashid Ali al-Gailani.

The Rashid Ali regime in Iraq was overthrown by the British after a brief military campaign in May–June 1941. Rashid Ali went to Berlin, where he spent the rest of the war as Hitler's guest with his friend the mufti of Jerusalem, Haj Amin al-Husseini. British and Free French forces then moved into Syria, transferring it to Gaullist control. In the years that followed the end of World War II, the British and the French departed, and after a brief interval the Soviets moved in.

The leaders of the Baath Party easily switched from the Nazi model to the communist model, needing only minor adjustments. This was a party not in the Western sense of an organization built to win elections and votes. It was a party in the Nazi and Communist sense, part of the government apparatus particularly concerned with indoctrination, surveillance, and repression. The Baath Party in Syria and the separate Baath Party in Iraq continued to function along these lines.

Since 1940 and again after the arrival of the Soviets, the Middle East has basically imported European models of rule: fascist, Nazi, and communist. But to speak of dictatorship as being the immemorial way of doing things in that part of the world is simply untrue. It shows ignorance of the Arab past, contempt for the Arab present, and unconcern for the Arab future. The type of regime that was maintained by Saddam Hussein—and that continues to be maintained by some other rulers in the Muslim world—is modern, indeed recent, and very alien to the foundations of Islamic civilization. There are older rules and traditions on which the peoples of the Middle East can build.

CHUTES AND LADDERS

There are, of course, several obvious hindrances to the development of democratic institutions in the Middle East. The first and most obvious is the pattern of autocratic and despotic rule currently embedded there. Such rule is alien, with no roots in either the classical Arab or the Islamic past, but it is by now a couple of centuries old and is well entrenched, constituting a serious obstacle.

Another, more traditional hurdle is the absence in classical Islamic political thought and practice of the notion of citizenship, in the sense of being a free and participating member of a civic entity. This notion, with roots going back to the Greek polites, a member of the polis, has been central in Western civilization from antiquity to the present day. It, and the idea of the people participating not just in the choice of a ruler but in the conduct of government, is not part of traditional Islam. In the great days of the caliphate, there were mighty, flourishing cities, but they had no formal status as such, nor anything that one might recognize as civic government. Towns consisted of agglomerations of neighborhoods, which in themselves constituted an important focus of identity and loyalty. Often, these neighborhoods were based on ethnic, tribal, religious, sectarian, or even occupational allegiances. To this day, there is no word in Arabic corresponding to "citizen." The word normally used on passports and other documents is *muwatin*, the literal meaning of which is "compatriot." With a lack of citizenship went a lack of civic representation. Although different social groups did choose their own leaders during the classical period, the concept of choosing individuals to represent the citizenry in a corporate body or assembly was alien to Muslims' experience and practice.

Yet, other positive elements of Islamic history and thought could help in the development of democracy. Notably, the idea of consensual, contractual, and limited government is again becoming an issue today. The traditional rejection of despotism, of *istibdad*, has gained a new force and a new urgency: Europe may have disseminated the ideology of dictatorship, but it also spread a corresponding ideology of popular revolt against dictatorship.

The rejection of despotism, familiar in both traditional and, increasingly, modern writings, is already having a powerful impact. Muslims are again raising—and in some cases practicing—the related idea of consultation. For the pious, these developments are based on holy law and tradition, with an impressive series of precedents in the Islamic past. One sees this revival particularly in Afghanistan, whose people underwent rather less modernization and are therefore finding it easier to resurrect the better traditions of the past, notably consultation by the government with various entrenched interests and loyalty groups. This is the purpose of the Loya Jirga, the "grand council" that consists of a wide range of different groups—ethnic, tribal, religious, regional, professional, and others. There are signs of a tentative movement toward inclusiveness in the Middle East as well.

There are also other positive influences at work, sometimes in surprising forms. Perhaps the single most important development is the adoption of modern communications. The printing press and the newspaper, the telegraph, the radio, and the television have all transformed the Middle East. Initially, communications technology was an instrument of tyranny, giving the state an effective new weapon for propaganda and control.

But this trend could not last indefinitely. More recently, particularly with the rise of the Internet, television satellites, and cell phones, communications technology has begun to have the opposite effect. It is becoming increasingly clear that one of the main reasons for the collapse of the Soviet Union was the information revolution. The old Soviet system depended in large measure on control of the production, distribution, and exchange of information and ideas; as modern communications developed, this became no longer possible. The information revolution posed the same dilemma for the Soviet Union as the Industrial Revolution did for the Ottoman and other Islamic empires: either accept it and cease to exist in the same manner or reject it and fall increasingly behind the rest of the world. The Soviets tried and failed to resolve this dilemma, and the Russians are still struggling with the consequences.

A parallel process is already beginning in the Islamic countries of the Middle East. Even some of the intensely and unscrupulously propagandist television programs that now infest the airwaves contribute to this process, indirectly and unintentionally, by offering a diversity of lies that arouse suspicion and questioning. Television also brings to the peoples of the Middle East a previously unknown spectacle—that of lively and vigorous public disagreement and debate. In some places, young people even watch Israeli television. In addition to seeing well-known Israeli public figures "banging the table and screaming at each other" (as one Arab viewer described it with wonderment), they sometimes see even Israeli Arabs arguing in the Knesset, denouncing Israeli ministers and policies—on Israeli television. The spectacle of a lively, vibrant, rowdy democracy at work, notably the unfamiliar sight of unconstrained, uninhibited, but orderly argument between conflicting ideas and interests, is having an impact.

Modern communications have also had another effect, in making Middle Eastern Muslims more painfully aware of how badly things have gone wrong. In the past, they were not really conscious of the differences between their world and the rest. They did not realize how far they were falling behind not only the advanced West, but also the advancing East—first Japan, then China, India, South Korea, and Southeast Asia—and practically everywhere else in terms of standard of living, achievement, and, more generally, human and cultural development. Even more painful than these differences are the disparities between groups of people in the Middle East itself.

Right now, the question of democracy is more pertinent to Iraq than perhaps to any other Middle Eastern country. In addition to the general factors, Iraq may benefit from two characteristics specific to its circumstances. One relates to infrastructure and education. Of all the countries profiting from oil revenues in the past decades, pre-Saddam Iraq probably made the best use of its revenues. Its leaders developed the country's roads, bridges, and utilities, and particularly a network of schools and universities of a higher standard than in most other places in the region. These, like everything else in Iraq, were devastated by Saddam's rule. But even in the worst of conditions, an educated middle class will somehow contrive to educate its children, and the results of this can be seen in the Iraqi people today.

The other advantage is the position of women, which is far better than in most places in the Islamic world. They do not enjoy greater rights—"rights" being a word without meaning in that context—but rather access and opportunity. Under Saddam's predecessors, women had access to education, including higher education, and therefore to careers, with few parallels in the Muslim world. In the West, women's relative freedom has been a major reason for the advance of the greater society; women would certainly be an important, indeed essential, part of a democratic future in the Middle East.

FUNDAMENTAL DANGERS

The main threat to the development of democracy in Iraq and ultimately in other Arab and Muslim countries lies not in any inherent social quality or characteristic, but in the very determined efforts that are being made to ensure democracy's failure.

The opponents of democracy in the Muslim world come from very different sources, with sharply contrasting ideologies. An alliance of expediency exists between different groups with divergent interests.

One such group combines the two interests most immediately affected by the inroads of democracy—the tyranny of Saddam in Iraq and other endangered tyrannies in the region—and, pursuing these parallel concerns, is attempting to restore the former and preserve the latter. In this the group also enjoys some at least tacit support from outside forces—governmental, commercial, ideological, and other—in Europe, Asia, and elsewhere, with a practical or emotional interest in its success.

Most dangerous are the so-called Islamic fundamentalists, those for whom democracy is part of the greater evil emanating from the West, whether in the old-fashioned form of imperial domination or in the more modern form of cultural penetration. Satan, in the Koran, is "the insidious tempter who whispers in men's hearts." The modernizers, with their appeal to women and more generally to the young, are seen to strike at the very heart of the Islamic order—the state, the schoolroom, the market, and even the family.

The fundamentalists view the Westerners and their dupes and disciples, the Westernizers, as not only impeding the predestined advance of Islam to final triumph in the world, but even endangering it in its homelands. Unlike reformers, fundamentalists perceive the problem of the Muslim world to be not insufficient modernization, but an excess of modernization—and even modernization itself. For them, democracy is an alien and infidel intrusion, part of the larger and more pernicious influence of the Great Satan and his cohorts. The fundamentalist response to Western rule and still more to Western social and cultural influence has been gathering force for a long time. It has found expression in an increasingly influential literature and in a series of activist movements, the most notable of which is the Muslim Brotherhood, founded in Egypt in 1928. Political Islam first became a major international factor with the Iranian Revolution of 1979. The word "revolution" has been much misused in the Middle East and has served to designate and justify almost any violent transfer of power at the top. But what happened in Iran was a genuine revolution, a major change with a very significant ideological challenge, a shift in the basis of society that had an immense impact on the whole Islamic world, intellectually, morally, and politically. The process that began in Iran in 1979 was a revolution in the same sense as the French and the Russian revolutions were. Like its predecessors, the Iranian Revolution has gone through various stages of inner and outer conflict and change and now seems to be entering the Napoleonic or, perhaps more accurately, the Stalinist phase.

The theocratic regime in Iran swept to power on a wave of popular support nourished by resentment against the old regime, its policies, and its associations. Since then, the regime has become increasingly unpopular as the ruling mullahs have shown themselves to be just as corrupt and oppressive as the ruling cliques in other countries in the region. There are many indications in Iran of a rising tide of discontent. Some seek radical change in the form of a return to the past; others, by far the larger number, place their hopes in the coming of true democracy. The rulers of Iran are thus very apprehensive of democratic change in Iraq, the more so as a majority of Iraqis are Shiites, like the Iranians. By its mere existence, a Shiite democracy on Iran's western frontier would pose a challenge, indeed a mortal threat, to the regime of the mullahs, so they are doing what they can to prevent or deflect it.

Of far greater importance at the present are the Sunni fundamentalists. An important element in the Sunni holy war is the rise and spread—and in some areas dominance—of Wahhabism. Wahhabism is a school of Islam that arose in Nejd, in central Arabia, in the eighteenth century. It caused some trouble to the rulers of the Muslim world at the time but was eventually repressed and contained. It reappeared in the twentieth century and acquired new importance when the House of Saud, the local tribal chiefs committed to Wahhabism, conquered the holy cities of Mecca and Medina and created the Saudi monarchy. This brought together two factors of the highest importance. One, the Wahhabi Saudis now ruled the holy cities and therefore controlled the annual Muslim pilgrimage, which gave them immense prestige and influence in the Islamic world. Two, the discovery and exploitation of oil placed immense wealth at their disposal. What would otherwise have been an extremist fringe in a marginal country thus had a worldwide impact. Now the forces that were nourished, nurtured, and unleashed threaten even the House of Saud itself.

The first great triumph of the Sunni fundamentalists was the collapse of the Soviet Union, which they saw—not unreasonably—as their victory. For them the Soviet Union was defeated not in the Cold War waged by the West, but in the Islamic jihad waged by the guerrilla fighters in Afghanistan. As Osama bin Laden and his cohorts have put it, they destroyed one of the two last great infidel superpowers—the more difficult and the more dangerous of the two. Dealing with the pampered and degenerate Americans would, so they believed, be much easier. American actions and discourse have at times weakened and at times strengthened this belief.

In a genuinely free election, fundamentalists would have several substantial advantages over moderates and reformers. One is that they speak a language familiar to Muslims. Democratic parties promote an ideology and use a terminology mostly strange to the "Muslim street." The fundamentalist parties, on the other hand, employ familiar words and evoke familiar values both to criticize the existing secularist, authoritarian order and to offer an alternative. To broadcast this message, the fundamentalists utilize an enormously effective network that meets and communicates in the mosque and speaks from the pulpit. None of the secular parties has access to anything comparable. Religious revolutionaries, and even terrorists, also gain support because of their frequently genuine efforts to alleviate the suffering of the common people. This concern often stands in marked contrast with the callous and greedy unconcern of the current wielders of power and influence in the Middle East. The example of the Iranian Revolution would seem to indicate that once in power these religious militants are no better, and are sometimes even worse, than those they overthrow and replace. But until then, both the current perceptions and the future hopes of the people can work in their favor.

Finally, perhaps most important of all, democratic parties are ideologically bound to allow fundamentalists freedom of action. The fundamentalists suffer from no such disability; on the contrary, it is their mission when in power to suppress sedition and unbelief.

Despite these difficulties, there are signs of hope, notably the Iraqi general election in January. Millions of Iraqis went to polling stations, stood in line, and cast their votes, knowing that they were risking their lives at every moment of the process. It was a truly momentous achievement, and its impact can already be seen in neighboring Arab and other countries. Arab democracy has won a battle, not a war, and still faces many dangers, both from ruthless and resolute enemies and from hesitant and unreliable friends. But it was a major battle, and the Iraqi election may prove a turning point in Middle Eastern history no less important than the arrival of General Bonaparte and the French Revolution in Egypt more than two centuries ago.

FEAR ITSELF

The creation of a democratic political and social order in Iraq or elsewhere in the Middle East will not be easy. But it is possible, and there are increasing signs that it has already begun. At the present time there are two fears concerning the possibility of establishing a democracy in Iraq. One is the fear that it will not work, a fear expressed by many in the United States and one that is almost a dogma in Europe; the other fear, much more urgent in ruling circles in the Middle East, is that it will work. Clearly, a genuinely free society in Iraq would constitute a mortal threat to many of the governments of the region, including both Washington's enemies and some of those seen as Washington's allies.

The end of World War II opened the way for democracy in the former Axis powers. The end of the Cold War brought a measure of freedom and a movement toward democracy in much of the former Soviet domains. With steadfastness and patience, it may now be possible at last to bring both justice and freedom to the long-tormented peoples of the Middle East.

Adrift on the Nile

The Limits of the Opposition in Egypt

Steven A. Cook

FOREIGN AFFAIRS, MARCH/APRIL 2009

It is hard to believe today, but just four years ago, the Arab world seemed on the brink of dramatic change. During the so-called Arab Spring of early 2005, Iraqis went to the polls for the first time since the demise of Saddam Hussein, Syria withdrew from Lebanon after one million protesters descended on central Beirut, and Saudi Arabia staged municipal elections. In Cairo, activists from across the political spectrum, having grown more confident and savvy, forced the regime of President Hosni Mubarak to cast itself as reform-minded, which loosened the reins on the opposition. The editorial pages of Western newspapers were asking triumphantly if the Middle East had finally arrived at that mythic tipping point.

Within the Bush administration, however, there was detectable unease, particularly when it came to the developments in Egypt. U.S. officials were worrying about how to react, not because they questioned President George W. Bush's "forward strategy of freedom" but because political transformation in Egypt presented a policy puzzle with no simple solution. On the one hand, Mubarak and his associates were profoundly

STEVEN A. COOK is Hasib J. Sabbagh Senior Fellow for Middle Eastern Studies at the Council on Foreign Relations.

unpopular; on the other, the opposition was thin on democrats and liberals and heavy on leftists, Nasserists, and Islamists, all deeply opposed to the United States. More broadly, the opposition was divided along fault lines that had vexed Egyptian politics for six decades. It was difficult to believe that these groups, acting alone or in a coalition, could dislodge Mubarak.

Since the July 1952 coup in which Colonel Gamal Abdel Nasser and his Free Officers dislodged King Farouk I, the central question confronting Egyptians has been, "what should the state's central ideology be?" At first blush, the answer seems obvious. Soon after seizing power, the Free Officers abandoned their plans to reform Egypt's political system in favor of a new order based on nationalism and an ill-defined variant of socialism, and they quickly established unrivaled authority, which their descendants still exercise today. Yet contemporary Egyptian leaders have repeatedly had to fend off deeply attractive alternatives to the regime built by the Free Officers. With the Egyptians preparing for an inevitable transition—this year, Mubarak will celebrate his 81st birthday and the 28th anniversary of his rule—the competition is on the upsurge. The main contender, as ever, is the Islamist movement.

Although the stakes of a change in leadership in Cairo are considerably lower for U.S. policymakers and analysts than for the Egyptians, the prospect has sparked a lively debate in Washington. A recent addition to the conversation is Bruce Rutherford's *Egypt After Mubarak: Liberalism, Islam, and Democracy in the Arab World*. Readers looking for the inside story on who will succeed Mubarak will be disappointed; there is little gossip in these pages. (Speculation is that Mubarak's son Gamal is being groomed for the top job.) But they will nonetheless be rewarded by Rutherford's ambitious effort to explain how significant political actors, specifically the Muslim Brotherhood, the judiciary, and the business sector, can work in parallel, if not exactly together, to influence the country's trajectory over time.

This is a novel approach to analyzing Egyptian politics, the conventional view being that although Egypt's leaders confront myriad economic and political challenges, the state is rarely, if ever, constrained; it just has too much firepower at its disposal.

BROTHERS' KEEPER

A perennial target of this firepower, sometimes literally, has been the Muslim Brotherhood, the Islamist group founded by Hasan al-Banna in 1928 to save Egyptian society from what he thought was the West's depraving influence. The Brotherhood's mission was to re-Islamize Egypt from below through preaching, education, good works, and even (between the 1940s and the 1960s) violence. It hoped to foster among the Egyptian masses so much demand for a system based on Islam that Egypt's leaders would have to either submit or be swept away. When the Free Officers Movement began to crystallize in the late 1940s, it found allies in the Brotherhood. Not all of the movement's members shared the Brotherhood's desire to build a society closely hewing to Islamic law, but they endorsed its abiding opposition to the West's colonial project in Egypt and the greater Middle East. The Free Officers and the Islamists embraced the same nationalist project.

In the almost 60 years since the Free Officers' coup, much has been written about the Brotherhood and its relationship to the Egyptian political system. Nowadays, Western observers tend to be split in their interpretation of the organization. At one end of the spectrum is *The Wall Street Journal*, which editorialized in the spring of 2005 that the Brotherhood represents a genuine political movement that Washington cannot ignore without undermining its case for promoting democracy in the Middle East. At the other end are the skeptics, who consider the Muslim Brothers to be extremists. Former Massachusetts Governor Mitt Romney summed up this sentiment during a

Republican presidential primary debate in 2007 by jumbling together Hezbollah, Hamas, al Qaeda, and the Muslim Brotherhood into what he called "the worldwide jihadist effort to try and cause the collapse of all moderate Islamic governments and replace them with a caliphate." Between these two groups are scholars with a more nuanced view, who claim that the organization has evolved, with its younger leaders embracing accountability, transparency, tolerance, and the rule of law as part of their project for Egypt. Others, although also recognizing recent changes in the Brotherhood, are less sanguine about the group; after all, it has never repudiated its historic goal of establishing an Islamic state based on an inherently antidemocratic interpretation of sharia.

For Rutherford, the Muslim Brothers' evolution into liberal reformers is demonstrable, with the notable exception of their position on women's rights. Putting his Arabic to good use, Rutherford examines firsthand the statements of leading Muslim Brothers to present a thorough account of the organization's record over the past 30 years. Rutherford's narrative is compelling because, unlike many Western analyses of the movement, which tend to portray the Brotherhood as static, it conveys a sophisticated understanding of the Brotherhood's development. Rutherford demonstrates not only that the organization has not engaged in violence during this time but also that it has managed to participate in highly circumscribed elections despite being outlawed by making alliances with parties of various ideological inclinations and proffering electoral platforms that have been in many ways unmistakably liberal.

Still, if Rutherford shows that the Muslim Brothers have earned reformist credentials, he fails to explain why they have so transformed themselves. At first glance, he seems to be making a case comparable to that of the political scientist Stathis Kalyvas, who argued in *The Rise of Christian Democracy in Europe* that the religious parties of nineteenth-century Europe eventually became the largely secular Christian Democrats of today for reasons that had very little to do with an ideological commitment to democratic principles. Rather, a combination of self-interest and political constraints confronting both party and church leaders unintentionally spawned the contemporary parties. Rutherford's account suggests that various political pressures and incentives have forced the leaders of Egypt's Islamist movement to pursue the path of moderation. This is an interesting insight, as it implies that the Brotherhood, like Europe's religious parties over a century ago (or, more recently, Turkey's ruling Justice and Development Party), could evolve into a political group only notionally tied to religion.

Unfortunately, Rutherford does not fully explore these potentially rich historical comparisons. Instead, he extensively examines four Islamist intellectuals—Yusuf al-Qaradawi, Tariq al-Bishri, Ahmed Kamal Abu al-Magd, and Muhammad Salim al-Awwa—who he claims have influenced the Brotherhood's thinking. Although this discussion will be extraordinarily valuable for non-Arabic speakers, who would not otherwise have access to these thinkers' work, Rutherford overstates their impact. Of this group, Westerners are most familiar with Qaradawi, the host of an extremely popular al Jazeera program called *Sharia and Life*. Qaradawi advocates treating all Israelis as legitimate targets of suicide bombers (since they all serve in the Israel Defense Forces) but holds progressive positions on family law, the status of women, and political reform (he recently told Egyptian government employees to pray less so as to improve their productivity). Central to the thinking of all four theorists, according to Rutherford, is a particularly flexible interpretation of sharia. Unlike the Taliban in Afghanistan or the Wahhabis in Saudi Arabia, Rutherford claims, the Muslim Brotherhood is interested in establishing a state based not on a strict reading of Islamic law but on principles inspired by it that are inclusive and compatible with modernity.

Rutherford is so confident in this interpretation that he overlooks an obvious red flag. The flexible understanding of sharia favored by Qaradawi and others is indeed alluring, especially to Western audiences, but this elasticity is inherently risky. It certainly makes good politics to paint contentious issues or concepts in broad strokes; doing so guarantees mass appeal and leaves room for political maneuvering. Rutherford seems blithely unaware that these theorists' protean notions can just as easily serve authoritarian policies as liberal ones. The leaders of the Egyptian regime, for example, speak openly about reform and democratization, but they do so with enough ambiguity to nonetheless pursue an inherently antidemocratic agenda. Perhaps the Brotherhood's embrace of liberal principles is more authentic than that of Mubarak and his associates; certainly, its delegates in the People's Assembly have distinguished themselves as serious legislators by holding the government's feet to the fire on a range of domestic and foreign policy issues. But whether the Muslim Brothers genuinely are liberals is an empirical question analysts will not be able to answer until they actually govern. In recent years, arguments such as Rutherford's have been used to make the case that the United States should engage the Brotherhood as a progressive force for modernization and political change. Yet so far, the Islamists' ostensible commitment to liberalism remains more assertion than fact.

LEGAL AID

Far more convincing is Rutherford's examination of the Egyptian judiciary's ongoing struggle to preserve its institutional prerogative; the judiciary's resistance, indeed, shows how groups armed with liberal principles can keep a regime in check. Although Egypt's Islamists have received the bulk of attention from policymakers, scholars, and journalists in recent years, the country's judiciary has for decades played a critical role in advancing the debate about power and legitimacy in Egypt's political system. In 1969, Nasser directly assaulted judges' independence and sought to establish a more politicized and pliant judiciary. He dissolved the board of the influential Judges Club and created the Supreme Judicial Council, granting the government control over the appointment and promotion of judges. The strategy was effective, but only to a point. The judges' continued resistance to being politicized forced the government to establish a parallel judicial system staffed with judges sympathetic to the regime: the state security courts and the supreme state security courts. Still, Egypt's regular courts have continued to constrain the Egyptian state in various ways. Since the 1980s, the Supreme Constitutional Court has forced the government to rewrite the country's electoral laws several times, ruling repeatedly that they violated the constitution. In 2005, the Judges Club demanded that it, rather than the Interior Ministry, supervise parliamentary elections, and it forced the government to hold that year's elections in three rounds and reduce the number of polling places from 54,000 to 9,000 so that the country's 8,000 judges could monitor the voting.

As with most things in Egypt, however, there are limits to the judges' power. During the spring of 2006, in a shocking demonstration of official hubris, thugs from the Interior Ministry and troops from the paramilitary Central Security Forces beat supporters of the judiciary who were demonstrating in the streets of downtown Cairo. The proximate cause of the confrontation was the fate of the respected jurists Hisham Bastawisi and Mahmoud Mekki, who risked losing their seats on Egypt's highest appeals court after having accused the government of fraud during the 2005 parliamentary elections. But the roots of the dispute could be traced back to the government's ongoing attempts to politicize the judicial branch and the judges' efforts to stand up for judicial independence and the rule of law.

The crisis was eventually defused. Bastawisi was slapped on the wrist, Mekki was absolved, and the government made a few cosmetic overtures in response to the judiciary's demands. That outcome did not satisfy the judges or the opposition, but it hardly undermined the significance of their activism: Egypt's judges had proved that they could in many ways act as the conscience of the Egyptian people, many of whom want a more open and democratic future. Without becoming partisan themselves or pouring into the streets as the lawyers of Pakistan regularly do, Egypt's judges can help shape Egypt's political future.

THE BUSINESS OF BUSINESS

The final, and perhaps least persuasive, part of Rutherford's examination of the opposition forces in Egypt concerns the country's business community. The conventional view holds that these movers and shakers ensure their wealth by operating at the nexus of business and politics; business leaders are not clients of the regime so much as integral components of it. The so-called economic dream team of Prime Minister Ahmed Nazif—Rasheed Mohamed Rasheed, the minister of trade and industry; Mahmoud Mohieddin, the minister of investment; and Youssef Boutros-Ghali, the minister of finance—which has been guiding Egypt's economic policy since 2004, is closely connected to Gamal Mubarak, who is one of the president's sons, his presumptive heir, and deputy chair of the ruling National Democratic Party. The NDP itself has very much become the party of big business, counting among its top ranks members of the business elite such as Ahmed Ezz, Egypt's steel magnate, and Taher Helmy, the president of the American Chamber of Commerce in Egypt. The blurring of lines between the private sector and the political class is not specifically Gamal's doing; the process began with former President

Anwar al-Sadat's *infitah* (opening) and has continued under Hosni Mubarak. The close connection between the NDP and big business today is simply the logical conclusion of a process that began 30 years ago.

And yet Rutherford sees Egypt's big business differently, less as an essential part of the regime than as an increasingly effective lobby championing liberal reforms. As evidence, he points to the fact that Egypt's private sector has grown considerably since Sadat implemented *infitah*—according to some analysts, it now accounts for 70 percent of the country's domestic production—that the country has become investment-friendly, that it boasts a flat tax, and that the privatization of state-owned industries has picked up in recent years. This is unpersuasive, not least because Rutherford overlooks the role of the International Monetary Fund, which in the late 1980s and early 1990s prodded Cairo to pursue liberal economic reforms. More than any domestic player, it is the IMF that has constrained the Egyptian government's economic policymaking. The interests of Egypt's industrial titans may be served by the reforms the Egyptian government has been forced to undertake, but that hardly makes them reformers or liberals. They welcome the modernization of the state's economic and administrative apparatus only because it allows them to use their privileged positions to make the most of the benefits of globalization.

FOREVER MORE

For Rutherford, Western analysts tend to be skeptical of the intentions of Egypt's business community because they are unable to think of "liberal" and "democratic" as discrete concepts. If one separates the two, Rutherford would say, it should become clear that the Muslim Brotherhood, the judiciary, and the business community are, indeed, liberal actors in Egypt. *Egypt After Mubarak* makes abundantly clear that none of these groups is much interested in democracy, but it suggests that a kind of collective liberalism emerges from their separate efforts to limit the Egyptian state's predatory policies. And if they continue to exert such influence, Rutherford argues, one day they could become catalysts for Egypt's present authoritarian system to become a liberal, if not a democratic, political order.

Given the current state of politics in Egypt, Rutherford's vision of a liberal nondemocratic system would be a vast improvement. Appealing as it is, however, the underlying patterns and processes of Egyptian politics will not allow it to be realized. As Rutherford acknowledges, after a short period of relative political openness between 2003 and early 2005, the political space available to Egypt's opposition has closed considerably. Bloggers, journalists, editors, democracy activists, and judges have been harassed, arrested, beaten, raped, and, in one high-profile case, driven out of the country. Egypt watchers have seen such openings and closings of the public sphere many times before, under Nasser, Sadat, and Mubarak. But the latest round of repression is different; as the opening act of the post-Hosni Mubarak drama, it suggests that the next order will look quite a lot like today's. This is especially likely since Egypt's new leader, be he Gamal or not, can be expected to launch his term by taking steps to consolidate his power. Just as Sadat and Mubarak first promised a more open political environment to garner the goodwill of the people but then quickly reneged, Egypt's next president will crack down as soon as openness threatens to morph into political challenge—a threshold that is easily met in Egypt.

Like advocates of change in earlier periods, the Muslim Brotherhood, the judiciary, the private sector, and other reform-minded groups in Egypt today probably will not be able to constrain the state in the way that Rutherford suggests. The Egyptian government is different from the communist regimes of central and Eastern Europe in 1989, which were buckling under the weight of their internal contradictions; it is both stronger and more flexible than Rutherford believes. Authoritarianism will not rule Egypt forever. But with a track record of some 7,000 years already, it could remain the law of the land for a very long time to come.

Is El Baradei Egypt's Hero?

Mohamed El Baradei and the Chance for Reform

Steven A. Cook

FOREIGNAFFAIRS.COM, MARCH 26, 2010

In an essay in *Foreign Affairs* last spring, I wrote about the obstacles impeding the emergence of a more liberal polity in Egypt. Although popular demands for political change have intensified in the past decade, the prospects for reform remain dim.

Over the years, foreign observers have argued that Egyptians favor political change by parsing the statements and actions of Egyptian activists of all stripes: the Islamists of the Muslim Brotherhood, a small group of liberals, Nasserist holdovers, judges, bureaucrats, and labor protestors. But these observers have never been able to identify an actual pathway to political reform. In fact, Egypt's political order has produced a system that seems impervious to change. The Egyptian regime of President Hosni Mubarak has proven adaptable to both internal and external pressures, not brittle and vulnerable to political challenges.

STEVEN A. COOK is Hasib J. Sabbagh Senior Fellow for Middle Eastern Studies at the Council on Foreign Relations.

In the last six weeks, however, two new developments have emerged with the potential to affect Egypt's political trajectory dramatically. In early March, Mubarak underwent an operation to remove either his gallbladder (according to the German hospital) or a benign tumor (as reported by the Egyptian press). He remained in intensive care for five days and continues to convalesce in Heidelberg University Hospital. Regardless of what ails him, Mubarak is now 81 years old, an age when people can die suddenly or never recover from seemingly routine illnesses or medical procedures. His extended stay in Germany has left many Egyptians wondering not only whether he will run for reelection in 2011 but who is actually running the country right now. Mubarak's illness has served to only intensify the decade-long national discussion of who will be his ultimate successor. Although the mechanics of the transition appear to have been determined, there remains uncertainty about precisely who will follow Mubarak. Much of the publicly available evidence, however, suggests that it will be his second son, Gamal Mubarak.

Perhaps more important was the return to Egypt in February of Mohamed El Baradei, the former head of the International Atomic Energy Agency (IAEA), after a 12-year absence. A lawyer and diplomat by training, El Baradei has always played the role of the ultimate international bureaucrat—a somewhat dour technocrat whose ties to his native country seemed purposely tenuous, to allow him to more freely contribute to improving global governance. This makes it somewhat surprising that El Baradei has caused a political sensation since his plane touched down in Cairo. Foreign news outlets estimated that as many as one thousand Egyptians turned out to welcome him home at Cairo's airport—and to implore him to run for president in Egypt's 2011 elections (a significant number given the government's record of intimidation and violence).

El Baradei did not douse his supporters' hopes. He coyly told the Egyptian and foreign press that he would consider running if the Egyptian government enacted electoral and party reforms to ensure truly free and fair elections. At the same time, he formed a new political organization called the National Front for Change, which encompasses a broad swath of Egypt's fractious but largely ineffective opposition movement. For its part, the Muslim Brotherhood has signaled its support for the Front, although this is likely a tactical move, considering that the Islamists' position in the political arena has recently become fragile under significant state pressure.

The creation of the Front, along with his tantalizing public statements, only amplified the El Baradei phenomenon. By late February, Egyptian bloggers and journalists were reporting that one thousand people were joining El Baradei's Facebook page every ten minutes. This story is surely apocryphal, but it is nonetheless worth noting that El Baradei currently has 82,069 Facebook supporters, compared to Gamal Mubarak's 6,583. Media coverage has contributed to El Baradei's apparent popularity and to the anticipation over his next moves. In a sign of his evident prestige, street art celebrating El Baradei has begun to appear in Cairo.

To be sure, the number of "friends" on a Facebook page is a crude metric of actual power or potential in Egypt's highly circumscribed political environment. The institutions of the Egyptian state are geared toward maintaining the status quo, making it difficult for the opposition to organize. Moreover, aspiring reformers challenge the legitimacy of the state at their own peril. El Baradei seems to understand this fact of Egyptian political life, which is why he will not commit to a presidential run. But he does appear to be the sort of political entrepreneur who can exploit the gap between regime rhetoric—about economic growth, political reform, and social progress—and empirical reality, which is dominated by political repression, poverty, substandard schools, and crumbling national infrastructure.

Of course, throughout Egypt's modern history there have been others who have sought to play this role. Two of the most prominent are Saad Eddin Ibrahim, a human-rights and democracy activist, and Ayman Nour, an independent member of parliament, both of whom served time in prison as a result of their activism. The Egyptian state was easily able to neutralize Ibrahim and Nour with false allegations and farcical court dramas that many members of the Egyptian elite were willing to believe, either out of self-preservation or personal animus toward the defendants.

El Baradei does not face the same vulnerability. What would seem to be his biggest weakness—his long absence from Egypt while heading the IAEA—is actually his greatest asset. His long tenure in Vienna means that the regime has nothing on him. It cannot taint him with charges of corruption, electoral malfeasance, financial chicanery, Islamist agitation, or of being a stooge of the United States. (In fact, El Baradei clashed repeatedly with Washington while at the IAEA.) Considering his stature and the predatory nature of the Egyptian regime, El Baradei's file with Egypt's domestic security services must be relatively thin.

Although initially surprised by the burst of interest surrounding El Baradei, the Egyptian government has started to develop a strategy for containing his nascent political momentum. The first hint came from the Egyptian president, who told a German reporter in early March that his country "does not need a national hero." Following suit, the country's state-directed press has done what it can to discredit El Baradei, suggesting that he provided the legal pretext for the U.S. invasion of Iraq in 2003 and is now seeking to inflame ethnic and sectarian differences in Egypt.

But it has become clear that although it continues to try to cut El Baradei down to size, the regime recognizes the difficulties of completely marginalizing him. In fact, Mubarak and his advisers may let El Baradei agitate, organize, and even run for president. An El Baradei candidacy could actually help the regime in one important way: without being totally disingenuous, Mubarak and others in government could use the existence of a credible presidential contender as a demonstration of Egypt's political reforms.

At the same time, an El Baradei candidacy would put enormous strains on Egypt's historically fractious opposition, with the resulting splits playing into Mubarak's hands. Not to mention that Egypt's Interior Ministry is well versed in the dark arts of vote rigging—though outright manipulation would be a more difficult endeavor if El Baradei indeed proves to be a widely compelling candidate. The regime in Cairo needs to look no further than Tehran's June 2009 electoral debacle to understand the risks involved.

The El Baradei phenomenon has led to inevitable questions about what Washington should do. Some observers, including the editorial page of *The Washington Post*, have argued that El Baradei's return has created an environment in which the United States can play a positive role in advancing the cause of reform if the Obama administration approaches the El Baradei "boomlet" with "less caution." Such statements suggest that the Egyptian public cannot help itself and has no agency, interests, or politics of its own, thereby requiring Washington to intervene. This is demonstrably untrue, making such a policy prescription unwise.

Further, Egypt's close relationship with the United States has become a critical and negative factor in Egyptian politics. The opposition has used these ties to delegitimize the regime, while the government has engaged in its own displays of anti-Americanism to insulate itself from such charges. If El Baradei actually has a reasonable chance of fostering political reform in Egypt, then U.S. policymakers would best serve his cause by not acting strongly. Somewhat paradoxically, El Baradei's chilly relationship with the United States as IAEA chief only advances U.S. interests now.

It is not surprising that Mubarak cannot accurately read Egyptian society's political desires and hopes. He is elderly, isolated, and has been out of touch for some time. Contrary to his recent declaration, Egyptians are looking for a hero. And they no longer want the false heroics of a discredited line of military officers. Instead, many seem deeply attracted to a bespectacled lawyer who appears to have the courage of his convictions. The El Baradei sensation may end up being little more than a minor diversion in the eventual ascension of Gamal Mubarak to his father's post, but it has revealed more than ever how thoroughly hollow and illegitimate the regime and its myths have become.

The Ice Breaks Up

Morning in Tunisia

The Frustrations of the Arab World Boil Over

Michele Penner Angrist

FOREIGNAFFAIRS.COM, JANUARY 16, 2011

Last Friday, Zine el-Abidine Ben Ali fled Tunisia after 23 years as president. He was driven out of the country by the cumulative pressure of a month of protests, sparked by a young man's economic despair and subsequent self-immolation. Much of the reporting on the demonstrations has emphasized Tunisians' economic grievances: unemployment, inflation, and the high cost of living.

But material difficulties were not the central driver in pushing Ben Ali from power. After all, economically motivated riots broke out in Tunisia in the early 1980s but did not bring down the government of then President Habib Bourguiba. And Ben Ali's promises in the middle of the most recent unrest to boost employment and cut the prices of basic goods could not stop the momentum of the protests.

On a more fundamental level, Tunisians are protesting dictatorship. They have had just two presidents since the

MICHELE PENNER ANGRIST is Associate Professor of Political Science at Union College. She is editor of *Politics and Society in the Contemporary Middle East* and co-editor of *Authoritarianism in the Middle East: Regimes and Resistance.*

country's independence from France in 1956. The first was Bourguiba, who led the independence battle against the French and then erected a secular, single-party authoritarian regime. The second was Ben Ali, who engineered Bourguiba's ouster in 1987, when it appeared that Bourguiba had grown too old and detached to govern effectively. Despite his early rhetoric emphasizing political pluralism, Ben Ali cracked down against free speech and any potential dissent. He cited the danger posed by the country's Islamists, who gave some cause for concern over the extent to which, if elected, they would respect democracy and the relatively equal rights Tunisian women had achieved after independence. During the 1990s, he eliminated the Islamist movement and consolidated an even darker and more repressive dictatorship than that of Bourguiba. Ben Ali retained Bourguiba's governing political party, renaming it the Constitutional Democratic Rally. The name was a cynical choice, for Ben Ali's Tunisia would come to have zero press freedoms, a censored Internet, monitored phone and e-mail communications, and only token opposition in a toothless parliament.

Yet these were not necessarily the features of the regime against which tens of thousands of Tunisians demonstrated last week. Ben Ali's was a particularly insulting dictatorship. The state-run media participated in grotesque displays of hagiography and helped produce a cult of personality around the president, whose portrait hung everywhere. The media lauded his initiatives as unambiguously and gloriously advancing the interests of all Tunisians, with Ben Ali the ever avuncular and enlightened ruler.

The reality was much more grim: dissidents were tortured and everyday Tunisians struggled to build livelihoods, while the families of the president and those connected to him enriched themselves and flaunted their wealth. The Ben Ali regime was contemptuous of its citizens, treating them as too unsophisticated to entrust with freedoms—and betting that they would be too meek to call the regime to account for its excesses.

This calculus held, however tenuously, for more than two decades. Few saw last week's events coming. In this regard, the fall of Ben Ali had much in common with the street protests that swept communist rulers from power in Eastern Europe in the late 1980s. No one predicted those governments would collapse, either—yet in 1989, the world witnessed what Timur Kuran, the Duke professor and economist, would later call "now out of never." Kuran argued that under such dictatorships, citizens are required to act in public as if they are content with the status quo. If they do not, the wrath of the security apparatus falls upon them.

But people bear an internal cost—to their sense of autonomy and personal integrity—of pretending that the status quo is acceptable. And when the cost of pretending becomes intolerably high for a few citizens, sudden and surprising mass protests can erupt. The actions of these few can trigger similar actions by others, who, when they see how many others feel as they do and are willing to show it publicly, join in the opposition. The larger the number of protestors becomes, the more others are willing to join them.

When Mohamed Bouazizi, distraught after authorities shut down his vegetable stall for operating without a license, set himself on fire in the city of Sidi Bouzid on December 17, 2010, the act was so dramatic—so beyond the parameters of normal experience—that for some Tunisians the costs of continuing to behave as if they approved of Ben Ali became unbearable. These were the first protestors, who rioted in the streets of Sidi Bouzid. Their actions triggered bandwagoning by thousands more who joined the demonstrations, emboldened by the sight of their fellow citizens daring to confront the regime.

As Ben Ali flew to exile in Saudi Arabia, Prime Minister Mohamed Ghannouchi assumed temporary command of the state; he quickly stepped down and ceded power to Fouad Mebazaa, the head of Tunisia's parliament. Mebazaa has assembled an interim coalition government and claims that new elections will be held in the coming months. Yet instability remains, with the military increasingly moving to confront and sideline the police and security services loyal to Ben Ali.

It is not yet clear how, or even if, the political dust will settle. Officials in the ruling party, the executive branch, and the security services have an enormous stake in the status quo and will try to preserve it. It appears that elements of the military pushed Ben Ali to depart the country, perhaps in the hope that sacrificing him and making modest concessions to the demonstrators—new elections, broader press freedoms, more leeway for the opposition, and so on—will suffice to restore order and leave the status quo more or less intact.

This will be a tough sell. In 1987, Ben Ali's rule was welcomed because most Tunisians were convinced that the aging and erratic Bourguiba was on a dangerous collision course with his Islamist challengers. Ben Ali retained grudging support throughout the 1990s because of the bloody civil war in neighboring Algeria between its secular single-party regime and its own Islamist opposition. To many in Tunisia, tolerating Ben Ali seemed like a small price to pay to avoid such a fate. But Algeria's war is long over; it provides no political cover to Ben Ali's successors and those in his inner circle who are attempting to cling to power. Although demonstrators did not articulate specific demands beyond Ben Ali's departure, cosmetic changes to the state are not likely to be enough to satisfy most Tunisians today.

But it is unclear who or what is a viable alternative. For a generation, Ben Ali suffocated the political arena to such a degree that there is no force capable of governing Tunisia other than the ruling party and the military. The country's handful of legal opposition parties has not been allowed to develop real constituencies and nationwide organizational structures. And the members of the Tunisian Islamist movement—which, for better or worse, constituted a real political alternative in the 1980s and early 1990s—are in no position to govern. Many of these Islamists have adopted more moderate views that could make them an attractive force, but these figures have been in exile for years. It is difficult to imagine a short-term future for Tunisia other than sustained instability as the protectors of the regime battle street protesters, or a military takeover to stem the anarchy threatening the nation.

Rulers of Arab countries whose political systems most resemble Tunisia's—the secular single-party authoritarian republics of Egypt and Syria—undoubtedly watched Ben Ali's fall with knots in their stomachs. Internet users and bloggers throughout the region reveled in what Tunisian protestors had achieved, calling for copycat actions elsewhere. The monarchies of Jordan, Morocco, and the Gulf states also have cause for concern.

Yet the dominoes may not fall so fast. Tunisia's military is smaller, more professional, and less politicized than the militaries in Egypt and Syria. Reports suggest that the Tunisian military refused to fire on citizen protestors; militaries in Egypt and Syria, however, are much closer to the ruling regimes and may not be so hesitant to shoot. They might not even need to—if Tunisia descends into anarchy, publics in nearby countries may be reluctant to destabilize their incumbent regimes.

Arab dictators have proven resilient in the face of similarly daunting challenges. In the 1980s and 1990s, as democratization spread across the globe, the rulers of Morocco, Tunisia, Egypt, Jordan, and Syria retained their power through combinations of modest liberalization, cooptation, and repression. At the same time, many Arab regimes enjoy Western support due to their moderate stances toward Israel, oil resources, assistance in the war on terror, and the fact that they face powerful domestic Islamist opponents whom Western governments are not eager to see take power.

True, Ben Ali's Western backers were not there for him in his hour of need: France would not receive him into exile, and U.S. President Barack Obama applauded the dignity and courage of the protestors. But Tunisia is a peripheral interest for Washington and its allies. It does not have much oil and has no Islamist movement waiting to assume power. Were the regimes in Egypt or Jordan on the line, Western support for the status quo might well be more vigorous.

For Washington, the quick fall of Ben Ali is a reminder that stability can be deceptive. Although it is necessary to work with existing, if unsavory, regimes to advance regional objectives, it is impossible to predict when these regimes' hold on power may unravel. And when it does, the absence of strong political institutions that are capable of managing transition can lead to a climate of dangerous instability. Atrophied, disorganized opposition groups make achieving stability even more difficult. Thus, although it may be a delicate and difficult task, the United States should encourage the development of stronger, more autonomous political institutions, as well as credible alternative power centers within its authoritarian allies.

Letter From Cairo

The People's Military in Egypt?

Eric Trager

FOREIGNAFFAIRS.COM, JANUARY 30, 2011

For a moment on Saturday afternoon, it seemed as though Egyptian President Hosni Mubarak had been ousted in a military coup. At approximately 1:30 PM, Al-Arabiya reported that a rift was developing between Defense Minister Mohammed Hussein Tantawi and Mubarak, and many speculated that Tantawi had refused the president's orders for the military to fire at protesters in downtown Cairo's Tahrir Square.

Then, 40 minutes later, the crowd hoisted a uniformed colonel on its shoulders and started cheering, carrying him all the way to a tank stationed in front of the Egyptian Museum. The people started chanting, "*Al-shaab wal-gaysh eed wahdah*"—"The people and the army are one hand"—and some wiped away tears of joy. Soaking up the adulation, the colonel mounted the tank and raised his arms victoriously.

The protesters cheered ecstatically. Like excited tourists, they began climbing tanks, posing for pictures, and hugging soldiers. One couple handed over their infant, and the soldier responded like a seasoned politician, cradling the baby in his arms and kissing it on the cheek as cameras kept flashing. Before long,

ERIC TRAGER is a Ph.D. candidate in political science at the University of Pennsylvania. He was a Fulbright Fellow in Cairo in 2006–7.

practically every tank in downtown Cairo had become a platform for protesters, and they stood, perhaps 20 at a time, on top of the tanks, holding posters and screaming anti-regime slogans. The soldiers, meanwhile, smiled but said little—a brilliant move, since the crowds took it as proof that the army was on their side against Mubarak.

To be sure, there was, in fact, no coup—the army was following Mubarak's orders. And if any rift between the military and Mubarak had emerged earlier in the day, Mubarak took important steps toward mending it when he appointed Omar Suleiman, a former general and security chief, as his vice president, and Ahmed Shafik, a former air chief of staff, as his prime minister. Yet many protesters still hoped that the military, seeing its immense popularity, would seize the moment, break with the regime, and oversee a political transition toward democracy.

But those hopes seem to be fading rather quickly among the protesters. Perhaps the best thing that the military has going for it is that it is—emphatically—not the police. The police, after all, have been the most frequent point of contact between the people and the regime, and they are famously corrupt and abusive. Operating under the Ministry of the Interior, the police include the Central Security Forces, who beat protesters all last week and blanketed Cairo in a cloud of tear gas on Friday; and State Security, which is responsible for monitoring and disrupting all political opposition activity through a vast system of informants. Meanwhile, to handle the messiest of anti-dissident jobs, the police frequently hire *balpagiya*—literally, gangsters, who are paid by the police to mete out punishment without dirtying the government's hands.

It was thus hardly surprising when Friday's protests became as much about fighting the police as they were about deposing Mubarak. The police were Mubarak's first line of defense against his domestic opponents, and the protesters confronted them defiantly, pelting police officers with rocks, throwing tear gas canisters back in their direction, charging at them en masse, and setting their vehicles on fire. The withdrawal of the police by Friday evening seemed to signify victory. Indeed, protesters in Tahrir Square spray-painted "THE END" on an abandoned police transport vehicle.

In contrast, ordinary Egyptians have only minimal contact with the army. Their primary experience with it is in grade-school curricula and at national monuments that emphasize great military victories—and, in particular, the Yom Kippur War of 1973, which Egyptians view, rather inaccurately, as a great military success against Israel. The army is thus portrayed as a proud, patriotic institution that is always on the side of the people. Even the most ardent anti-regime protesters endorse this grandiose view of the military.

"The army is the symbol of our country," one protester said. "They are leaders for us. Everything that has to do with the army is good for us. They always attack the enemies. They are the enemies of our enemies." A member of the liberal Ghad party put it more succinctly. "It's our army," he said.

Yet beyond its storied history, the army's quasi-mythic status within Egyptian society can be explained by severe government restrictions on criticizing it. The army, after all, is the backbone of the regime, and attacking it is as forbidden as attacking Mubarak himself. In turn, opposition groups have been prevented from examining army budgets, inquiring about military-owned business enterprises, investigating corrupt officer land sales, and even second-guessing military strategy. And most ironically, the government institutions responsible for enforcing these prohibitions have been the police and State Security, which hound opposition newspaper editors and can threaten all kinds of retribution if this "redline" is crossed.

In other words, the police state that the protesters so furiously decry has nearly been the first line of defense for Egypt's military regime. So there is good reason to believe that, with the police state having been peeled away, the military will emerge as a target of criticism.

To some extent, this is already happening. For many protesters, the selection of Suleiman as vice president served as a quick reminder that the military is as foundational to the regime as the much-hated police forces. As one protester in Tahrir Square said, Suleiman is "a man of the army, a man of the regime, and a man of the system" and therefore unacceptable to a movement that seeks political change. Another protester said that he opposed Suleiman, in part because he wanted "someone from civil society and not the army."

But the real challenge to the army's popularity came yesterday, when it began repeatedly flying F-16 fighter jets and military helicopters over Tahrir Square, in an apparent effort to disperse the crowds as a 4:00 PM curfew loomed. The protesters did not take kindly to this and started screaming in dismay. "He is doing this to threaten us," one protester said, referring to Mubarak. "They're freaking us out!" another exclaimed.

As sonic booms continued to reverberate in the protesters' ears, the pro-military chants ceased entirely. And suddenly, a classic Middle Eastern revolutionary slogan made its somewhat predictable return: "*Allahu Akbar! Allahu Akbar!*" "When I pray, I say, '*Allahu Akbar*,'" a protester explained. "It means that I have one God. It means that God is greater than the president."

Just like that, the army had become another face of the regime rather than its alternative. And as two F-16s continued to circle menacingly over Tahrir Square, emitting sonic booms every 30 seconds or so, the people looked to the sky defiantly. "*Hua yemshi, mish hanemshi*," they said. "He will go, we won't." Just as they once defied Mubarak's police, they were now defying Mubarak's military.

The longer that the military serves as the primary enforcer of Mubarak's strict curfews, the faster its goodwill will evaporate.

And this could have serious repercussions for its ability to control the politics of any transition. Rather than looking to the military, people may look to civilian leaders, such as Mohamed El Baradei, the former International Atomic Energy Agency director, and Amr Moussa, the Arab League's secretary-general, among other possibilities.

Many protesters are already heading in that direction. "I agree that the protesters and soldiers are brothers," said Mahmoud Diab, the chief of the Cairo Lawyers Syndicate, a major locus of opposition activity. "That doesn't mean that we agree that the rules and the system are directed by soldiers. The people should choose a committee of intellectuals to make a constitution that gives the authority to the people and not the president, regime, or government."

Luckily for the military, its moment as Mubarak's domestic enforcer may soon be ending. Today, the police returned to the streets—except in Tahrir Square, which the army will continue to patrol. The situation in Egypt is extremely fluid, and the military's popularity—like that of other figures and institutions—is bound to swing wildly in the coming days and weeks. There's no way to know what direction the army will take going forward, but for now, it is standing with the regime. And the protesters are beginning to resent it.

The U.S.-Egyptian Breakup

Washington's Limited Options in Cairo

Steven A. Cook

FOREIGNAFFAIRS.COM, FEBRUARY 2, 2011

With Hosni Mubarak's announcement yesterday that he would not seek a new term as president, the Mubarak era in Egypt came to an ignominious end. Although the Egyptian military may yet find a way to allow for a relatively graceful exit, Mubarak's historical legacy is sure to be colored by the very factors that led to his downfall: political alienation, economic dislocation, corruption, and the precipitous decline in Egypt's regional influence. After the chaos of this past week, not even his claim to have brought stability to Egypt will survive.

Yet the seeds of Mubarak's demise were sowed long ago. Although he came to power promising reform and vowing not to seek more than one term, Mubarak quickly became enamored with the power of the presidency and saw himself as indispensable to Egypt's future. He had witnessed first hand the drawbacks of Gamal Abdel Nasser's experiments with socialism and Arab nationalism and Anwar Sadat's efforts to correct the excesses of both. Instead, Mubarak eschewed ideology for

STEVEN A. COOK is Hasib J. Sabbagh Senior Fellow for Middle Eastern Studies at the Council on Foreign Relations.

a bland pragmatism that emphasized "stability for the sake of development"—hardly an appealing political vision. He built a small, narrow constituency for his rule among big business, the police, and the army and relied on force and the threat of violence to keep the population under control.

By the end, Mubarak's disdain for the Egyptian people was so complete that last November, when the opposition sought to establish a shadow parliament after stunningly fraudulent parliamentary elections, he smirked and declared before his rubber-stamp People's Assembly, "Let them have fun."

The United States was not responsible for the inequity of Mubarak's rule, but it did enable and benefit from it. Mubarak was long Washington's man in Cairo: he kept open the Suez Canal, repressed the Islamists, and maintained peace with Israel. In return, the United States provided much for Egypt, contributing billions in economic assistance over the years to build up the country's infrastructure, agricultural technology, and public health programs. Yet this U.S. assistance, while certainly contributing to Egypt's development, also served to undermine the nationalist legitimacy of the regime. After all, how could Mubarak boast of Egyptian pride and ability when USAID employees were nestled in many government ministries?

At the same time, Egyptians came to see that their country's foreign policy was being warped for the sake of U.S. largesse—and that the jackboots of the Interior Ministry awaited those who objected too loudly to this bargain. The original sin was Sadat's separate peace with Israel, which Mubarak inherited and scrupulously upheld.

From the perspective of many Egyptians, this arrangement hopelessly constrained Cairo's power while freeing Israel and the United States to pursue their regional interests unencumbered. Without the threat of war with Egypt, Israel poured hundreds of thousands of Israelis into settlements in the West Bank and the Gaza Strip, invaded Lebanon (twice), declared Jerusalem its capital, and bombed Iraq and Syria. For the United States, Mubarak was pivotal in creating a regional order that made it easier and less expensive for Washington to pursue its interests, from the free flow of oil to the protection of Israel and the prevention of any one country in the region from becoming too dominant. The benefits to Mubarak were clear: approximately $70 billion in economic and military aid over 30 years and the ostensible prestige of being a partner of the world's superpower.

For Egypt, the particular policy ramifications of this deal have been plentiful, including Egypt's deployment of 35,000 troops to Saudi Arabia in the Gulf War of 1991, its quiet support for the 2003 invasion of Iraq, its implicit alliance with Israel during the war in Lebanon in 2006, and its complicity with Israel in the ongoing blockade of Gaza. Mubarak believed that these policies served Egypt's interests—at least how he defined them—but they ran directly against the grain of Egyptian public opinion.

Mubarak thus faced two irreconcilable positions: he could either be Washington's man or a man of the people—but not both. He chose the former and tried to fill in the resulting legitimacy gap with manipulation and force.

It is no surprise, then, that the relationship between Egypt and the United States runs like a live wire through the popular opposition to Mubarak's rule. As protesters in Cairo declared in March 2003, just as U.S. forces were pouring into Iraq, only a democratic Egypt would be able to resist Israeli and U.S. policies in the Middle East. More recently, opponents of Mubarak expressed a similar sentiment, calling Mubarak's presidency the "Camp David regime."

No Egyptian leader will make Mubarak's mistake again, which does not portend well for Washington's position in the Middle East. In the coming days, analysts and policymakers in the United States will voice loud recriminations of decades of U.S. policy. This debate will not focus on finding out who "lost"

Egypt; Mubarak had become odious to most in the United States except his paid consultants and a few remaining die-hard supporters. Instead, commentators will argue over how to deal with the sudden explosion of Arab people power and how to fortify Washington's allies in the region. Yet simply retooling U.S. assistance to focus on promoting democracy, creating benchmarks for a new Egyptian government, and making Washington's expectations (whatever they are) known to Egyptian political actors is unlikely to influence the trajectory of Egypt's transition.

The United States should greatly lower its expectations of what is possible in the post-Mubarak era and come to terms with the end of the strategic relationship. Expecting the new Egyptian president—whoever that may be—to carry on a partnership with Washington is like Václav Havel asking the Soviets for assistance after Czechoslovakia's Velvet Revolution in 1989. To be sure, there are no Havels in Egypt, and Washington is not Soviet-era Moscow—but the analogy rings true enough for those people in Cairo's Tahrir Square or the Alexandria corniche who saw U.S.-made F-16s fly overhead or were choked by tear gas produced in the United States.

The urge among many in Washington to try to shape Egyptian political change betrays the belief that Egyptians have no agency, politics, or interests of their own. This attitude is the product of an old canard, popular among regime loyalists and some old Middle East scholars, that Egyptians are preternaturally passive and will always seek stability. Yet the nationalist revolution in 1919, the Free Officers' coup in 1952, the student revolts in 1968 and 1972, the broad-based opposition to Sadat at the end of his tenure in the early 1980s, and the last decade of street protests suggest otherwise. Clearly, Egyptians can help themselves.

Where, then, does this leave Washington? The best the United States can do to salvage its position in Egypt is for President Barack Obama to make a statement in support of a democratic, tolerant, and pluralist Egypt—and then get out of the way to let Egyptians build a new political system. Obama's statement calling for a "meaningful transition" was particularly important, because it indicates that Washington will not look kindly upon a shift from Mubarak to Omar Suleiman or some other regime figure.

Washington has become such a negative factor in Egyptian politics that it risks doing more harm than good if U.S. officials give in to the temptation to do much more than emphasize so-called "first principles" on a peaceful, orderly, and transparent political change. Implicit demands that call into question the continuation of the U.S. assistance package or even suggestions on how Egyptians should proceed after the Mubarak era will be met with tremendous resistance from those seeking to lead, if only because Egypt's politicians will need to demonstrate their nationalist credibility.

But such restraint seems beyond the U.S. diplomatic character, especially if the Egyptian political arena gets messy. Still, Washington would be wise to remember that a handful of grants from the Middle East Partnership Initiative, a few USAID projects, and expressions of deep concern are unlikely to have much influence as Egypt's disparate political groups wage a struggle among themselves.

What sort of political future will emerge in Egypt is hard to predict. At the very least, however, Egypt does have a parliamentary history. The country's 1923 constitution established a parliament that functioned on and off to varying degrees until the Free Officers' Revolution in 1952. This era was destabilized by the British presence in Egypt, which ultimately ushered in Nasser and his comrades, who constructed the regime against which Egyptians are currently rebelling. Washington does not occupy Egypt, but it risks playing a malevolent role in the transition if it tries to interfere. The United States should learn the lessons of the past, stand aside, and let the Egyptians pick up where they left off when the Free Officers took over.

The Muslim Brotherhood After Mubarak

What the Brotherhood Is and How It Will Shape the Future

Carrie Rosefsky Wickham

FOREIGNAFFAIRS.COM, FEBRUARY 3, 2011

With the end of the Mubarak era looming on the horizon, speculation has turned to whether the Muslim Brotherhood will dominate the new Egyptian political landscape. As the largest, most popular, and most effective opposition group in Egypt, it will undoubtedly seek a role in creating a new government, but the consequences of this are uncertain. Those who emphasize the risk of "Islamic tyranny" aptly note that the Muslim Brotherhood originated as an anti-system group dedicated to the establishment of sharia rule; committed acts of violence against its opponents in the pre-1952 era; and continues to use anti-Western, anti-Zionist, and anti-Semitic rhetoric. But portraying the Brotherhood as eager and able to seize power and impose its version of sharia on an unwilling citizenry is a caricature that exaggerates certain features of the Brotherhood while ignoring others, and underestimates the extent to which the group has changed over time.

CARRIE ROSEFSKY WICKHAM is Associate Professor of Political Science at Emory University.

Founded by Hasan al-Banna in 1928, the Muslim Brotherhood has had the longest continuous existence of any contemporary Islamist group. It was initially established not as a political party but as a *da'wa* (religious outreach) association that aimed to cultivate pious and committed Muslims through preaching, social services, and spreading religious commitment and integrity by example. The group saw its understanding of Islam as the only "true" one and condemned partisanship as a source of national weakness. It called on Egyptians to unite to confront the forces of Zionism and imperialism and pursue economic development and social justice.

The Free Officers' Movement, which seized power in Egypt in 1952, was influenced by the Brotherhood and shared many of its concerns. But the new regime headed by Colonel Gamal Abdel Nasser did not support the Brotherhood's call for sharia rule and viewed the group as a potential rival. After a member of the Brotherhood attempted to assassinate Nasser in 1954, Nasser had the pretext he needed to try to crush the organization—interning thousands of its members in desert concentration camps and forcing others into exile or underground.

The leaders of the Brotherhood learned very different lessons from their experience during the Nasser years. Some, like the Brotherhood ideologue Sayyid Qutb, became radicalized and concluded that the only way to confront the vast coercive powers of the modern state was through jihad. Hasan al-Hudaybi, who succeeded Banna as the Brotherhood's General Guide, or leader, advocated moving toward greater judiciousness and caution. Umar Tilmisani, who succeeded Hudaybi in 1972, renounced violence as a domestic strategy altogether when then President Anwar el-Sadat allowed the group to join the political fold.

Beginning in 1984, the Brotherhood started running candidates in elections for the boards of Egypt's professional syndicates and for seats in parliament—first as junior partners to legal parties and later, when electoral laws changed, as independents. Some of the group's leaders opposed participation, fearing that the Brotherhood would be forced to compromise its principles. But Tilmisani and others justified political participation as an extension of the Brotherhood's historic mission and assured critics that it would not detract from the Brotherhood's preaching and social services.

Although the Brotherhood entered the political system in order to change it, it ended up being changed by the system. Leaders who were elected to professional syndicates engaged in sustained dialogue and cooperation with members of other political movements, including secular Arab nationalists. Through such interactions, Islamists and Arabists found common ground in the call for an expansion of public freedoms, democracy, and respect for human rights and the rule of law, all of which, they admitted, their movements had neglected in the past.

By the early 1990s, many within the Brotherhood were demanding internal reform. Some pushed for revising the Brotherhood's ideology, including its positions on party pluralism and women's rights. Others criticized the old guard's monopoly of power within the Brotherhood's Guidance Bureau, demanding greater transparency, accountability, and stricter conformity with the internal by-laws governing the selection of leaders and the formation of policy.

In 1996, increasingly frustrated with the old guard's inflexible leadership, some prominent members of the "reformist" wing broke from the Brotherhood and sought a government license to form a new political party, Hizb al-Wasat (Center Party). Wasat leaders who used to be in the Brotherhood, along with a few reformers who remained in its fold, helped launch the cross-partisan Movement for Change, known by its slogan, *Kefaya* (Enough) between 2004 and 2005. They worked with secular democracy activists on such projects as creating a civic charter and a constitution, preparing for the time when a new democratic government came to power. During the past week of protests, members of these cross-partisan groups were able to quickly reactivate their networks to help form a united opposition front. These members will likely play a key role in drafting Egypt's new constitution.

Meanwhile, the Brotherhood itself has been stunted in comparison to its analogues in Morocco and Turkey because of its constant vulnerability to repression combined with the parochial mindset of its aging leaders. Nevertheless, important changes, representing a departure from the group's anti-system past, have occurred. Over the last 30 years, Brotherhood leaders have become habituated to electoral competition and representation, developed new professional competencies and skills, and forged closer ties with Egyptian activists, researchers, journalists, and politicians outside the Islamist camp. Calls for self-critique and self-reform have opened heated debates on policy matters that were once left to the discretion of the General Guide and his close advisers. And although the Brotherhood was never a monolith, its leadership is more internally diverse today than ever before.

The factions defy easy categorization, but there seem to be three major groups. The first may be called the *da'wa* faction. It is ideologically conservative and strongly represented in the Brotherhood's Guidance Bureau and local branch offices. Its main source of power is its control over bureaucratic operations and allocation of resources. Because it has also managed to control the socialization of new recruits, it has cultivated loyalty among the youth, particularly in rural areas. The second faction, who we might call pragmatic conservatives, seems to be the group's mainstream wing. This group combines religious conservatism with a belief in the value of participation and engagement. Most of the Brotherhood's members with legislative experience, including such long-time parliamentarians as

Saad al-Katatni and Muhammad Mursi, fall into this category. The final faction is the group of reformers who chose to remain with the Brotherhood rather than breaking off. Advocating a progressive interpretation of Islam, this trend is weakly represented in the Guidance Bureau and does not have a large following among the Brotherhood's rank and file. Yet 'Abd al-Mun'em Abu Futuh, arguably the Brotherhood's most important reformist figure, has become an important model and source of inspiration for a new generation of Islamist democracy activists—inside and outside the Muslim Brotherhood. Interestingly, Futuh first suggested that the Brotherhood throw its weight behind a secular reform candidate last February, prefiguring the Brotherhood's support for Mohamed El Baradei, the opposition's de facto leader, today.

Individuals affiliated with the reformist faction of the Brotherhood, whether still active in the group or not, appear to be the most involved in leading Egypt's popular uprising. It is not surprising, for example, that the reformist blogger Mustafa Naggar is one of the chief spokesman for El Baradei's National Coalition for Change. Still, the Brotherhood's participation has been low profile. It did not officially mobilize until January 28, days after the protests began. And unlike in previous demonstrations, when members of the Brotherhood held up copies of the Koran and shouted slogans such as "Islam is the solution," religious symbols have been conspicuously absent this time.

The Brotherhood knows from experience that the greater its role, the higher the risk of a violent crackdown—as indicated by the harsh wave of repression that followed its strong showing in the 2005 parliamentary elections. Its immediate priority is to ensure that President Hosni Mubarak steps down and that the era of corruption and dictatorship associated with his rule comes to an end. To achieve that, the Brotherhood, along with other opposition groups, is backing El Baradei. The Brotherhood also knows that a smooth transition to a democratic system will require an interim government palatable to the military and the West, so it has indicated that it would not seek positions in the new government itself. The Brotherhood is too savvy, too pragmatic, and too cautious to squander its hard-earned reputation among Egyptians as a responsible political actor or invite the risk of a military coup by attempting to seize power on its own.

Still, it is unclear whether the group will continue to exercise pragmatic self-restraint down the road or whether its more progressive leaders will prevail. Such reformers may be most welcome among the other opposition groups when they draft a new constitution and establish the framework for new elections, but they do not necessarily speak for the group's senior leadership or the majority of its rank and file. It remains to be seen whether the Brotherhood as an organization—not only individual members—will accept a constitution that does not at least refer to sharia; respect the rights of all Egyptians to express their ideas and form parties; clarify its ambiguous positions on the rights of women and non-Muslims; develop concrete programs to address the nation's toughest social and economic problems; and apply the same pragmatism it has shown in the domestic arena to issues of foreign policy, including relations with Israel and the West. Over time, other parties—including others with an Islamist orientation—may provide the Brotherhood with some healthy competition and an impetus to further reform itself.

The Brotherhood has demonstrated that it is capable of evolving over time, and the best way to strengthen its democratic commitments is to include it in the political process, making sure there are checks and balances in place to ensure that no group can monopolize state power and that all citizens are guaranteed certain freedoms under the law. In the foreign policy domain, the Brotherhood rails against "U.S. and Zionist domination," demands the recognition of Palestinian rights, and may one day seek to revise the terms of Egypt's relationship with Israel through constitutional channels. The Brotherhood will likely never be as supportive of U.S. and Israeli interests in the region as Mubarak was. Yet here too, the best way for the United States to minimize the risk associated with the likely increase in its power is to encourage and reward judiciousness and pragmatism. With a track record of nearly 30 years of responsible behavior (if not rhetoric) and a strong base of support, the Muslim Brotherhood has earned a place at the table in the post-Mubarak era. No democratic transition can succeed without it.

Egypt's Democratic Mirage

How Cairo's Authoritarian Regime Is Adapting to Preserve Itself

Joshua Stacher

FOREIGNAFFAIRS.COM, FEBRUARY 7, 2011

Despite the tenacity, optimism, and blood of the protesters massed in Tahrir Square, Egypt's democratic window has probably already closed.

Contrary to the dominant media narrative, over the last ten days the Egyptian state has not experienced a regime breakdown. The protests have certainly rocked the system and have put Mubarak on his heels, but at no time has the uprising seriously threatened Egypt's regime. Although many of the protesters, foreign governments, and analysts have concentrated on the personality of Egyptian President Hosni Mubarak, those surrounding the embattled president, who make up the wider Egyptian regime, have made sure the state's viability was never in question. This is because the country's central institution, the military, which historically has influenced policy and commands near-monopolistic economic interests, has never balked.

JOSHUA STACHER is Assistant Professor of Political Science at Kent State University. He is writing a book comparing authoritarianism in Egypt and Syria.

As the headquarters of the ruling National Democratic Party burned to the ground, NDP members chaotically appeared on TV with a pathetically incoherent message; meanwhile, the message from the ruling military elite was clear, united, fully supportive of Mubarak, and disciplined practically down to a man. Indeed, this discipline could be seen throughout the military ranks. Despite the fact that a general with a megaphone stated his solidarity with the protesters while other protesters painted "Down to Mubarak" on tanks across central Cairo, no acts of organizational fragmentation or dissent within the chain of command have occurred.

Since January 28, the Mubarak regime has sought to encircle the protesters. Egypt's governing elites have used different parts of the regime to serve as arsonist and firefighter. Due to the regime's role in both lighting the fire and extinguishing it, protesters were effectively forced to flee from one wing of the regime to another. This occurred on two levels: first, the regime targeted the protesters, using the police as its battering ram. During the first days of demonstrations, uniformed officers fired rubber bullets and tear gas into the crowds. Beginning on February 2, plain-clothes officers posing as Mubarak supporters—some on horseback and camels—carried whips and sticks to intimidate and injure those protesting against the system, teaching them a repressive lesson.

Although it is impossible to say that every single member of the "pro-Mubarak" crowd was in the security forces, enough of them had their credentials taken to illustrate an indisputable police presence. Moreover, the violence has been selective and targeted, not chaotic, as Mubarak has described. The disappearance of police officers on January 29, leaving the neighborhoods to criminal elements and neighborhood watch groups, and their reappearance 24 hours later suggest that they were acting on orders, rather than haphazardly dispersing and returning.

While the army kept order in the streets, the Interior Ministry and police were functioning as the regime's repressive arm, performing the dirty work of trying to force the protesters from Tahrir back into their homes.

The military's rank and file, who are deployed on the streets, became part of a different regime strategy. There is no doubt that solidarities developed between protesters and soldiers as fellow citizens, but the army's aloof neutrality underscores that its role on the sidelines was intentional. This was prominently on display when the "pro-Mubarak" demonstrators attacked antigovernment protesters in Tahrir on February 2. That the siege of a major city square took place over the course of 16 hours, leaving 13 dead and more than 1,200 wounded, according to the Egyptian Ministry of Health, suggests that the military's orders were conceived to cast its officers as potential saviors from the brutal violence.

This containment strategy has worked. By politically encircling the protesters, the regime prevented the conflict from extending beyond its grasp. With the protesters caught between regime-engineered violence and regime-manufactured safety, the cabinet generals remained firmly in control of the situation.

The generals that now man the cabinet also sought to wage a war on the non-protesting population, and they did so without firing a single shot. As the state framed the demonstrators as troublemakers, non-protesting Egyptians experienced the uprising's effects. Banks have been closed since January 27, ATMs have been emptied of their cash, and the prices of food and staples have slowly risen at a time when school is cancelled, offices are closed, and curfews are in effect. Similarly, the Internet and cellular networks were shut off and have been patchy at best since their return.

Although some of these citizens may have sympathized with the protesters initially, their mood appears to be shifting. People are tired of being cooped up in their apartments, made anxious as their stockpiles of food and money decrease, and they are ready for a sense of "normalcy" to return. Ironically, the normalcy they pine for resembles the police state so many tried to banish just thirteen days ago. This method of wearing down the non-protesting public seems just as strategic as the violence employed on those airing their grievances in the streets.

The story that the news media have largely crafted is that of the good protesters pitted against the bad Mubarak dictatorship. Despite the accurate reporting of incidents and often horrifying images, the fact that the Egyptian regime has played a good-cop, bad-cop routine to contain the situation remains lost in the din of 24-hour coverage. Despite many of the protesters pointing out this dynamic, such as Hossam el-Hamalawy and Mahmoud Salem, it has failed to take hold as the prevailing thread.

Nevertheless, as the crisis has deepened, the push for Mubarak's resignation has intensified. According to *The New York Times*, the Obama administration will seek to have Mubarak retire early instead of waiting until the September election. The United States has repeatedly insisted on an "orderly transition."

If those guiding the transition choose to direct it toward a democratic end, then it will have to include forces that are currently banned in the country, such as the Muslim Brotherhood, and individuals who have been tortured or imprisoned, such as Ayman Nour. It will have to include the youth elements from the street organizing committees as well as the irrelevant figures that head the country's existing opposition parties. Managing such a transition from dictatorship to democracy is a massive challenge even in the best of times. The leader of the transition will therefore determine whether it results in a genuine democracy or continuous authoritarian rule. If that person is General Omar Suleiman, who was sworn in as vice president on January 30, the prospects for democracy are grim.

Suleiman is cut from the same undemocratic cloth as Mubarak. They have collaborated since 1993, and Suleiman shares many of Mubarak's policy preferences and his worldview. He is known for his skill as a negotiator and his disdain for the Muslim Brotherhood. Although the vice president may now seem a stabilizing force for the Egyptian state during a transition period, U.S. officials should consider that he might seek to stay in power long beyond September.

Indeed, some of Suleiman's earliest public statements since becoming vice president do not bode well for democracy. In fact, they sound eerily familiar. On February 2, the bloodiest day in Tahrir Square to date, Suleiman said the regime now refuses to negotiate until "the Egyptian street returns to normal." Sensing that the regime had the upper hand, Suleiman declared that a new constitution is out of the question in advance of the presidential election later this year and asserted that the unrest had been the result of "a conspiracy" directed by "foreign countries, the Muslim Brothers, and some parties." Lastly, echoing the paternalistic tone that Mubarak has employed for nearly 30 years, Suleiman recommended, "We will ask [protesters] to go home. And we'll ask their parents to ask them to go home." Hence, he effectively called out potential transition partners as traitors and children before pledging to conduct another presidential election under a desperately flawed constitution.

The protesters have been given an ambiguous choice about this transition. Go home and—perhaps—be invited to the negotiating table later, or continue protesting and be excluded from Suleiman's negotiations. Some independent figures, such as Amr Moussa and Nabil Fahmy, have broken ranks with the protesters and met with Suleiman. Given that many of these individuals held previous appointments in Mubarak's Egypt, protesters will likely be skeptical of their intentions as agents of change.

There is no doubt that the post-Mubarak era is afoot, but it is not necessarily a democratic one. The Egyptian military leaders that are governing the country seem content to leave

Mubarak in his place so Suleiman can act as the sitting president. Indeed, even leading government officials, including U.S. Secretary of State Hillary Clinton, have begun to direct their concerns to Suleiman's office. Hence, as the protesters in Tahrir Square—and the non-protesters facing empty refrigerators and wallets at home—have begun to feel the state's squeeze, the regime has so far maintained its ability to control how the conflict is unfolding.

When the uprising began in Egypt, many linked the events in Tunis and Cairo and declared that 2011 might be the Arab world's 1989. Instead, 2011 is showing just how durable and adaptable the authoritarian regimes of the Arab world truly are. Faced with real challenges and moments of potential breakdown, Egypt's military did not hesitate or even break a sweat. In fact, the regime remained cohesive throughout by pursuing a sophisticated strategy of unleashing violence upon the people and then saving them from it.

This latest adaptation of autocracy in the Arab world is more honest than its previous incarnations. Before the uprising in Egypt began, the military ruled from behind the curtain while elites, represented by public relations firms and buoyed by snappy slogans, initiated neoliberal economic policies throughout Egypt. In this latest rendering, with Suleiman at the helm, the state's objective of restoring a structure of rule by military managers is not even concealed. This sort of "orderly transition" in post-Mubarak Egypt is more likely to usher in a return to the repressive status quo than an era of widening popular participation.

Overcoming Fear and Anxiety in Tel Aviv

How Israel Can Turn Egypt's Unrest Into an Opportunity

Aluf Benn

FOREIGNAFFAIRS.COM, FEBRUARY 8, 2011

The revolt against President Hosni Mubarak in Egypt invokes fear and anxiety among Israelis. Mubarak, Israel's oldest neighbor, is suddenly moving out, and Israelis are afraid of the consequences: Who will be the new tenants next door? Will they keep the long-standing peace treaty with Israel? Is a new Iran emerging across the border, with the long-forgotten southern front coming back to life? To a nation built around survival, these questions are extremely worrying.

True to form, Israeli Prime Minister Benjamin Netanyahu has highlighted those fears in public, particularly the threat of Egypt turning into a new Iran. Yet a more optimistic analysis suggests that the Israeli government could leverage the Egyptian crisis to seek new opportunities—a window to restart the peace process with the Palestinians or Syria, or a chance to support the spread of democracy in the region. Israel's establishment, however, has thus far opted for entrenchment.

ALUF BENN is Editor-at-Large of *Haaretz*.

For three decades, Mubarak has been a fixture of Israel's geostrategic landscape. Israel replaced eight prime ministers, fought several wars, and engaged in peace talks with multiple partners, and Mubarak was always there. He personified regional stability.

To be sure, Mubarak has kept his distance from Israel. Unlike his predecessor, Anwar Sadat, who came to Jerusalem to make peace, Mubarak stubbornly refused to pay an official visit to Israel, coming only once to attend Israeli Prime Minister Yitzhak Rabin's funeral and insisting at the time that "this is not a visit." Mubarak's governments were vocally critical of Israeli policies vis-á-vis the Palestinians and waged endless diplomatic campaigns against Israel's nuclear program.

But Israeli leaders were willing to accept these minor insults, knowing that Israel had no better ally than Mubarak on big-picture issues. They could go to war in Lebanon and Gaza and expand the West Bank settlements, freed from having to devote a substantial force to the southern front.

Yet as Mubarak grew older, Israel's leaders began worrying about who would succeed him. Given the obvious sensitivities—Israel could not speculate openly about an ally's coming demise—the issue was rarely discussed in public or even among diplomatic circles. When asked about it, Israeli officials hinted at Omar Suleiman, intelligence chief (and now Egypt's vice president), or at Gamal Mubarak, the president's son and heir apparent, as their preferred successors to the aging leader. The alternatives to these comfortable candidates left many Israeli leaders unsettled. They believed that Mubarak and his police state were barriers to chaos that, if removed, would be succeeded by an Iranian-style Islamic Republic—one directly neighboring Israel and armed with state-of-the-art U.S. weaponry.

In the Israeli collective memory, 1979 marks a major strategic turning point. Until then, Iran was Israel's key regional ally and energy supplier, and Egypt its chief adversary. In the span of six weeks that year, however, the Shah's regime in Iran gave way to the rule of the fiercely anti-Israel Ayatollah Ruhollah Khomeini, and Israel signed its peace treaty with Egypt. Thus, Iran and Egypt switched roles, with the former becoming Israel's enemy and the latter turning into its strategic ally and energy supplier. "There was a country that we had peace with, an extraordinary de-facto peace," Netanyahu told a gathering of Israel's ambassadors in December 2010. "Meetings between leaders, security and economic cooperation. This country was named Iran. It is still named Iran. And one day, one day, it changed." The same happened with Turkey, added Netanyahu, "not overnight, but it changed very fast due to domestic changes unrelated to us." The lesson, according to Netanyahu, was that all alliances are temporary and might collapse as a result of uncontrollable domestic forces.

Israel's regional ties have always been with the ruling elites, the military commanders, and the intelligence communities. Public opinion in the Arab world has been traditionally hostile to Israel. Civil society groups in Egypt and Jordan, in particular, largely reject their countries' respective peace treaties with Israel. Israelis, for their part, hardly cared about people-to-people contacts; not many Israeli Jews bother to learn Arabic and immerse themselves in the neighboring culture. Most Israelis viewed the peace process as a means for bettering relations with Europe and the United States and not as a channel to regional acceptance.

It is little wonder, then, that the Israeli political-military establishment has viewed Arab democracy as a dangerous adventure. The mainstream belief is that if allowed to choose, the Egyptian public would bring the Muslim Brotherhood to power—and throw the peace treaty with Israel to the shredder. Hamas' victory in the Palestinian election of 2006 and its subsequent takeover of Gaza serve as the most compelling evidence for this mindset. Israeli leaders saw U.S. President

George W. Bush's support for democratization in the Middle East as the ultimate expression of American naiveté.

Netanyahu has in the past called democracy the ultimate foundation of peace, arguing that Israel cannot relinquish territory to nondemocratic countries because they are untrustworthy. But given the slim chances of a true democracy appearing in Israel's neighborhood, his argument was interpreted as an appealing—if unconvincing—excuse against territorial compromise. In recent years, however, following the electoral rise of Hamas, Netanyahu changed his tune. He stopped calling for Arab democracy and, like his predecessors, learned to appreciate the familiar dictators. Indeed, after returning to office in 2009, Netanyahu enthusiastically befriended Mubarak. The two met frequently to discuss their concerns about Iran and Gaza and Israeli-Palestinian peace negotiations. It was not an unequivocal love affair: according to a cable released by WikiLeaks, Mubarak described Netanyahu as elegant and charming, but unable to keep promises. Yet the two leaders forged a good working relationship that seemed likely to endure. Netanyahu wanted his friend to stay in power as long as possible.

The Tunisian tempest that has nearly ousted Mubarak took the Israeli government by surprise. Even after the Tunisians overthrew their despot, Zine el-Abidine Ben Ali, Israel's intelligence chiefs and Arab affairs experts argued that the Egyptian regime was stable. When reality swept away the rosy predictions, Netanyahu begged Western leaders to lend a hand to his besieged friend Mubarak. At first, they would not listen, but after several days the Obama administration appeared to heed the Israeli call and opt for a gradual transition in Egypt.

As his nightmare of losing Mubarak came true, Netanyahu warned of an Islamic takeover in Egypt. He demanded that the international community call on any Egyptian government to abide by its peace treaty with Israel. The undertone of his message reflected a growing doubt among Israeli policymakers about the value of U.S. pledges of support. If the United States was so willing to abandon its longtime Egyptian protégé, Israelis are wondering, can its commitments be trusted? And if Israel's oldest and strongest peace treaty, that with Egypt, cannot withstand a change in government, how could Israel sign similar land-for-peace agreements in the future?

Netanyahu's warning notwithstanding, an Egyptian repeat of the Iranian ally-to-enemy scenario is unlikely. Mubarak's successor would likely cool off the alliance with Israel. But rather than follow Khomeini and Iranian President Mahmoud Ahmedinejad, the next Egyptian leader could imitate Turkish Prime Minister Recep Tayyip Erdogan: keep the formal structure of relations with Israel, do away with the strategic alliance, and criticize Israel's treatment of the Palestinians and its use of force. This policy has bought Erdogan immense popularity with the Arab public, even as Israel's embassy in Ankara remains open and Israelis travel freely to Istanbul.

Even if Egypt's new leadership takes this more moderate path, Israel faces a difficult security dilemma. Rebuilding a large ground force to anticipate the possible resurrection of an Egyptian adversary is both costly and risks an unwanted arms race. Neglecting to do so, however, could be risky if the Muslim Brotherhood assumes power in Cairo. And even if Egypt abides by the current security structure—a demilitarized Sinai—Israeli uncertainty over its behavior would limit Israel's freedom of action in other fronts. Netanyahu is unlikely to bomb Iran's nuclear facilities if he cannot trust the Egyptians to look the other way, as they did when Israeli Prime Minister Menachem Begin bombed the Iraqi nuclear reactor at Osirak in 1981.

Mubarak's departure would strip Israel of its most important regional ally. But it would also leave the United States without a trustworthy "pillar of stability" in the region. This friendless situation could push Obama and Netanyahu into closer cooperation, despite their rocky relationship to date.

The Egyptian revolt also opens up new opportunities for peacemaking elsewhere. Israel wants to break away from its growing diplomatic isolation, having just lost its Turkish alliance last year, and now watching its Egyptian alliance hang in the balance. Its interlocutors in Syria and the Palestinian Authority are afraid that they are next in line to face popular revolts. Peace deals can serve both sides' interest, with the added strategic bonus for Israel of preventing encirclement on multiple fronts.

Israel could offer new peace proposals to the Palestinians and Syria, or demonstrate renewed interest in the 2002 Arab Peace Initiative, which hinged a comprehensive settlement between Israel and the Arab world on the creation of a Palestinian state. By proposing a serious blueprint to Palestinian statehood and pulling Syria away from Iran's orbit through negotiations, Israel would not only defuse animosity against it in the Arab street, but also take part in the rebuilding of the Middle Eastern community in the wake of Egypt's unrest.

Alas, such ideas are far from the minds of Israel's current leaders. The instinctive and expected Israeli reaction to the upheaval in Egypt has been to try to preserve the status quo for as long as possible while planning a defense budget increase. A collapse or cooling of the peace treaty between Egypt and Israel would bolster the right-wing argument that Arabs cannot be trusted and that peace with the Arab world is impossible. A more sober analysis could leverage the current crisis into a new opportunity for Israel. This, however, entails a change from the siege mentality underlying Netanyahu's foreign policy.

Mubarakism Without Mubarak

Why Egypt's Military Will Not Embrace Democracy

Ellis Goldberg

FOREIGNAFFAIRS.COM, FEBRUARY 11, 2011

Egyptian President Hosni Mubarak gave into the demands of the protesters today, leaving Cairo and stepping down from power. That came hours after a speech, broadcast live across the world yesterday, in which he refused to do so. Earlier that day, the Supreme Military Council released a statement—labeled its "first" communiqué—that stated that the military would ensure a peaceful transition of Mubarak out of office. In practice, it appears that power has passed into the hands of the armed forces. This act was the latest in the military's creep from applauded bystander to steering force in this month's protests in Egypt. Since the protest movement first took shape on January 25, the military has, with infinite patience, extended and deepened its physical control of the area around Tahrir Square (the focal point of the protests) with concrete barriers, large steel plates, and rolls of razor wire. In itself, the military's growing

ELLIS GOLDBERG is Professor of Political Science at the University of Washington and at the American University in Cairo.

footprint was the next act in a slow-motion coup—a return of the army from indirect to direct control—the groundwork for which was laid in 1952.

The West may be worried that the crisis will bring democracy too quickly to Egypt and empower the Muslim Brotherhood. But the real concern is that the regime will only shed its corrupt civilians, leaving its military component as the only player left standing. Indeed, when General Omar Suleiman, the recently appointed vice president to whom Mubarak entrusted presidential powers last night, threatened on February 9 that the Egyptian people must choose between either the current regime or a military coup, he only increased the sense that the country was being held hostage.

The Egyptian political system under Mubarak is the direct descendant of the republic established in the wake of the 1952 military coup that brought Gamal Abdel Nasser and the Free Officers to power. Nasser and the officers abolished Egypt's limited parliamentary monarchy and ousted an entire generation of civilian political and judicial figures from public life. They created their own republic stocked with loyal military figures. Their one experiment with technocratic governance, allowing Egyptian legal experts to write a new basic document, was a failure. The experts' draft had provisions for a strong parliament and limited presidency, which the officers deemed too liberal. They literally threw it into the wastebasket and started over, writing a constitution that placed immense power in the hands of the president.

Such an arrangement would prove to work out well for the military, as every Egyptian president since 1953 has been an army officer. For two generations, the military was able, through the president, to funnel most of the country's resources toward national security, arming for a series of ultimately disastrous wars with Israel. These defeats, combined with the government's neglect of the economy, nearly drove the country to bankruptcy. Popular revolt erupted between 1975 and 1977 over the government's economic policies. To regain control, the military turned its attention away from war and toward development. It gradually withdrew from direct control over politics, ceding power to domestic security forces and the other powerful backer of Egypt's ruling party—small groups of civilian businessmen who benefited from their privileged access to government sales and purchases to expand their own fortunes.

In the 1990s, Mubarak waged a domestic war against Islamists, and the role of the military evolved further. As the government became dependent on an expanded domestic police force, the army was reduced in size and importance. Over time, the police and the Ministry of the Interior supplanted the armed forces and Ministry of Defense as the keystone of the regime. Meanwhile, the factions of the business elite that fed on the state, such as the now disgraced steel magnate and former ruling party leader Ahmed Ezz, grew more powerful. Mubarak gave them privileged access to the ruling National Democratic Party, which they convinced to open the Egyptian economy to world trade—enriching them even further.

The officer corps was appeased to some degree, however, by its own economic good fortune. Throughout the 1990s, the army expanded its involvement in the economy. By this decade, industries owned by the military were estimated to control 5 to 20 percent of the entire Egyptian economy; likewise, army officers receive a variety of benefits, such as special preference in access to goods and services.

Today, the army presents itself as a force of order and a neutral arbiter between contending opponents, but it has significant interests of its own to defend, and it is not, in fact, neutral. The basic structure of the Egyptian state as it now exists has benefited the military. The practical demands of the protesters seem fairly simple: end the state of emergency, hold new elections, and grant the freedom to form parties without state interference. But these demands would amount to opening up the political space to everyone across Egypt's social and political structure. That would involve constitutional and statutory changes, such as reforming Egypt as a parliamentary rather than a presidential system, in which a freely elected majority selects the prime minister (who is now appointed by the president). These changes would wipe away the power structure the army created in 1952 and has backed since.

A freely elected parliament and a reconstituted government would weaken the role of the presidency, a position the military is likely to try to keep in its portfolio. Moreover, open elections could hand the new business elites power in parliament, where they could work to limit the role of the army in the economy. This would put the army's vast economic holdings—from the ubiquitous propane cylinders that provide all Egyptian homes with cooking gas to clothing, food, and hotels—in jeopardy. Moreover, the army has always preferred that the country be orderly and hierarchical. It is uncomfortable with the growing participatory festival on the streets, and even if the officers were to tolerate more contestation than their grandfathers did in the 1950s, they would likely try to limit participation in politics to those whose lives have been spent in the military by retaining the system of presidential appointment for government ministers.

Indeed, instead of pursuing institutional change, leading military figures will likely try to satisfy the public with symbolic gestures. They would surely investigate the most corrupt businessmen and their ministerial associates for the misuse of public funds and public property. At the same time, there will likely be an investigation of the former minister of interior for deliberately murdering demonstrators during the crisis.

If the military takes further control, two of the players currently on the scene will be crucial. First, Suleiman, who has strong ties to the military, is at the center of every negotiation among the opposition factions and is almost constantly on television. Unsurprisingly, he has made it clear that he has no intention of reforming the presidential system. Playing for time, he has consistently insisted that even negotiations should be strictly limited to changing the three articles of the constitution that deal with elections.

Second, although Egypt's defense minister, Field Marshal Hussein Tantawi, has been much less visible, he is no less important. He is behind the army's announcement that it would not, unlike the hated security police, fire on Egyptians. In fact, the army fired on neither the demonstrators nor on the thugs who attacked them, and even went so far as to announce that the protesters had legitimate demands. I have heard accounts of the army arresting some protesters and members of human rights groups. Some of those who have been arrested and released report that a faction of army officers remain sympathetic to Mubarak's appeals that he has a mission to carry out. Still, under Tantawi, the army will likely try to at least appear neutral while negotiating with the rest of the opposition to manage a transition, even as Suleiman works to ensure that reform is limited.

The Mubarak regime as it has existed for the last decade—an increasingly corrupt and incompetent government that has conferred immense economic advantages on a handful of politically connected businessmen—has been shattered. A more open political system and a responsive government that ensures its own safety by trimming back the power and privileges of the military could still emerge. And the army may step in as a transitional power and recognize that, as much as it might like to, it cannot return to complete control. The Egyptian military is far more professional and educated than it was in the 1950s, so many officers may recognize the benefits of a democracy. More likely, however, is the culmination of the slow-motion coup and the return of the somewhat austere military authoritarianism of decades past.

Reflections on the Revolution in Egypt

Richard N. Haass

PROJECT SYNDICATE, FEBRUARY 13, 2011

Revolutions happen for a reason. In the case of Egypt, there are several reasons: more than 30 years of one-man rule; Hosni Mubarak's plans to pass the presidency on to his son; widespread corruption, patronage, and nepotism; and economic reform that did not benefit most Egyptians, but that nonetheless contrasted sharply with the almost complete absence of political change.

The net result was that many Egyptians felt not just alienated, but also humiliated. Humiliation is a powerful motivator. Egypt was ripe for revolution; dramatic change would have come at some point in the next few years, even absent the spark of Tunisia or the existence of social media.

Indeed, social media are a significant factor, but their role has been exaggerated. It is hardly the first disruptive technology to come along: the printing press, telegraph, telephone, radio, television, and cassettes all posed challenges to the existing order of their day. And like these earlier technologies, social media are not decisive: they can be repressed by governments as well as employed by governments to motivate their supporters.

RICHARD N. HAASS, formerly director of policy planning in the U.S. State Department, is president of the Council on Foreign Relations.

Timing counts for a lot in politics. Mubarak's announcement that he would not seek re-election would likely have averted a crisis had he issued it in December. But, by the time he did say it, the mood of the street had evolved to the point that he could no longer placate it.

The initial success of revolutions is determined less by the strength of the protesters than by the will and cohesion of the regime. Tunisia's collapse came quickly, because its president lost his nerve and the army was weak and unwilling to stand by him. Egypt's establishment and its military are demonstrating far greater resolve.

Mubarak's departure is a significant but not decisive development. To be sure, it closes a prolonged era of Egyptian politics. It also marks the end of the first phase of Egypt's revolution. But it is only the end of the beginning. What begins now is the struggle for Egypt's future.

The objective must be to slow the political clock. Egyptians need time to build a civil society and open a political spectrum that has been mostly closed for decades. A hybrid, caretaker government, including military and civilian elements, may be the best way forward. To slow the clock is not to stop it, however. A genuine political transition needs to move ahead, albeit at a measured pace.

Early elections should be avoided, lest those (such as the Muslim Brotherhood) who have been able to organize over the years enjoy an unfair advantage. The Muslim Brotherhood should be allowed to participate in the political process so long as it accepts the legitimacy of that process, the rule of law, and the constitution. The history and political culture of Egypt suggest a natural limit to the Brotherhood's appeal if Egyptians can bridge their most important differences, maintain order, and restore economic growth.

Constitutional reform is critical. Egypt needs a constitution that enjoys broad support—and that includes checks and balances that make it difficult for minorities (even those who command the support of a plurality of voters) to rule majorities.

Revolutionary movements invariably split into factions. Their sole common objective is the ouster of the existing regime. As soon as this goal comes close to being achieved, elements of the opposition begin to position themselves for the second phase of the struggle and the coming competition for power. We are already beginning to see signs of this in Egypt and will see more in the days and weeks to come.

Some in Egypt will be satisfied only with full democracy; others (probably a majority) will care most about public order, greater official accountability, a degree of political participation, and economic improvement. It is never possible to satisfy the demands of all protesters, and regimes should not try.

Egypt will face enormous economic difficulties, exacerbated by recent events, which have frightened off tourists, deterred investment, and kept many from working. The challenges of a fast-growing population, inadequate education, insufficient jobs, corruption, bureaucracy, and rising global competition constitute the greatest threat to the country's future.

Outsiders have had and will have only limited influence over the course of events. Over the past 30 years, intermittent calls by the United States for limited political reform were largely rebuffed. Once the crisis began, the people in the streets, Mubarak himself, and above all the army have been the principal protagonists. Moving forward, it will again be Egyptians who will largely determine their own path.

In this vein, outsiders should be careful of intervening too much, especially in public. It is up to Egyptians to define for themselves how much and what kind of democracy is established. Outsiders can assist—for example, with ideas for constitutional reform or voting procedures—but this should be done privately and as suggestions, not demands.

Developments in Egypt will have uneven consequences in the region. Not every country will be affected equally. True monarchies, like Jordan, have a legitimacy and stability that the leaders of faux monarchies (Syria, Libya, and Yemen), as well as the Iranian regime, do not. Much will depend on what transpires and how.

Change in Iraq was imposed from the outside by force, whereas change in Egypt has come from within and has largely been accomplished by consent rather than coercion. But it is too soon to know whether change in Egypt will be far-reaching and lasting, much less positive, and thus too soon to assess its historic impact.

Postcolonial Time Disorder

Egypt and the Middle East, Stuck in the Past

James D. Le Sueur

FOREIGNAFFAIRS.COM, FEBRUARY 14, 2011

Gamal Abdel Nasser pledged to thrust Egypt into the postcolonial time zone in 1952, when he wrested control of the government from the Egyptian monarch and the British Empire. As he wrote in his autobiographical essay, *Egypt's Liberation*, "The revolution marked the realization of a great hope felt by the people of Egypt since they began, in modern times, to think in terms of self-government and to demand that they have the final say in determining their own future." Unfortunately, almost 50 years later, Egyptians are still struggling to determine their own future. And now, with President Hosni Mubarak deposed, the aspirations of the people once again rest in the hands of the military.

Mubarak was just 24 years old when Nasser took power. He was part of a generation of leaders in the developing world who, like Nasser, came to view hegemonic nationalism as necessary and used the military to secure national unity at the expense

JAMES D. LE SUEUR is Professor of History at the University of Nebraska at Lincoln. He is the author of *Algeria Since 1989: Between Terror and Democracy*.

of civic freedoms. When Mubarak took office after Anwar al-Sadat was assassinated, he rolled back Sadat's interior political reforms and repressed his political opponents, especially the Muslim Brotherhood.

It is safe to say that most of the protesters who filled Tahrir Square had an altogether different view of nationalism, the military, technology, ideology, and most important, time. Mubarak, however, subscribed to an outdated nationalist ideology that did not tolerate democratic discussion and was trapped in a view of the world that refused to account for change. For Mubarak, time stood still, so protesters clamoring for change made no sense historically to him.

Likewise, xenophobic Egyptian state propaganda presented the protesters as part of a foreign, almost neocolonial, conspiracy meant to undo the nation. As a result, the military—which has been the beneficiary of autocracy and generous foreign aid packages from the United States and elsewhere—found itself straddling the past and the future as it faced its first true crossroads since 1952. It had to make a decision about its place in time.

Many leaders within and outside the Middle East suffer from the same type of historical jetlag as Mubarak. As a result, they are similarly unable to keep pace with younger populations demanding political reform. Last month, activists in Tunisia chased 74-year-old Zine el-Abidine Ben Ali into exile, which emboldened Egyptians to get rid of Mubarak. With both men out of power, leaders from Algeria and Libya to Yemen have been put on notice.

Like Mubarak, other "presidents for life" see popular challenges to state authority as inauthentic and conspiracy-driven—an understandable worldview, since many of them cut their teeth during decolonization. They suffer from what can be called postcolonial time disorder, or PTD, meaning that they still subscribe to an out-of-date philosophy of governance, according to which authoritarianism is the only cure for external or internal political challenges. They have a Manichean inability to think outside the logic of totalizing state power.

PTD originated in countries' efforts to jump-start history during the anticolonial national liberation movements before and after World War II, when the great European empires ran the show and stamped out democratic movements. Decolonization and the postcolonial periods were so hard fought that states could claim that only their uncontested authority would prevent a return to the past.

In various ways, PTD affects how such leaders as Algerian President Abdelaziz Bouteflika, Libyan leader Muammar al-Gaddafi, Iranian President Mahmoud Ahmadinejad, Zimbabwean President Robert Mugabe, and Myanmarese President Thein Sein run their countries. All of them contend that their uncontested powers shield their people from the dangers of a neocolonial world. Ben Ali viewed his unflinching stranglehold on the population as a quasi-divine nationalist right. Mubarak was one of decolonization's last men standing and served as the secretary-general of the Non-Aligned Movement, an artifact of the Cold War. Now that he has fallen, it is possible that the paradigm of unchecked state power—which has prevented time from moving forward and blocked democratic enfranchisement—will also implode.

Now that the clock has finally struck for Mubarak in Egypt, other states in the region suffering from PTD remain vulnerable to revolution. Algeria—a regional power, U.S. ally, and major energy producer—is foremost among them. Protesters there, who went to the streets on February 12 in much smaller numbers than in Tunisia and Egypt, hope to catch a lift from their neighbors. But it is not clear if Algerians have the stomach to pull off what the Egyptians and the Tunisians have done.

After massive riots caused the one-party state to collapse in 1988, Algeria failed to become a democracy, and the military took power in 1992. What followed was the decade-long Algerian civil war. Algerian civil society has only just begun to emerge from the trauma of that war, which left 200,000 people dead. To date, it remains the region's most violent conflict between militants and the state. As was the case in Egypt, public protests in Algeria are prohibited under state-of-emergency measures, which have allowed the government to engage in heavy-handed censorship and the abuse of civil liberties. And like Mubarak, following the revolution in Tunisia and flashes of protests in Algeria, Bouteflika vowed to lift the existing state-of-emergency measures. But he has not yet done so.

One of the key moments of decolonization came in February 1960, four years after Nasser's nationalization of the Suez Canal, when British Prime Minister Harold Macmillan delivered his "wind of change" speech to the South African parliament in Cape Town. The speech signaled that the United Kingdom was willing to accept the loss of its African colonies, and it set in motion a wave of decolonization. Today, the Middle East might be experiencing another "wind of change" moment, with the people rejecting regimes that are out of sync with time, fueled by corruption, reliant on brutal police regimes to suppress dissent, and determined to stay in power at all costs.

As the dust settles, all eyes are turning to the military elite. For Egypt, the question is how the military will facilitate a democratic process and whether it will remain, as it is often described, the people's army. In South Africa, it should be remembered, Macmillan's speech gave the apartheid state justification to retreat from foreign criticism and leave the Commonwealth of Nations to create the Republic of South Africa in 1961. The country was betting against time, and it took another 30 years to break the hold of PTD on its leaders. After the downfall of Mubarak, it is doubtful that the Egyptian military will dig in and resist efforts to reform the one-party police state.

To stay with the South African example, Nelson Mandela said many times that while in prison he saw too many postcolonial leaders come to power only to abuse their people and rob them of the promises of liberation. In this sense, Mandela is one recent leader who understood the dangers of PTD and inoculated himself from its effects by embracing national reconciliation and democracy after he was elected president in 1994. Given the brutality of the South African regime he was succeeding, this was by no means an easy strategy. Nevertheless, he overcame his rage and set the South African clocks forward with a program of national reconciliation, complete with trials and forgiveness for willing participants. And he oversaw the implementation of the most liberal constitution in the world, which ensured multiparty competition.

If Egypt—and, indeed, other governments in the region whose leaders still have untreated PTD—is to move forward, its future leaders must be sure not to inherit PTD from past leaders. In the West's rush to prejudge the various movements that might be involved in the new government in Egypt, it is worth remembering that both Ronald Reagan and Margaret Thatcher initially insisted that Mandela was a communist-backed "terrorist." All the while, the United States and the United Kingdom were supporting radical Islamists, including Osama bin Laden, as anticommunist allies fighting in Afghanistan against the Soviets. The fact that Mandela became the most important man of peace of his generation and bin Laden became the greatest terrorist is cause for skepticism and patience.

The legacy of Mubarak's oppressive rule will make it difficult for Egyptians to fight off the desire for revenge. To overcome that impulse, the military will have to provide security and the space Egyptians need to consider constitutional reforms like those South Africa enacted, which protected civil liberties for all citizens. The newly reconstituted Egyptian state must also allow journalists, activists, and historians to do their jobs, since, as South Africa demonstrated, historical awareness and civic-minded democratic activism is vital for any state to move forward after decades of distrust. From all the evidence so far, the Egyptian activists appear well-positioned to keep track of the military's progress toward reform.

Egypt's Constitutional Ghosts

Deciding the Terms of Cairo's Democratic Transition

Nathan J. Brown

FOREIGNAFFAIRS.COM, FEBRUARY 15, 2011

Egyptians seeking to build a new future after the rule of Hosni Mubarak hope to draw on, as well as correct, the flaws in the country's longstanding constitutional tradition. In the days since a military council took power from Mubarak, the country's political opposition has been quick to articulate its demands in the language of dry legal texts and procedures.

The current constitution was first enacted in 1971 and amended several times in the years afterward, but its precursors date back to a century before. Egypt's first constitutional effort came in 1882, when an assembly approved a basic law to govern its relationship with the cabinet. In 1923, when the country gained its independence from the British Empire, a second and more comprehensive document was written to combine, however uneasily, a parliamentary system with a monarchy.

NATHAN J. BROWN is Professor of Political Science and International Affairs at George Washington University and a nonresident Senior Associate at the Carnegie Endowment for International Peace.

When the 1923 constitution was scrapped in the wake of a 1952 military coup, Egypt's legal scholars set to work designing a republican constitution based on liberal and democratic values. Their work was shelved in 1954, however, by the country's new military rulers, who issued instead a series of documents to serve their own ideological and institutional needs. These new rules delivered the Egyptian polity into the hands of a one-party system in which all power rested with Gamal Abdel Nasser, Egypt's president until his death in 1970.

In 1971, Egypt received a new constitution, which would prove to be a more complicated and long-lived document. When Anwar al-Sadat succeeded Nasser, he found himself with rivals in various institutions, such as in the sole political party and the security apparatus. At the same time, he looked to recalibrate the regime's ideology, moving gently away from socialism and toward religion. Both problems, he realized, could be addressed with a new constitution. Sadat convened a large and remarkably diverse committee: feminists, Islamic legal scholars, liberals, socialists, nationalists, and representatives of the Christian church were all represented. On the whole, the group moved in the direction Sadat wanted: weakening the party, nominally strengthening legal institutions, and promising Egyptians a move away from the harshest aspects of Nasserist authoritarianism.

The result was a document that promised a little bit to everybody—but everything to the president. The constitution contained guarantees for individual freedoms, democratic procedures, and judicial independence. It made nods toward socialism and Islam. But for every commitment, there was also a trap door; for every liberty, there was a loophole that ultimately did little to rein in the power of the president or the country's determined security apparatus.

Over the next four decades, Egypt's presidents tinkered with the text. Sadat took further steps against socialism and made greater concessions to Islam; he dismantled the single-party system and replaced it with a nominally pluralistic political order in which the party of the president—today's collapsing National Democratic Party—enjoyed a dominant role. For every step forward, there was a step back: after the single party that had controlled the press was disbanded, authority was handed, in 1980, to a new state press council.

Mubarak left the constitution alone for most of his presidency, arguing that Egypt needed stability rather than further ideological and institutional gyrations. But Egypt did change in some gradual ways, sometimes toward liberalism. Mubarak widened the limited party pluralism allowed by Sadat; he permitted an opposition press to grow in the 1980s and an independent press to flourish in the 2000s.

Yet the country's political movement was far from linear. In the 1980s, the state's reliance on harsh authoritarian tools gradually abated; yet in the 1990s, these repressive tools were resurrected and used not just against radical Islamists but also the far tamer Muslim Brotherhood.

But on the whole, beginning in the 1980s, some of constitution's liberal elements began to come to life, largely led by Egypt's judiciary. A new judicial law in 1984 gave Egypt's civil and criminal judiciary more autonomy, and the State Council—a set of courts that have jurisdiction over cases in which a state body is a party—proved surprisingly friendly to ordinary citizens.

Most striking was the Supreme Constitutional Court, a structure originally designed to keep the rest of the judiciary in check. But as it gained an autonomous voice during the 1980s and 1990s, it actually began to enforce some of the rights and freedoms embedded in the Egyptian constitution. A set of court decisions on electoral laws, for example, forced a more open balloting process. By 2005, parliament had one-fifth of its seats controlled by the Muslim Brotherhood. Most of the other deputies were allied with the regime, but a looser party system made them more difficult to control.

In 2007, the Mubarak regime introduced a series of constitutional amendments that slammed shut most of the liberal openings in the 1971 constitution. The changes took elections away from full judicial supervision and placed them under the control of regime-dominated commissions; allowed multicandidate presidential elections on paper but sharply restricted viable candidacies in practice; constitutionally barred the Brotherhood from forming a political party; and took steps to insert formerly extraordinary emergency measures (such as the president's ability to refer cases to military courts for swift and reliable convictions) into the constitutional text.

It should be no surprise, therefore, that the protest movement that brought down Mubarak no longer looked to the constitution for guidance. For years, opposition activists and reform figures focused their efforts on a few constitutional provisions in the hope that fixing those could bring the liberal and democratic elements of the 1971 constitution back to life. But the 2007 amendments had carefully placed booby traps throughout the document. Tinkering was no longer enough. When Egypt's opposition leaders began talking of "revolution," they wanted not only to end the Mubarak presidency but also to sweep aside the 1971 constitution.

Thus, the crowds in Tahrir Square were elated by the abandonment of constitutional procedures on February 11 and the suspension of the constitution on February 13. If the country is to be governed by a military junta, then fundamental restructuring would seem to be on the table. This is an extremely risky strategy for the opposition, however, since it depends on the regime's willingness to negotiate with the opposition and agree to a truly inclusive process of political reconstruction.

It might seem that the past century would make Egyptians cynical about the power of paper to build a proper political order. But just the opposite seems to be the case: it has taught them that they need to pay far more attention to the fine print. Today there is a remarkably wide consensus on the elements of a new constitutional order. Almost all political forces outside of the regime—from the Muslim Brotherhood to labor-oriented activists—would agree on a general package of reform.

The opposition would like to see a whittling down of the powers of the presidency; firm institutional guarantees of judicial independence, largely in the form of a more autonomous and powerful judicial council; judicial monitoring of elections; an end to exceptional courts and Egypt's state of emergency (in nearly continuous effect since 1939); more robust instruments for protecting rights and freedoms; and a truly pluralist party system.

Taken together, the proposed changes would have three effects. First, they would greatly increase accountability of existing institutions to the people. Second, they would give real protection to individual freedoms and provide guarantees for a pluralist political system. Third, they would activate mechanisms of horizontal accountability, so that Egypt's various constitutional institutions could patrol one another.

In this third element, Egyptians show a sophisticated understanding of their constitutional past. Egypt is a state of institutions—but those institutions have all been accountable to the presidency. By giving these institutions true autonomy, the vague promises of a constitutional text can take on real meaning. This does not necessarily suggest a U.S.-style system of "checks and balances," however—Egyptian constitutional architects are more likely to speak of "separation of powers," in which institutions are contained within well-defined boundaries.

Is this a quixotic task? There are two reasons for hope. First, Egypt has a strong set of constitutional institutions with deep roots and professional standards. Second, there is a remarkable degree of consensus on what needs to be done. Of course, any constitutional process will spark symbolic debates about identity and Islam, but even on these potentially contentious issues, some version of the formulas in the country's current constitution are acceptable to most political camps.

The real obstacles to Egypt's constitutional revolution lie elsewhere. For starters, there is no real procedure in place for writing a new constitution. If Egypt starts from scratch, how is it to proceed? Past constitutions have been drafted by committees working in private. The country has no tradition to draw on for more protracted and inclusive practices, such as an elected constituent assembly. The only way to design such procedures is to bring all parties to the negotiating table and agree on the process. Yet this will be difficult because as much as they might agree on matters of substance, the diffuse nature of the opposition makes agreement on tactics and procedures slow and arduous.

Such consensus will become even more difficult if the military rulers push for a less radical solution. And this is the most significant obstacle by far: the Egyptian state is currently controlled by a committee of military leaders who have made very polite general sounds but suggested very limited intentions. Indeed, they have given strong signs that they wish simply to amend the current draft, and they have shown little inclination toward either a democratic or an inclusive process. Such a procedure looks suspiciously like the ones used to change the constitution or elect the president in the past—the people are invited to vote only after their leaders have made their choices for them. To be fair, the apparent appointment of Tariq al-Bishri, a leading public intellectual with a reputation for integrity and independence, as chair of the new constitutional committee is a very hopeful sign.

At this point, much depends on the intent of the Egyptian military leaders. They still have the chance to correct a mistake that some of their predecessors made. In 1952, the group of officers that overthrew the regime was headed by General Mohammed Naguib, who promised a return to civilian rule. Most of the work on the draft liberal constitution was performed under Naguib's presidency.

But Nasser deposed Naguib in 1954 and set to work building the system that the Egyptian revolutionaries have just brought to its knees. If the Egyptian revolution is to succeed in building a new system, Naguib's ghost will have to work its magic on the generals who now control the country.

A Tunisian Solution for Egypt's Military

Why Egypt's Military Will Not Be Able to Govern

Clement M. Henry and Robert Springborg

FOREIGNAFFAIRS.COM, FEBRUARY 21, 2011

The popular uprisings that swept Egypt and Tunisia this winter were remarkably similar, but their immediate outcomes have been quite different. In Tunisia, civilian politicians and technocrats quickly took the helm of the country in the wake of the revolution. In Egypt, by contrast, the military's Supreme Council is slated to rule the nation for six months, and whether it stays in power or returns to the barracks, it will surely try to ensure that civilians do not subordinate its role in politics. Given the nature and history of the two countries' militaries, this divergence is not surprising. Still, Egypt's military may not have the stranglehold on power that many think, and a

CLEMENT M. HENRY is Professor Emeritus of Government and Middle East Studies at the University of Texas at Austin. ROBERT SPRINGBORG is Professor of National Security Affairs at the Naval Postgraduate School and Program Manager for the Middle East at the Center for Civil-Military Relations. They are co-authors of *Globalization and the Politics of Development in the Middle East.*

real Tunisian solution—a civilian government free of military involvement—could form in Egypt as well.

Under President Zine el-Abidine Ben Ali, Tunisia was a police state. The president relied on his handpicked security and intelligence forces in the Interior Ministry to maintain his rule. Mistrustful of large militaries, he purposefully ensured the weakness of the army. With merely 50,000 in uniform, the army, as a proportion of the population, is among the smallest in the Arab world. Denied significant amounts of the foreign assistance that came into Tunisia, undersupplied, poorly equipped, and excluded from Ben Ali's patronage network, it was not invested in the regime. Meanwhile, over the past few decades, Ben Ali had effectively placed it under U.S. tutelage, where it was given training and modest arms transfers. This was a hedge against the French, who retained some influence over the police after Tunisian independence. They supplied and trained the security and intelligence forces, and even helped the government suppress an uprising in 1955. U.S. involvement with the military, Ben Ali supposed, would prevent the French from having a monopoly of influence over his country's means of coercion. At the same time, it meant that the army, which already had little loyalty to Ben Ali and no economic interest in maintaining his regime, became the one well-trained and highly professional force in the country.

It is not surprising, then, that when Ben Ali ordered the Tunisian army's chief of staff, Rachid Ammar, to fire on the protesters as the Jasmine Revolution gained momentum, the general refused. Likewise, Ben Ali's order to dismiss Ammar was ignored. The military instead turned its guns on the security and intelligence forces and the gangs of hooligans that Ben Ali loyalists had sent into the streets to sow panic. The French foreign minister, of course, suggested that France reinforce the police to help Ben Ali suppress the crowds. The police, however, were not reinforced, and Ben Ali, left without protection, had no choice but to flee. Soon after, Ammar conspicuously stepped aside to allow for the creation of a new civilian government.

By contrast, former President Hosni Mubarak's Egypt was a military state to which the police were subordinate. Although outnumbering military troops three to one (a staggering 1.5 million to 450,000), the security and police forces were underequipped, poorly paid, and viewed with contempt by the military. And unlike in Tunisia, the Egyptian military was allowed—indeed encouraged—to develop its own economic empire, which alleviated some of the institution's expenses for the government and, more important, generated a patronage network to buy the loyalty of the officer corps.

Since the military was considered above such matters as crowd control, Mubarak called on the security and intelligence forces to subdue the protests when they erupted in Cairo. Those forces soon began to crack, creating a security vacuum into which the government poured thugs, officers out of uniform, and hired criminals. Unlike the Tunisian army in comparable circumstances, the Egyptian military stood aside, failing to protect civilians. Only when it became clear that Mubarak's tactics had failed, did it step in. On February 11, the Supreme Council of the Armed Forces assumed control of the country and immediately began issuing proclamations as the new de facto government.

It appears that the Egyptian military has won the cake, at least for the time being, but eating it is going to be difficult. Although its size and strength are widely recognized, the Egyptian army is not the tight professional force that many consider it to be. It is bloated and its officer core is indulged, having been fattened on Mubarak's patronage. Its training is desultory, maintenance of its equipment is profoundly inadequate, and it is dependent on the United States for funding and logistical support. But even weapons systems the United States has given the Egyptian army, such as F-16s and M1A1 tanks, are underutilized. Many are also comparatively ineffective, in part because Minister of Defense Muhammad Tantawi, acting on behalf of Mubarak, denied them vital, state-of-the-art communication capacities. He did so to impede lateral communications within the officer corps and to prevent interoperability with nominally allied forces, including those of friendly Arab countries. The raison d'être of the military was always to support the Mubarak regime, not defend the nation.

As presently constituted, the military will also not be able to meet many of the protesters' demands. It cannot allow the core of the anti-Mubarak movement, such as the National Association for Change associated with Muhammad El Baradei, to play a leading role in forming a new government. Nor can it allow a parliament to have real power. The anti-Mubarak opposition and an empowered legislative branch would seek at least an oversight role and ultimately try to subordinate the military to the civilian government. This would be unacceptable to the military, which knows that its patronage network and economic influence would dry up if civilians took control. It will also try to deny calls for a full-scale investigation into the "economic crimes" of the ancien régime, for it has been involved in many of them.

But there has been a revolution, and re-imposing military control behind a civilian facade will now be extremely difficult, especially since the opposition seems to see through the military's strategies. The opposition's massive gathering in Tahrir Square on February 18, one week after Mubarak's ouster, for example, was a warning that it would force the military to share power with civilians. For its part, the military will likely try to maintain power and justify crackdowns by appealing to the need for order; steer a fellow traveler into the presidency, such as Amr Moussa, an Egyptian diplomat and the current secretary-general of the Arab League, or the current prime minister and a former general, Ahmad Shafiq; limit constitutional changes aimed at achieving a more democratic balance of power between the executive and legislative branches; and orchestrate economic show trials.

But Egypt faces dire economic conditions, and the military may already be jeopardizing the country's future and discouraging foreign direct investment by targeting some of the old regime's liberal economic elite, such as the former minister of trade and industry, Rachid Mohamed Rachid. The military high command may try to counter the lack of investment by calling for renewed economic nationalism, but that will condemn Egypt to economic stagnation, similar to that which it experienced in the mid-1960s. In addition to mobilizing the middle class seeking freedom and jobs, the revolution energized the poor, who joined in the protests to demand dignity, justice, and bread. If the economy worsens and the military overstays its welcome, the Egyptian people may well return to the streets.

Established military rule in Egypt is certainly not in the Egyptian people's interest, but neither is it in the United States' or any other country's interest. It would be politically unstable in the short term, and over the longer haul would likely lead to a repetition of this past month's events. The United States must encourage the institutionalized political participation of those who drove—and are still driving—the revolution. And rather than continuing to support the military, as the Obama administration has promised to do, the United States needs to signal that an overgrown, overfed, and largely useless Egyptian military is not acceptable. Aid the United States does send should be geared toward helping the Egyptian military deal with real national security interests, such as disaster relief, air and sea rescue, and cooperative engagement with allied military forces. And, as in the case of Tunisia, U.S. training certainly has a role to play. Through professional military education, the United States can assist Egypt's military in developing professional norms, which are supportive of civil-military relations within a democratic framework. To recall a chant inciting Cairo's January 25 movement: "Tunisia is the solution."

The Fall of the Pharaoh

How Hosni Mubarak's Reign Came to an End

Dina Shehata

FOREIGN AFFAIRS, MAY/JUNE 2011

For almost 60 years, Egyptians have celebrated Revolution Day on July 23, to commemorate the day in 1952 when Gamal Abdel Nasser and the Free Officers overthrew the monarchy to establish a republic. Next year, the country will celebrate Revolution Day on January 25—the first day of the mass protests that forced Hosni Mubarak, the country's president for 30 years, from power.

For the 18 days from January 25 to February 11, when Mubarak finally stepped down, millions of Egyptians demonstrated in the streets to demand, as many chanted, "*isqat al-nizam*," "the fall of the regime." The Mubarak government first met these protests with violence, but its vast security apparatus soon crumbled in the face of an overwhelming numbers of protesters. Then, the state attempted to use propaganda and fear-mongering to scare the population back into its embrace, but this, too, failed. Finally, the Mubarak regime resorted to making concessions. However, these were too limited, and the death toll from the protests had already grown too high.

DINA SHEHATA is Senior Researcher at the Al-Ahram Center for Political and Strategic Studies in Cairo.

Fearing that more violence would hurt the military's legitimacy and influence, the army broke with Mubarak and forced him to leave office.

The immediate trigger for the outbreak of protests in Egypt was the Jasmine Revolution in Tunisia in mid-January, which demonstrated that sustained and broad-based popular mobilization can lead to political change, even in a police state such as Tunisia. But other factors had long been at work in Egyptian politics and society. In particular, Mubarak's downfall was the result of three factors: increasing corruption and economic exclusion, the alienation of the youth, and the 2010 elections and divisions among the Egyptian elite over questions of succession. When these currents came together, they inspired a broad cross section of Egyptian society to achieve the unthinkable: removing Mubarak from power.

But the revolution did not lead to full regime change. Instead, it has achieved partial change: the military and the state bureaucracy remain in control and are likely to dictate the terms of the country's political transition over the coming months. What follows this transition will depend on whether the forces that staged the revolution can remain united and organized or whether some groups, such as the Muslim Brotherhood, strike a separate deal with the military. If this were to happen, the secular and youth movements that were the driving force behind the January 25 revolution would be effectively marginalized.

NASSER'S BARGAIN

In the 1950s and 1960s, the Nasser regime, which was at once authoritarian and populist, forged a ruling bargain with labor and the middle class. All political parties were banned and all civil-society organizations, including trade unions, came under the direct control of the regime. In return, the state provided social and welfare services in the form of government employment; subsidies for food, energy, housing, and transportation; and free education and health care.

In the early 1990s, a looming economic crisis caused by unsustainable levels of external debt forced Mubarak's government to sign an agreement on economic reform with the World Bank. Over the next two decades, the Egyptian government undertook a series of structural adjustments to the economy that reduced spending on social programs; liberalized trade, commodity prices, and interest rates; suspended the longtime guarantee of government employment for university graduates; privatized a number of public-sector companies; and suspended subsidies for many commodities. As state expenditures declined, public spending on social services—including education, health care, transportation, and housing—stagnated, and the quality of these services deteriorated.

Factory workers, landless peasants, government employees, and those who produce goods for the local market (as opposed to for export) suffered most. They depended on government services and subsidies, as well as on market protections, and many saw their fortunes fall as a result of the economic liberalization. At the same time, a new Egyptian business elite emerged: some people exploited the period of economic reform and openness to turn their contacts with the regime and international markets into vast fortunes. Just below this newly minted business aristocracy, a well-off middle class also began to develop. Thus, there soon emerged a two-tiered society: the majority of the Egyptian population was increasingly marginalized, while a small minority prospered like never before. Moreover, economic reform and liberalization led to the emergence of an unholy alliance between the ruling elite and the business elite. A select few—those closely aligned with the ruling National Democratic Party (NDP)—found themselves with special privileges to buy up public lands and public companies or put on a fast track to obtain state licenses and contracts.

Over the past five years, many workers—both blue-collar laborers and educated professionals—took to organizing strikes and other protests to show their anger at their economic disenfranchisement. These protests took place outside the control or leadership of the country's labor unions and professional syndicates, which were constrained by laws that limited their freedom to strike or carry out any protest. In 2008, property-tax collectors established Egypt's first independent trade union since 1959, the year that all such unions were brought under the control of the state. In 2010 alone, there were around 700 strikes and protest actions organized by workers across the country. However, these protests tended to focus exclusively on labor-specific demands and to shy away from political issues.

YOUNG MAN'S BURDEN

Egypt, like much of the Middle East, is in the middle of a dramatic and growing youth bulge. Today, more than half the total population of the Arab countries is under the age of 30; in Egypt, more than one-third of the population is between 15 and 29.

This demographic group faces a particularly frustrating paradox: according to the World Bank, the Middle East has both the fastest-rising levels of schooling and the highest level of youth unemployment in the world (25 percent, compared to a global average of 14.4 percent). Youth unemployment is highest among those with more education: in Egypt in 2006, young people with a secondary education or more represented 95 percent of the unemployed in their age group. Those who do find jobs often work for low pay and in poor conditions. This combination of high unemployment and low pay has kept many young Egyptian men from marrying and forming families. Approximately half of all Egyptian men between the ages of 25 and 29 are not married.

As a result of constraints on political life and civil society, youth in Egypt have been denied outlets for political and civic participation. Most cannot remember a time before the country's emergency law was last imposed, in 1981, which allowed the regime to freely persecute its challengers. Less than 5 percent of young people in Egypt belong to political parties, and less than 45 percent have ever participated in elections.

Partly because of such limitations, religious groups such as the Muslim Brotherhood were able to capitalize on widespread social grievances to recruit and mobilize young people in large numbers during the 1980s and 1990s. But after the state's harsh persecution of Islamists in the 1990s, youth activists began to express their grievances through a new generation of protest movements open to members of all ideological backgrounds and to those without any particular ideology at all.

One such movement is Kefaya, which has attracted legions of previously apolitical youth. In 2004 and 2005, it organized a series of high-profile protests calling for the end of Mubarak's presidency and the country's emergency law. In 2008, youth activists from Kefaya formed the April 6 Movement in solidarity with textile workers who were planning a strike for that date. The movement attracted 70,000 members on Facebook, making it the largest youth movement in Egypt at the time. Members of both the April 6 Movement and Kefaya were behind the creation of another popular Facebook group, one supporting Mohamed El Baradei, the former head of the International Atomic Energy Agency, who returned to Egypt in February 2010.

Perhaps the most important Facebook group would arise some months later when, in June 2010, activists associated with the El Baradei campaign created a Facebook page called "We are all Khaled Said" in memory of a young man who was beaten to death by police officers in Alexandria. Their page attracted more than one million supporters and became the focal point for a number of large protests against state abuses in the summer of 2010. By the end of 2010, Egypt's youth activists had succeeded in bypassing many of the long-standing constraints on political and civic life in the country. Although they may not have fully realized it at the time, all they needed to see their mission to the end was a final, triggering event—and that was gathering momentum some 1,300 miles away, in Tunisia.

THE EDIFICE CRACKS

As labor and youth unrest grew, another struggle was taking shape between Egypt's old guard, representing the military and the bureaucracy, and the new guard, representing Mubarak's son Gamal and his supporters in the business community and the ruling party.

Beginning in the mid-1970s, in an attempt to bolster his legitimacy both at home and abroad, then Egyptian President Anwar al-Sadat began to liberalize the political system. He allowed opposition parties and movements to gain some representation in the country's elected assemblies. As long as the ruling NDP maintained its two-thirds majority and its control over the real levers of power, the Egyptian opposition could contest elections and maintain a limited presence in parliament and in civil society. When Mubarak came to power, he continued to follow this same formula with few adjustments.

However, over the last five years, the Mubarak regime began to violate this implicit agreement, by imposing renewed constraints on the ability of political parties and movements to organize and to contest elections. Moreover, the state heavily manipulated the 2010 parliamentary elections in favor of the NDP, effectively denying all opposition groups any representation in parliament. (With opposition groups represented on the ballot but prevented from winning any races, the NDP won 97 percent of the seats.) For some in the opposition, the fraudulent elections of 2010 marked a departure from the limited political pluralism instituted by Sadat. The New Wafd party and the Muslim Brotherhood, among others, began to reconsider the utility of participating in elections under such conditions.

The regime's tactics in the 2010 elections were part of a broader plan to ensure a smooth succession from Mubarak to his son Gamal during the upcoming presidential election in 2011. This plan was the pet project of a group of businessmen closely associated with Gamal—such as Ahmed Ezz, a steel tycoon and a leading figure in the NDP—who had come to assume greater influence over the ruling party and the government in recent years. Not only did the country's opposition strongly oppose the succession plan, but many important factions within the state bureaucracy and the military were also skeptical. As 2010 came to a close, the country's ruling edifice was beginning to crack.

These underlying forces in turn spurred on the groups that participated in the mass protests in January and February: youth movements, labor groups, and the political parties that were excluded from joining parliament in 2010, including the Muslim Brotherhood. Youth activists agreed to hold protests against state brutality on Police Day, January 25. This demonstration begat others, and as the size and momentum of the protests grew, these activists formed the Coalition of January 25 Youth to present a series of demands to the regime: the resignation of Mubarak, the lifting of the state of emergency, the release of all political prisoners, the dissolution of parliament, the appointment of a government of independent technocrats, the drafting of a new constitution, and the punishment of those responsible for violence against the protesters. Egypt's youth activists refused to negotiate with Omar Suleiman, a Mubarak confidant who was appointed vice president on January 29 as a means of appeasing the protesters.

At the outset, Egypt's opposition was divided over whether to participate in the demonstrations. Some groups, such as Kefaya, the National Association for Change, the Democratic Front Party, the Tomorrow Party, and the New Wafd Party, endorsed and joined the January 25 protests, whereas other groups, such as the Muslim Brotherhood and the leftist Tagammu Party, did not officially join the protests until January 28 (although many of their younger members participated on January 25).

Many of the political groups taking part in the uprising disagreed over their demands and over how best to achieve them. Groups such as Kefaya, the National Association for Change, and the Democratic Front Party and individual leaders such as El Baradei and Ayman Nour endorsed the demands of the youth coalition and refused to negotiate with the regime until after Mubarak stepped down. Others, however—the Muslim Brotherhood, the New Wafd Party, the Tagammu Party, and a number of independent public figures—agreed to enter into negotiations with Suleiman. These talks turned out to be short-lived: the regime refused to make any real concessions, and the protests on the street continued to escalate.

For its part, the Muslim Brotherhood threw its full weight behind the protests but purposefully kept a low profile. Its young members were an integral part of the coalition that had organized the protests, and according to some of the organizers, Brotherhood supporters constituted about one-third of the crowd occupying Tahrir Square. Muslim Brothers made up a large share of the protesters in those cities where the group has long had a large following, such as Alexandria and El Mansura. However, throughout the protests, the Brotherhood was careful not to use religious slogans or to overshadow the secular, pro-democracy activists who were driving the demonstrations.

During the first two weeks of the revolution, labor movements and professional groups did not play a visible role, partly because the regime had shut down all economic activity during this time. However, during the final week, as economic activity resumed, workers and professionals began to organize strikes. In the two days preceding Mubarak's resignation, the country was approaching a state of total civil disobedience, with workers striking en masse in the transportation, communications, and industrial sectors. Judges, doctors, university professors, lawyers, journalists, and artists also organized protests. According to Shady El Ghazaly Harb, a leading Egyptian youth activist, it was this development that finally convinced the military to oust Mubarak and assume control.

LAST DAYS OF THE PHARAOH

During the three weeks of protests in January and February, groups that had previously competed with one another—Islamists and secularists, liberals and leftists—joined forces against the regime. There were fears that the opposition would fragment and that some factions would strike a separate deal with the regime, but such a turn of events never happened—although this had more to do with the Mubarak government's refusal to make any concessions and its apparent willingness to use violence. In the end, it was the unity of the opposition and broad-based popular mobilization that forced the military to oust Mubarak.

Unlike the opposition, the regime suffered from multiple divisions during the crisis. In the first week, the state tried to defuse the protests by sacking Gamal Mubarak as assistant secretary-general of the NDP and purging the businessmen closely associated with him from the ruling party and the cabinet. This effectively aborted the much-despised succession scenario and removed the new business elite from its privileged economic and political position.

Mubarak hoped that by removing Gamal and his business cronies, the protests would begin to lose steam. Indeed, these measures seemed to satisfy the majority of Egyptians; many observers in the media and even some opposition figures predicted that the revolution would come to a halt. However, the next day, after Mubarak announced that he would step down in September, security forces and hired vigilantes violently cracked down on the protesters—11 were shot and killed in Tahrir Square alone—turning the momentum back against the regime. Demands for Mubarak's immediate resignation intensified, and at that point, many new groups, mainly workers and professionals, joined the protests in large numbers.

The military, which until then had backed Mubarak while refraining from using force against the protesters, began to show signs of sedition. Throughout the crisis, the protesters had welcomed the presence of the military on the streets and urged it to side with them against Mubarak, as the military had done in Tunisia just weeks earlier. But until the last days of the crisis, the military seemed to back Mubarak's plan to remain in power until September and oversee an orderly transition to democracy. It took new groups joining the protests and the rising prospect of a confrontation between the protesters and the presidential guard for the military to finally break with Mubarak. On February 10, a spokesperson for the High Council of the Armed Forces delivered a communiqué that stated that the council supported the legitimate demands of the people. Mubarak was expected to resign that same night, but he did not. The next day, the military ousted him. The High Council of the Armed Forces assumed control of the country, and one week later, it announced the suspension of the constitution and the dissolution of both houses of parliament.

DEMOCRACY'S UNFINISHED BUSINESS

The revolution that pushed Mubarak from office has resulted in only a partial dissolution of his regime. The primary victims of this turn of events have been Mubarak's family, the business elites closely associated with it, leading figures in the state bureaucracy and the NDP, and members of the much-despised state security apparatus. The regime's basic structure remains largely intact, however: the military and the state bureaucracy are still in firm control of the country and in a position to dictate the course of the transition in the coming months. As of this writing, the High Council of the Armed Forces rules Egypt. The state bureaucracy, which comprises some six million people, remains in place, with state ministries and agencies largely unchanged and still responsible for managing day-to-day affairs.

Two scenarios seem possible. The first scenario involves speedy elections held over the summer, both parliamentary and presidential. This option appears to be favored by the military and the Muslim Brotherhood, but it is rejected by most of the groups that took part in the revolution. Such a schedule would benefit only those individuals and groups that are already positioned to achieve electoral success in the near future—namely, those associated with the NDP and the Muslim Brotherhood, the only two political organizations in Egypt with long-standing networks and bases of support that could be mobilized on short notice. Were such elections held, the outcome would probably be a power-sharing arrangement between the regime (or some new incarnation of it) and the Muslim Brotherhood, leaving little representation for the secular and youth groups that drove the revolution.

The second scenario would see the appointment of a three-member presidential council made up of two civilians and a military figure and the formation of a new cabinet composed of technocrats not affiliated with any one party. This option has been put forward by El Baradei and is the apparent preference of the country's secular political parties and youth movements. The next step would be to hold presidential elections, followed by direct elections for an assembly that would then draft a new constitution. Until these elections were held, the presidential council would lift all constraints on political parties, the media, and civil-society organizations, which would allow secular forces the chance to organize themselves and attract voters. Parliamentary elections would follow the new constitution and the creation of new political parties, likely within one or two years. Such an arrangement would level the playing field and would allow secular parties and movements to compete more effectively with the NDP and the Muslim Brotherhood.

There are fears that if the first scenario prevails, the democratic revolution will be aborted and the old regime—under the guise of NDP loyalists in an alliance with the Muslim Brotherhood—will reassert itself. A new parliament, dominated by former NDP members and the Muslim Brotherhood would guide the drafting of the new constitution and would set the parameters of a new political system. Some important liberalization measures might be adopted to quell popular discontent, but full democratization would be unlikely.

If, however, Islamists and secularists remain united, the street stays mobilized, and international pressure is applied to the military, the second scenario may prevail. In this case, the various groups that drove the revolution would have the time to organize themselves into viable political parties—and only that can produce genuine democratic change.

The Black Swan of Cairo

How Suppressing Volatility Makes the World Less Predictable and More Dangerous

Nassim Nicholas Taleb and Mark Blyth

FOREIGN AFFAIRS, MAY/JUNE 2011

Why is surprise the permanent condition of the U.S. political and economic elite? In 2007–8, when the global financial system imploded, the cry that no one could have seen this coming was heard everywhere, despite the existence of numerous analyses showing that a crisis was unavoidable. It is no surprise that one hears precisely the same response today regarding the current turmoil in the Middle East. The critical issue in both cases is the artificial suppression of volatility—the ups and downs of life—in the name of stability. It is both misguided and dangerous to push unobserved risks further into the statistical tails of the probability distribution of outcomes and allow these high-impact, low-probability "tail risks" to disappear from policymakers' fields of observation. What the world is witnessing in Tunisia, Egypt, and Libya is simply what happens when highly constrained systems explode.

NASSIM NICHOLAS TALEB is Distinguished Professor of Risk Engineering at New York University's Polytechnic Institute and the author of *The Black Swan: The Impact of the Highly Improbable*. MARK BLYTH is Professor of International Political Economy at Brown University.

Complex systems that have artificially suppressed volatility tend to become extremely fragile, while at the same time exhibiting no visible risks. In fact, they tend to be too calm and exhibit minimal variability as silent risks accumulate beneath the surface. Although the stated intention of political leaders and economic policymakers is to stabilize the system by inhibiting fluctuations, the result tends to be the opposite. These artificially constrained systems become prone to "Black Swans"—that is, they become extremely vulnerable to large-scale events that lie far from the statistical norm and were largely unpredictable to a given set of observers.

Such environments eventually experience massive blowups, catching everyone off-guard and undoing years of stability or, in some cases, ending up far worse than they were in their initial volatile state. Indeed, the longer it takes for the blowup to occur, the worse the resulting harm in both economic and political systems.

Seeking to restrict variability seems to be good policy (who does not prefer stability to chaos?), so it is with very good intentions that policymakers unwittingly increase the risk of major blowups. And it is the same misperception of the properties of natural systems that led to both the economic crisis of 2007–8 and the current turmoil in the Arab world. The policy implications are identical: to make systems robust, all risks must be visible and out in the open—*fluctuat nec mergitur* (it fluctuates but does not sink) goes the Latin saying.

Just as a robust economic system is one that encourages early failures (the concepts of "fail small" and "fail fast"), the U.S. government should stop supporting dictatorial regimes for the sake of pseudostability and instead allow political noise to rise to the surface. Making an economy robust in the face of business swings requires allowing risk to be visible; the same is true in politics.

SEDUCED BY STABILITY

Both the recent financial crisis and the current political crisis in the Middle East are grounded in the rise of complexity, interdependence, and unpredictability. Policymakers in the United Kingdom and the United States have long promoted policies aimed at eliminating fluctuation—no more booms and busts in the economy, no more "Iranian surprises" in foreign policy. These policies have almost always produced undesirable outcomes. For example, the U.S. banking system became very fragile following a succession of progressively larger bailouts and government interventions, particularly after the 1983 rescue of major banks (ironically, by the same Reagan administration that trumpeted free markets). In the United States, promoting these bad policies has been a bipartisan effort throughout. Republicans have been good at fragilizing large corporations through bailouts, and Democrats have been good at fragilizing the government. At the same time, the financial system as a whole exhibited little volatility; it kept getting weaker while providing policymakers with the illusion of stability, illustrated most notably when Ben Bernanke, who was then a member of the Board of Governors of the U.S. Federal Reserve, declared the era of "the great moderation" in 2004.

Putatively independent central bankers fell into the same trap. During the 1990s, U.S. Federal Reserve Chair Alan Greenspan wanted to iron out the economic cycle's booms and busts, and he sought to control economic swings with interest-rate reductions at the slightest sign of a downward tick in the economic data. Furthermore, he adapted his economic policy to guarantee bank rescues, with implicit promises of a backstop—the now infamous "Greenspan put." These policies proved to have grave delayed side effects. Washington stabilized the market with bailouts and by allowing certain companies to grow "too big to fail." Because policymakers believed it was better to do something than to do nothing, they felt obligated to heal the economy rather than wait and see if it healed on its own.

The foreign policy equivalent is to support the incumbent no matter what. And just as banks took wild risks thanks to Greenspan's implicit insurance policy, client governments such as Hosni Mubarak's in Egypt for years engaged in overt plunder thanks to similarly reliable U.S. support.

Those who seek to prevent volatility on the grounds that any and all bumps in the road must be avoided paradoxically increase the probability that a tail risk will cause a major explosion. Consider as a thought experiment a man placed in an artificially sterilized environment for a decade and then invited to take a ride on a crowded subway; he would be expected to die quickly. Likewise, preventing small forest fires can cause larger forest fires to become devastating. This property is shared by all complex systems.

In the realm of economics, price controls are designed to constrain volatility on the grounds that stable prices are a good thing. But although these controls might work in some rare situations, the long-term effect of any such system is an eventual and extremely costly blowup whose cleanup costs can far exceed the benefits accrued. The risks of a dictatorship, no matter how seemingly stable, are no different, in the long run, from those of an artificially controlled price.

Such attempts to institutionally engineer the world come in two types: those that conform to the world as it is and those that attempt to reform the world. The nature of humans, quite reasonably, is to intervene in an effort to alter their world and the outcomes it produces. But government interventions are laden with unintended—and unforeseen—consequences, particularly in complex systems, so humans must work with nature by tolerating systems that absorb human imperfections rather than seek to change them.

Take, for example, the recent celebrated documentary on the financial crisis, *Inside Job*, which blames the crisis on the malfeasance and dishonesty of bankers and the incompetence of regulators. Although it is morally satisfying, the film naively overlooks the fact that humans have always been dishonest and regulators have always been behind the curve. The only difference this time around was the unprecedented magnitude of the hidden risks and a misunderstanding of the statistical properties of the system.

What is needed is a system that can prevent the harm done to citizens by the dishonesty of business elites; the limited competence of forecasters, economists, and statisticians; and the imperfections of regulation, not one that aims to eliminate these flaws. Humans must try to resist the illusion of control: just as foreign policy should be intelligence-proof (it should minimize its reliance on the competence of information-gathering organizations and the predictions of "experts" in what are inherently unpredictable domains), the economy should be regulator-proof, given that some regulations simply make the system itself more fragile. Due to the complexity of markets, intricate regulations simply serve to generate fees for lawyers and profits for sophisticated derivatives traders who can build complicated financial products that skirt those regulations.

DON'T BE A TURKEY

The life of a turkey before Thanksgiving is illustrative: the turkey is fed for 1,000 days and every day seems to confirm that the farmer cares for it—until the last day, when confidence is maximal. The "turkey problem" occurs when a naive analysis of stability is derived from the absence of past variations. Likewise, confidence in stability was maximal at the onset of the financial crisis in 2007.

The turkey problem for humans is the result of mistaking one environment for another. Humans simultaneously inhabit two systems: the linear and the complex. The linear domain is characterized by its predictability and the low degree of interaction among its components, which allows the use of mathematical methods that make forecasts reliable. In complex systems, there is an absence of visible causal links between the elements, masking a high degree of interdependence and extremely low predictability. Nonlinear elements are also present, such as those commonly known, and generally misunderstood, as "tipping points." Imagine someone who keeps adding sand to a sand pile without any visible consequence, until suddenly the entire pile crumbles. It would be foolish to blame the collapse on the last grain of sand rather than the structure of the pile, but that is what people do consistently, and that is the policy error.

U.S. President Barack Obama may blame an intelligence failure for the government's not foreseeing the revolution in Egypt (just as former U.S. President Jimmy Carter blamed an intelligence failure for his administration's not foreseeing the 1979 Islamic Revolution in Iran), but it is the suppressed risk in the statistical tails that matters—not the failure to see the last grain of sand. As a result of complicated interdependence and contagion effects, in all man-made complex systems, a small number of possible events dominate, namely, Black Swans.

Engineering, architecture, astronomy, most of physics, and much of common science are linear domains. The complex domain is the realm of the social world, epidemics, and economics. Crucially, the linear domain delivers mild variations without large shocks, whereas the complex domain delivers massive jumps and gaps. Complex systems are misunderstood, mostly because humans' sophistication, obtained over the history of human knowledge in the linear domain, does not transfer properly to the complex domain. Humans can predict a solar eclipse and the trajectory of a space vessel, but not the stock market or Egyptian political events. All man-made complex systems have commonalities and even universalities. Sadly, deceptive calm (followed by Black Swan surprises) seems to be one of those properties.

THE ERROR OF PREDICTION

As with a crumbling sand pile, it would be foolish to attribute the collapse of a fragile bridge to the last truck that crossed it, and even more foolish to try to predict in advance which truck might bring it down. The system is responsible, not the components. But after the financial crisis of 2007–8, many people thought that predicting the subprime meltdown would have helped. It would not have, since it was a symptom of the crisis, not its underlying cause. Likewise, Obama's blaming "bad intelligence" for his administration's failure to predict the crisis in Egypt is symptomatic of both the misunderstanding of complex systems and the bad policies involved.

Obama's mistake illustrates the illusion of local causal chains—that is, confusing catalysts for causes and assuming that one can know which catalyst will produce which effect. The final episode of the upheaval in Egypt was unpredictable for all observers, especially those involved. As such, blaming the CIA is as foolish as funding it to forecast such events. Governments are wasting billions of dollars on attempting to predict events that are produced by interdependent systems and are therefore not statistically understandable at the individual level.

As Mark Abdollahian of Sentia Group, one of the contractors who sell predictive analytics to the U.S. government, noted regarding Egypt, policymakers should "think of this like Las Vegas. In blackjack, if you can do four percent better than the average, you're making real money." But the analogy is spurious. There is no "four percent better" on Egypt. This is not just money wasted but the construction of a false confidence based on an erroneous focus. It is telling that the intelligence analysts made the same mistake as the risk-management systems that failed to predict the economic crisis—and offered the exact same excuses when they failed. Political and economic "tail events" are unpredictable, and their probabilities are not scientifically measurable. No matter how many dollars are spent on research, predicting revolutions is not the same as counting cards; humans will never be able to turn politics into the tractable randomness of blackjack.

Most explanations being offered for the current turmoil in the Middle East follow the "catalysts as causes" confusion. The riots in Tunisia and Egypt were initially attributed to rising commodity prices, not to stifling and unpopular dictatorships. But Bahrain and Libya are countries with high GDPs that can afford to import grain and other commodities. Again, the focus is wrong even if the logic is comforting. It is the system and its fragility, not events, that must be studied—what physicists call "percolation theory," in which the properties of the terrain are studied rather than those of a single element of the terrain.

When dealing with a system that is inherently unpredictable, what should be done? Differentiating between two types of countries is useful. In the first, changes in government do not lead to meaningful differences in political outcomes (since political tensions are out in the open). In the second type, changes in government lead to both drastic and deeply unpredictable changes.

Consider that Italy, with its much-maligned "cabinet instability," is economically and politically stable despite having had more than 60 governments since World War II (indeed, one may say Italy's stability is because of these switches of government). Similarly, in spite of consistently bad press, Lebanon is a relatively safe bet in terms of how far governments can jump from equilibrium; in spite of all the noise, shifting alliances, and street protests, changes in government there tend to be comparatively mild. For example, a shift in the ruling coalition from Christian parties to Hezbollah is not such a consequential jump in terms of the country's economic and political stability. Switching equilibrium, with control of the government changing from one party to another, in such systems acts as a shock absorber. Since a single party cannot have total and more than temporary control, the possibility of a large jump in the regime type is constrained.

In contrast, consider Iran and Iraq. Mohammad Reza Shah Pahlavi and Saddam Hussein both constrained volatility by any means necessary. In Iran, when the shah was toppled, the shift of power to Ayatollah Ruhollah Khomeini was a huge, unforeseeable jump. After the fact, analysts could construct convincing accounts about how killing Iranian Communists, driving the left into exile, demobilizing the democratic opposition, and driving all dissent into the mosque had made Khomeini's rise inevitable. In Iraq, the United States removed the lid and was actually surprised to find that the regime did not jump from hyperconstraint to something like France. But this was impossible to predict ahead of time due to the nature of the system itself. What can be said, however, is that the more constrained the volatility, the bigger the regime jump is likely to be. From the French Revolution to the triumph of the Bolsheviks, history is replete with such examples, and yet somehow humans remain unable to process what they mean.

THE FEAR OF RANDOMNESS

Humans fear randomness—a healthy ancestral trait inherited from a different environment. Whereas in the past, which was a more linear world, this trait enhanced fitness and increased chances of survival, it can have the reverse effect in today's complex world, making volatility take the shape of nasty Black

Swans hiding behind deceptive periods of "great moderation." This is not to say that any and all volatility should be embraced. Insurance should not be banned, for example.

But alongside the "catalysts as causes" confusion sit two mental biases: the illusion of control and the action bias (the illusion that doing something is always better than doing nothing). This leads to the desire to impose man-made solutions. Greenspan's actions were harmful, but it would have been hard to justify inaction in a democracy where the incentive is to always promise a better outcome than the other guy, regardless of the actual, delayed cost.

Variation is information. When there is no variation, there is no information. This explains the CIA's failure to predict the Egyptian revolution and, a generation before, the Iranian Revolution—in both cases, the revolutionaries themselves did not have a clear idea of their relative strength with respect to the regime they were hoping to topple. So rather than subsidize and praise as a "force for stability" every tin-pot potentate on the planet, the U.S. government should encourage countries to let information flow upward through the transparency that comes with political agitation. It should not fear fluctuations per se, since allowing them to be in the open, as Italy and Lebanon both show in different ways, creates the stability of small jumps.

As Seneca wrote in *De clementia*, "Repeated punishment, while it crushes the hatred of a few, stirs the hatred of all . . . just as trees that have been trimmed throw out again countless branches." The imposition of peace through repeated punishment lies at the heart of many seemingly intractable conflicts, including the Israeli-Palestinian stalemate. Furthermore, dealing with seemingly reliable high-level officials rather than the people themselves prevents any peace treaty signed from being robust. The Romans were wise enough to know that only a free man under Roman law could be trusted to engage in a contract; by extension, only a free people can be trusted to abide by a treaty. Treaties that are negotiated with the consent of a broad swath of the populations on both sides of a conflict tend to survive. Just as no central bank is powerful enough to dictate stability, no superpower can be powerful enough to guarantee solid peace alone.

U.S. policy toward the Middle East has historically, and especially since 9/11, been unduly focused on the repression of any and all political fluctuations in the name of preventing "Islamic fundamentalism"—a trope that Mubarak repeated until his last moments in power and that Libyan leader Muammar al-Qaddafi continues to emphasize today, blaming Osama bin Laden for what has befallen him. This is wrong. The West and its autocratic Arab allies have strengthened Islamic fundamentalists by forcing them underground, and even more so by killing them.

As Jean-Jacques Rousseau put it, "A little bit of agitation gives motivation to the soul, and what really makes the species prosper is not peace so much as freedom." With freedom comes some unpredictable fluctuation. This is one of life's packages: there is no freedom without noise—and no stability without volatility.

The Cracks Spread

Why Jordan Is Not a Regional Domino

Robert Danin

CFR.ORG, FEBRUARY 1, 2011

The Jordanian government's fall in Amman today appears to be the latest in the series of dominoes that first fell in Tunis and appears poised to tip over in Cairo. At first glance, there are similarities: Thousands of protesters have taken to the streets of Amman, Karak, Salt, and Irbid protesting difficult economic conditions, tax policies, government corruption, and other domestic maladies. Demonstrators called for their leaders' resignation, tanks deployed to the cities, and barricades were erected.

Yet the government's toppling in Amman is not regime change and does not presage it. Instead, it is the removal of a government that leaves the throne well intact. The demonstrators in Jordan did not call for King Abdullah's removal; they called for better governance, economic reform, and the removal of Prime Minister Samir Rifai, who is blamed for rising commodity prices and political stagnation. Even demonstrating Islamists remain loyal to the monarchy. They want policy changes, not regime change.

Monarchies like Jordan are better insulated to absorb the wave of discontent sweeping the Arab world today. This is true for

ROBERT DANIN is Eni Enrico Mattei senior fellow for Middle East and Africa studies at the Council on Foreign Relations.

most of the monarchies in the Arab world, such as Morocco, Saudi Arabia, and Qatar. While the king retains ultimate control, power is also more diffused, allowing for a buffering of rage and resentment, and greater potential for real politics. It also means greater government accountability; the prime minister and his cabinet are not the venerated unassailable symbols of the nation, as many republican autocrats elsewhere in the region have come to view themselves. Jordanians can criticize their government without being accused of being disloyal to Jordan.

Such is not the case in Cairo, where criticism of the president long ago came to be viewed by the leadership as tantamount to criticism of Egypt. Such centralization of power in one set of hands, and the juxtaposition of fealty to the leader with loyalty to the state, does not bode well for authoritarian strongmen in Libya, Syria, or Sudan.

The peaceful change of government in Jordan does not mean that all is well. One of the core demands of the demonstrators—elections to choose a new prime minister—was not met. Moreover, the new prime minister—Marouf al-Bakhit—may not be the right man for the hour. He is an ex-general whose previous term as prime minister from 2005 to 2007 was not marked by promised reforms, but by perceived inaction. Upon announcement of Bakhit's appointment, opposition leaders criticized the choice of a non-reformist. They did not, however, criticize the Hashemite leader.

Ultimately, to maintain the basic compact that exists between the monarchy and the people, King Abdullah may yet need to institute greater and more fundamental change—new elections, more governance reform, rapid economic reform, greater social safety nets—lest Jordanians begin to question the legitimacy of his rule and propel Jordan onto the wave that is sweeping other parts of the Arab world.

Green Movement 2.0?

How U.S. Support Could Lead the Opposition to Victory

Geneive Abdo

FOREIGNAFFAIRS.COM, FEBRUARY 18, 2011

Taking a cue from the Egyptian revolution, opposition activists in Iran reinvigorated their beleaguered movement on Monday, getting thousands of protesters onto the streets despite the regime's year-long crackdown and ban on demonstrations. Their chants were telling. Referring to Supreme Leader Ali Khamenei, demonstrators chanted, "Mubarak, Ben Ali—it's your turn, Seyyed Ali!" and "Whether Cairo or Tehran, death to tyrants!" In an interview posted on InsideIran.org, a student who helped organize the protests said, "People don't realize how tense the situation is in Tehran. It is a powder keg and only needs a trigger."

Such sentiments were similar to those in 2009, when Iran also seemed on the verge of change after the so-called Green Movement took to the streets to protest President Mahmoud Ahmadinejad's disputed reelection. At the time, members of the Green Movement were conflicted about whether an endorsement from the United States would help or hurt their cause. And for its part, Washington was hesitant to support

GENEIVE ABDO is Director of the Iran Program at the National Security Network and the Century Foundation. She is the author of *Answering Only to God: Faith and Freedom in Twenty-First-Century Iran*.

the movement, fearing that it might taint the opposition if its involvement created the impression that the United States was behind the protests. In the end, the state cracked down, the protests lost momentum, and the movement failed.

The uprising in Egypt has put to rest some of the Iranian opposition's fears: observing the support U.S. President Barack Obama gave Egyptians at critical moments in their three-week uprising, many Iranian activists were convinced that Obama's backing of their cause would give the opposition the push it needs to confront its authoritarian rulers over the long haul. Of course, Obama waited days to endorse the Egyptian uprising, but when he did it sent the message that the United States would not pressure Egypt's military to keep former President Hosni Mubarak in power. This alone heartened Egypt's opposition. A similar endorsement could do the same for Iran's.

It is also far less true today than in 2009 that U.S. support would tarnish Iran's opposition movement: it is already clear that the Egyptian uprising and revolts unfurling across the Arab world are popular, local, and independent of the United States. Nonetheless, it remains to be seen whether the United States is prepared to lend the same support to the Green Movement that it did to the Egyptian protesters. Many inside the Washington Beltway believe that, despite the current flare-up, the Green Movement is long dead and not worth the risk of further alienating the Iranian regime. But the United States was too quick to write off the Green Movement in 2009 in the first place. Fundamental change takes time and, more than a lack of will, the Green Movement is plagued by a lack of means to confront a security apparatus far more effective and brutal than that in Egypt. Indeed, Iranians may need U.S. support to face their regime more than the Egyptians did.

After the protests in 2009, the Islamic Revolutionary Guards Corps established a cyber defense command to counter online political activism, making Facebook and Twitter inaccessible to those without filter proxies bought in the West. On Monday, the regime banned Iranians from organizing; blocked BBC Persian, a main source of information in Iran (much as Al Jazeera is in the Arab world); and put the de facto leaders of the Green Movement under house arrest. Iranian leaders have announced that they will create a special court focusing on "media crimes," a move that will surely deter even more journalists and citizens from using the Internet to disseminate information about the protests. Even the regime's moderate conservatives, such as Parliamentary Speaker Ali Larijani, have been quick to demand that opposition leaders face trial for the most recent protests, some even calling for their execution. Of course, the Egyptian government also shut down the Internet—but only for one day during the heat of the protests. And unlike Egypt's military, the Iranian Revolutionary Guard cannot be counted on to sit on the sidelines.

Even so, tens of thousands of Iranians reportedly protested on February 14. But if world leaders were to support civil disobedience, for example by making sophisticated technology available to Iranians to counter the regime's manipulation of the internet, the momentum could build for future demonstrations even if the violent security forces started to crack down.

At the moment, Iran's opposition is far less unified in its goals than the Egyptian opposition was during its protests. Some factions want only to reform Iran's theocracy, while others (particularly the younger activists) want to dismantle supreme clerical rule altogether and establish a parliamentary democracy. The West's endorsement of the movement could strengthen Iran's opposition as a whole but only as long as Washington does not talk of trying to supplant the regime with a Western-style democracy. The leaders of the Muslim Brotherhood have made clear that Egypt will be a democracy that reflects the religious and cultural values of Egypt, and the United States should not try to dictate Iran's future form of governance.

Washington's public support, moreover, would deprive the Iranian regime of one of its weapons: anti-Americanism. For example, the Iranian government has tried to convince its people that U.S. sanctions are designed to hurt them, not the regime. Some Iranians have been left believing that the United States cares more about security issues—in particular preventing Iran from developing a nuclear weapon—than their well-being. But far from wanting the United States to back off entirely, a majority say that they would like closer ties with the West, according to a recent poll from the International Peace Institute.

To be sure, Washington has started to take a firmer stance against the Iranian regime as uprisings sweep through the Middle East. U.S. officials have even said that tougher rhetoric will now be part of Washington's official approach toward the country. And this is indeed a shift in policy; in 2009, the United States resisted even rhetorical support for the demonstrators. Speaking this week about Monday's protests, U.S. Secretary of State Hillary Clinton said, "There needs to be a commitment to open up the political system in Iran to hear the voices of the opposition and civil society." U.S. officials have also noted the hypocrisy of the Iranian regime's support for the Egyptian uprising. Throughout Egypt's revolt, Iran's leaders praised the uprising as part of a new "Islamic awakening" in the region, crediting the unrest to their own 1979 revolution. In a statement condemning Iran's blocking of BBC Persian, Tommy Vietor, a spokesman for the National Security Council, said, "For all of its empty talk about Egypt, the government of Iran should allow the Iranian people the same universal right to peacefully assemble, demonstrate, and communicate in Tehran that the people are exercising in Cairo."

Opposition activists are seeking much more. They want the international community to draw attention to Iran's human rights violations. Indeed, in the International Peace Institute poll, 55 percent of all respondents said that the West should speak out against the regime's human rights violations. This is an area in which the government is vulnerable. Iran has managed to convince at least a sizable portion of the population that the crackdown and repression after the 2009 movement have been necessary to preserve the country. If the United States makes clear that it condemns repression and supports the aspirations of the Iranian people, it could inspire young non-ideological Iranians—who have much in common with their Egyptian counterparts—to confront the security forces. One step further, which some U.S. senators have already backed, would be to establish an independent UN human rights monitor to track the situation in Iran and publicize violations.

Iranians look with sadness and regret as they see Arabs liberating themselves from long-standing dictatorships. "For the first time in history, the Iranians are envious of the Arabs," said one activist, referring to Persians' historic sense of superiority to Arab countries. But Monday's demonstrations, just like those in 2009, are giving the Iranian opposition hope again. This time, with talks over Iran's nuclear program at a stalemate and fears of tainting the movement gone, there should be no debate about endorsing it. In a not-so-subtle rebuke during a visit to Tehran on Monday, Turkish President Abdullah Gül said that "without exception" all states in the Middle East must listen to their people and implement their demands. And if even Iran's allies can stand behind the protesters, the United States should be able to as well. At any rate, the more pressure the Iranian regime encounters from all angles, the more tools the opposition will have to confront the regime.

Iran's Protests and Economic Realities

Interview with Suzanne Maloney

CFR.ORG, FEBRUARY 22, 2011

Iran's hardline regime has cracked down on opposition protests in the wake of sweeping regional protests following revolutions in Egypt and Tunisia. Internal economic and political pressures, as well as a new wave of international sanctions against Iran, have prompted questions about how long the Iranian regime can hold onto power. But the Brookings Institution's Suzanne Maloney says a number of factors work in the regime's favor, including the Iranian military's greater ability to repress the public and its allegiance to the regime; an ability to block the public's access to technology; and opposition leaders' loyalty to the idea of preserving an Islamic Republic. International sanctions have also increased domestic political support for needed economic reforms that may actually strengthen the Iranian regime's hold on power, she says. Maloney notes that, unlike in Egypt, heavy reliance on public sector jobs has dampened public support for political upheaval. "When your job comes from the state, it's much more difficult to go out to the streets because you risk losing your livelihood as well as endangering your own safety."

SUZANNE MALONEY is a senior fellow at the Brookings Institution. (Interview conducted by Roya Wolverson.)

There have been a flurry of comparisons between Egypt and Iran. Considering these, is Iran also ready to fall?

What made Egypt a successful and relatively blood-free revolution was the presence of a large, mobilized, well-prepared young population that had access to technology and had a very coherent, tactical plan for driving an opposition movement. They were also disconnected from the interests of, or need to bargain with, the government. You don't have those factors in Iran today. The Iranian regime is deeply paranoid and watching the youth because they played such an important role in the 1979 Iranian Revolution. Their access to technology is frequently constrained and the surprise factor that facilitated some of the stumbles of the Egyptian and Tunisian regimes simply isn't present.

There is also a much greater repressive capacity and fear factor in the population's relationship with the military. The Egyptians saw the military as potentially an honest broker, which wouldn't happen in Iran.

Finally, Iranian reformists Mehdi Karoubi and Mir Hossain Mousavi have yet to disavow the Islamic Republic as a model, even as they press for greater democracy. And so their involvement makes it more likely that what you will see in Iran is a sort of pacted transition, rather than a full-scale upheaval. In Egypt, so much of the change was driven by those outside the political establishment.

Why don't Mousavi and Karoubi go the extra step to fully challenge the regime?

They are full-fledged opposition figures. But they are still identified with the regime. They still have decades of history with the supreme leader and the political establishment. For them to disavow the regime altogether is a more complex and dangerous act. It doesn't necessarily make for a worse transition, but it alters the parameters for opposition.

We don't know the extent to which there is a new generation of leadership emerging in Iran, as emerged in Egypt and Tunisia. Young people were armed with technology and able to evade the restrictions of the regime, capable of thinking tactically to outfox even the regime's repressive capabilities. If those people exist, we won't recognize what they're up to until we see it play out on the streets. It's an opposition movement we can neither orchestrate nor anticipate. Because of the restrictions they must function under, they have to operate in a very opaque fashion.

How does the youth bulge in Egypt and elsewhere in the Arab world differ from Iran?

Iranians have shifted their demographic policy in a fairly radical fashion. [Iran has experienced the fastest decline in fertility of any country over the last two decades due to government-led family planning measures.] As a result, the youth bulge has a termination point for Iran. At a certain stage, Iran is going to be facing a sort of Japan problem where they have a very old population with a much smaller number of young people to support it. Right now, Iran is at the height of its youth bulge. But they've already been shuttering elementary schools that are no longer needed, because they had built for the widest part of the bulge. It changes the level of activism and the potential for a long-term pressure compared to Egypt and elsewhere in the region.

How long can President Mahmoud Ahmadinejad buy public support with cash payments to poor Iranians before the economy reaches a crisis point?

It's remarkable that the regime has been able to implement the [cash payments and subsidies removal] program as widescale as it has. This has involved setting up bank accounts for millions of people, transferring funds, raising prices, and dictating the prices of a number of domestic products, consumer products. It's also remarkable that there has been so little public reaction. Funds are now going into the pocketbooks of average Iranians, which enables them to make their purchasing decisions. They can continue to spend on the same basket of goods, in particular gasoline. Or they can reorient their purchases, save some of the funds, invest in small businesses. There's some anecdotal evidence that that's actually having a very positive effect on the economy. If Iran is able to make this transition successfully, and eliminate some of the very costly subsidies that have been a drag on the economy, it would have a very powerful effect on the economy and on the political stability of the regime.

Shedding some of the costs of subsidies and reinvesting them in productive sectors of the economy also helps insulate the regime from sanctions and from popular pressures of a citizenry concerned about rising prices, as we've seen elsewhere in the Middle East. So there is a positive dimension of this program for the Iranian economy and, paradoxically, for the regime. What drew the political sector together despite objections to the reform program was the looming specter of international sanctions and financial pressures on Iran. International financial pressure has produced some rationalization of the Iranian economy and may in the end help improve the economy's performance, which is not the intention of the sanctions.

Haven't sanctions also helped Ahmadinejad channel more economic power into the hands of Iran's Revolutionary Guard?

The Revolutionary Guard is primarily benefitting from the exclusionary effect of sanctions, as international firms have left the Iranian marketplace—particularly in the oil sector, but also in other major dimensions of the economy. The Revolutionary Guard is best positioned to move in and appears to be receiving some degree of preferential treatment when it comes to building on projects and obviously access to capital and technology. So, they are a privileged sector of the economy. This isn't unique to the Islamic Republic. Militaries across the world have an economic dimension to them. And particularly in this part of the world, in the Middle East, militaries have sought to become self-sufficient and sought to involve themselves in all varieties of sectors of the economy. But the concerns about the Revolutionary Guard's role come from its increasingly political dimension. The extent to which the Revolutionary Guard is a political power with an economic capital unto themselves makes it a really independent power center within Iran and evokes concerns from across the political spectrum, and of course from average Iranians as well.

Are targeted sanctions against the Revolutionary Guard having the intended effect?

U.S. officials are generally pleased when they see the Revolutionary Guard expanding its role in the Iranian economy because it has been a major focus of targeted sanctions over the past several years, and because there is widespread international concern about its role and about its perspective. It makes it easier to gain international support for sanctions where you see the Revolutionary Guard taking a stronger role. But this is one of the areas where we have to be concerned about unintended consequences. If what we're driving is a military takeover of the Iranian state, the long-term consequences for the Iranian people are not going to be positive. In effect, what we've done is to force the regime to rely more on the Revolutionary Guard, which is ultimately more problematic for the United States.

Can Iran's growing trade relations with countries like China ultimately insulate the regime?

We're already seeing some problems with the approach of trying to use China as a substitute for European firms and European investors. There are political constraints: a lot of backlash by Iranian merchants to the overwhelming role of Chinese products that have come into the marketplace and to the quality of those goods. There's been outcry in the press about sectors of the economy that have been shut down by low-cost, low-quality competition from China. And there have been moves to ban a number of goods coming in from China because of quality concerns.Those concerns as well as the political relationship—for example backlash about Chinese support for intensified sanctions on Iran in mid-2010—produced some calls for a change in relationship between the two countries from various parts of the Iranian political establishment. So this won't be a perfectly untroubled relationship.

Of course, the Iranians value the extent to which the Chinese are disinterested in political issues in their business dealings. They're unlikely to express concerns about human rights and about democracy, a major sticking point in the expansion of trade relations with Europe.

Will Iran's economic woes be the downfall of the regime, as was the case in Egypt?

It isn't the economy that drives people to the streets. The economy has been a persistent issue within Iran, but it is one that Iranians have become somewhat inured to. Unless we see some sort of dramatic deflation, dramatic change in the status of the Iranian currency, then it's unlikely, in part because so many Iranians have an economic connection with this regime. Or if we saw the price of oil drop to somewhere in the $20 to $40 a barrel range, which would impose severe constraints for the Iranian economy. And that's unlikely because of the worldwide demand for petroleum now. The public sector has ballooned under the Islamic Republic, and many other Iranians are in some way interconnected with a private sector that really isn't private, but is a kind of crony capitalist or parastatal sector. And when your job comes from the state, it's much more difficult to go out to the streets because you risk losing your livelihood as well as endangering your own safety.

The Arab Turmoil and Palestinians

Interview with Rashid I. Khalidi

CFR.ORG, FEBRUARY 25, 2011

The turmoil in the Arab world, particularly the overthrow of President Hosni Mubarak of Egypt, has "excited" most Palestinians, says Rashid Khalidi, co-director of Columbia's Center for Palestine Studies. But the U.S.-led negotiations for a two-state solution between Palestinians and Israel has foundered, which was underscored by the U.S. veto in the Security Council against a resolution to condemn Israeli settlements in the West Bank. He says the veto—the only one among Council members—will "intensify a sense in the Arab world generally and among Palestinians as well that a resolution to this conflict does not lie through this bankrupt, failed negotiation process." He says a rethink of U.S. policy in the region is necessary. "[Obama] has to make a decision on whether he wants to act on the basis of what most people would agree are American interests: a rapid resolution of this conflict and removing the impression that most people in the world have of the United States' being on the wrong side of this."

RASHID I. KHALIDI is Edward Said professor of modern Arab studies at Columbia University. (Interview conducted by Bernard Gwertzman.)

Much of the attention in the Middle East in recent years has been over Israeli-Palestinian negotiations, which have proceeded without achieving any breakthrough. And now, suddenly there is turmoil in the Arab world that has diverted attention away from the Israeli-Palestinian issues. How do you see this, as a Palestinian?

I think most Palestinians are very excited about what's happening because they felt that the old Arab order helped to keep them down [and] was complicit with the United States and Israel. Palestinians were thrilled with what happened in Tunisia and ecstatic about what happened in Egypt. Most Palestinians will be very happy to see [Muammar] Qaddafi bite the dust. The so-called "peace process" has not been something that most Palestinians believed in since late in the 1990's. Most Palestinians believed that this was not a process that had anything to do with peace or conflict resolution. It had to do with conflict management and expansion of occupied Israeli settlements. It was clear that these talks were not leading to self-determination or statehood. It was clear it was not leading to an end of the occupation. Most Palestinians were very disenchanted with the whole process.

Now, in the midst of the upheavals in the Arab world, the Palestinians tried to get a UN Security Council resolution passed last Friday, which would have condemned the Israeli settlements. It was approved by every member of the Security Council except the United States, which by voting no, vetoed the resolution. What's been the reaction?

I think it will intensify a sense in the Arab world generally that a resolution to this conflict does not lie through this bankrupt, failed negotiation process. We may be seeing its last days. This veto clarified matters. It shows what we've known since the days of President Harry Truman [who recognized the State of Israel in 1948 against the advice of the State Department]. Clearly, domestic [pro-Israel] concerns trump everything.

People's opinions are changing. But Congress hasn't changed and the media to a very large extent hasn't changed. So, the administration responds to that [pro-Israel] sentiment. They aren't responding to reality, unfortunately. Sooner or later it's going to catch up with them. But who knows when?

At the Security Council last week, the British ambassador said that the EU was looking forward to admitting a Palestinian state to the UN by September. Is there really any possibility of a separate Palestinian state emerging?

The reality is that there has been one sovereign power since June 1967 between the Jordan River and the Mediterranean Sea, and that sovereign power is Israel. And any declaration of a Palestinian state would fly in the face of that reality. European powers may be irritated enough over the U.S. policy to take a separate course, but I'll believe that when I see it.

But isn't Salem Fayyad, the prime minister of the Palestinian Authority, working toward a Palestinian state?

The whole Arab constellation is changing. We really don't know where we're going to end up in as little as a few weeks and certainly a few months. So that may have been, and may indeed still be, the intention of Fayyad. But he's also been talking about elections and reconciliation between Hamas [in Gaza] and the Palestinian Authority [on the West Bank], and I'm not sure how you square that with such a declaration. It may be that it would be something that would appeal to a coalition government after elections, but I don't know.

What about the July elections proposed by President Mahmoud Abbas? I take it Hamas is opposed to them.

Yes, and they seem to argue that you have to have an agreement before you can have elections. Given the fact that everything is changing in the Arab world, I would suggest that there may be developments in this regard yet to come. The Egyptian regime was an enormous prop of the Palestinian status quo in its closure of Gaza and in its blockade of Gaza with Israel. All this is changing now. So, I would hesitate to suggest that we could say much definitively about this right now.

Could you see an uprising in Gaza?

The only demonstrations have been in Ramallah [the capital of the Palestinian Authority in the West Bank], and they haven't been opposing the authority but were calling for Palestinian reconciliation. I'm sure that any attempts to demonstrate in Gaza would be repressed. But the ground is moving under the feet of these two weak authorities, both of which lack legitimacy. I don't think the Gaza/Hamas authority is very popular, and I know the Ramallah authority is not popular either. That's not to say that those two parties are not going to do well in elections. They have the party machines to get out votes and know how to raise an election.

Are there some Palestinian leaders who we don't know about who are more popular?

A large chunk of Palestinian leadership at any moment is either under administrative detention, on trial, or has been sentenced or awaiting sentence. And there are a lot of people in prison. Americans and Westerners are dying to see a new Palestinian leader. The most irritating question I've gotten about Egypt is, "Who are the leaders? Where are the leaders? Why don't we see the leaders?" Well, it seems to me that one of the things that people who have been organizing this uprising in Egypt have been careful to do is to avoid appearing as leaders. In fact, somebody said on Egyptian television that the days of Egyptian strongmen are over. That period in Arab history has passed. Perhaps it's an exaggeration, but I think that what you're seeing in both Tunisia and Egypt is a fairly well-organized movement that has been very reluctant to produce a charismatic leader. I'm not sure that's germane to the Palestinian case, but I don't think we should necessarily be looking for a new leader, although many potential leaders are in prison.

I take it that George Mitchell's peace mission is dead, right?

It very much depends on what the president directs [Mitchell] to do. If he tells him to keep doing what he's been doing, I can't see that there's much point to it. A negotiation between a party under occupation and a sovereign power—which has nuclear weapons and is one of the strongest countries in the world militarily—is not a negotiation. And if the greatest superpower in the world puts its thumb on the Israeli side of the scale to boot, it's a travesty. It's not even in the realm of negotiations.

That has been the policy since Secretary of State James Baker in 1990–91, and it has just not worked. In 1991, there were a couple hundred thousand settlers, and now there's well over half a million. That has been the policy that the president essentially asked Mitchell to continue. It is a policy whereby the United States essentially endorses whatever Israel chooses to throw in the way of the Palestinians, and if the Palestinians don't accept it, then the United States wanders off and pays attention in another two months. There's no point to anyone continuing with that. That is not a peace process. That is not a negotiation. That is not going to resolve the conflict. That is simply a means of enabling Israel to continue the expansion of its settlement and occupation, which is now in its forty-fourth year [since the 1967 war]. I think it's insane for both American and Israeli interests. It's obviously not good for the Palestinians, and allowing it to continue for two years of the Obama presidency leaves a bad mark on this presidency.

If Obama called you and asked for advice on what to do, what would you recommend?

I would suggest that a fundamental rethinking of the U.S. approach is necessary. [Obama] has to make a decision on whether he wants to act on the basis of what most people would agree are American interests: a rapid resolution of this conflict and removing the impression that most people in the world have of the United States being on the wrong side of this, [which is] that we're in favor of settlement, in favor of unending occupation, and in favor of Israel dictating terms. I would suggest to him that we have to decide whether we really believe that following a policy that would serve the interest of the United States as well as the interests of Israelis and Palestinians would, in fact, lose him votes. I would be very surprised if it didn't win him votes. It would serve the national interests of the United States and the Middle East. And I would say to him that there's a huge untapped reservoir of support for a just, equitable, rapid solution of this conflict.

What would be the basis of an equitable settlement in your mind?

You would have to say settlement and occupation are illegal and should be ended as rapidly as possible. That's how you have to start it. You take note of Resolution 242, which ended the 1967 war and called an end to "territories occupied," and you take the Fourth Geneva Convention against moving populations to occupied territories. That would be a very simple and clear way to start. And how you work from there to a settlement, I don't know. But I think status quo is the starting point.

Talk about the Israeli settlements.

The settlements are illegal. Forcing Israelis to face the fact that they have to obey international law may shake up the people in Israel who really are not in favor of the settlement or the settlers. The majority of Israelis don't really believe that the settlements are in Israel's interests. But they don't get any support from the United States. The settlers get support from the United States. The only people in Israel who are happy with this U.S. veto were the settlers. The United States is in support of the settlers and not in support of the Israeli majority that's against settlement? That's what our policy, in effect, says.

But hasn't Obama inveighed pretty strongly against the settlements?

His speeches are one thing and his Security Council veto is another thing. I think his veto has a lot more weight than a lot of hot air, don't you?

Letter From Sana'a

Saleh on the Edge

Abdullah al-Qubati

FOREIGNAFFAIRS.COM, FEBRUARY 25, 2011

Last Friday, hundreds of students and activists gathered in Sana'a University's square in Yemen to call for the ouster of President Ali Abdullah Saleh. "Ali, leave, leave—your seat has oxidized!" they shouted. After an hour of protests, a thousand armed tribesmen—supporters of Saleh—surrounded the stage and attacked the demonstrators with knives, batons, and stones, injuring dozens. Known as *baltagia* ("thugs" in Arabic), the men were mercenaries paid by Saleh's party, the General People's Congress. Government officials transported the men to the university and provided them with weapons and banners supporting the president.

That violent incident was but one in a number of antigovernment protests that have expanded throughout Yemen, as the main opposition factions have joined the students to call for the end of Saleh's regime. Tens of thousands of demonstrators have been camping in Yemen's largest cities—Taiz, Aden, Ibb, and the capital, Sana'a—refusing to return home until their demand for Saleh's exit is met.

Saleh, however, is showing no sign of capitulation—and he appears willing to use lethal force. A government supporter

ABDULLAH AL-QUBATI is a freelance journalist in Yemen.

threw a grenade on a massive demonstration in Taiz last Friday, killing two and injuring 85. Clashes on Wednesday in Sana'a between antigovernment demonstrators and Saleh loyalists left at least one protester dead. All in all, the president's security forces have killed 15 protesters since February 16. The violence spurred seven members of Yemen's parliament to resign in protest from the government and the ruling party.

The protests in Yemen truly began on January 16, when hundreds of young liberal students from Sana'a University, inspired by the uprising in Tunisia against the now-deposed Zine el-Abidine Ben Ali, demonstrated at the university square to call for Saleh and his family to leave power. Radda al-Salami, a student protester, explained their actions by telling me that he "lost the ability to continue life as it should be." "I could not complete my university education due to lack of expenses for housing, food, books, and fees," he said. Angry at the concentration of power and wealth in the Saleh regime, this student movement organized a number of subsequent demonstrations that then drew the attention of Yemen's established opposition parties.

Wary of his country going the way of Egypt, Saleh announced on February 2—as former Egyptian President Hosni Mubarak's regime lifted its ban on Internet access—that he would not seek reelection when his current presidential term ends in 2013. Furthermore, he declared that he would not pass control to his family after leaving office. He also postponed national parliamentary elections, originally scheduled for April 27, to reenter dialogue with the opposition parties over electoral issues.

Yet Saleh's concessions did not mollify the protesters. "Our main demand is to overthrow the backward system in order to replace it with a modern civil national Yemeni state," said Mizzar al-Jonaid, a leader of the student movement, following Saleh's speech. Another key activist in the movement, Fakhr al-Azzab, said, "The sole incentive behind these protests is that we—as Yemeni youth—want a homeland that is large enough for our hopes, and regime step-down is our goal, as [it] is responsible for the current situation in the country."

Once others joined the protests, the demonstrating parties fell into three lines. The first involves the established opposition factions: the Joint Meeting Parties (JMP), which includes six main parties, and the Preparatory Committee for National Dialogue (PCND), a broad network of alliances that includes the JMP as well as other opposition parties, the Houthis in the north, civil society organizations, and several tribes.

Founded in 2003 to balance Saleh's one-party system, the JMP is the largest Yemeni opposition bloc and includes secular parties as well as the moderate Islamic party Islah. It holds 57 of the 301 seats in Yemen's parliament, chiefly dominated by Islah and several socialist parties. At first, the JMP refrained from calling for Saleh's ouster, instead demanding that he abandon his attempt to amend Yemen's constitution to make himself president for life. "The JMP's agenda focused on changing the nature of the political system, its form and performance," said Abdu Salem, a leading member of Islah. Yet in recent protests, JMP leaders have bowed to pressure from grass-roots activists and appealed for Saleh to leave office immediately.

The PCND formed in June 2008 out of a JMP initiative to unite Yemen's disparate opposition and civil society factions. It has played a key role in the most recent rallies by mobilizing demonstrators from Yemen's northern provinces as well as powerful tribal forces, which rarely get involved in political protests. It has also helped to sustain the momentum of the protest movement, which in Sana'a alone is attracting thousands of people every day.

In a second wave of unrest, demonstrators in the southern part of the country have organized a string of semi-daily protests to call for further autonomy from the north. North and South Yemen unified in 1990, after a civil war between the two former states ended with the victory of Saleh's northern forces. Since then, however, southern Yemenis have remained wary of unification, unhappy with perceived employment discrimination, the wholesale looting of southern natural resources by the north, and political exclusion.

On February 11, factions in the south held a "day of rage" inspired by the Egyptian protests. Tens of thousands participated, despite the use of live fire by security forces. Khalid al-Faiadhi, a leading member of the movement in the Yemeni city of Abyan, confirmed that protest organizers have decided to shift demonstrations from the minor areas to the main cities in the south, including Aden and Al-Mukalla.

The third, and perhaps most crucial, protest faction is a group of liberal youth that have coalesced in the wake of Tunisia and Egypt. Since February 11, the group, called Irhal, has drawn tens of thousands of protesters to camp on the streets of Taiz. Irhal's spokesman, Bushra al-Maqtari, confirmed the group's resolve: "We will continue sit-ins until our demands are achieved, including departure of the symbols of corruption and looters of public money, land, and life."

Yet many observers doubt the possibility of a successful revolt, believing it unlikely that the protests will gain the momentum of a mass national movement, given the fragmented, rural nature of Yemeni society and the high rates of illiteracy, poverty, and political disenfranchisement in the country. Yemen is wracked with internal divisions, with a Shiite rebellion operating in the north since 2004 and secessionist voices in the south only growing stronger as a result of the recent protests. Approximately 70 percent of the population is rural, as opposed to 35 percent in Tunisia and 56 percent in Egypt. Yemen's poverty rate stands at over 46 percent, compared to Egypt's 20 percent and Tunisia's 3.8 percent as of last year. These obstacles will make it difficult for the country to achieve the national unity that is likely necessary to unseat Saleh.

The possibility still exists, however, for Yemen's protesters to succeed—albeit in a different manner than in Tunisia or Egypt. Yemen may need far more time to erase the sharp divisions within its social structure—a healing process required to unite against the Saleh regime and establish democratic institutions. The process and speed of change will depend on the opposition forces in the north and south joining to form new alliances, and the ability of new movements to maintain the interest and support of Yemen's population.

Much as Ben Ali in Tunisia and Mubarak in Egypt did, Saleh maintains Western support by raising the specter of extremism overtaking the country should his regime fall. Western policymakers should ignore this threat and support the protest movements in their attempts to develop Yemeni civil society. If the West fails to do so, Yemen will not be the next Egypt. It will be the next Somalia.

Bahrain's Shia Question

What the United States Gets Wrong About Sectarianism

Kristin Smith Diwan

FOREIGNAFFAIRS.COM, MARCH 2, 2011

The spirit of Cairo's Tahrir Square was reborn on February 16, as a diverse group of Bahrainis gathered in Pearl Square in Manama, the country's capital. Two days before, a Facebook-organized "Day of Rage" had ended in two deaths as security forces cracked down on protesters. Now, the demonstrators marched from the funeral toward Pearl Square's traffic roundabout, determined to continue the fight for a new Bahrain. Officials from the main Shia political society, the Islamic National Accord Association (Al-Wefaq) brought cleaning supplies to scrub graffiti off the Pearl Square fountain. The leader of the leftist secular National Democratic Action Society (Wa'ad) movement spoke of Bahrain's proud history of cross-sectarian labor activism and proposed the formation of a new national organization to press for a genuine constitutional monarchy. Shia and Sunni prayed together. By nightfall, thousands of unaligned Bahrainis had crowded the square to join what, by then, felt like a celebration.

KRISTIN SMITH DIWAN is Assistant Professor of Comparative and Regional Studies at the School of International Service at American University.

Yet that celebration was cruelly extinguished at three in the morning by a surprise police attack on the sleeping encampments. Security forces wounded hundreds and killed four in the brutally efficient raid. Even health workers seeking to aid the wounded were attacked. By morning, the space where Bahrain's pro-democracy activists, Shia and Sunni, had come together was encased in barbed wire. The ruling al-Khalifa monarchy did not want that unity to continue.

Like much of the news media covering Bahrain's uprising, it prefers a simpler narrative of Shia against Sunni. Just as Hosni Mubarak held Egypt hostage for decades to a false choice between staying loyal to his regime or facing an Islamist takeover, the ruling al-Khalifa family resisted democratic reform by presenting themselves as protectors of the Sunni community against the Shia majority. The extraordinary meeting of foreign ministers of the Gulf Cooperation Council (GCC) in Bahrain on the same day as the Pearl Square raid both reinforced and broadened this threat by sharply denouncing foreign (read: Iranian) intervention in Gulf countries. During the meeting and since, the GCC have been reviving the fear that plagued the region after Iran's 1979 Islamic revolution—that Iran would foment unrest among Shia communities of the Gulf.

The GCC warning resonates in the United States, which bases its Fifth Naval Fleet in Bahrain and is locked in its own confrontation with Iran. But it should not. In fact, separate from the Iranian question, the empowerment of the Shia majority is a necessary component of political liberalization. Shias should be able to engage as full citizens, and their role in building Bahrain should be respected. This would be the best way to curb Iranian influence. A more democratic Bahrain that fully integrates its Shia public would be less susceptible to appeals from the Islamic Republic. Over time, the political relevance of Shia identity might even decrease, since Shias would have less reason to seek communal protection from a discriminatory state.

Contrary to Western fears and the Bahraini regime's announcements, the country's largely Shia opposition movement is not an Iranian implant. Indeed, its strength is a product of the Bahraini government's own policies. Al-Wefaq, for example, is a deeply communal movement that emerged in the wake of the violent suppression of a Shia uprising in the 1990s. When I met with the movement's quietly charismatic leader, Sheikh Ali Salman, a number of years ago, he explained that "the best democracy is practiced on the street," meaning that the key to effective political change is constant communication with the people. It is this connection, combined with its religious legitimacy, that allows Al-Wefaq to mobilize Bahrainis so impressively when it wants to. Even in 2005, it drew more than 50,000 Shia—nearly one in ten Bahrainis—to a demonstration in support of constitutional reform, a demand that still unites protesters of all factions today.

Those protests were ultimately unsuccessful. In 2006, Al-Wefaq ended a four-year boycott of the parliament, demonstrating a willingness to work within a flawed system and accept the necessity of incremental reform. The move was costly for the Shia opposition. One of Al-Wefaq's founders, Hassan Mushaima, left in protest to form a rival organization, the Haq Movement for Liberty and Democracy. This would have been a tremendous opportunity for the al-Khalifa government to broaden its legitimacy, but instead of reaching out to Al-Wefaq—inviting cooperation to lessen systematic discrimination against Shias in housing, government hiring practices, and political districting—the ruling family worked to isolate the Shia opposition. So although it portrayed the Shias as dangerously sectarian, in reality it was the one fomenting sectarian distrust.

By gerrymandering districts and holding strategic naturalizations of Sunnis from neighboring states, the regime prevented Al-Wefaq from gaining its rightful majority position in the elected lower house. At the same time, the government prevented the popular leftist cross-sectarian opposition headed by Wa'ad from gaining any parliamentary seats. As a result, the 2006 parliament was a strictly sectarian affair in which Sunni Islamists from both the Salafi and Muslim Brotherhood traditions faced off against the cleric-led Al-Wefaq. This composition belied the diverse views of the Bahraini public and solidified sectarian identities in the formal political sphere.

Still, the al-Khalifa regime's strategy did little to advance its stability. Indeed, it ultimately cost it a precious asset: a legitimate national Shia movement willing to work within the system. Al-Wefaq's minority position in parliament left it burdened with the responsibility of governance without the structural power to force accountability and change. Former supporters decried Al-Wefaq's inability to curb royal corruption while at the same time supporting the implementation of the Gulf's first income tax. Disillusionment returned to the Shia street—a wave of tire-burning protests hit Shia villages, and the popularity of Haq rose. The organization's confrontational program of civil disobedience and international human rights activism siphoned support from al-Wefaq, particularly among the youth. The regime responded forcefully and brutally in 2010, arresting 23 dissidents, including human rights workers and a well-known blogger, allegedly subjecting some to torture while in detention.

The outbreak of the Arab revolutions this year, then, came at a critical point in the evolution of Bahrain's opposition politics. By providing a model of regime change through mass protest, the Tunisian and Egyptian examples reinforced the Bahraini opposition's drift away from formal politics back into the street. The protests across the Arab world returned the opposition's focus to core democratic issues: freedom and dignity. The al-Khalifa regime's lethal crackdown hardened its resolve. Many in Bahrain now want more than constitutional reformation. They want to achieve what Tunisia and Egypt have done—to fell the regime.

After the violence in Pearl Square, King Hamad bin Isa al-Khalifa apparently regained control from a hard-line faction of the ruling family that had been running the crackdown, and tried to appease demonstrators by calling for national unity and a dialogue among all parties. To entice the opposition to enter negotiations, the King has met two of their key demands—withdrawing troops from the streets, allowing the protesters to retake the symbolic Pearl Square, and releasing hundreds of prisoners, including the prominent Shia dissidents he had accused of plotting terrorism. But by calling all Bahraini factions to the table to talk, the regime has effectively diluted the opposition's power by adding more conservative and pro-monarch parties to the conversation.

The rival rallies held on February 21 by the opposition in Pearl Square and by monarchy loyalists in Al-Fateh mosque reinforced the image of a society hopelessly divided between Shia democrats and Sunni monarchists. The potential for sectarian polarization to harden to the point where compromise is impossible is real, but it belies the fluid situation on the ground. Fearing the loss of national unity, all sides present themselves as speaking for all Bahrainis, regardless of religion. The mass of people in control of Pearl Square still contains a number of cross-sectarian democratic and labor movements. And even the ostensibly pro-monarchy gathering at Al-Fateh mosque challenged the monarchy to enact deeper social and political reforms.

As attention drifts elsewhere in the Middle East, the Bahraini public is still politically mobilized to an astonishing degree. It will take tremendous skill to find a solution that will avoid dangerous sectarian polarization and further bloodshed. Not having taken advantage of Al-Wefaq's parliamentary inclusion, the al-Khalifa family now faces the street. The street wants revolution, but the majority of the Sunni community will not support the fall of the monarchy, and Saudi Arabia, just across the causeway, will not allow it. The best solution is reform—substantial reform—to put the island on the path of genuine constitutional monarchy.

The U.S. confrontation with Iran has heightened sectarian tensions across the Middle East. Bahrain offers an opportunity to push back against this dangerous trend. The promise of the Pearl uprising—that Bahraini Shia could be integrated through a broader democratic movement—should be realized. Although the empowerment of Shias poses some risks, the alternative is much worse. If the Gulf's first attempt at an Egypt-inspired democratic revolution ends in sectarian strife and violent suppression of the Shia majority, the unrest will not be restricted to the tiny island. And the government in Iran will find a much more receptive political environment across Arabia for its hard-line message.

Rage Comes to Baghdad

Will Iraq's Recent Protests Lead to Revolt?

Raad Alkadiri

FOREIGNAFFAIRS.COM, MARCH 3, 2011

Saddam Hussein may have been overthrown in 2003, but the dawn of more representative government in Iraq has not inoculated the country from the popular unrest now sweeping through the Arab world. Over the past month, demonstrations protesting the woeful lack of services and widespread corruption have taken place throughout the country. These culminated in a violent "day of rage" in a number of Iraqi cities, including one in Baghdad on February 25 that left more than 20 protesters dead.

These protests have not reached the scale of those witnessed in Egypt, Libya, and Tunisia, and demonstrators have not demanded regime change per se. Nonetheless, the tight security measures taken to contain the "day of rage" protests in Baghdad—including blocking access to the city and putting a tight military cordon around Tahrir Square, the focal point of the demonstrations—and Prime Minister Nouri al-Maliki's efforts to link the unrest to al Qaeda and Baathist provocateurs

RAAD ALKADIRI is a Partner at PFC Energy. He was Assistant Private Secretary to the United Kingdom Special Representative to Iraq from 2003 to 2004 and Political Adviser to the United Kingdom's Ambassador to Iraq from 2006 to 2007. The views expressed here are his own.

suggest that his government is rattled. And with good cause, because if Baghdad cannot respond effectively to popular demands, the current government's political survival is no less at stake than those in Cairo, Tripoli, and Tunis.

Although there is undoubtedly an element of contagion influencing events in Iraq, which began with small demonstrations in Baghdad led by intellectuals and professionals, the protests there are driven by local grievances. Popular anger at the persistent lack of services—especially electricity—has been rising steadily over the past few years. Demonstrations protesting power shortages occurred in Basra last summer, expressing a frustration common to Iraqis across the country; some parts of Baghdad, for example, received around two hours of electricity per day from the national grid in early February. Iraqis also share growing resentment toward pervasive government corruption, a factor that has been particularly important in driving demonstrations against the regional administration in Kurdistan. Iraq ranked 175 out of 178 countries on Transparency International's 2010 corruption index. Meanwhile, there is broad resentment of the high salaries and generous benefits that public officials have granted themselves, especially given the government's apparent ineptitude.

None of these grievances is new; Iraqis have complained about poor services and unresponsive government since the U.S. invasion in 2003. But in the bloody, chaotic years that followed Hussein's fall, security was the biggest popular concern. Now that levels of violence have diminished, Iraqis' patience with their government's inadequacies is wearing thin.

Iraq's leaders were slow to recognize this simmering popular frustration. In the early days of unrest in Egypt and Tunisia, Iraqi officials were blasé and almost smug, lecturing their Arab counterparts on the need for democratic government and dismissing the chances of similar disturbances in Iraq. The warnings that were issued over the risk of domestic turbulence had a clear political bent and seemed to be aimed more at casting aspersions on Maliki's leadership than anything else.

Consequently, Baghdad was caught unawares when protests did break out in the capital and in cities such as Mosul in early February, and its initial response was rather panicked. Following a now well-trodden path, Maliki announced on February 5 that he would not seek reelection for a third term, only for his official spokesman to claim a day later that the prime minister had been misquoted. Maliki, his cabinet ministers, and members of the Council of Representatives also discussed slashing their salaries. As a temporary measure to compensate for the poor state of services, the government pledged free electricity for approximately one million of Iraq's poorest families. Maliki also promised that every person would be given 15,000 dinars (roughly $13) as compensation for deficiencies in the national ration card system, a program to supply basic foodstuffs that was first introduced by Saddam Hussein in the early 1990s, when Iraq was under international sanctions.

Faced with continuing protests, the government followed up with a slew of other initiatives, including shifting spending priorities in the 2011 budget. The state will double its spending on the national ration card and increase capital spending on infrastructure projects at the expense of current spending (although its room for maneuver is limited, as the latter is dedicated mostly to salaries and wages). Most government officials have escaped salary reductions for the moment, but the prime minister, president, and speaker of the Iraqi parliament will assume 20 percent pay cuts. To address energy concerns, Maliki separately announced that factories will be removed from the national electricity grid between May and September to divert more power to households, and he has proposed a plan to distribute small generators to villages to supplement patchy national distribution.

These proposals have yet to mollify the protesters. And although the initiatives look good on paper, the government faces a steep challenge in implementing them. Twenty years of war, sanctions, and invasion have hamstrung the fledgling Iraqi government. Maliki must confront a debilitating set of political and administrative weaknesses that severely undermines his government's capacity to design and implement policy. Maliki himself has been the first to acknowledge that his new cabinet, much like its predecessor, sacrifices effectiveness for political inclusiveness. All the main parties and blocs in the Council of Representatives are represented in the new government—including Ayad Allawi's Iraqiya party, which narrowly defeated Maliki in last year's elections—largely because the factions feared being marginalized in opposition. But they have not committed to a common program, and political differences among them remain stark. Maliki may have secured his post by outmaneuvering his opponents, but his actions merely increased their distrust of him—and, in some cases, their determination to weaken and even unseat him.

Compounding these political problems is the diminished capability of Iraq's public service ministries. The overall quality of the country's civil servants has steadily deteriorated over the past eight years. Although violence and de-Baathification have taken a toll, time itself is an enemy. Iraq's most capable technocrats—many of whom came from the last generation to be educated abroad in the mid-1980s—have passed retirement age. Many of the current senior civil servants are simply out of their depth, having suffered through years of isolation under sanctions and having been promoted rapidly, as a result of political connections or the need to fill the leadership vacuum. Moreover, they are forced to operate in ministries that—particularly in the case of service branches—have become political fiefdoms serving party or constituency interests rather than the country at large. Such provincialism results in little or no coordination between ministries and undermines the capacity for broad strategic planning and implementation—both of which are necessary to solve the country's infrastructure and services deficits.

None of this is to suggest that Iraq is on the brink of collapse. With continued oil revenues—conservatively estimated at around $70 billion this year but liable to rise if crude oil prices remain at their current elevated levels—the government will retain a powerful means of increasing social spending and, more important, protecting the crucial patronage networks relied on by various ruling parties to preserve their influence. At the very least, these funds will help the government maintain the status quo.

But the threats posed by the protest should not be underestimated. It is possible that the shock of the protests, combined with the impending loss of the safety net that U.S. troops have provided for the past eight years, will force Iraq's leaders to assume greater responsibility. This shift would not immediately change conditions on the ground, but it could improve the government's administrative capacity and nudge it toward more realistic and manageable policies to address Iraq's social and infrastructure challenges.

Or, more worringly, Iraq's dearth of administrative and technocratic capabilities could remain an obstacle to implementing even small-scale government initiatives. Worse still, Maliki's rivals may begin to try to take political advantage of the current protests. Leaders from across the political spectrum sense the opportunity, and some, Iraqiya, are already hinting at a parliamentary vote of no confidence against the prime minister. The Shiite cleric Muqtada al-Sadr's call last week for his followers to give the government a six-month grace period in which to improve services seemed to provide Maliki with some respite, especially as the Sadrists are a key government ally, representing some of the poorest and potentially most disruptive parts of Iraqi society. But even this reprieve has been temporary. Sadr and his lieutenants have joined a chorus of attacks on the prime minister sung in recent days by many of the other major parties. The fact remains that Maliki has made a host of enemies among rival political blocs over the past five years, all of whom would be happy to see him fall.

Consequently, unless conditions improve in Iraq, Maliki may face the unpalatable choice of allowing himself to be replaced or clinging to power through authoritarian means. It is by no means clear that he will choose the former. As he showed during the nine months of painful negotiations over government formation last year, he will not yield power easily, and his reaction to the recent "day of rage" was a reminder of his authoritarian streak. In the time-honored fashion of Arab strongmen, the prime minister has sought to establish personal control over Iraq's security services over the past few years, and his instinctual response to the latest crisis has been to consider further centralizing his control by establishing overseers for each ministry based in his office and appointing special representatives in the ministries themselves.

Such actions would have a corrosive impact on the country's representative politics. Iraqis have already shown unmistakable signs of disillusionment with the new order. Voter participation has dropped over the last five years—official turnout fell from 79.6 percent in 2005 to 62.4 percent last year—and many of those who did vote in last year's general elections expressed their frustration with business-as-usual politics through a clear anti-incumbency vote for Allawi's Iraqiya party. The fact that incumbents—Maliki chief among them—were largely able to protect their power and prerogatives simply widened the chasm between Iraq's rulers and its ruled. The Maliki government's failure to respond effectively to the latest protests will expand that gap further. An Egypt- or Tunisia-style revolution is not in the cards for Iraq—at least not yet. But if Iraqis are forced to endure another hot summer without sufficient electricity supplies, protests will continue and pressure on the government will grow. Worse yet, the Iraqi people may lose faith altogether in electoral politics, which would put not just Maliki's future at risk but also the stability of the entire post-2003 political order.

The Sturdy House That Assad Built

Why Damascus Is Not Cairo

Michael Bröning

FOREIGNAFFAIRS.COM, MARCH 7, 2011

As revolutions rocked authoritarian regimes from Tunis to Manama, pundits were quick to identify Syria's leadership as the next to fall. Like other countries in the region, Syria is deeply impoverished. And on the face of it, the similarities between Damascus' authoritarian system and those of Tunisia, Egypt, and Libya are striking. Just as in Tunisia and Egypt, a single-party regime has ruled Syria with an iron fist for years. For the past five decades, it has kept the country under permanent emergency law, which, like in its North African counterparts, has been used to suppress calls for greater political participation. Yet despite various parallels, a closer look at Syria reveals that the Assad regime—led for the past decade by Bashar al-Assad—is unlikely to fall. Paradoxically, Syria's grave economic situation and its Alawi minority rule, which has been safeguarded by repressive mechanisms, will prevent oppositional forces from gaining critical mass in the near future.

MICHAEL BRÖNING is Director of the East Jerusalem office of Friedrich-Ebert-Stiftung, a German political foundation affiliated with Germany's Social Democratic Party. He is the author of *The Politics of Change in Palestine: State-Building and Non-Violent Resistance*.

Syria has recently experienced annual economic growth rates of around 4 percent, but the country is still plagued by staggering unemployment, increasing costs of living, stagnating wages, and widespread poverty. Although official data from Damascus (which is notorious for its overly optimistic calculations) lists unemployment in the first quarter of 2010 at eight percent, independent estimates hover around 20 percent, with even higher rates among the younger generation. Because underemployed and disillusioned youth comprised one of the driving forces of revolutions in Tunisia and Egypt, observers have enthusiastically noted Syria's youth unemployment rate as a signal of potential revolt.

Syrian youth certainly share the economic grievances of young people in Tunisia and Egypt, but widespread poverty and unemployment are unlikely to catalyze sudden regime change now. Despite the policy of cautious economic liberalization that Assad initiated after taking office in 2000, Syrian society continues to be defined by its high degree of egalitarianism. True, Western luxury goods are increasingly available to elites, and some members of Assad's extended family have been accused of nepotism and profiteering. However, the accumulation of excessive wealth in the hands of an oligarchic political elite has been more an exception than a rule. Political isolation and domestic authoritarianism have severely restricted the development of a politically conscious and economically empowered middle class. As such, the situation in Damascus differs significantly from pre-revolutionary Tunisia, Egypt, and Libya. In all three countries, public fury was fueled by a highly visible and ever-increasing status gap between a large elite class and a marginalized majority. Unlike Syrians, protesters in Tunisia, Egypt, and now Libya perceived their poverty to be relative rather than absolute—and thus as an injustice caused by the regime.

During its decades of rule, moreover, the Assad family developed a strong political safety net by firmly integrating the military into the regime. In 1970, Hafez al-Assad, Bashar's father, seized power after rising through the ranks of the Syrian armed forces, during which time he established a network of loyal Alawites by installing them in key posts. In fact, the military, ruling elite, and ruthless secret police are so intertwined that it is now impossible to separate the Assad regime from the security establishment. Bashar al-Assad's threat to use force against protesters would be more plausible than Tunisia's or Egypt's were. So, unlike in Tunisia and Egypt, where a professionally trained military tended to play an independent role, the regime and its loyal forces have been able to deter all but the most resolute and fearless oppositional activists. In this respect, the situation in Syria is to a certain degree comparable to Saddam Hussein's strong Sunni minority rule in Iraq. At the same time, it is significantly different from Libya, where the military, although brutal and loyal to the regime, is a more disorganized group of militant thugs than a trained and disciplined army.

Indeed, the regime's use of force against opponents has not been merely hypothetical. In 1982, Hafez al-Assad infamously suppressed an uprising of the Muslim Brotherhood in the city of Hama, resulting in thousands of civilian deaths. More recently, in 2004, Bashar al-Assad's security forces violently quelled Kurdish protests, leaving dozens dead. The likelihood of the regime resorting to such violence again is increased by Syria's isolation. Unlike in Egypt, where a strong history of friendly bilateral relations and a U.S.-led diplomatic effort shaped the military's response to growing protests, or Tunisia, where the military received intensive U.S.-training, the West has very little leverage over Syria. The consequences of such political isolation can be seen on the Libyan streets: with no one able to stop him, the equally ostracized leader Muammar al-Qaddafi has opted to use sheer force to maintain his hold on power. For many Syrians, the Libyan regime's violent response is a stark reminder of the suffering a determined tyrant can inflict on his people.

Another Syrian particularity is Assad's affiliation with a religious minority: the Alawi sect. Political observers have established a near-unanimous consensus that his minority status has severely jeopardized long-term stability. This assessment is plausible but fails to account for Syria's specific circumstances.

It is true that Assad has even fewer enthusiastic supporters beyond his small group of co-opted elites than did former Tunisian President Zine el-Abidine Ben Ali and former Egyptian President Hosni Mubarak, but the regime's opposition has even less popular support. Unlike other dictators in the region, Assad is seen by many as a counterweight to sectarian disintegration rather than as a champion of sectarian interests. Moreover, Syrians have had frequent and direct exposure to the devastating outcomes of sectarian conflicts in Iraq and Lebanon. In 2005 and 2006, hundreds of thousands of Lebanese and Iraqi refugees flowed into Damascus, reminding Syrians of the dire consequences of religiously fueled carnage. And seeing how sectarianism has stunted Lebanon and Iraq, Syria's equally pluralist society has good reason to acquiesce to Assad's leadership.

Moreover, Assad's relative youth (he is 45, Ben Ali is 74, Mubarak is 82, and Qaddafi is 68) and his record of staunch anti-Westernism give him a layer of protection that the other leaders did not enjoy. Many Syrians perceive his opposition to the U.S.-led invasion of Iraq and his anti-Israel policies as desirable and in the national interest. In fact, Assad's reputation in the West as an unyielding pariah has translated into popularity in his own country. In a somewhat twisted way, his willingness to stand up to the United States comports with the theme of Arab dignity that has rallied protesters throughout the region. While a similar anti-Western stance was taken by Qaddafi, Syria's geographical proximity to the Arab-Israeli conflict (and its direct involvement) has lent Assad's rhetoric of resistance much greater credibility than Qaddafi's, especially after Qaddafi improved relations with the United States in the 2000s.

This is not to say that the Syrian regime has demonstrated complete indifference to regional developments. Indicating at least some uneasiness at the toppling of his counterparts in Tunisia and Egypt, Assad recently promised reforms "to open up society" and "start dialogue." So far, his reforms have been limited to ad hoc increases in certain wages and the (surprising) unlocking of social media networks. Still, Syrians will likely prefer to pin their hopes on a slow but stable process of reform rather than an uncertain and violent revolution. Calls on Facebook for a "day of rage" have until now remained unanswered.

Certainly, an early test of whether Assad's promise of reforms was sufficient will be seen in municipal and parliamentary elections scheduled for later this year. However these elections turn out, it seems that the current wave of anti-authoritarianism will continue to largely pass Syria by. Ironically, the one Arab regime Western leaders would probably most like to see ousted from power may very well end up relatively strengthened compared to the fledgling regimes in the rest of the region. This is especially worrisome, given the possibility that an unshaken regime in Damascus might seriously consider a rapprochement with a newly elected Egyptian leadership. The question of how the West should engage Assad, now bolstered by the demise of Western-backed leaders in Tunisia and Egypt, will thus soon reemerge with even greater acuteness.

Rageless in Riyadh

Why the Al Saud Dynasty Will Remain

F. Gregory Gause III

FOREIGNAFFAIRS.COM, MARCH 16, 2011

Earlier this month, Saudi Arabia's opposition bloggers and Facebook users called for a "day of rage" to be held on Friday, March 11, modeled after those in neighboring Bahrain, Egypt, Tunisia, and Yemen. There was no reason to think that Saudi Arabia would be immune to the protest contagion. After all, the problems facing Saudi Arabia are similar in kind (if not extent) to those of the other Arab states. Saudi Arabia has a demographic youth bulge. Like other Arab nations, it has a serious youth unemployment problem. It has an autocratic government that prevents serious political participation. It is a rich country but with low per capita income compared to its smaller Gulf neighbors. Even Bahrain, wracked with protests, has a higher per capita GDP, $40,400 compared to Saudi Arabia's $24,200. And the positive response of thousands of Saudis to online petitions for political reform, especially on Dawlaty.info and Saudireform.com, indicates that plenty of people in the country want some kind of change.

But the calls for a "day of rage" met with almost no response except for a few relatively small protests in Shiite-majority areas

F. GREGORY GAUSE III is Professor of Political Science at the University of Vermont.

of the Eastern Province. The Saudi media, which had studiously ignored the online calls, crowed on Saturday about the protests' failure, mocking the "day of rage" as a "day of calm" and a "day of reassurance."

Perhaps we should not have been so surprised. In late January, all of the elements for popular mobilization against the regime appeared to be in place. In Saudi Arabia's second-largest city, Jeddah, there was devastating flooding, during which at least ten people died, many more were injured, and millions of dollars in property was damaged. This followed even more damaging flooding in late 2009. This manifest government failure occurred just as the rest of the Arab world was exploding: protesters in Tunisia had just driven their president, Zine el-Abidine Ben Ali, from power (to exile in Jeddah, of all places), and Egyptians were mobilizing by the hundreds of thousands in Tahrir Square. But very little happened in Jeddah. There were a few protests, about 50 people arrested, and no ripple effects elsewhere in the country.

So what makes the Saudi case different from the others? First, the Saudi government has plenty of ready cash and has shown itself willing to spend it to deflect political mobilization. No other Arab regime has been able to throw money at its problems quite like the Saudi one. Three weeks ago, for example, the government announced a set of salary increases, unemployment benefits, loan forgiveness, consumer subsidies, and other measures totaling $36 billion. This package will not solve Saudi Arabia's long-term economic problems, of course, but it certainly cushions the blow of rising inflation, a housing shortage, and youth unemployment.

Second, Saudi Arabia's security forces are a strong deterrent. There are a number of Saudi security agencies tasked with maintaining order, but the National Guard ultimately guarantees domestic security and regime stability. Exclusively Sunni, it is largely comprised of recruits from the tribes of central and western Arabia and of nontribal recruits from the central Arabian heartland, the base of Al Saud power. There is no doubt that members of the guard would obey the regime's orders to suppress demonstrations in the Shia towns of the Eastern Province (as they did in 1979 and 1980) and in the cities of western Saudi Arabia (Jeddah, Mecca, and Medina). Unlike the Egyptian and Tunisian armies, which felt kinship with the demonstrators in their capitals and refused to fire on them, Saudi security forces would likely view demonstrators anywhere outside of Riyadh and central Saudi Arabia as strangers. Whether they would be as reliable against protesters in Riyadh or central Arabia is an open question and not one that the regime has had to answer yet. Still, its security apparatuses were out in force on March 11, including in Riyadh, and they did not hesitate to use violence against small demonstrations in Shia towns the day before.

Third, the opposition is still too divided to offer a real threat. This stands in contrast to Tunisia and Egypt, where people from across classes, sects, and ideologies mobilized to oust Ben Ali and former Egyptian President Hosni Mubarak. At the topmost level, Saudi political activists are beginning to bridge differences in sect, region, and ideology. Since 9/11, there has been more cross-sectarian and cross-ideological dialogue than in the past, some of it even sponsored by the government through its national dialogue initiative. But this is not the case throughout the population. It is instructive that there have been two major online petition movements rather than a single one representing the broad range of political currents. The two petitions share a number of points—most notably their calls to give the elected legislature real oversight of government ministries—but one was more reflective of the Wahhabi intellectual current, and the other of a more liberal (in the Saudi context) current. Wahhabi sheikhs might occasionally visit Shia discussion groups, but the chance that a single street protest could bring together large numbers of both groups is slim.

Finally, the Saudi regime has had weeks to digest the reasons for and consequences of the Tunisian and Egyptian revolutions, something that Ben Ali entirely lacked and Mubarak was too set in his ways to appreciate. Despite the advanced age and infirmity of their top leaders, members of the Saudi elite have proved fairly nimble. They threatened punishment for any opposition (but not so much as to excite protesters), and they balanced their threats with promises of rewards for cooperation. They were also deft at getting the religious establishment to come to their aid, by issuing fatwas declaring street demonstrations to be in violation of Islam. It is unclear how many Saudis still pay attention to state-appointed arbiters of religion, but it certainly does not hurt the Saudi leadership to have them on its side.

Meanwhile, local regime officials engaged in fairly active outreach on behalf of their constituents. A government delegation from Qatif, the most important Shia city in the Eastern Province, met with the Saudi king a few days before the scheduled "day of rage," although the purpose of the visit was not made public. Prince Muhammad bin Fahd bin Abdul Aziz Al Saud, the governor of the Eastern Province, spoke with local Shia leaders earlier last week and made a few gestures of good faith, including releasing a number of prisoners. Similarly, Prince Khalid al-Faisal, the governor of Mecca (who also has jurisdiction over Jeddah), met very publicly with activists and has since rolled out a high-profile campaign to show that the government is serious about fixing Jeddah's water drainage infrastructure. It is possible that the local and national leadership could also announce some small steps on the political front: a cabinet shake-up, municipal council elections, perhaps even elections to the national *shura* (consultative) council.

Yet the Al Saud are certainly not out of the winter of Arab discontent. On March 13, hundreds demonstrated in front of the Interior Ministry in Riyadh to demand the release of prisoners captured during the government's years-long fight against al Qaeda in the Arabian Peninsula. There were demonstrations of similar size in Shia towns that day as well. And having just deployed troops to support the monarchy in Bahrain, the Saudis have placed themselves in a tricky situation; as Saudi forces help suppress the Bahraini protesters, the vast majority of whom are Shia, they could provoke serious protests among Saudi Arabia's own Shia population. But, at least so far, Saudi Arabia is among the ranks of Syria and Morocco—the other major Arab states least affected by the wave of Arab upheaval.

Syria's Assad No Longer in Vogue

What Everyone Got Wrong About Bashar al-Assad

Tony Badran

FOREIGNAFFAIRS.COM, MARCH 25, 2011

It was slow in coming, but the Arab revolutionary wave of 2011 has reached Syria. Its arrival has forced a reassessment of the Bashar al-Assad regime's domestic legitimacy and prospects for survival. Over the past few months, many commentators have maintained that the regime would remain sheltered from regional turmoil. As the prominent Syrian dissident Suhair Atassi lamented, her country is "a kingdom of silence" dominated by fear.

Now, the story line has changed dramatically. Events in the southern city of Deraa have challenged the conventional wisdom about Syria's stability. Protests began on March 18, after security forces detained 15 children for spraying anti-regime graffiti on walls there. Seeking to nip any ideas of revolution in the bud, Assad's security forces attacked the protesters, killing four.

TONY BADRAN is a Research Fellow at the Foundation for Defense of Democracies.

The next day, thousands took to the streets, torching the ruling Baath Party headquarters, several other government buildings, and the local branch of the country's main cell phone company, Syriatel, which is owned by Assad's cousin, Rami Makhlouf, whom the protesters singled out by name, calling him a "thief." They also defaced many of the ubiquitous posters of Assad that the regime, Soviet-style, hangs in public places, and tore down a statue of Hafez al-Assad, Bashar's father.

The regime's heavy-handed crackdown on the children lit the fuse on the Syrian people's political and economic grievances. They initially demanded an end to the emergency laws first enacted 48 years ago when the Baath Party seized power in Syria. But by March 19, they were calling for "revolution." The old regime-sanctioned chants of "God, Syria, and Bashar only" had been replaced with "God, Syria, and freedom only."

The regime attempted to calm the situation by sending to Deraa a delegation headed by Faisal al-Miqdad, the deputy foreign minister, to offer condolences and promise an investigation into the deaths of the four protesters. It also pledged to release the original 15 detainees. But the delegation was not well received, and the riots continued and spread to some neighboring towns.

By March 22, the regime judged the situation in Deraa to have gotten out of hand and dispatched several tanks and helicopters to seal off the city. Although they were initially repelled, the security forces subsequently made a final push against the protesters at dawn on March 23, resulting in what dissidents have called a "massacre." According to human rights activists and witnesses, more than 100 people were killed. Rumor has it that the push was undertaken by the Republican Guard—a force tasked with protecting the Assad regime commanded by Bashar's brother, Maher.

Despite the bloody crackdown, the protesters continued to come out in the thousands, expressing their resolve to push ahead. In particular, the regime was clearly concerned about plans for a major rally on March 25 after Friday prayers, and about the prospect of it spreading beyond Deraa. In a desperate attempt to head it off, Assad's spokesperson, Bouthaina Shaaban, made public statements promising that the regime would "study" lifting the emergency laws. By all indications, however, her statement only increased the protesters' determination to press on. To the protesters, such gestures may simply be too little, too late.

According to many observers, Assad was supposed to be immune to this kind of popular movement. His anti-American policies and enmity toward Israel were thought to boost his legitimacy in the eyes of his people. Compared to the advanced age of Egypt's former president, 82-year-old Hosni Mubarak, and Tunisia's ex-president, 74-year-old Zine el-Abidine Ben Ali, Assad's relative youth at 45 was also thought to be an asset. One Syria specialist, Joshua Landis, noted that unlike the aging Mubarak, the young Assad was "popular among young people" who "tend to blame [corruption] on . . . the 'old guard.'" An unfortunately timed puff piece on Asma al-Assad, the president's glamorous wife, in the current issue of *Vogue*, spoke of the "first lady's central mission . . . to change the mind-set of six million Syrians under eighteen [and] encourage them to engage in what she calls 'active citizenship.'" It gave plausibility to the claim that the Assads are a fresh breeze blowing through a decrepit house.

Ironically, the basis for such arguments was Assad's own public relations strategy. When Assad inherited power from his father in 2000, he adopted the "old versus new guard" theme to cultivate his image as a reformer and bolster his legitimacy at home and abroad. For a brief period, he allowed dissidents to criticize corruption openly. But this so-called Damascus Spring was a cynical mirage. In the past decade, Syria has not seen a single meaningful act of reform.

The truth is that Assad could not have pursued such reform even if he had wanted to, as this would have meant taking on the corruption of his immediate family. Assad's cousin, the billionaire Makhlouf, is widely considered to be the second-most powerful man in the country, even though he holds no official title. He is essentially the economic arm of the regime, using his business empire to co-opt the Sunni merchant class. (Makhlouf, Assad, and most of the ruling elite and high-ranking officers are Alawites, a minority sect.) When the people of Deraa set fire to the Syriatel office, they were not targeting the old guard; they were targeting the very heart of the current regime, or, as one Syrian activist in Deraa told Reuters, the very symbols of oppression and corruption.

The idea that Assad's anti-Western ideology is popular enough to shield him from public discontent comes from him as well: in an interview with *The Wall Street Journal* in late January, he explained that the Mubarak regime was unpopular due to its alliance with the United States and its peace treaty with Israel. By contrast, he suggested, the Syrian regime was ideologically united with the people. As Assad put it, Syrians "do not go into an uprising," because "it is not only about [their] needs and not only about the reform. It is about the ideology." Assad's foreign policy and ideology of "resistance" may indeed be popular in Syria. But the protests are driven by concerns over domestic issues. The idea that ideology and foreign policy trump concerns about lack of freedom, economic opportunity, and political participation has proved wrong.

Other commentators who dismissed the likelihood of the Assad regime falling pointed to solidarity among the Alawite elite. Unlike the Egyptian army, which functioned independently of Mubarak and broke with him at a key moment, the Syrian brass, as part of a small religious minority, views its fate and safety as inextricably linked to Assad's and therefore will not fail to crack down on protests.

Still, that threat has not deterred all the protesters. And on March 22, the sectarian dimension of the conflict became explicit: the Deraa demonstrators broke a long-standing taboo, chanting, "No to Iran, no to Hezbollah, we want a God-fearing Muslim"—by which they meant, "We want a Sunni Muslim running the country." In a show of solidarity with the regime, Alawites replaced their own headshots on Facebook with pictures of Bashar.

It has been suggested that the best way for Assad to deal with sectarian tensions would be to reform and democratize. But to democratize is to take the Alawite hand off the tiller. And, the bankrupt regime's latest concession to quell the unrest—the announcement of a salary increase for state employees—suggests that even Assad's supposed economic rationalization is over. With its sources of legitimacy badly undermined, brute force is the only tool left to secure the regime's rule.

On March 24, U.S. Secretary of Defense Robert Gates urged that Syria follow Egypt's example. However, as the protests spread throughout the rest of Syria, Assad will surely follow another example: Hafez al-Assad who set the precedent, in 1982, when he pulverized Hama, a Muslim Brotherhood rebellion city, killing nearly 20,000 to secure his rule. That legacy has kept the Syrians fearfully silent—until now.

The regime's concern about the Friday protests was justified. Today, demonstrations have erupted everywhere, including in major cities, such as Aleppo, Damascus, Homs, Latakia, and Qamishli. Chants of "Down with Bashar's regime" have been heard regularly. The regime's response continues to be violent repression coupled with attempts at political maneuvering. It is hard to predict where the demonstrations will go after today. If unrest takes hold in the northeast (among the Kurds) and northwest (in large Sunni areas), it will be a sign that the Assad regime's grasp on power is weakening. The people of Deraa have shown that the population's barrier of fear can be broken. That is something that Assad cannot allow to persist and take root. Whether he manages to reinstill it will prove decisive for his family's rule.

Meanwhile in the Maghreb

Have Algeria and Morocco Avoided North Africa's Unrest?

Azzedine Layachi

FOREIGNAFFAIRS.COM, MARCH 31, 2011

In Arabic, the Maghreb means "where and when the sun sets." The region, which includes Algeria, Libya, Morocco, and Tunisia, is part of both Africa and the Arab world, and it enjoys a special relationship with Europe, thanks to geographical proximity, colonial history, and economic ties. The Maghreb is where the Arab world's recent dramatic political upheaval first began (Tunisia) and where it has reached its most violent climax (Libya). Of the four countries, Algeria and Morocco have been the least shaken by these events—but this calm may not hold for long.

After gaining independence from their colonial masters in the 1950s and 1960s, Algeria, Morocco, Tunisia, and Libya opted for different economic development strategies and political systems. But they all ended up with authoritarian regimes that relied on repression and paternalistic rule.

AZZEDINE LAYACHI is a Professor of Government and Politics at St. John's University.

Algeria, which was governed by a one-party system under military control from independence in 1962 until 1989, now has a multiparty system in which political parties do not matter as much as the military. In Morocco, King Mohammed VI oversees a nominal multiparty system under an absolute monarchy. He appoints key members of the government, including the prime minister, and has the power to dissolve parliament and impose a state of emergency. No one is allowed to criticize him or question his religious leadership as the "commander of the faithful."

All four Maghrebi countries made major headway in economic and social development since their independence. They improved social services, education, employment, health care, and national income. In the last two decades, however, the limits of such progress became apparent. They could not keep up with their growing populations.

In Algeria, economic liberalization magnified the effect of global economic shocks, which made it difficult to maintain the welfare system that was behind the country's tacit social contract. In Morocco, however, this contract has been more limited: the monarch simply provided security and national unity (not material comforts) in exchange for loyalty and obedience. This began to change some as power passed from King Hassan II, who died in 1999, to his son, Mohammed VI. In contrast to the outright neglect of Hassan, Mohammed made some efforts to address his country's economic and social ills.

Following serious economic crises, both Algeria and Morocco privatized some public companies, reduced subsidies, and lifted some price controls as part of structural-adjustment programs sponsored by the IMF and the World Bank. These reforms helped to stave off economic decline, but they did not do enough to improve living conditions, unemployment, and income disparity.

In Algeria, a large sector of society has seen its living standards decrease (23 percent live below the poverty line). Foreign exchange reserves, meanwhile, reached $157 billion in 2010, thanks to oil exports. This paradox has become untenable—especially when combined with a housing crisis, a failing school system, and rampant unemployment among the youth (above 20 percent). In Morocco, which, unlike Algeria and Libya, does not have the benefit of hydrocarbon income, similar conditions have created a sense of desperation among the large number of unemployed youth, several thousands of whom are college graduates.

Whereas Libya under Colonel Muammar al-Qaddafi and Tunisia under Zine el-Abidine Ben Ali repressed all political opposition and relied on extensive security services, Algeria and Morocco have enacted some important political reforms but without changing the nature of their regimes.

In Algeria in the late 1980s, the political system was opened to the opposition under President Chadli Bendjedid; nowadays, it even includes small moderate Islamist parties such as the Movement of Society for Peace (MSP), Islah, and Ennahda. This does not mean that the country is a democracy by any definition. The system remains controlled by three key centers of power: the military, the president and his close allies, and the National Liberation Front, which controls a pro-government coalition in parliament.

In Morocco, a multiparty system has existed since the country's independence in 1956, but it has been more pro forma than real because most of the power has always been in the hands of the monarch. In 1998, under Hassan II, the Union of Socialist Forces party (once a bitter enemy of the monarchy) was allowed to lead the government, and moderate Islamists were permitted to enter parliament—but none of this fundamentally changed the system.

Over the past two decades in the Maghreb, authoritarian regimes have used the fight against Islamist extremism to justify the hardening of their rule. Algeria, for example, was until

February 24, 2011, under a state of emergency for 19 years. The emergency law was put in place in 1992 to deal with a rising and violent Islamist challenge and was used throughout the 1990s to arrest and detain people without due process and to muzzle the press.

In the name of security and counterterrorism, the Moroccan state also clamped down on both religious and secular opposition, detaining suspects without due process and, up to the late 1990s, restricting political dissent. More recently, Morocco, a willing partner in the U.S.-led "war on terror," became a destination country for suspects detained under the United States' "extraordinary rendition" program. By participating in various security agreements with Washington, Morocco received military hardware and training for its security forces—and earned the silence of Western governments regarding abuses of human and political rights.

Given this collective backdrop, the outbreak of protests in Algeria and Morocco was no surprise. Indeed, Algeria's riots in January were the culmination of a decade-old pattern of almost daily protests in many towns and villages against poor government services, injustice, and corruption. But these riots took place on a scale that had not been seen since the historic upheaval of October 1988, which ended the one-party system.

The Algerian riots of January 2011 spread quickly—but also ended quickly, after the government reduced the price of basic food items. The rioters did not have a wider political agenda or slogan, and no major political party or organization joined them. It was not until the protests in Tunisia that some opposition figures in Algeria formed the National Coordination for Change and Democracy on January 21 to call for large-scale demonstrations. The resulting protests, however, failed to bring out a large number of people and were restricted by anti-riot police. They had little effect, largely because they lacked clarity and details and were led by the Rally for Culture and

Democracy, a party known for having supported the government's cancellation of the 1991 elections and repression of the Islamists. Moreover, the leaders of the protest movement underestimated the reluctance of people to confront the state so soon after a decade-long war that traumatized the entire population and killed 200,000 people.

In Morocco, the demonstrations of February 20 attracted a few thousand people but lacked the energy and zest of the revolts of Tunisia and Libya and even the much smaller protests in Algeria. The Moroccan demonstrators demanded a new government, a constitutional reform that would limit the powers of the king, an end to corruption, the improvement of living conditions, and social justice. They did not target Mohammed VI himself. Since ascending to the throne in 1999, the king has enacted several reforms, such as his 2004 changes to the *moudawana*, or family code, which improved the legal status of women, and programs to alleviate poverty and illiteracy. These moves served to enhance his legitimacy even if they did not actually improve living conditions or create jobs.

Yet with Ben Ali and Mubarak gone, and Qaddafi's regime under assault, leaders of Algeria and Morocco are nonetheless nervous. Both regimes recently promised cuts in food prices and reforms that would create more jobs and enhance political freedom.

The Algerian government, for its part, finally lifted the 19-year-old state of emergency on February 24 and promised more political freedoms and economic reforms. To thwart the possibility of social upheaval in Morocco, Mohammed VI announced a plan to reform the constitution, giving more power to parliament and the prime minister and his cabinet. He also promised more political freedom and more jobs. But the protest did not end—more people than ever took to the streets to demand immediate economic reforms and a say in the process of reforming the constitution, rather than leaving this process solely to a commission entrusted by the king.

In both countries, substantial power is held by important, and virtually unaccountable, behind-the-scenes players. In Algeria, they are known as *Le Pouvoir* and in Morocco as the *Makhzen*. Even if formal political structures are reformed, there will be no serious change unless both *Le Pouvoir* and the *Makhzen* are discarded. This is one of the reasons why protesters in Algeria are not likely to accept cosmetic changes. In Morocco, constitutional reforms may make for a good start, but such steps are not likely to be enough without taking on the elusive powers of the *Makhzen*.

As Tunisia builds a new governing system and the Qaddafi regime remains under a dual assault of internal rebellion and Western airstrikes, the Maghreb is experiencing a period of unrest and uncertainty. If Qaddafi is eventually overthrown and Libya democratizes, both Algeria and Morocco will face increasing pressure to liberalize, too. But if the Libyan revolt fails to dislodge the Qaddafi regime, Algeria's and Morocco's rulers may decide that holding out against popular protest is a tenable strategy. The future of Algiers and Rabat may very well be affected by what happens in Benghazi and Tripoli.

Bahrain's Base Politics

The Arab Spring and America's Military Bases

Alexander Cooley and Daniel H. Nexon

FOREIGNAFFAIRS.COM, APRIL 5, 2011

U.S. policymakers have long struggled to reconcile their support for friendly authoritarian regimes with their preference for political liberalization abroad. The ongoing upheavals in the Middle East, like so many developments before them, shine a bright light on this inconsistency. In Egypt, the Obama administration struggled to calibrate its message on the protests that toppled longtime ally Hosni Mubarak; in Libya, it leads a multinational coalition intent on using airpower to help bring down Muammar al-Qaddafi; and in Bahrain, the United States stands mostly silent as Saudi troops put down popular protests against the ruling al-Khalifa family.

Washington's balancing act reflects more than the enduring tensions between pragmatism and idealism in U.S. foreign policy. It highlights the specific strains faced by defense planners as they attempt to maintain the integrity of the United

ALEXANDER COOLEY is Associate Professor of Political Science at Barnard College and a member of Columbia University's Arnold A. Saltzman Institute for War and Peace Studies. DANIEL H. NEXON is Associate Professor in the School of Foreign Service and the Department of Government at Georgetown University.

States' worldwide network of military bases, many of which are hosted in authoritarian, politically unstable, and corrupt countries. Now, with the "Arab Spring" unfolding, even U.S. basing agreements with some of its closest allies are vulnerable.

Until the recent revolutions in the Middle East, Bahrain's relative stability and loyalty to the United States provided comfort to Pentagon officials. The U.S. Navy's Fifth Fleet—which brings with it several thousand onshore personnel and dependents, about 30 warships, and roughly 30,000 sailors—has its headquarters in Juffair, a suburb of Bahrain's capital, Manama. The Fifth Fleet patrols the Arabian Sea, the Red Sea, the western part of the Indian Ocean, and the Persian Gulf, ensuring that sea-lanes remain open, protecting the flow of oil, conducting anti-piracy operations, and acting as a check against Iran's regional influence. Bahrain also hosts the United States' Naval Forces Central Command (NAVCENT)—the maritime component to the U.S. Central Command—and offers U.S. forces the Isa Air Base and space at Bahrain International Airport.

During the 1940s and 1950s, Bahrain was a British protectorate, and the U.S. military operated out of the country through a leasing arrangement with London. When Bahrain became independent in 1971, the United States agreed to pay $4 million a year in exchange for continued basing rights. After the 1973 Arab-Israeli war, Bahraini authorities evicted the U.S. Navy, only to grant it reduced facilities following protracted negotiations. In 1977, Manama insisted that U.S. forces move their headquarters back on board ship.

The U.S. military maintained a low profile in Bahrain until the 1990 Persian Gulf crisis, when the country acted as a major naval base that hosted 20,000 U.S. troops and served as a hub for air operations against Iraq in Operation Desert Storm. After the war ended, in 1991, Washington and Manama negotiated a ten-year Defense Cooperation Agreement (DCA), and four years later the U.S. military's footprint expanded when Bahrain became the headquarters of the Fifth Fleet and NAVCENT. In 2001, the United States renewed the DCA. In addition to a $6.7 million annual lease payment, the United States now provides Bahrain with military aid—ranging from $6 million in 2006 to $18 million in 2010—and security pledges.

The current political upheaval in Bahrain began as a nonviolent protest by a diverse coalition, but the government and its allies have done their best to frame it as a purely sectarian conflict. Shiites comprise 60–70 percent of the country's 500,000 citizens (another 500,000 are foreign workers), yet they currently enjoy little political representation and few economic opportunities. Since independence, the al-Khalifi family has zealously guarded its power, failing to deliver on repeated promises to introduce significant political reforms. In the run-up to parliamentary elections last year, the regime arrested 23 opposition leaders and hundreds of activists, and charged them with such crimes as terrorism and conspiracy to overthrow the government.

On February 14 of this year, inspired by the movements in Tunisia and Egypt, Bahrainis took to the streets, congregating around the Pearl Roundabout in central Manama. Three days later, the security services cracked down, killing five demonstrators and injuring hundreds. King Hamad bin Isa al-Khalifa offered limited concessions, but the protesters, incensed by the regime's violence, demanded the end of the monarchy altogether. On March 15, Saudi Arabia and the United Arab Emirates intervened under the auspices of the Gulf Cooperation Council, deploying 1,000 troops, 500 security personnel, and more than 100 armored vehicles to quash the demonstrations. The king declared a three-month state of emergency and imposed martial law.

The use of force and foreign troops against peaceful demonstrators in a country with a major U.S. military presence necessarily implicates Washington. Even though U.S. officials maintain that they were informed of Riyadh's decision to intervene but not consulted about it, such a nuanced distinction will do little to remove the perception of U.S. complicity in the crackdown. Rumors now circulate that the United States green-lighted Saudi intervention in return for Riyadh's support for a no-fly zone in Libya. And the question of whether Bahraini security forces used U.S. military hardware and equipment against protesters remains open, as Washington and Manama have launched investigations into the conduct of the security services.

These developments have raised concerns that regime change in Bahrain will lead to the eviction of U.S. forces. The United States' relative silence gives further credibility to the idea that Washington sees a trade-off between political stability and democratic reform, and that it opposes the latter for fear of jeopardizing U.S. security interests. But the "base politics" of Bahrain are part of a broader pattern.

In Kyrgyzstan last year, accusations that the United States had been too accommodating toward President Kurmanbek Bakiyev, who was forced out of office that April, put the fate of the critical U.S. military's Manas Air Base in jeopardy. In Uzbekistan, human rights groups now accuse U.S. officials of dampening their criticism of the government in order to safeguard U.S. supply routes through the country to Afghanistan. Djibouti, host to the largest U.S. military base in Africa, may prove the next flash point in the Middle East; its president, Ismail Omar Guelleh, recently arrested major opposition leaders and cancelled a U.S. election-monitoring mission. In the Persian Gulf, Oman, the United Arab Emirates, Qatar, and Kuwait all host U.S. military installations, although none has faced mass protests along the lines of those that emerged in Bahrain.

The global landscape is changing in ways that threaten to undermine U.S. basing agreements in many parts of the world. One shift is that people are more aware than ever before of the activities of U.S. bases in their countries. In 1986, a U.S. State Department memo described U.S.-Bahraini military relations as "warm, quiet and based on a long history of mutual trust and understanding." But today, satellite television, blogs, and social media have made it harder to keep the U.S. basing footprint quiet. From Ecuador to Japan to Kyrgyzstan, U.S. military bases have quickly become sources of contention when opposition leaders and activists politicize the U.S. presence. In the wake of the crackdown in Bahrain, Shia-backed regional groups, such as the Hezbollah Brigades in Iraq, have called for retaliation against U.S. troops and military installations.

Moreover, U.S. policymakers have found it harder to compartmentalize the terms of bilateral basing agreements. In theory, when negotiating bilateral agreements, the United States has the upper hand: it can tailor terms to the specific needs of a relationship, and its partners lack information about the "going rate" of what the United States is willing to bear in terms of monetary assistance, security guarantees, and concessions to host-nation sovereignty. In practice, however, this information now flows not only to elites in different host countries but also to activists, political opponents, and interest groups. This change means the United States will find itself making greater concessions and exposing itself more to charges of hypocrisy when it behaves inconsistently.

Further complicating base politics are transnational political movements, which can overwhelm the traditional U.S. policy of promoting incremental political reform in authoritarian partners. A few years ago, the so-called color revolutions diffused across Eurasia. Although the revolutions resulted in pro-U.S. regimes in Ukraine and Georgia, by throwing a light on the authoritarian practices of Washington's allies in Central Asia, they also politicized U.S. basing arrangements in the region. Following Western criticism of the Uzbek government's crackdown on demonstrators in May 2005, Uzbek

President Islam Karimov became concerned that the United States was plotting another regional regime change. In July 2005, the government of Uzbekistan evicted the U.S. military from its facility at Karshi-Khanabad, a disturbance that continues to complicate U.S. basing arrangements in Central Asia. When political movements like these arise, as they now have in the Arab world, the United States cannot count on being able to distance its bases simultaneously from unpopular host government policies and elite fears across host countries that Washington is ready to throw its autocratic friends under the bus.

It is time for U.S. officials to reconsider their basing policies. First, they should create broader constituencies for the continued presence of the U.S. military in host countries. In Bahrain, this means U.S. policymakers should do their best to ensure that the Shia community garners economic benefits from the naval base and its related facilities, rather than allowing those benefits to be monopolized by a handful of elites. The base contributes about $150 million annually to Bahrain's economy, or about one percent of GDP. Last May, U.S. officials announced a plan to double the size of the base by 2015, with the intent of spending an additional $518 million. Given the precarious current political environment, U.S. planners should ensure that Bahraini Shia companies and workers gain a large share of the resulting contracts.

Second, Washington needs to avoid thinking about its basing arrangements in terms of a simple trade-off between pragmatism and idealism. As recent events suggest, traditional strategies of binding the United States to loyal strongman regimes can undermine both U.S. interests and values. Defense officials and U.S. diplomats can best preserve security contracts and commitments by broadening their engagement with a wide variety of political, social, and economic actors, even over the initial objections of authoritarian elites.

Third, U.S. officials should make efforts to decouple the rationale of a given basing relationship from support for a particular regime. This means creating political space between Washington and the policies of authoritarian host countries whenever possible. With respect to Bahrain, U.S. officials should make clear that the U.S. military maintains its facilities for the defense of its territory and for regional stability—not for the purposes of propping up the ruling family. At the same time, Washington needs to signal that it believes that both countries' interests are best served by greater political liberalization.

Abandoning the idea of a zero-sum trade-off between pragmatism and idealism is particularly important when considering U.S. policy toward Bahrain. Some see Bahrain as a proxy state in the struggle among Saudi Arabia, the United States, and Iran, and so they believe that further pressuring Manama to democratize will open the door to Iranian domination. But this misreads the national loyalties of Shia Bahrainis and confuses the main source of current Iranian influence. Bahrain's Shiites have shown little interest in allying themselves with the deeply reactionary regime in Tehran. Indeed, the more Washington promotes the inclusion of Shiites in Bahrain's political system, the less of a political opening Tehran will have.

Some observers raise legitimate concerns about such hedging strategies, on the grounds that the United States should avoid reinforcing suspicions among its strategic partners that it will abandon them in a political pinch. But a nimbler approach to relations with host countries and their citizens would not mean abandoning autocratic allies. Ensuring that the benefits of U.S. bases are more broadly distributed, cultivating ties with a larger swath of host countries' civil societies, and clarifying the nature of the strategic relationship are all prudent steps that should do little to jeopardize strategic relationships that often pay significant dividends for the host countries.

Of course, Washington's ability to hedge its bets will differ from strategic partner to strategic partner; U.S. officials will always have to tread carefully lest they push too far and overly antagonize current governments. But it is better to gain flexibility before the next political crisis hits than be forced to scramble after it is under way.

Let Them Eat Bread

How Food Subsidies Prevent (and Provoke) Revolutions in the Middle East

Annia Ciezadlo

FOREIGNAFFAIRS.COM, MARCH 23, 2011

For two days, people poured into the streets of Cairo, burning buses and trams, government buildings, and expensive cars. In Tahrir Square, troops fired tear gas at the demonstrators. Cairenes cheered from balconies and rooftops while their comrades in the streets below chanted antigovernment slogans: "You dress in the latest fashions," they roared at their president, "while we sleep 12 to a room!"

It was 1977, and revolution was in the air. When an already unpopular government tried to rescind food subsidies—meaning massive price increases for staples like bread, rice, and cooking gas—riots erupted. By the time they were over, hundreds of buildings were burned, 160 people were dead, and Egyptian President Anwar Sadat had learned an essential lesson for the modern Arab dictator: let them eat bread. Lots of cheap bread.

Change is sweeping through the Middle East today, but one thing remains the same: the region once known as the Fertile Crescent is now the world's most dependent on imported grain.

ANNIA CIEZADLO is the author of *Day of Honey: A Memoir of Food, Love, and War*. She has reported from the Middle East as a special correspondent for *The Christian Science Monitor* and *The New Republic*.

Of the top 20 wheat importers for 2010, almost half are Middle Eastern countries. The list reads like a playbook of toppled and teetering regimes: Egypt (1), Algeria (4), Iraq (7), Morocco (8), Yemen (13), Saudi Arabia (15), Libya (16), Tunisia (17).

For decades, many of these regimes relied on food subsidies to ensure stability—a social contract so pervasive that the Tunisian scholar Larbi Sadiki described it as *dimuqratiyyat al-khubz*, or "democracy of bread." But over the past several years, grain prices reached record levels, and these appeasement policies lost their luster. In Tunisia, pro-democracy demonstrations began in late December 2010 with protesters brandishing baguettes. In just a few months, a wave of uprisings rippled across the region, toppling Tunisian President Zine el-Abidine Ben Ali and Egypt's longtime ruler, Hosni Mubarak.

The revolutions, of course, are about more than just bread. Middle Easterners want basic human rights, dignity, and a chance at a decent future—good jobs at livable wages. But when a government puts those things out of reach for the majority of its citizens, using handouts or subsidies as a substitute for democratic or economic reforms, bread becomes a powerful symbol of all they cannot have. Today, the protests have spread all the way to Yemen, where demonstrators are baking loaves of bread that spell out the command "leave" in Arabic. The message could not be clearer: the very commodity that Arab regimes once used to ensure obedience has now become a symbol and source of defiance.

The bread wars go back to the Cold War era, when the two superpowers wooed smaller nations with guns, grain, and other goods. It was during this time that many Arab regimes instituted social safety nets based on the Soviet model of centralized bread distribution. In 1950s Egypt, the populist President Gamal Abdel Nasser began the practice of subsidizing daily bread in exchange for social peace. "They adopted this because this was one way of buying loyalty from the society," says

Ibrahim Saif, an economist and the secretary-general of the Economic and Social Council of Jordan. "It's the patronage system that prevailed for some time: I am the state, I take care of you, and you don't question my political behavior."

By the late 1970s, the International Monetary Fund (IMF) was urging Arab countries to rid themselves of the "subsidy burden." Cairo's 1977 "bread intifada" was only one of many across the region: throughout the 1980s, protests erupted in Morocco, Tunisia, Algeria, and Jordan whenever rulers tried to lift food subsidies. When Sadat was assassinated in 1981, his successor, Mubarak, remembered the lesson of the bread riots: he made sure that Egyptians had plenty of cheap, government-subsidized bread, and other Middle Eastern regimes did the same.

For the next three decades, U.S. taxpayers helped buy that bread. According to the Congressional Research Service, the United States provided Egypt with $4.6 billion in loans and grants under the U.S. Agency for International Development's Food for Peace program, most of it flowing between 1979 and 1997. Mubarak was not the only autocrat who developed a taste for cheap American wheat; Iraq's Saddam Hussein received billions of dollars' worth of surplus American wheat through grants and loan guarantees, and Jordan, Yemen, and other Middle Eastern countries got lesser amounts. For decades, the United States considered that a small price to pay for keeping friendly dictators in power.

But the cheap wheat came at a high cost: unemployment. The dependence on foreign largesse, coupled with the low price of global grains, encouraged many Middle Eastern regimes to hollow out their agricultural sectors. Throughout the 1980s and 1990s, trade liberalization programs pushed Egypt and Morocco, among others, into a dangerous dependence on cheap carbohydrates from abroad. Encouraged by the IMF and the World Bank to lift tariffs and import bans, and discouraged (or even restricted) from investing in their own agricultural sectors, they went from being net agricultural exporters to net importers—especially of subsidized American wheat. In 1960, Egypt was producing enough wheat to be almost self-sufficient; by 2010, it was importing roughly half the country's total intake (nine billion tons), making it by far the biggest wheat importer in the world.

By 2010, the Egyptian government was subsidizing bread to the tune of about $3 billion a year, mostly by selling flour to local bakeries—a complicated, inefficient system that lent itself to massive corruption. The higher global prices rose, the more incentive bakers had to resell subsidized flour and bread into the black market, where they could go for five or more times the subsidized rate.

As expensive as they are, bread subsidies do not succeed in lifting people out of poverty; in fact, by discouraging domestic agricultural investment, they have often hurt the very people they are intended to help. According to the United Nations' 2009 Arab Human Development Report, the Middle East is the only region outside of sub-Saharan Africa where the number of malnourished people has risen since the early 1990s. In recent years, the standard of living for most Egyptians declined, even as elites thrived and external economic measurements appeared healthy: according to a Gallup study published last month, both Egypt and Tunisia saw a significant decline in living standards for all income groups except the top 20 percent—even as GDP increased. By early 2008, about 40 percent of Egyptians were living on less than two dollars a day.

When the price of grain began to skyrocket, the "democracies of bread" began to show cracks. In 2008, a wave of small bread riots began in Jordan, Morocco, Algeria, Lebanon, Syria, and Yemen. Governments responded by raising wages, increasing subsidies, or handing out cash—solutions that proved unsustainable in the long run. In Egypt, bread prices rose by 37 percent between February 2007 and February

2008. More people became dependent on subsidized bread than before. This meant longer bread lines, and by March 2008 about a dozen people had died in Egypt's bread lines—some in fights, others from the sheer exhaustion of standing for hours to get bread.

The public was outraged over these "bread martyrs." Mubarak ordered the army to take over the baking and distribution of subsidized bread to the public, effectively militarizing bread production. But this bizarrely symbolic decree came too late: on April 6, 2008, tens of thousands of students, unemployed Egyptians, and textile workers in the textile-mill town of Al-Mahalla al-Kubra staged a protest against unemployment, high food prices, and widespread police torture. Young protesters broadcast cell phone videos of the uprising on Facebook and YouTube, which helped spread the protests to other parts of Egypt. Eventually, the youth activists coalesced into the April 6 Movement, named after the Al-Mahalla al-Kubra uprising, which in turn grew into the revolt that would eventually topple Mubarak.

Over the next two years, a combination of factors—drought, wildfires, ethanol subsidies, and more—converged into a global food crisis. By early 2011, the United Nations' Food and Agriculture Organization announced that food prices had reached an all-time high, surpassing even 2008 levels.

When young Egyptians took to the streets in January—many of them from the April 6 movement—they crafted slogans that translated justice and democracy into the language of food: "They are eating pigeon and chicken," they chanted, "and we are eating beans all the time." Others protested, "Oh my, ten pounds can only buy us cucumbers now, what a shame, what a shame." Arab regimes scrambled to keep the peace as they always had: with handouts. Algeria, Tunisia, and Morocco lifted import tariffs and customs duties on wheat and other food imports. Egypt, Jordan, and Yemen upped their food subsidies. Jordan unveiled a $125 million subsidy package for sugar, rice, and fuel. Saudi Arabia announced a package of cash grants. And even Syrian President Bashar al-Assad rolled back subsidy cuts.

On February 15, World Bank President Robert Zoellick released data showing that 44 million people had been pushed into extreme poverty since June 2010, and he warned that global food prices had reached "dangerous levels." Zoellick asked countries not to impose policies that would further exacerbate price volatility, such as export bans or price fixing. But he might also have mentioned massive subsidy programs, which are helping to drive up grain prices worldwide.

Economically, import subsidies have precisely the same effect as export restrictions: because "democracies of bread" depend on food subsidies to stay in power, they create a demand that is relatively inelastic—demand will not go down when prices rise. That additional demand makes the marginal quantity of wheat still available even more expensive; and that, in turn, helps keep global prices high at a time when people in danger of starving need grains to survive. "We are not supposed to say this," one senior international economist told me in mid-January, before the revolution in Egypt had even begun, "but we have countries where hunger is really endemic, where you have massive undernutrition and shortage of food. And the problem is that those countries like Egypt who have these subsidies—not necessarily because they have a food security problem but because they want to ensure that everything's stable in the country and they have no food riots—are one of the biggest factors contributing to it."

Mubarak and Ben Ali are history, but it is worth taking a hard look at some of the other wheat importers on that list—particularly Yemen, a corrupt, U.S.-backed dictatorship where one in three citizens suffers from acute hunger. Even if strong democratic institutions emerge from the current upheaval, the region's dependence on wheat from abroad will continue to create crises for years to come. The solutions are simple: the United States and the international banking community should encourage its Middle Eastern allies to develop their own agricultural sectors, where economic growth is far more effective at lifting people out of poverty than in other sectors. The United States should also stop sending agricultural surplus abroad as foreign aid, which depresses prices in the countries that receive it and drives farmers further into poverty (the Obama administration has taken steps toward ending this practice).

Perhaps the United States, and the Middle Eastern regimes it supports, can learn something from Mubarak's demise. It seems obvious that countries such as Egypt, Iraq, and Yemen cannot stop their bread subsidies overnight. But it seems equally obvious that propping up dictatorships with cheap bread is a shortsighted policy: in the near term, it helps keep global prices high, and in the long run it does not even guarantee stability.

Demographics of Arab Protests

An Interview with Ragui Assaad

CFR.ORG, FEBRUARY 14, 2011

From Tunisia to Egypt, youth have become the face of dissent against longstanding autocratic regimes in the Arab world. The region is facing a demographic bulge in which youth aged fifteen to twenty-nine comprise the largest proportion of the population. These young people, frustrated with lack of jobs, have been at the forefront of anti-government protests. Ragui Assaad, a professor at the Humphrey School of Public Affairs at University of Minnesota and a nonresident senior fellow at Brookings, says the region has to move toward greater democratic systems and open economies "to allow these young people to vent and have a say in their future." He predicts the youth bulge will be a destabilizing factor in Yemen and will lead to further unrest in Iran with calls for regime change. Migration, he says, will emerge as yet another important issue with youth bulges in the Mideast and an aging population in Europe. "There needs to be international agreements to regulate migrant flows," he adds.

How significant has the role of demographics been in the protests across the Middle East?

RAGUI ASSAAD is a professor at the Humphrey School of Public Affairs, University of Minnesota. (Interview conducted by Jayshree Bajoria.)

Demographics have played an important role, not because they are the problems themselves but because they have exacerbated other serious problems that youth are having in the way that they have been affected by the reforms that have occurred over the past three years in the Middle East. So, demographics, simply by having large numbers of people who are very frustrated at their inability to turn their education into productive jobs, has really exacerbated the problems.

The entire region is experiencing a pronounced "youth bulge," where the proportion of young people is significantly larger compared to other age groups. Is this an opportunity or a challenge?

Currently it's proving to be a challenge, but it's not necessarily a challenge. In other parts of the world, the youth bulge phenomenon has been an opportunity. In East Asia and Southeast Asia with their open economies and good education systems, they've been able to use the youth bulge as an advantage. In the Middle East, unfortunately, it's turning out to be a challenge because of the governments' inability to put together economic policies that make use of these human resources. When you have people whose expectations have risen because of their education, and then these expectations are shattered, they become very angry and dangerous to the regimes.

But these countries in the Middle East—Tunisia, Egypt, and even Yemen—that are facing popular uprisings are at different stages of demographic transition, right?

They are definitely. Tunisia is ahead of the game. Its fertility started declining earlier than in either Egypt or Yemen, and its youth bulge is kind of passing at this point. The young people are moving on to their thirties and later. However, that group was not very well treated by the transition that occurred in Tunisia from public sector–led economies to a more market-driven economy, and their dissatisfaction is still there.

However, as a demographic phenomenon, it's been getting less extreme.

Egypt is very close to the peak of its youth bulge. These last few years, the youth bulge is beginning to decline as the share of fifteen to twenty-nine year-olds starts to decline. However, that group of young people is making its way into the labor market right now and putting a lot of pressure in the form of unemployment and informalization of the labor market as they get poor jobs.

Yemen is going to have a problem for a very long time because the fertility in Yemen has not declined yet or has declined very little. So, Yemen is going to have a youth bulge that is going to continue well into the future, probably for another thirty years. That is going to be highly destabilizing in Yemen for a long time.

Are youth generally more given to revolutions than other age groups?

One can argue that the youth protests and unrest that occurred in the United States and in Europe in the late sixties was driven by the baby boom that occurred after the Second World War, which was a youth bulge in its own right. So, it is not uncommon for youth bulges to cause unrest. Sometimes it's in the form of peaceful protest, and sometimes it's in the form of civil conflict and other times it's in the form of more serious forms of violence. I think that in a sense we are lucky that in Tunisia and Egypt, the conflict that is resulting is peaceful in the form of these demonstrations. It could have been much worse.

What do these large populations of youth mean for the future and for the security of the region?

Governments have to devise political systems that allow these youth to be represented, to have a voice in the running of their country. And they have to devise economic systems that make good use of these productive resources that the youth potentially are. However, if that doesn't happen, there is going to be a generation of people who are going to continue to be frustrated and continue to be a source of instability. The region definitely has to move toward more democracy, more freedom to allow these young people to vent and have a say in their future.

Are there things the West should be worried about in relation to these large youth populations in the Middle East, things they should be watching for?

What the West needs to watch for is cases in which political regimes are extremely weak and the countries are very fragmented, [because then] these youth bulges can result in extended civil conflict and potentially a failure of the state. I think Yemen is at risk of that, and maybe there are other places. Clearly, the situation in Palestine is very worrying, as very pronounced youth bulges with unresolved conflict with Israel could portend future problems.

However, in countries like Tunisia and Egypt, if the West can support the transition to democracy, then there are very good potential long-term implications in terms of making youth move into adulthood and become productive members of their societies. That's going to make the societies richer in general.

Do you think the events in the Mideast have implications for other countries in the vicinity, such as Iran, Pakistan, and Afghanistan, which also have very high youth populations and are struggling to provide basic needs and stability to their populations?

Absolutely, Iran is the perfect example. Iran has the most pronounced youth bulge of anywhere in the world because Iran not only had this reduction in mortality rate that resulted in more young people surviving, but it also had an increase in fertility after the Iranian Revolution. These two factors together produced a very pronounced youth bulge, which is at its peak right now but is expected to decline very fast because of the rapid decline in fertility that occurred in Iran post-1990. These are the young people who were fueling the protests that we saw two years ago in Iran, and they're going to be continuing to fuel protests. These are people who are born after the revolution. They do not necessarily support the Islamic regime there. But they are going to be demanding change for quite some time. So we haven't seen the [last] of youth unrest and calls for change in Iran.

Pakistan also has a pronounced youth bulge, and Pakistan ostensibly has a democratic system in which some of these frustrations can be vented. But especially if there are regional issues and there are issues in the northwest area of Pakistan, it could cause of instability in parts of Pakistan.

In general, the whole region has this demographic phenomenon occurring, but it does not have to be a problem if it is handled properly and if it's considered to be a resource that is used for productive purposes.

To get dividends from these youth populations, what do you think these countries must do?

They must pursue development strategies that bring the benefits of development to the [majority] of the population, especially ones that promote labor intensive and job creating growth. So far the development strategies in many of these countries have benefited a few cronies—a few people close to the regime have become extremely rich basically at the expense of the rest of the population.

They [also] have to provide political systems that allow these young people to have a voice in the future of their country. They have to open economies because that's the way they're going to be able to specialize in those activities that make use of labor intensively, just the way that Southeast Asia and East Asia have done.

Another issue that needs to be on the table is the possibility of migration. Many of the developed countries, but in particular Europe, have a deficit of young people, and there's going to be tremendous pressure for migration from the countries in the southern Mediterranean and elsewhere in the Middle East and Asia to migrate. We have to find ways to allow this migration without creating anti-migrant backlashes in Europe or creating problems with absorption of migrants in European countries.

What role can the international community play here?

There needs to be international agreements to regulate migrant flows. We need to strengthen international organizations for migration. Like there are trade treaties that govern trade between countries, there need to be migration treaties as well. The economic forces for greater migration are extremely powerful—as the European population ages and there is the graying phenomenon that occurs in Europe—but still the cultural and social factors of fear of migrants in Europe are going to create problems.

Are the Mideast Revolutions Bad for Women's Rights?

Isobel Coleman

WASHINGTON POST, FEBRUARY 20, 2011

On Friday, Egyptians again gathered in Cairo's Tahrir Square, this time in a victory celebration, one week after their revolution unseated President Hosni Mubarak. Tunisians have also been sampling new freedoms of speech and press along a boulevard that is no longer a war zone. But even as the exultation lingers, women in both countries have launched new protests. They want to make sure that democracy does not erode their rights.

In Tunisia, several hundred women have already taken to the streets to voice their concern about what an Islamic revival, should it come, could mean for them. In Egypt, women's rights activists immediately mounted a petition drive when the committee named to draft a new constitution included not a single woman (although many noted female Egyptian lawyers could easily serve on that committee).

In both countries, there is popular support for a broader establishment of sharia, or Islamic law, developed from the

ISOBEL COLEMAN is senior fellow for U.S. foreign policy; director of the Civil Society, Markets, and Democracy initiative; and director of the Women and Foreign Policy program at the Council on Foreign Relations.

Koran and religious writings. Of course, there is no single sharia; interpretations vary throughout the Middle East and are subject to change. Morocco, for example, sets the legal age of female marriage at 18, based on its more progressive version of sharia, whereas in Saudi Arabia girls as young as 8 are married to much older men, based on its version. As new leaders in the region grapple with how to blend some version of sharia with some version of democracy, women's rights will become a central element of the debate.

The laws affecting women in Tunisia, and to some extent in Egypt, are among the most progressive in the Middle East, so the potential for backsliding under Islamic pressure in those countries is real. And women in Yemen, Bahrain, Libya and Iraq, where the spreading unrest has been met with government force, have also struggled for their rights and likewise have reason to be concerned if their governments fall or start handing out concessions.

Tunisia, in particular, has been a bastion of women's rights in a region known for the opposite. Shortly after independence in 1956, President Habib Bourguiba, the country's secular authoritarian leader, pushed through a Personal Status Code which was remarkably liberal for its time. It granted women equal divorce rights to men, abolished polygamy, set minimum marriage ages, allowed access to birth control and even some access to abortion. Bourguiba modeled himself on Mustafa Kemal Ataturk, Turkey's founder who force-marched his country into the modern age through a painful process of secularization—"for the people, despite the people," as he once quipped.

The result is that Tunisian women today enjoy relatively high literacy and have achieved broad gains in law, medicine, business, academia and media.

Islam, meanwhile, has been tightly regulated; in Zine el-Abidine Ben Ali's police state, it was not uncommon for the authorities to question a person for switching mosques or attending one more than once a week. Popular Islamist leaders were arrested and exiled. Still, many women in Tunisia wear the headscarf despite its ban in public places. Enforced secularism never succeeded in stamping out religiosity.

Democracy will inevitably bring Islamist groups into Tunisia's political mainstream. A few conservative voices have already made rumblings about revising aspects of the Personal Status Code, whereas moderate Islamists are quick to express support for women's rights and adherence to the current code. Rachid Ghannouchi, head of the formerly banned Islamist party Nahda, was once critical of the Personal Status Code and the country's anti-polygamy laws on religious grounds, but by the late 1980s he had come to terms with it. He recently returned to Tunisia after exile in London and has again reaffirmed his support for women's rights. The question is whether Ghannouchi's brand of moderate Islamism will carry the day in Tunisia.

In Egypt, democracy will also create important openings for Islamist groups, especially the Muslim Brotherhood. In a 2007 Gallup survey, 64 percent of Egyptians polled said that sharia should be the only source of law in the country; an additional 24 percent said it should be a source of legislation. (There was little variation by gender.)

Still, Egyptians' desire for sharia is balanced by a strong demand for modernization and a distaste for theocracy. Women's rights will be a litmus test for the new government—a sign of where the country is headed. The Muslim Brotherhood unleashed a sea of controversy in 2007 when it released its party platform excluding women (and non-Muslims) from the presidency, and calling for a group of Islamic scholars to review and veto legislation that does not conform to religious rules. These conservative positions confirmed critics' worst fears of the Brotherhood, and led to some soul-searching within the organization itself, especially among younger members who disagreed with the hard-line positions of their elders.

So far, no women have been named to the small panel revising Egypt's constitution; hence the petition to the ruling Army Council. "We collected more than 11,000 signatures in a few days," Iman Bibars, a prominent women's rights activist in Cairo, told me by phone. "That's a huge number in such a short amount of time." Bibars is sanguine about prospects for women in the new Egypt, although realistic too. "We will have to fight for our rights," she said. "It will be tough, and require lobbying, but that's what democracy is all about."

The constitutional reform process presents challenges for women's rights. Some role for sharia is inevitable in the new Egyptian constitution, as the existing one already establishes Islamic law as the main source of legislation. The real issue is what kind of Islam will exert most influence.

The rise of Salafism, a particularly conservative form of the faith propagated by Saudi Arabia, should worry Egyptian women's groups. In recent years, tensions between secularists and Salafis have been rising, with Salafis calling for full veiling of women and gender segregation in universities. The Salafis' following is evident in the rising number of Egyptian women wearing the niqab, the face-covering veil, long black abayas and even gloves on their hands to avoid physical contact with men.

Wearing the veil has become popular in Tunisia and Egypt for a variety of reasons, including as an expression of religious identity, conforming to social pressures and as a statement against the secular authoritarianism of the government. (The irony is that Egypt is the birthplace of Arab feminism, which in the first half of the 20th century put much energy into unveiling women.)

With Hosni Mubarak gone, activists will now have to contend with hard-core politics in a way that has been missing from Egypt's Potemkin parliament. Controversial legislation, like the equal right to divorce that was passed in 2000, will come under pressure from Islamist lawmakers who fiercely opposed the bill. (Tunisia is the only other Arab country that grants women the right.) Women's groups can no longer fall back upon a sympathetic Mubarak regime, which often sided with their cause.

In a more fluid democratic system, women's groups in Tunisia and Egypt will have to forge alliances with moderate religious leaders who promote progressive interpretations of sharia. Women's groups in countries such as Morocco, Jordan and, to some extent, Iran have succeeded in doing so, harnessing critical support on legislation affecting their rights.

If a brave new world of electoral politics does emerge, women's rights activists will have to be savvy—commanding international support without raising fears of undue Western influence. When women in Iraq and Afghanistan, for example, have faced disastrous rollbacks of their rights in the name of religion, they have called in the international media and shamed their governments into backing down.

Tunisian and Egyptian activists should know that women's rights often become bargaining chips for some other agenda. In Iraq, the American-appointed Governing Council wasted no time in trying to rescind the Baathists' progressive family law and replace it with religious law. Only a backlash from women's groups, and a U.S. veto, prevented the move. In the months ahead, women in Tunisia and Egypt must be ready to face similar watershed moments.

Intervention in Libya

Our Bargain With the New Gadhafi

Elliott Abrams

WALL STREET JOURNAL, FEBRUARY 25, 2011

The man Ronald Reagan called "the mad dog of the Middle East" is living up to that title these days, launching bloody assaults on his own population and reminding us of why we hated him for so long. Moammar Gadhafi is the man behind the bomb that brought down Pan Am flight 103 in 1988, killing 270 people (190 Americans). He is also behind the 1986 bombing of the La Belle discotheque in Berlin, killing several Americans and wounding 229 people. By the time Reagan left office, we had a total trade ban on Libya and had, in response to the attack on La Belle, bombed targets near Tripoli and Benghazi.

Two decades later we have come full circle, watching Gadhafi on TV with horror. On Tuesday he said, "I call on those who love Moammar Gadhafi, who represents glory . . . to come out of your houses and attack" the anti-regime demonstrators. He would not resign, he said, because "Moammar Gadhafi is not the president, he is not a normal human being."

That is clear, but for most of the past decade we made believe he was. After the U.S. Army made short shrift of Saddam

ELLIOTT ABRAMS is senior fellow for Middle Eastern studies at the Council on Foreign Relations.

Hussein's forces in 2003, Gadhafi approached British intelligence and sought to come in from the cold. He agreed, after negotiations conducted largely by the CIA and London's MI6, to abandon terrorism and hand over to the U.S. his programs for developing missiles and weapons of mass destruction.

He kept his part of the bargain: Those materials reside at a military base in the U.S., and he has stayed away from terrorist groups. Libya began making payments to the families of those killed on Pan Am 103, ultimately reaching an agreement with all but one family and handing over a total of $1.5 billion.

In exchange, the U.S. sent an ambassador to Tripoli and allowed Libya to open an embassy in Washington. Gadhafi's son Saif al-Islam visited Washington, and his suave and murderous intelligence chief Musa Kusa (Michigan State University class of '78, and more recently Libya's foreign minister) was allowed back into the U.S. All sanctions ended. The U.S. stopped blocking Libyan efforts to join United Nations committees, and in 2008 Libya served for a month as president of the Security Council. That same year, Secretary of State Condoleezza Rice visited Libya.

The U.S. also restrained its criticism of Gadhafi's internal repression. The agreement with Gadhafi came in 2003, the same year that President George W. Bush delivered his speech at the National Endowment for Democracy saying that "Sixty years of Western nations excusing and accommodating the lack of freedom in the Middle East did nothing to make us safe—because in the long run, stability cannot be purchased at the expense of liberty."

How did we square that circle when it came to Gadhafi? We hoped that our embassy folks, visitors, academics and businessmen would—in the long run—pull Libya toward being a more open society. And we suspended disbelief about the intermittent promises of reform, usually delivered by Saif al-Islam, that change was on the way.

Our annual human rights reports told the truth, but there was no question that the Bush administration (and the Obama administration that followed) felt limited by Gadhafi's adherence to the bargain. We had not promised to be silent about human rights abuses, and we were not, but there was no real energy behind our statements. We were doing business with Gadhafi, not trying to overthrow him. The fate of Fathi Eljahmi, one of Libya's most prominent dissidents, was symbolic: Bush and Obama administration pressure was insufficient to free him from prison until just before his death in 2009.

Seen from this bloody February of 2011, the agreement with Libya was still the right policy. Gadhafi in his bunker with control over missiles, chemical weapons and a rudimentary nuclear program is a terrifying thought. So is a Libya after regime collapse with those materials available to the highest bidder.

Had we reneged—taken Libya's weaponry but then started a campaign against Gadhafi's rule—he'd have re-armed fast and gone back to terrorism. It's also not clear what more strenuous and public efforts to promote change in Libya would have achieved. It's not as if one could reason with Gadhafi.

Gadhafi's vicious regime has left Libya far worse than he found it on the day of his coup in 1969. King Idriss was at least a unifying figure for a country that had not long been unified and had been independent only since 1951. Gadhafi has established no national institutions, not even allowing a fake parliament of the Mubarak or Ben Ali variety that could perhaps be turned into something real.

Nor is there an army such as in Egypt, with the prestige and unity to intervene, restore calm and (we all hope) set the country on a better path. Gadhafi, who took power in a military coup, was too clever to allow a well-organized army that might do the same to him. Many units are organized along tribal lines, which has kept Gadhafi safe but may be his undoing now. If the tribes are central to defeating him, the next government will have to balance them carefully, using Libya's oil wealth to buy support and time to address its many crises.

Like Idi Amin and Emperor Bokassa, Gadhafi will soon join the pantheon of grotesque dictators who leave their countries in ruins. Given the last years—when quiet disapproval replaced forceful denunciation as U.S. policy—we can only hope that Libyans remember the decades when we were Gadhafi's worst enemy.

Libya's Terra Incognita

Who and What Will Follow Qaddafi?

Frederic Wehrey

FOREIGNAFFAIRS.COM, FEBRUARY 28, 2011

After Libyans, and much of the civilized world, rejoice in the seemingly inevitable fall of Muammar al-Qaddafi, the country will face the difficult task of repairing a society long traumatized by the Middle East's most Orwellian regime. Libya lacks both legitimate formal institutions and a functioning civil society. The new, post-Qaddafi era, therefore, is likely to be marked by the emergence of long-suppressed domestic groups jostling for supremacy in what is sure to be a chaotic political scene.

For four decades, Libya has been largely terra incognita, a place where the outsized personality of its quixotic leader and a byzantine bureaucracy obscured an informal network of constantly shifting power brokers. Even before the current unrest, working with these figures was uncertain at best—"like throwing darts at balloons in a dark room," as one senior Western diplomat put it to me in 2009.

In the near future, even with Qaddafi gone, the country may face a continued contest between the forces of a free Libya and the regime's die-hard elements. In particular, Qaddafi's sons—Saif al-Islam, Khamis, Al-Saadi, and Mutassim—and

FREDERIC WEHREY is a Senior Policy Analyst at the RAND Corporation. He recently returned from Libya.

their affiliated militias may not go quietly into the night; the struggle to root them out may be violent and protracted (think, for example, of Saddam Hussein's sons, Uday and Qusay). Saif al-Islam, who was known for years in the West as Libya's supposed champion of reform, revealed his true character as a reactionary much like his father by promising a "bloodbath" in a televised speech last week. On the ground, many of the attacks against demonstrators and their suspected sympathizers are being ordered by Captain Khamis al-Qaddafi, who heads the 32nd Brigade, the regime's best-trained and best-equipped force. As the current unrest unfolded, Al-Saadi's star was on the rise: as a brigadier in the special forces, he was dispatched to placate and then suppress the brewing revolt in Benghazi on February 16. Lastly, Mutassim, Libya's National Security Council adviser, reportedly sought in 2008 to establish his own militia to keep up with his brothers and has strong ties to a number of hard-liners.

Lined up against these Qaddafi holdouts are the members of the Libyan military and officer corps who have joined the opposition. Beginning in the early 1990s, Qaddafi deliberately weakened the Libyan officer corps after a succession of coup attempts by lower-ranking officers from the al-Warfalla and al-Magariha tribes, which had grown increasingly marginalized by Qaddafi's own tribe, al-Qaddadfa, and were angered by his disastrous war against Chad in the early 1980s. From this point onward, Qaddafi kept the general military underfunded while devoting resources and training to elite units that were comprised of tribal allies of the al-Qaddadfa. He would later entrust these units to his sons.

Over the years, the regular military's infrastructure has become dilapidated and its budget so meager that generals and colonels wear civilian attire to preserve their uniforms. Some of the most senior officers—among them even those who supported Qaddafi in the 1969 coup—were forced into early retirement after the Tunisian and Egyptian uprisings to prevent them from leading any opposition. Nevertheless, the officer corps, weak as it is, may be the only formal body capable of representing an impartial Libyan national interest in a post-Qaddafi era and, importantly, preventing an outbreak of revenge violence.

Libya's tribes will also be critical for governance and reconciliation. Qaddafi's 1969 coup overturned the traditional dominance of the eastern coastal tribes in Cyrenaica in favor of those drawn from the west and the country's interior. Although the Qaddafi regime was, at least in theory, opposed to tribal identity, its longevity depended in large measure on a shaky coalition among three principal tribes: the al-Qaddadfa, al-Magariha, and al-Warfalla.

In 1993, Qaddafi took steps to harness the power of the tribes for the revolutionary bureaucracy by creating "popular social leadership committees," which were responsible for maintaining local order. This move was a tacit admission not only of the importance of tribes and traditional elites in Libyan politics but also that the regime's longstanding instruments of state power—the despised revolutionary committees—had grown too corrupt and sclerotic to control the population.

In the post-Qaddafi era, the recently defected tribal bulwarks of the ancien régime—the al-Magariha and the al-Warfalla—will play a critical role in lending legitimacy and unity to a new government. That said, the weakness and fragmentation of the military and the tempting availability of oil resources highlight the very real threat of tribal warlordism.

Tribal clout, however, is tempered by other affiliations: a strong middle class and, increasingly, religion. Among Libya's Islamists, the Libyan Islamic Fighting Group has long attracted the attention of the West because of its association with al Qaeda. But after Qaddafi, the less visible, non-Salafi networks will matter more—namely, the Sufi orders and the

Muslim Brotherhood. The revivalist Sanussiya Sufi order has featured prominently in the country's collective memory. It provided the organizational base for the Libyan resistance to the Italian occupation and was the pillar of support for the monarchy under King Idris, who held sovereign power from 1951 until 1969.

Although long hostile to Sufism as a potential threat to his authority, Qaddafi himself had begun a policy of bolstering Sufi charitable networks as a buffer against radical Salafism. The long-suppressed Muslim Brotherhood may also reemerge as a potent force. It is perhaps significant that this organization was among the first Libyan groups to offer congratulations to the new regime in Egypt.

All these influences are underpinned by a historic split along the Mediterranean seaboard that runs between Tripoli and the eastern province of Cyrenaica, the historic base of the Sanussi monarchy. The two regions are divided by linguistic and cultural differences, as well as a vast stretch of desert. The east shares tribal ties with Egypt and even the Arabian Peninsula rather than with the Maghreb. After toppling the monarchy, Qaddafi shifted political power and economic resources to Tripoli, which further exacerbated the regional divide.

In post-Qaddafi Libya, Cyrenaica will be tempted to reassert its historic primacy. For starters, the area produces the country's oil wealth. It also bears the proud legacy of having led not one but two resistance struggles: the anti-Italian guerrilla campaign under the direction of the Sufi leader Omar al-Mukhtar and now the February 17 "Day of Rage," which was christened by its organizers—not accidentally—as the Mukhtar Revolution.

The sparsely populated and ill-governed southern periphery will also contend for resources and influence in the new state. Non-Arab ethnic groups with transnational ties across the Sahel and Saharan belt—the Amazigh (Berbers), Tuareg, and Toubou—were marginalized under Qaddafi. They will undoubtedly now seek to redress this injustice, and they have the means to make their concerns felt. Immediately before the Benghazi unrest, activism among the Amazigh was Qaddafi's primary security concern. The Tuareg waged a long-running rebellion that stretched across Algeria, Niger, and Mali, and the disaffected Toubou have staged periodic riots in southern towns. Going forward, strong but equitable administration will be essential to incorporate these peripheral groups and also prevent al Qaeda in the Islamic Maghreb from enjoying newfound maneuverability in the area by exploiting longstanding grievances.

The new Libya will need pluralistic institutions, a constitution, and resource-sharing mechanisms to ensure that a Tripolitan-Cyrenaican rivalry, excessive tribal power, and ethnic grievances do not unravel the gains of recent weeks. On this point, the constitution of 1951 is a useful starting point: it established a federal structure that provided a degree of provincial autonomy and a rotating capital between Benghazi and Tripoli (this was amended in 1963 in favor of a more centralized system), and a bicameral legislature.

The leaders of the new state will also need to adopt a magnanimous view toward the remnants of the old bureaucracy. The National Oil Corporation, the Libyan Arab Foreign Investment Company, and the various popular committees may be arms of the Qaddafi-run state, but they are also reservoirs of technocratic, administrative, and economic expertise. The Sanussi monarchy, which has been exiled from Libya since Qaddafi took power in 1969, should also be included—but with the understanding that its legitimacy among many Libyans has been diminished by its long absence from the country.

Most important, the Libyan army and security apparatus will have to develop their own identities that both respect and dilute the affiliations of tribe and geography. They will need to extend the writ of the post-Qaddafi government into the country's hinterlands and secure its borders. But above all, the country's security institutions have to rebuild themselves in a way that is unconditionally subordinate to civil authority. They must ensure that praetorianism and officer privilege, which spawned the nightmare of Qaddafi in the first place, are never allowed to emerge again.

What Intervention Looks Like

How the West Can Aid the Libyan Rebels

Robert E. Hunter

FOREIGNAFFAIRS.COM, MARCH 16, 2011

With Muammar al-Qaddafi now closing in on a final campaign to defeat the rebels opposing his regime, the world's attention has centered on what the United States and others should do—or even can do—to aid those who are trying to bring down the Qaddafi government. Some observers caution that any sort of intervention would be unwise, if not dangerous. They warn that arming the Libyan rebels today could empower the next Osama bin Laden, who could one day use Western-supplied arms and training against his benefactors. Others cite the disastrous U.S.-led intervention in Somalia in the early 1990s and the ongoing difficulties of fostering civil society in Afghanistan. Even imposing a no-fly zone over Libya could require, as U.S. Secretary of Defense Robert Gates has cautioned, destroying Qaddafi's air defenses, an act of military aggression against a sovereign state that is not at war with the United States. And such actions could call to mind the U.S.-led

ROBERT E. HUNTER is a Senior Adviser at the RAND Corporation. He was U.S. Ambassador to NATO and a Director of Middle East and North African Affairs on the National Security Council.

invasion of Iraq in 2003, an event that still has negative resonance in much of the Arab and Muslim world, to say the least.

But of all the possible historical analogies for the dilemma facing the United States, the most useful one may be the case of Bosnia from 1993 to 1995. At that time, I was U.S. ambassador to NATO. I negotiated eight different decisions to use NATO airpower, but most of these came to naught: only the last time—after the massacre at Srebrenica—did NATO carry out decisive air strikes. Several NATO members, notably the United Kingdom, resisted NATO's use of force for more than two years. They worried about "proportionality," "even-handedness," the precedent of acting beyond NATO's formal area of commitment, and assuming responsibility for Bosnia's future.

What finally caused NATO to act was not the mounting human toll alone but also the realization that unless NATO stopped the worst killing on Europe's doorstep since World War II, neither it nor the European Union would have the credibility needed to undertake other tasks for the future of European security and cooperation. The same calculus was true for Kosovo three years later.

Also, Bosnia and Kosovo are in the close backyard of both NATO and the European Union. The same could be said about Libya: refugees from the current conflict would spill over into Europe, just as Bosnians, Kosovars, and others from the former Yugoslavia did in the 1990s.

What happened in Bosnia (and, later, in Kosovo) also demonstrated the importance of formal legitimacy in international law for military action. Such legitimacy is generally understood to come from a resolution of the UN Security Council under Chapter VII, the enforcement provisions of the UN Charter. Although the United States argues that NATO can act without such outside authority, almost all of NATO's European members insist upon it. NATO acted militarily in Bosnia with the full blessing of the United Nations, which gave it authority to establish a no-fly zone over Bosnia and use airpower to protect so-called safe areas. The United States and its coalition partners had similar legal authority in the invasion of Afghanistan in 2001 and during the Persian Gulf War of 1991. By contrast, there is still debate over whether UN Security Council resolutions justified the invasion of Iraq in 2003. And there was no such blessing for the NATO-run air campaign against Serbia in 1999 to stop the ethnic cleansing of Kosovo. For the Western powers, the dilemma arises when they want to act but there is no UN Security Council resolution to provide formal legitimacy.

Much as Russia and China opposed the use of NATO airpower in Kosovo, they appear ready to veto any UN resolution calling for the imposition of a no-fly zone over Libya today. They would almost certainly oppose an even more vigorous application of military power if that proved necessary to stop Qaddafi from crushing the Libyan opposition. In Bosnia, the no-fly zone also proved insufficient, and it became necessary to carry out air attacks on Serbia-backed forces.

Three years after the fighting stopped in Bosnia, Serbia's leader, Slobodan Milosevic, expelled as many as one million Kosovars. By early 1999, NATO members came to the unanimous conclusion that this could not be tolerated. As in Bosnia, if the West did not act, then both NATO and the European Union would appear feckless and thus diminished as security institutions with a valid role in the post-Cold War era. Caught between the need to take military action and the lack of a UN mandate, the NATO allies agreed among themselves that each member could decide for itself the legal basis for air strikes. All did so—even Greece, despite its close relations with Orthodox Serbia. At the same time, most of the allies vowed that they would never again act without formal UN sanction. (This was one reason so much of Europe opposed the U.S. invasion of Iraq in 2003.)

Nevertheless, if NATO wanted to impose a no-fly zone over Libya, the act would not be totally illegitimate. Although Beijing's and Moscow's recalcitrance means that the UN Security Council is not likely to act, the next best source of legitimacy in the current situation has spoken: the Arab League. Its support for a no-fly zone has been buttressed by similar calls from two other institutions that also have political standing within the Arab world: the Organization of the Islamic Conference (OIC) and the Gulf Cooperation Council (GCC). In fact, last week the GCC went so far as to call the Qaddafi regime "illegitimate." This is a remarkable turn of events, given that all three organizations have members that are deeply concerned that the current unrest in the Arab world could spread to their own countries and, in some cases, already has. Such approval would be proof against any future claims by Arab states or other parties, such as al Qaeda, that acting against Qaddafi was a renewal of Western colonialism.

Yet what if a no-fly zone proved less than effective? Are NATO countries ready to step up military intervention to secure Qaddafi's defeat? In both Bosnia and Kosovo, Milosevic sued for peace before NATO had to face that choice. But since Qaddafi is fighting for his survival and has a long history of brutality, Washington and Brussels must be aware that compromise with him is almost certainly impossible. The question, then, is whether stopping the fighting—which could also require forcibly removing Qaddafi—is worth the price of deep military engagement and responsibility for Libya's postwar future.

U.S. President Barack Obama seems to have made his decision, saying that "It is in the interest of the United States, and more importantly, in the interest of the Libyan people for Mr. Qaddafi to leave." (This is the logical conclusion of his commitment to put the United States "on the right side of history.") If the United States is indeed resolute in achieving that goal, the rest, then, is a question of tactics.

A no-fly zone can be imposed in a matter of hours, likely with low military risk, as NATO demonstrated over Bosnia in the mid-1990s and as a coalition did over Iraq after 1991. As Gates argued, this might also require suppressing Libyan air defenses—but that is also a relatively straightforward military proposition.

In sum, the course is clear. Washington should push for the rapid institution of a no-fly zone against the Qaddafi regime. This no-fly zone could be undertaken by NATO, the European Union, or by a "coalition of the willing" that includes the United States, France, the United Kingdom, and a few others. This could prove necessary if, despite the backing of the Arab League, the GCC, and the OIC, some NATO allies still do not want to act. Both Turkey and Germany remain reluctant—Ankara because of the precedent of the 2003 invasion of Iraq, and Berlin out of its historic reluctance to use force. They may have some silent partners among other NATO allies.

At the same time, the West should begin arming the rebels and trying to peel off Qaddafi supporters, by publicly declaring that those who desert Qaddafi now will not be excluded from roles in Libya's post-Qaddafi future. U.S. and European military planners should also prepare for more robust military action, including air strikes, if that becomes necessary to depose Qaddafi and stop the fighting. Meanwhile, the European Union should take the lead in planning for Libya's post-Qaddafi era (as well as in adjacent Egypt and Tunisia). It is now time for Europe to demonstrate whether it is serious about its attempts to forge a common foreign and security policy: the region is on its doorstep, refugees are most likely to flow north, and the EU members have both the resources and experience to make an impact. Libyans will need the help of the West not just in getting rid of Qaddafi but also in building their lives after him.

The Folly of Protection

Is Intervention Against Qaddafi's Regime Legal and Legitimate?

Michael W. Doyle

FOREIGNAFFAIRS.COM, MARCH 20, 2011

In classic United Nations Security Council language, Resolution 1973, passed on March 17, 2011, authorized UN member states to "take all necessary measures . . . to protect civilians and civilian populated areas" in Libya by establishing a no-fly zone and enforcing an arms embargo against Colonel Muammar al-Qaddafi's regime. The resolution gave teeth to the much-heralded "responsibility to protect"—which, according to the 2005 UN World Summit Outcome, is the responsibility of the international community to "help protect populations from genocide, war crimes, ethnic cleansing, and crimes against humanity."

The UN General Assembly adopted the principle of the responsibility to protect—or RtoP, its UN abbreviation—in 2005 in a unanimous resolution advocated by nongovernmental organizations; UN Secretary-General Kofi Annan and the high-level panel he appointed in 2005 to investigate how the

MICHAEL W. DOYLE is Harold Brown Professor of International Affairs, Law, and Political Science at Columbia University and Chair of the United Nations Democracy Fund Advisory Board.

United Nations could pursue reform; and Gareth Evans and Mohamed Sahnoun, co-chairs of the International Commission on Intervention and State Sovereignty, whose 2001 report urging adoption of RtoP drove the campaign for the concept. The 2005 document articulating RtoP carefully deliniated grounds for action under the doctrine, limiting it to four situations suitable for intervention: genocide, war crimes, ethnic cleansing, and crimes against humanity. The Libyan intervention represents only the third time since 2005 that the Security Council has invoked RtoP to enforce the protection of civilians. The second case occurred just weeks ago, when the Security Council's first resolution targeted Qaddafi's crackdown against Libya's rebellion by calling for financial sanctions and an arms embargo. Resolution 1973, however, marks the first Security Council approval of force in the name of RtoP.

In passing RtoP, the Security Council helped bridge the gap between so-called legitimate (ethically justifiable) and legal (legally authorized) intervention. The Kosovo Commission, a group of independent experts under the chairmanship of the South African justice Richard Goldstone, first identified this dichotomy in 1999 while investigating the North Atlantic Treaty Organization's intervention in Kosovo. It deemed NATO's actions "illegal but legitimate," in the sense that the Western countries had performed a legitimate rescue of oppressed Kosovars likely to suffer ethnic cleansing under Slobodan Milosević's leadership but had done so without the Security Council's legal sanction (unavailable due to the threatened Russian and Chinese vetoes). To gain approval for their current intervention in Libya, however, Western nations secured a resolution that passed with ten votes in favor, no vetoes, and five abstentions from Brazil, China, Germany, India, and Russia.

By invoking RtoP for the intervention in Libya, the Security Council narrowed the divide between legitimacy and legality. Yet the ethical and legal justifications for both elements remain murky. Most significantly, a legitimate and lawful outcome to the operation is far from assured.

The true complexity of the UN action against Qaddafi's regime can be understood only by investigating the UN Charter, which specifies that "nothing contained in the present Charter shall authorize the United Nations to intervene in matters which are essentially within the domestic jurisdiction of any state." The only exception to this principle falls under Chapter VII of the charter, which authorizes the Security Council to "determine the existence of any threat to the peace, breach of the peace, or act of aggression" and act to "maintain or restore international peace and security." Internal abuses by states—including the slaughter of civilians—do not automatically qualify as "international" threats under the charter.

Nonetheless, the Security Council has, in practice, claimed wide discretion to interpret events as "threats to the peace" that did not necessarily qualify as dangers to "international peace." This phenomenon became particularly acute following the Cold War, when the Security Council further diluted the requirement of "international threat" by endorsing a wide range of other triggers for successful Chapter VII sanctions. It authorized arms embargoes, trade sanctions, no-fly zones, and even armed intervention against various acts of genocide, ethnic cleansing, interference with the delivery of humanitarian supplies, violations of cease-fires, collapse of civil order, and coups against democratic governments and war crimes in Haiti, Cambodia, Iraq, Liberia, Rwanda, Somalia, and the former Republic of Yugoslavia.

RtoP, responding to the sense that these domestic harms warranted international response, solidified the Security Council's claims to wider discretion. Yet it also restricted its ability to sanction intervention to the four situations listed in the RtoP document—genocide, war crimes, ethnic cleansing, and crimes against humanity—and thus precluded, for example, intervention in cases of civil disorder and coups. Although the resolution authorizing force against Libya will certainly further entrench the principle of RtoP, it will not completely resolve the tension between RtoP—in itself only a General Assembly recommendation—and the UN Charter itself, which, according to the letter of the law, limits action to "international" threats. Equally significant, the Libyan resolution authorizes only a no-fly zone and the protection of civilians, not the ouster of Qaddafi that U.S. President Barack Obama has called for and which is most likely to resolve the crisis politically.

The no-fly zone itself faces questions of ethical legitimacy as well. An old tradition of ethical and practical lessons, dating at least as far back as the writings of the British philosopher John Stuart Mill in the middle of the nineteenth century, argues against armed intervention for the sake of protecting civilians and promoting human rights and democracy. For anyone committed to human dignity, this tradition claims, democracy and human rights must derive from self-government, not laws and regulations imposed by foreigners, however well meaning. And imposing democracy from the outside tends to fail. Democracy is not only government for the people; it is also government of and by the people. Unless citizens view themselves as a collective body and are prepared to pay taxes, defend their borders, and abide by majority rule, democracy is unsustainable. These attributes are more often achieved by long national struggles and wars of liberation than foreign intervention.

Thus, when foreigners seek to liberate a country whose people have been unable to liberate themselves, they often fall into one or more of three traps. First, the leadership that replaces the former regime finds that it cannot rule because it has not been able to mobilize the support to win on its own, and, as in Iraq, civil strife follows the liberating invasion. The new leadership finds itself in the second trap when it can only remain in power thanks to ongoing foreign support. As a result, it renders the country a client state rather than a free nation. The third trap occurs when the leadership learns that it can only govern as the previous dictator did—by force. The liberating invaders are thus responsible not only for the monetary and human costs of the invasion but for having produced a civil war, a colony, or one more tyranny with a new ideological label attached.

Foreign states must sometimes override or disregard these traps. The national security interests of a given country may require intervention, or the casualties being suffered or likely to result from a domestic conflict are so large as to demand a humanitarian rescue (such as in Rwanda in 1994). Such humanitarian rescue offers the best justification for the current intervention in Libya. Yet legitimate armed interventions must be proportional, in the sense that they will actually cost fewer lives than they save. The no-fly zone is saving the rebels and their civilian supporters at the moment, but their current preservation may simply set the stage for a prolonged and costly civil war.

Military action should also not be undertaken unless it is likely to be successful. Success with regard to the Libyan intervention has yet to be defined. Qaddafi probably would have been able to conquer the rebel capital Benghazi with his air force, artillery, and armor, but the commencement of allied intervention will destroy the air force and protect the civilian population from large-scale ground attacks. However, it does not appear that the rebels can conquer the country even if Qaddafi's air force is neutralized unless they are aided by international arms or forces on the ground—assistance not authorized by Resolution 1973.

The current intervention in Libya, then, seems to wed legality with ethical legitimacy. But it strains against the letter of the UN Charter law on intervention and will remain ethically problematic unless it can help resolve the crisis without further substantial loss of life. This uncertainty will pose intricate problems for policymakers and negotiators in the weeks and months ahead. If Qaddafi retains power while the rebels maintain their own territory, will partition provide a workable solution? If Qaddafi and the rebels cannot achieve any political agreement, can the international community continue its involvement while the two sides battle it out with small arms? Or will the interveners brush aside the restrictions of the Security Council resolution and topple Qaddafi—and thereby discredit the legal authorization of RtoP? Regardless, the intervention in Libya is sure to shape how RtoP is applied in the future.

To the Shores of Tripoli

Why Operation Odyssey Dawn Should Not Stop at Benghazi

Dirk Vandewalle

FOREIGNAFFAIRS.COM, MARCH 21, 2011

As Catherine Ashton, the European Union's high representative for foreign affairs and security policy, wrote in a March 18, 2011, *New York Times* editorial about the European Union's options in Libya, "sometimes the toughest question in world politics is: 'And then what?'" In light of the furious pace of the negotiations surrounding the previous day's adoption of UN Security Council Resolution 1973—which extended a no-fly zone over Libya and authorized the international community to take whatever additional measures necessary to protect the country's population short of sending ground troops—it is not surprising that no one had really stopped to consider her question. Indeed, more time seems to have been spent getting the European Union, the Arab League, the G-8, and the Security Council to agree on the language than on the content. Still, if those hurried diplomatic negotiations seemed a Herculean task, they may pale in comparison to the challenge that comes next: keeping Libya intact and on the road to recovery.

DIRK VANDEWALLE is Associate Professor of Government at Dartmouth College.

For his part, U.S. President Barack Obama promised that intervention would be short—a matter of "days, not weeks." And British Prime Minister David Cameron admonished that international involvement should be limited to stopping Colonel Muammar al-Qaddafi's violence. Both caveats will prove unrealistic.

At this point, the international community has two options: to either protect the opposition movement in Cyrenaica, the vast eastern province in which Benghazi is located, but not force Qaddafi out of power, or make Qaddafi's ouster an explicit goal. The former seems to be what Cameron had in mind when he spoke of selective containment—perhaps in an attempt to sanitize international involvement. It was also echoed in Obama's call for short-term intervention. Still, this kind of containment is neither possible nor feasible. Indeed, it would defeat the very logic of Resolution 1973.

Of course, ongoing military strikes will undoubtedly strengthen the rebels' resolve. Seeing the destruction wreaked by the international coalition, Qaddafi loyalists are unlikely to put up much opposition. Even if the strikes stopped in the course of a cease-fire, rebels would likely take advantage of Qaddafi's weakness to try to push the remnants of his assault forces westward, reigniting the fighting.

If international action simply contained Qaddafi by halting his advance, he would be left in control of Tripolitania, the northwestern province in which Tripoli is located, leaving Cyrenaica effectively independent. The two provinces are divided by long-standing tensions. Qaddafi historically neglected the economy of Cyrenaica, because he judged the tribes in those areas to be potentially disloyal. And tensions between the two provinces were further exacerbated by Qaddafi's attempts to play each off the other in order to stay in power. Protecting half of the country while leaving the other to Qaddafi would harden the provinces' resolve to go their own ways. And economically speaking, that would be possible; both provinces have oil fields to rely on for revenue.

But politically speaking, such a division would be disastrous. In Tripolitania, Qaddafi would still have the resources and territory to continue to wage war against the opposition. If the brutal state terrorism Qaddafi instituted in the 1980s to secure Libya' position in the region is any indication, he would not hesitate to do so. Even if he does observe a future cease-fire, selective containment would allow him to play a long-term cat-and-mouse game, stopping violence while surreptitiously extending his reach into the eastern part of the country by manipulating or buying such Cyrenaican tribes as the Warfalla, a powerful group that has so far adopted a cautious wait-and-see policy.

Meanwhile, the weapons that flowed through Libya's porous borders and into the hands of Cyrenaican opposition forces during the anti-Qaddafi campaign will leave the regional tribes substantially more powerful than before. Having suffered through Qaddafi's violence against them and then emboldened by Western intervention on their behalf, they would be ready to fight back at all cost. Thus the specter of all-out intertribal and interprovincial warfare would rise once more.

A Libya with Qaddafi in even partial control would be unacceptable to the international community; the country would be highly unstable and a real liability to North Africa and Europe. The world's inability or unwillingness to displace an unreconstructed Qaddafi would give succor to a number of groups, including al-Qaeda, that could seize chaos in Libya and North Africa as an opportunity to extend their influence. Indeed, Qaddafi's threat to turn the Mediterranean into a zone of instability is a reminder of precisely what a divided Libya could yield.

Internal instability aside, there is another reason why selective containment is unwise: it would severely constrain the international community's future options. It seems inevitable that EU and U.S. efforts will successfully drive Qaddafi's forces from Benghazi. But selective containment would require them to stop there. Given Qaddafi's rhetoric of the past few weeks, it seems unlikely that they would be able to pressure him into any kind of settlement from such a position. Further, it is improbable that, having achieved the limited objective of securing Cyrenaica relatively quickly, the United Kingdom and France, the leaders of the intervention forces, would be content to settle rather than march on to Tripoli to dislodge Qaddafi himself.

Of course, the alternative, forcing Qaddafi out of power, is fraught with its own problems and complications. Qaddafi's departure would leave behind a political vacuum that would need filling as soon as possible. The choice of local interlocutors would be key. For all the sympathy the international community may currently feel for the opposition movement headed by the Libyan National Council, the provisional government, it would have to be cautious about unconditionally supporting it. Indeed, the threats that the LNC is already issuing should give the international community doubts about its readiness to lead in democratic government. Throughout the conflict, the LNC has threatened that there will be dire consequences for those countries in the West that had not sufficiently supported the rebel side if it won.

It is worth noting that although there is as yet no other opposition group, the LNC is national only in its aspirations. Much of Tripolitania still genuinely supports Qaddafi and would likely be resentful of whatever took his place and refuse to join an LNC-led government. To overcome antagonism between the provinces and to guide the country through the arduous process of state building and reconstruction that would follow Qaddafi's departure, institutions would need to be truly national and representative. Since the settling of scores seems inevitable in Libya after decades of Qaddafi's deliberate divide-and-rule policies, the international community would need to help establish a Libyan version of the Truth and Reconciliation Commission that brought political opponents in South Africa to some kind of understanding. Meanwhile, the international community would also have to steer the development of democracy and good governance in a country that has not known anything except tyranny for decades.

It is only such a process of democratization and reconstruction that would truly lessen the salience of Libya's enduring divisions. The reintegration of Libya with its North African neighbors after decades of self-enforced isolation under Qaddafi would also help. After years of ostracism, reintegration in the region could bring some measure of pride and responsibility to Libyans.

For all of this to happen, Libya, in addition to removing Qaddafi from power, needs what Ashton called in her article a "Marshall plan for North Africa" that would help a post-Qaddafi Libya (and other countries in the region) start building their states, developing their economies, and improving democratic governance through a number of educational, economic, and political initiatives. Libya's survival as a unified country will not only depend on how its own citizens deal with its long-standing fissures but also on the careful planning of outside powers.

Unless the United States and the European Union reach a decision quickly, they may wind up in a self-imposed stalemate that Qaddafi could exploit. The international community needs a proactive agenda and a clear plan for the intervention, starting now.

A New Lease on Life for Humanitarianism

How Operation Odyssey Dawn Will Revive RtoP

Stewart Patrick

FOREIGNAFFAIRS.COM, MARCH 24, 2011

The United States and its coalition partners' decision to launch Operation Odyssey Dawn to enforce a no-fly zone in Libya on March 19 was a vindication of the fragile "responsibility to protect" (RtoP) norm. The diplomatic process to build a consensus about intervention was messy, involving protracted negotiations among multiple parties, and the military outcome in Libya remains uncertain. Still, the Obama administration was correct to champion RtoP's basic principle: state sovereignty is not a license for a dictator to murder his citizens.

When it was endorsed unanimously by heads of state at the 2005 World Summit, RtoP was the biggest challenge to state sovereignty in three and a half centuries. It makes a state's presumed right of nonintervention contingent on its ability and willingness to protect its citizens and threatens "collective,

STEWART PATRICK is a Senior Fellow and the Director of the Program on International Institutions and Global Governance at the Council on Foreign Relations. He is the author of the forthcoming *Weak Links: Fragile States, Global Threats, and International Security.*

timely, and decisive action" if it does not. Until recently, however, putting this norm into practice proved tougher than enunciating it. UN member states repeatedly failed to intervene in even the most egregious situations—such as in Darfur, Sri Lanka, and the Democratic Republic of the Congo—and left hundreds of thousands of civilians at the mercy of genocidal leaders and armed militias. Given its seeming unenforceability, RtoP risked becoming a twenty-first century version of the 1928 Kellogg-Briand Pact, which "outlawed war" as an instrument of national policy.

In invoking "the Libyan authorities' responsibility to protect its population" in UN Security Council Resolution 1973, which prompted Operation Odyssey Dawn, the Security Council has seemingly given RtoP a new lease on life. How strengthened RtoP will be depends both on how well the Libya case fits its mandate and how well the intervention turns out.

RtoP was never intended as a license to go after every misbehaving regime. It applies only to those committing mass atrocities—genocide, war crimes, crimes against humanity, and ethnic cleansing. Although there is no consensus on the body count needed to trigger RtoP, the actions and intentions of Libya's leader Colonel Muammar al-Qaddafi have provided ample justification. Qaddafi's own security forces and the mercenaries he imported from Mali, Niger, Chad, and other sub-Saharan African countries have used indiscriminate force against civilians, massacring hundreds, perhaps more than a thousand, Libyans. They have also committed gross violations of human rights, the laws of war, and humanitarian law, such as using live ammunition against peaceful protesters, employing civilians as human shields, and denying relief to affected populations. On February 22, Qaddafi even pledged to "cleanse Libya house by house" of antigovernment protesters. Resolution 1973 noted that these "systematic attacks against the civilian population may amount to crimes against humanity," and, pursuant to a

Security Council request, Luis Moreno-Ocampo, chief prosecutor of the International Criminal Court (ICC), has already opened an investigation into Qaddafi's actions.

Even in the face of atrocities, RtoP envisions military action as a last resort after diplomatic efforts and sanctions have failed. In this, too, Operation Odyssey Dawn meets RtoP's standards. Before authorizing military intervention, the international community took numerous other steps to dissuade Qaddafi from committing further atrocities, including imposing an arms embargo, a travel ban, and an asset freeze; condemning Libya within (and ejecting it from) the UN Human Rights Council; and referring the Libyan case to the ICC. Qaddafi's continued defiance left the Security Council with the choice between escalating military intervention and tolerating, in the words of Resolution 1973, additional "gross and systematic violations of human rights, including arbitrary detentions, enforced disappearances, torture and summary executions."

Of course, Qaddafi did himself no favors by to "have no mercy and no pity" in Benghazi, the opposition movement's stronghold. As U.S. Secretary of State Hillary Clinton correctly observed from Paris on March 19, "We have every reason to fear that, left unchecked, Qadaffi will commit unspeakable atrocities." The dictator's large stockpile of chemical weapons raised the stakes even further.

For an RtoP intervention to be legitimate, it has to have international support, which the United States was prudent to secure before launching military operations. Critics, such as former UN ambassador John Bolton and Kori Schake, a research fellow at the Hoover Institution, have bemoaned the administration's willingness to allow other countries, particularly France, to spearhead the intervention as a retreat from leadership. They decry its insistence on seeking a UN imprimatur and warn of the dangers of war by NATO committee. But a U.S.-led intervention in Libya without Security Council authorization would have been disastrous, fanning the flames of anti-Americanism in the region, upending the narrative of this year's protests as an indigenous "Arab awakening," and saddling the United States with exclusive responsibility for yet another Muslim-majority country.

Attacking Libya without international backing, moreover, would also have done grievous damage to the RtoP norm, allowing critics to frame it as window-dressing for Western interventionism. Security Council authorization provided critical legitimacy for the United States and its allies to combat Qaddafi's atrocities. The endorsement of the no-fly zone by the Arab League, Organization of the Islamic Conference, and Gulf Cooperation Council was also crucial. None of these bodies has ever lifted a finger against regional tyrants, but this time their members made a different calculation, presumably reflecting a collective distaste for Qaddafi and their vulnerability to democratic aspirations sweeping the region.

One key aspect of successful intervention is clarity of political goals. In this respect, the United States and its partners' dithering over Operation Odyssey Dawn's aims is disturbing. In early March, the Obama administration signaled multiple times that it wanted full regime change in Libya. U.S. President Barack Obama has since vacillated, insisting in a March 19 address that the United States would not use force "beyond a well-defined goal—specifically, the protection of civilians in Libya."

Unfortunately, the notion that any country could impartially intervene on behalf of civilians is a delusion. Using military force to protect beleaguered civilian populations invariably means taking sides—a lesson it took years for the West to learn in Bosnia. And war involves other uncertainties: coalition aerial attacks could cause civilian casualties, and Arab League support could evaporate. If Qaddafi's forces dig in and hold their forward positions, they could still exact revenge against rebels in areas left under their control. The conflict could settle into a bloody, inconclusive stalemate, or alternatively, Qaddafi could abruptly fall from power and victorious rebel forces could launch their own round of score-settling. Given the likely possibility that at least one of these things will happen, the Obama administration is kidding itself if it believes that it can hand Libya over to coalition allies or victorious protesters after a few days, without any involvement in the endgame. As the only power with the strength to respond to these various contingencies, the United States will need to see this through to the end.

The "responsibility to protect" implies a responsibility to rebuild once the shooting stops. Although Resolution 1973 explicitly rejects foreign occupation of any part of Libyan territory, stabilizing the country for the long term will likely require a multinational peacekeeping force. Ideally it would be authorized by the United Nations and include significant contingents from the Arab world. Such long-term tasks as reconstructing Libya's economy and political institutions would only be possible with major commitments of financial resources from the European Union, the World Bank, the African Development Bank, wealthy Gulf sheikhdoms, and the United States.

In a seminal *Foreign Affairs* article in 2002, Gareth Evans, then president and CEO of the International Crisis Group, and Mohamed Sahnoun, who was special adviser on Africa to the UN secretary-general, argued that any military intervention to support RtoP must satisfy six principles: the cause must be just, the intentions of the interveners must be pure, the use of force should be a last resort, it should be sanctioned by the Security Council, it must be undertaken with proportional means, and it should have reasonable prospects of success. The imposition of the no-fly zone in Libya has met the first five of these criteria. But its ultimate success will depend on meeting the sixth. To do that, the United States and its allies must show more willingness to remove the Qaddafi regime and then rebuild a war-torn Libya.

In Libya, How Obama Can End a Mission That Started Badly

Gideon Rose

WASHINGTON POST, MARCH 25, 2011

American presidents are better at starting wars than ending them. In Libya, the Obama administration may prove the rule once again—in a particularly egregious way.

The central strategic challenge of any war is how to use military means to achieve political ends. The failure to think clearly about this challenge is the main reason America's leaders have had so much trouble closing out military conflicts smoothly and effectively in the past. Trapped in a fog of war, they have stumbled across the finish line without a clear sense of where they were going or how they advanced American interests amid all the chaos.

Past U.S. wars offer straightforward guideposts for success. First, set out a vision of a stable postwar political situation and develop a plan that gets you there. Second, define your goals precisely—avoiding cheap talk, simplistic analogies, and abstract concepts such as "victory" or "democracy"—and frame your political objectives in terms of what specifically will happen on the ground once military operations are finished.

GIDEON ROSE is the Peter G. Peterson chair and editor of *Foreign Affairs*.

Finally, prepare at least rudimentary backup plans for what to do if things go better, worse or differently than expected.

If this sounds like common sense, that's because it is. But in war, as in life, common sense is quite uncommon. Presidents have violated each of these "best practices" in every American war over the past century—and sometimes several of them in a single conflict.

Woodrow Wilson fought World War I to make the world "safe for democracy," but he never asked himself what democracy actually meant and whether, say, a constitutional monarchy in Germany would fit the bill. Franklin Roosevelt's administration never considered what would happen to its postwar arrangements if its alliance with the Soviet Union fell apart. Harry Truman and his secretary of state, Dean Acheson, made voluntary prisoner repatriation (the offer of asylum to enemy prisoners of war in U.N. hands) a key war aim in Korea but never asked themselves whether such a demand would block an armistice—which it did for almost a year and a half. The Kennedy and Johnson administrations dug themselves deeper and deeper into Vietnam without any strategy for victory or withdrawal.

George H.W. Bush assumed that Saddam Hussein would fall as a result of defeat in the Persian Gulf War but thought little about what to do if he did not. And George W. Bush made sure that Hussein's regime toppled but paid scant attention to what might follow.

Now, in the first war—or "kinetic military action"—that President Obama can truly call his own, his administration seems determined to best its predecessors by violating all of the maxims simultaneously.

In Libya, instead of starting with the desired end state and working back to develop a strategy for achieving it, the administration has launched the United States into battle with no clear vision of what a successful and stable outcome looks like. Instead of defining postwar goals precisely and matching means to ends, different officials have set out a range of objectives, from narrow (protecting civilians) to broad (ousting Libyan leader Moammar Gaddafi), even as they have announced severe restrictions on the military measures being considered to achieve them (no ground troops and no lengthy U.S. involvement). And if there has been any contingency planning for what happens should Gaddafi not fold or fall quickly, it is the only U.S. diplomatic secret yet to be leaked.

The Obama administration's efforts to gain international authorization of the operation have been deft. But procedural triumphs such as Security Council Resolution 1973, the approval of the Arab League or a transfer of responsibility for the no-fly zone to NATO will be of little cheer once the mission's substantive flaws come to the fore. Failure, after all, is usually an orphan.

Administration officials and their supporters counter that such criticisms don't apply to this operation, because it is not a war, but a "time-limited, scope-limited military action," in the words of White House spokesman Jay Carney. Conventional strategic reasoning is irrelevant to Operation Odyssey Dawn, the argument runs, because the operation's official goal is narrow and pure: the protection of innocent civilians from Gaddafi's threatened reprisals.

Letting events play out would indeed have yielded some sort of tragedy (although almost surely not the "massacre" of "100,000 people," as National Security Council staffer Dennis Ross has claimed). But the humanitarian issue emerged only because of a prior and larger political issue. The rebels are at risk of retaliation by Gaddafi because they rose up against his regime and were unable to topple it on their own. His opponents will be at risk so long as Gaddafi remains in power.

The true question at hand, therefore, is who will rule Libya? Whatever the Obama administration may be telling itself, by intervening to help one side in a civil war, it is now embroiled in Libya's political future to a vastly greater extent than it was two weeks ago.

The administration insists that, in the final analysis, it will have provided only some small and brief help in launching the operation, and that it will be able to hand off the Libya mission to other coalition members. Soon, we are assured, they will be the ones setting policy, executing it and bearing the accountability for whatever follows. "In some ways, how it turns out is not on our shoulders," an administration official told the *New York Times* on Thursday.

If only it were that simple. In insisting that it is only a little bit pregnant—or that it will not be, or be held to be, responsible for supporting its offspring—the administration is kidding itself (or us). If France, Britain or the Arab League could conduct lengthy, complex military operations or major nation-building efforts by themselves, they would do so. Then-Secretary of State Madeleine Albright's 1998 comment about the United States being "the indispensable nation" was not a boast but a statement of fact, one that has become more accurate in the years since.

Absent a significant escalation in the scale or duration of U.S. involvement, four possible outcomes lie ahead for Libya. Washington and its allies could get lucky and see Gaddafi's support collapse quickly, with a relatively quick transition to some better regime taking place under the supervision of a broad international coalition. Unfortunately, this best-case scenario is the least likely—for reasons including Gaddafi's zeal for power, the absence of strong institutions in Libya and probable divisions within the Libyan opposition.

Three far worse outcomes are more likely: a humiliating Western climb-down from the goals of civilian protection or regime change; a military stalemate and a de facto partition of the country between east and west, with outside forces garrisoning a rump mini-state until the situation changes; or post-Gaddafi political turmoil, with Libya at risk of becoming a failed state.

"No one starts a war—or rather, no one in his senses ought to do so—without first being clear in his mind what he intends to achieve by that war and how he intends to conduct it," noted the 19th-century military theorist Carl von Clausewitz. Bringing a war to a successful close, he said, requires a "thorough grasp of national policy." Unfortunately, at this point, such a policy is precisely what the Obama administration seems to lack.

This is why its first order of business now should be to settle on an actual goal for Libya's future order. It must decide, for example, whether Gaddafi will be allowed to stay in power under any circumstances—and if not, what local political and security arrangements will follow his departure, and who will maintain them and how. The president's address to the nation on Monday night would be an ideal opportunity to lay out such a policy publicly. But regardless of whether he does so then, the challenge will remain. Only once he establishes a target will Obama be able to aim properly and hope to finish well what he started so badly.

The Mythology of Intervention

Debating the Lessons of History in Libya

Micah Zenko

FOREIGNAFFAIRS.COM, MARCH 28, 2011

When considering how the United States should deal with persistent foreign policy problems, history can be instructive. Distorted or misremembered history, however, is dangerous. Unfortunately, in the recent debate over U.S. intervention in Libya, journalists and analysts have propagated an array of falsehoods and mischaracterizations about the United States' uses of military force since the end of the Cold War. Believing in these myths—particularly in their supposedly successful outcomes—leads to a misunderstanding of contemporary problems and to a more interventionist U.S. foreign policy.

The first myth is that the combination of NATO airpower and a Kosovo Liberation Army (KLA) ground offensive drove Serbian President Slobodan Milosevic out of Kosovo in 1999. Today, proponents of intervention in Libya, such as Max Boot at the Council on Foreign Relations and Peter Juul at the Center for American Progress, have advocated replicating this

MICAH ZENKO is a Fellow at the Center for Preventive Action at the Council on Foreign Relations. He is the author of *Between Threats and War: U.S. Discrete Military Operations in the Post-Cold War World*.

supposed success. They argue that Libyan rebel forces, fighting with close air support from Western fighter planes, could wage an effective ground offensive all the way to Tripoli and force Libya's Muammar al-Qaddafi from power.

But a U.S. Air Force review of its precision airpower campaign in Kosovo revealed a much darker picture than NATO's glowing initial assessment: 14 tanks were destroyed, not 120, as previously reported; similarly, 18 armored personnel carriers, not 220, and 20 mobile artillery pieces, not 450, were eliminated. During the campaign, the Serbian military quickly adapted to NATO's operations by constructing fake "artillery" from logs and old truck axles, and "surface-to-air missiles" made of paper.

Furthermore, the KLA failed to mount a credible and sustained opposition to the disciplined, ruthless, and better-armed Serbian ground forces. Ultimately, it was NATO's escalation of air strikes against the Serbian military and the civilian infrastructure in Serbia proper—combined with Russia's withdrawal of its support for Serbia—that caused Milosevic to capitulate.

Second, many in and outside of government, including Senator John McCain (R-Ariz.) and the diplomat and academic Philip Zelikow, have called for a so-called no-drive zone, in which Libyan armored divisions would be prohibited from any movement around the country, or at least from movement against civilian populations. They cite the successful use of such a policy by U.S. forces in Iraq after the first Gulf War. In Libya, this thinking goes, a no-drive zone could be relatively easy to set up and would neutralize Qadaffi's conventional ground capabilities and alter the military balance between the regime and rebels.

Yet there never was a no-drive zone in Iraq. In fact, in October 1994, Saddam Hussein dispatched 70,000 troops, led by two Republican Guard divisions, toward the Kuwaiti border. There, they joined six Iraqi army divisions already stationed below the 32nd parallel, the geographic marker that cordoned off the southern no-fly zone. To safeguard Kuwaiti and Saudi oil, the Clinton administration responded with Operation Vigilant Warrior, which rapidly deployed U.S. ground forces and armored equipment to the Persian Gulf. Deterred, Hussein quickly pulled his Republican Guard divisions back to central Iraq, where they stayed. In addition, UN Security Council Resolution 949 demanded the "withdrawal of all military units recently deployed to southern Iraq." Washington and London used that resolution as justification for formal diplomatic warnings to Baghdad that it could not augment its ground forces beneath the 32nd parallel. But this policy applied only to military units that arrived in the region after October 1994: in other words, although Hussein may have withdrawn his two Republican Guard divisions, six Iraqi Army divisions remained and freely attacked foes of the Baghdad regime.

Third, many military analysts, along with U.S. Senator John Kerry (D-Mass.), seem to believe that no-fly zones protect civilians on the ground. But this is often not the case. Despite the rosy memories of some interventionists, the no-fly zones over Bosnia-Herzegovina (1992–95) and northern and southern Iraq (1991–2003) failed to protect civilian populations.

In Bosnia-Herzegovina the no-fly zone went largely unenforced (with one notable exception, when NATO shot down four Serbian planes in February 1994). As Madeline Albright, then U.S. ambassador to the United Nations, wrote in her memoir: "We voted to enforce no-fly zones, but the Serbs violated them hundreds of times without paying a significant price." To a lesser degree, Croatian and Bosnian Muslim airplanes and helicopters also violated the no-fly zone. Even if it had been enforced, the no-fly zone would have been impotent against the brutal counterinsurgency attacks conducted by Serbian ground forces, which massacred 9,000 unarmed Bosnian Muslims at Srebrenica.

Within both the northern and southern no-fly zones in Iraq, Saddam's ground forces attacked any group that opposed the regime. In the south, in the years after the failed Shia uprising in 1991, Hussein initiated a brutal counterinsurgency campaign. His troops destroyed the marshlands that were part of the historical ecosystem of southern Iraq, building roadways through some so they could bring artillery within range of Shia insurgents and draining others so as to eliminate rebel hiding places. At the same time, Iraqi security forces cordoned off suspected rebel areas and controlled the movement of people. In the north, in August 1996—with the no-fly zone in full operational force—Hussein viciously put down a short-lived Kurdish uprising with 40,000 troops, 300 tanks, and 300 pieces of artillery.

Outside powers, meanwhile, routinely violated the Iraqi no-fly zones. In southern Iraq, Iranian jets penetrated Iraqi airspace to bomb camps run by Mujahideen-e Khalq (an armed, Shia, anti-Tehran opposition group), which housed both civilians and fighters. In northern Iraq, Turkish fighter planes repeatedly bombed villages suspected of harboring Kurdistan Workers' Party terrorists. According to the U.S. State Department's 2000 report on human rights, in one of these attacks, Turkish planes accidentally killed 38 civilians. As one U.S. commander of the northern no-fly zone told me: "We would fly over the Kurds in F-16s to protect the population and assure humanitarian supplies. Then the Turks would bomb the Kurds with F-16s."

The fourth myth of U.S. intervention is that NATO established a no-fly zone over Kosovo in the 1990s—which then did not stop Serbian soldiers and paramilitaries from forcibly displacing hundreds of thousands of Kosovar Albanians and killing 10,000 others. In debating a no-fly zone in Libya, commentators in *The Washington Post* and *The Wall Street Journal*, among others, invoked this supposed fact, which suggested that no-fly zones were impotent, as a reason why they would fail in Libya.

In reality, after small skirmishes between Serbian forces and the KLA in early 1998, in July and August of that year, NATO debated a number of preventive deployments—such as placing military observers in Albania and Macedonia—and more intrusive measures, including a phased air campaign and the incursion of up to 200,000 NATO troops into Kosovo. Before Operation Allied Force began on March 24, 1999, however, NATO neither debated implementing a no-fly zone over Kosovo nor did it impose one.

Lastly, many believe the myth that killing political leaders neutralizes the threat their regimes pose. Citing the recent success of unmanned drone strikes in killing suspected al Qaeda and Taliban operatives in Pakistan, many, including British Foreign Secretary William Hague, have asked, "Why don't we just assassinate Qadaffi?" Although this may appear to be an easy solution, the targeted killing of political leaders does not work.

Recent, comparable efforts to use cruise missiles or bombs to eliminate U.S. adversaries—including Qadaffi himself in 1986 and again by the British last Monday, Osama Bin Laden in 1998, Milosevic in 1999, and Saddam Hussein in 1991 and 2003—all failed. Despite the United States' intelligence capabilities, political leaders who believe they are targeted are adaptive, resilient, and hard to kill from a distance. The U.S. record of failure in this regard is even worse than the historical average. Of the 298 publicly reported assassination attempts on national leaders between 1875 and 2004, less than 20 percent were successful. Furthermore, while decapitating the leadership certainly generates confusion, the aftermath is rarely positive—as with the killing of South Vietnamese President Ngo Dinh Diem in 1963, when the United States plunged deeper into a civil war on behalf of incompetent generals in Saigon. However unpleasant a truth it may be, nothing short of a full-scale invasion can assure regime change, as shown everywhere from Grenada to Panama and Iraq to Afghanistan.

Even when accurate, historical analogies can be a double-edged sword. As Ernest May and Richard Neustadt argued in their book, *Thinking in Time: The Uses of History for Decision Makers*, well-deployed and critically examined historical references can enhance decision-making (the Kennedy administration relied on the lessons of World War II to avoid a nuclear war with the Soviet Union during the Cuban missile crisis), or degrade it (the Truman administration misunderstood Nazi and fascist expansionism, which led it to miscalculate in Korea).

In the debate over whether, and how, to intervene in Libya, opponents and proponents called on historical examples to bolster their case. Too often, these examples were historically inaccurate and were misapplied to Libya's unfolding civil war. If the legacy of recent uses of U.S. military force demonstrate anything, it is that regardless of whether the objective is to protect civilians on the ground, precipitate Qaddafi's removal from power, or stabilize a postconflict Libya, more force, time, attention, and resources will be needed than the international community has thus far proven willing to commit.

Flight of the Valkyries?

What Gender Does and Doesn't Tell Us About Operation Odyssey Dawn

Charli Carpenter

FOREIGNAFFAIRS.COM, MARCH 28, 2011

Last week, U.S. President Barack Obama decided to send fighter planes to Libya in an effort to protect civilians from the predations of Colonel Muammar al-Qaddafi. In doing so, he sided with Secretary of State Hillary Clinton, Senior Director for Multilateral Affairs Samantha Power, and UN Ambassador Susan Rice over Counterterrorism Chief John Brennan, National Security Advisor Thomas Donilon, and Secretary of Defense Robert Gates.

As a result, commentators are falling over themselves to explain the "gender divide" among Obama's staff, particularly the apparently astonishing fact that several key pro-intervention voices came from women. The Daily Beast's John Avlon claimed that the bellicosity of female presidential advisers was historically unprecedented. Invoking the dual hawk-dove/woman-man dichotomy in *The New York Times*, Maureen Dowd called the presence of strong female politicians "mythological." *The*

CHARLI CARPENTER is Associate Professor of Political Science at University of Massachusetts-Amherst and the author of two books on the protection of civilians. She blogs about human security at DuckofMinerva.blogspot.com and LawyersGunsMoneyBlog.com.

Nation's Robert Dreyfuss, meanwhile, perhaps captured the pundits' astonishment the best, writing, "We'd like to think that women in power would somehow be less pro-war, but . . . ."

These discussions reveal far more about gender misconceptions among foreign policy journalists than about the preferences or influence of Obama's female foreign policy staff. Avlon, Dowd, Dreyfuss, and others apparently subscribe to the classic gender myth that women are generally more diplomatic and opposed to war than men. This myth is widespread in the foreign policy establishment. Indeed, Francis Fukuyama, Swanee Hunt, and Isobel Coleman have all made the case for women's inherent pacifism in *Foreign Affairs* in recent years. In other forums, so have a variety of nongovernmental organizations, the United Nations Security Council, and some feminist international relations theorists, such as Betty Reardon and Sara Ruddick, who argue that women's maternal impulses translate into a greater reluctance to solve problems through armed violence.

But the wider scholarship on gender and international affairs—to say nothing of the historical record—provides plenty of evidence that thoroughly refutes the association between women and peace. In 2003, U.S. Secretary of State Condoleezza Rice pushed for war in Iraq. In 1998, U.S. Secretary of State Madeline Albright and a significant faction of U.S. feminists strongly advocated for military intervention in the Balkans. Jeane Kirkpatrick, President Ronald Reagan's foreign policy adviser and later U.S. ambassador to the United Nations, was never known for pacifist views. Nor are women associated with the "security mom" movement, which, in the wake of 9/11, harnessed maternal fears of terrorist attacks to influence elections. Their calls for a tough foreign policy to protect America's young infused former Vice-Presidential candidate Sarah Palin's rhetoric and launched women such as the conservative blogger Michelle Malkin to national prominence.

The myth of female nonviolence is also countered by studies on female violence, such as *Mothers, Monsters, Whores*, by political scientists Laura Sjoberg and Caron Gentry, and "Countering Female Terrorism," an essay by Karla Cunningham, who works as a political scientist at the RAND Corporation. In *War and Gender*, Joshua Goldstein, a professor at University of Massachusetts-Amherst, has documented the historical role of some civilian women in shaming men into war, even as other women support peace movements. Finally, the feminist writer Cynthia Enloe explained in her book *Maneuvers* how women may become complicit in war through the state militarization of the roles they play in society. Think, for example, of military wives and mothers, women who depend on jobs in munitions factories, or those who design the uniforms worn by military men and women.

Of course, it is never a good idea to make broad inferences from case studies of particular wars and historical eras, but more systematic social science studies have also shown that the "women and peace" myth is partially correct at best. Strong evidence suggests that it is not sex but gender ideology that correlates with more pacifist views. In surveys conducted throughout the Middle East, the political scientists Marc Tessler and Ina Warriner found that both men and women who generally value gender equality also generally value non-violent resolutions to international disputes such as the Palestinian conflict. And Mary Caprioli, a researcher at University of Minnesota has found that a higher level of gender inequality within a country yields a greater likelihood of militarized international disputes, even when controlling for democracy.

But all this is a far cry from claiming that women per se are likely to oppose war. Although there is a small gap in foreign policy attitudes about war between men and women in the general population—with men generally supporting war about 12 percent more often than women—it is far from cut and dry.

In a 2003 analysis of U.S.-based surveys, Richard Eichenberg, an associate professor at Tufts University, found that the "gender gap" varies considerably depending on the reason for war: women are about as comfortable as men with using force to protect civilians from atrocities, and as a group they feel more strongly about it than men do. So it is really no surprise that U.S. feminists were among those who championed intervention in Bosnia to halt mass human rights abuses in the 1990s, and that certain female politicians are among those now pushing for the protection of civilians in Libya.

But gender trends are only probabilities: they have very little to say about what policies an individual woman or man would prefer once in power, or about the extent to which she or he will succeed in pursuing those preferences. And fixation on the sex of the pro-intervention voices in this case overlooks a far more fundamental difference between the hawks and doves on the Libyan issue: in the hawks' view, the national interest included both human and national security.

And this political preference of Clinton, Rice, and Powers—which was similar to some men but different from others—is as likely a result of their professional histories as of their sex. All three moved into the foreign policy establishment through political, diplomatic, or academic circles in the late 1990s, when the idea of humanitarian intervention as being a part of protecting the national interest was nearing its heyday. Many men with the same background and social networks share their views on intervention. John Prendergast, a human rights activist, and Ramesh Thakur, a political scientist and peace researcher, have both spoken out in support of a muscular U.S. human security policy. And within the White House debate last week, Dowd's mythical Valkyries had like-minded men on their side as well, including Ben Rhodes, Obama's foreign policy speechwriter, and ultimately, the president himself, who made the final decision.

By contrast, Gates and Brennan were socialized into foreign affairs though careers in the Central Intelligence Agency during the Reagan era, when counterterrorism and nuclear deterrence took precedence over genocide prevention and the concept of human security had not yet been popularized. Perhaps as a result, they lacked personal experience with, or investment in, the "responsibility to protect" doctrine, one of the chief justifications of the Libya intervention.

Reconciling individuals' competing conceptions of the national interest is an essential part of foreign policy decision-making, not a sign of weakness on Obama's part. Of course, it will take some time for the full details behind the Libya intervention to come out, but it is likely that Obama sided with Clinton, Powers, and Rice because their way of looking at war resonated with him. Rather than being henpecked, perhaps he is simply sympathetic to the "responsibility to protect" doctrine—as he indicated when he said in his 2010 Oslo speech, "Those who claim to respect international law cannot avert their eyes when those laws are flouted," and spoke sternly about the need to rein in "those who violate international laws by brutalizing their own people." Or perhaps he was truly conflicted over intervention but judged that in the case of Libya—now a humanitarian problem, not a terrorism problem—he should assign more weight to the opinion of his UN ambassador and multilateral affairs director than to his counterterrorism specialists.

Far from being "pusillanimous," to quote the conservative radio host Bill Bennett, Obama's apparent last-minute decision may have in fact been carefully calculated to encourage Western allies to take the lead first. If his actions were meant to balance commitments to multilateralism, the protection of civilians, and a withdrawal from the role of single-handed global policeman, they may have been his savviest yet.

Of course, what gets all the attention is the supposed Amazon-woman aspect of the Obama administration's decision-making.

Ultimately, it does not matter whether a political actor is male or female; it matters whether social expectations about gender roles shape or frame policy choices. It is unlikely that the sex of these policymakers alone determined their preferences, and it is unclear if it influenced their authority in briefings with the president. It is, however, apparent that gender expectations—based on myths and stereotypes—have influenced the interpretation of these events. And if such spin damages Obama's credibility in the eyes of U.S. allies or adversaries, the responsibility is on the spin doctors, not the policymakers.

Qaddafi Must Go

Max Boot

WEEKLY STANDARD, MARCH 28, 2011

Better late than never, the United States and her allies finally have acted to stop the slaughter in Libya. With strong American, British, and French support, the United Nations Security Council on March 17 approved a Lebanon-sponsored resolution authorizing member states to use "all necessary measures . . . to protect civilians and civilian populated areas under threat of attack" in Libya.

Only hours before, Muammar Qaddafi had been issuing blood-curdling threats, promising to go "house by house, room by room" and vowing "we will have no mercy and no pity on them." Yet as soon as the U.N. resolution passed, Qaddafi's foreign minister announced an immediate cease-fire—although there were reports that offensive operations were still continuing.

Qaddafi may be a "mad dog" (as Ronald Reagan called him), but he is also shrewd and ruthless enough to have held on to power for 41 years. His ruthless streak has been on ample display in recent weeks as his armed forces have been on a rampage through rebel-held towns. Now we are seeing his pragmatic streak—the same instinct he displayed in 2003, after the U.S. invasion of Iraq, when he suddenly decided to give up his weapons of mass destruction program and support of terrorism.

MAX BOOT is Jeane J. Kirkpatrick senior fellow for national security studies at the Council on Foreign Relations.

Presumably Qaddafi realizes that overwhelming military forces are marshaling against him and that his best bet is not to provoke the American-led coalition.

But while the cease-fire, if real, is good news—it gives breathing room to the rebels in Benghazi, Libya's second city, which Qaddafi had been on the verge of assaulting—it should not lead to complacency on the part of the West and our Arab allies. We cannot be content with the current stalemate, with Qaddafi holding Tripoli and most other cities while the rebels are ensconced in Benghazi and Tobruk in the east. We do not want to divide Libya indefinitely (unless its people vote to do so). Most of all, we do not want to get into a situation like that in Iraq between 1991 and 2003, when the United States had to devote considerable resources to maintaining a no-fly zone.

The longer Qaddafi stays in power, the more suffering he can inflict on the people under his control, and the more mischief he can inflict on other countries—including the United States. He has already threatened to retaliate against "all air and maritime traffic in the Mediterranean Sea." That is no idle threat, given that in the past he has been responsible for numerous acts of terrorism, including the midair bombing of Pan Am flight 103 in 1988.

The only way this crisis will end—the only way we and our allies can achieve our objectives in Libya—is to remove Qaddafi from power. Containment won't suffice. We must make "rollback" the international strategy.

Such a goal is not compelled, but is permitted, under U.N. Security Council resolution 1973. That resolution "stresses the need to intensify efforts to find a solution to the crisis which responds to the legitimate demands of the Libyan people" and which leads to "a peaceful and sustainable solution." The Obama administration should argue that the only "peaceful and sustainable solution" would be for Qaddafi to abdicate power—as the president has already demanded (a demand he pointedly did not reiterate yesterday though he did say Qaddafi has lost "the legitimacy to lead").

Now we need to muster the will and the resources to oust the dictator. Resolution 1973 gives authority for a wide variety of actions. The only step which is explicitly excluded is "a foreign occupation force of any form on any part of Libyan territory," although it is not impossible to imagine a future U.N. resolution authorizing the dispatch of an international peacekeeping force to help Libya make the transition from Qaddafi's heinous rule. The immediate need is for the U.S., British, and French armed forces—along with, we hope, Arab allies—to unleash a devastating fusillade from the air and the sea to cripple Qaddafi's ability to threaten Libyan civilians. We should target not only his military forces but also their command and control infrastructure—including Qaddafi himself. The Libyan state is a one-man operation. Eliminate that man and the whole edifice may come tumbling down.

We should also dispatch special forces and CIA operatives to meet with the resistance and assess their needs. There is an obvious need for outside specialists to help train the rebels and to coordinate any offensive they undertake with allied forces. We saw in Afghanistan in the fall of 2001 how devastating an indigenous force can be when backed by precision American airpower directed by tactical air controllers on the ground. A similar combination should work as well in Libya's deserts as it did in Afghanistan's mountains—especially considering the fact that Qaddafi has significantly fewer supporters than the Taliban had. Few if any Libyans have been converted to the loopy gospel of Qaddafi's "Green Book." The bulk of his forces are mercenaries. It is doubtful that they will fight to the death. Many will desert once they see they are backing a losing cause.

We don't want to discount the difficulties of toppling Qaddafi. Like any other military operation, it will be filled with risks, costs, and hardships. In many ways, however, the harder issue will be cobbling together a post-Qaddafi government. The Transitional Council, under the leadership of Qaddafi's former justice minister, Mustafa Abdul Jalil, has made a good start in Benghazi. Behind the scenes, we and our allies should be working to build the most durable and democratic regime possible—while assuring Qaddafi's allies, especially in the army, that they will be welcome in the new Libya. A good start would be to recognize the Transitional Council as Libya's lawful government, as France already has done.

The passage of U.N. Security Council resolution 1973 is a step in the right direction. But it is only the beginning—not the end. Much dangerous and difficult work remains to be done to create a decent post-Qaddafi state where (in the words of the U.N. resolution) civilians will not have to fear "attacks" and "abuses."

Winning Ugly in Libya

What the United States Should Learn from Its War in Kosovo

Michael O'Hanlon

FOREIGNAFFAIRS.COM, MARCH 30, 2011

The Obama administration has come under fire for its slowness in responding to the Libyan crisis, its apparent unenthusiastic stance once it did get involved, and its desire to hand off the mission to Europeans as quickly as possible. The administration has also been criticized for failing to involve Congress in the decision-making leading up to the military operation and for its apparent failure to develop a clear road map for what to do next.

Most of these criticisms have a kernel of truth—indeed, although the mission has been effective in averting a humanitarian debacle so far, it has been ugly in some ways. But as Ivo Daalder, now the U.S. ambassador to the North Atlantic Treaty Organization, and I argued about the Kosovo war a dozen years ago in our book, *Winning Ugly: NATO's War to Save Kosovo*, an ugly operation is not the same as a failed operation. In fact, even a mission that starts off badly can turn around if policymakers start to give thought to the full range of outcomes that will be acceptable and what it will cost to achieve them. It is

MICHAEL O'HANLON is the Director of Research and a Senior Fellow of Foreign Policy at the Brookings Institution.

far too early to say for certain that Operation Odyssey Dawn will turn out as well as the 1999 war designed to stop Slobodan Milosevic's violence against ethnic Albanians in what was then the Serbian province of Kosovo. Much can still go wrong, as it did in Kosovo. But on balance, this operation is off to a far better start than that one.

In the run-up to the Kosovo war, there was less disagreement among NATO members about getting involved, although Greece was more opposed to war then than Turkey is today. Still, given Russia's opposition to using any force against its long-standing ally in Kosovo, NATO had to launch its operation without a UN Security Council resolution, which only complicated the mission at the end, when Russia unsuccessfully tried to compete with NATO for control over northern Kosovo in the postwar peacekeeping mission. And the war got off to a terrible start: rather than protecting ethnic Albanians, the initial campaign instead prompted Milosovic to intensify his pogrom against them, as he realized that the alliance had not planned a militarily effective operation. Indeed, NATO's leaders had predicted that a few days of pinprick attacks would be enough to stop the Serbian thug, and they had failed to plan for any possible escalation if they were not. Tellingly, the United States had even redeployed its only aircraft carrier stationed in the Mediterranean just a few days before initiating hostilities; keeping to the Navy's schedule for ship rotations apparently mattered more than keeping ready combat power in the region.

This time, the United States has been more careful. Both here and in Europe, military leaders have not promised that the mission would be a military cakewalk. In the U.S. debate, Daalder, Secretary of Defense Robert Gates, and Admiral Michael Mullen, the chairman of the Joint Chiefs of Staff, have all warned about the limited effectiveness of no-fly zones. Some have interpreted their statements as hedges against the possible failure of a military mission that they did not want to conduct, but the remarks should in fact be read as a combination of prudence and public education. Their statements have certainly been vindicated. The imposition of the no-fly zone has been a violent affair that has produced no quick victory despite already having gone well beyond standard procedure to include destroying much of the Libyan air force and attacking ground combat vehicles. It has so far provisionally achieved its core goal of protecting the rebels and civilians in pro-rebel areas. And although Libya's Colonel Muammar al-Qaddafi has certainly not backed down, he has not escalated his onslaught, as Milosevic did, nor has he even repeated his threats to show "no mercy" to insurgents. In both Kosovo and Libya, the United States has walked a strategic middle path between decisive force and passivity.

In both cases, the U.S. president ruled out any use of ground troops early on. That decision was likely ill-advised in Kosovo, especially when combined with the United States' other signs of irresoluteness in the war's early days, but it is probably correct in Libya, since airpower will be more potent in the country's open terrain (and is already being used to greater effect). But even though they were reluctant to commit troops, both U.S. Presidents Bill Clinton and Barack Obama felt the need to do something—Clinton because he regretted standing by early on as the conflict in Bosnia started and during the 1994 Rwandan genocide, Obama largely because he is advised by several of the same people who experienced the Bosnia and Rwanda debacles firsthand.

Yet the impulse to do something, as Colin Powell, then chairman of the Joint Chiefs of Staff, famously warned in the early 1990s, can be dangerous. Allied help, a balanced approach, and noble intentions do not necessarily add up to guaranteed victory. The Kosovo war would have been a debacle had it ended after the first month, as Milosevic drove hundreds of thousands from their homes. This scenario looked entirely possible until NATO dramatically intensified its operations and started to hint at a possible ground invasion. And the Libyan engagement, although effective so far in stemming Qaddafi's onslaught, could still produce a stalemate that leaves him temporarily in power in Tripoli and its environs. Perhaps a worse outcome would be if the United States helped the rebels just enough to keep them fighting but not enough to resolve the conflict. Libya might become a bleeding ulcer that al Qaeda could try to exploit. In war, it is not enough merely to make a good effort; a good outcome is also a necessity.

It would be preferable, of course, that Qaddafi leave. And it seems plausible that he could be driven from power partly as a result of the military operation. To raise the probability of that happening, some steps that go beyond the Kosovo precedent, including transferring defensive arms, communication gear, and logistical support to the rebels are worth considering. But in the end, Libya is not important enough and Qaddafi is probably not dangerous enough for the United States and its allies to require his unconditional surrender if it proves difficult to get. If the war seems headed for stalemate, there is a range of other outcomes that Washington could live with, just as the United States eventually lived with only achieving limited aims on the battlefield in Kosovo.

Again, that case is instructive. In Kosovo, the United States obtained its initial goal of protecting the Kosovar Albanian population, but only after it almost failed. Although the campaign is considered a success, it was initially disastrous in its net effect on the population and, in the end, came short of achieving what many would surely have preferred—Milosovic's immediate ouster. In Libya, a simple cease-fire (rather than a peace deal formalizing Qaddafi's continued role) might be acceptable. It would allow the United States to formally hew to its earlier position that Qaddafi eventually go, while recognizing that it was not in a position to make that happen immediately. Qaddafi would have to accept international monitors to observe his compliance to cease-fire lines. The rebels could pump oil from their respective parts of the country to fill their coffers; by contrast, the world might place sanctions on what Qaddafi could sell. The ultimate U.S. goal would explicitly be reunification but with an understanding that it could take months or even years to achieve that outcome, since Qaddafi's departure from the scene might be a necessary prerequisite and the United States would be using only economic, diplomatic, and legal means to achieve it.

The United States could also accept a government of national unity between the Qaddafi loyalists and the rebels that would give Qaddafi some symbolic role, provided that international monitors are allowed in the country and that loyalists in the military are removed so that Qaddafi would be less able to relaunch war. His duplicity in the 1980s, when he promised to end Libyan operations in Chad, only to resume them later, should be kept in mind, as Kenneth Pollack, the director of the Saban Center for Middle Eastern Affairs at the Brooking Institution reminded at an American Enterprise Institute talk on March 27th. Alternatively, the United States could insist that Qaddafi step down from the national government but allow him some titular role such as "mayor of Tripoli." The national government would then hold elections to replace him in perhaps one to three years.

These are not the full range of acceptable options, but they do indicate that there are end states in Libya that—however much they may make the United States and its allies hold their noses—would still be preferable to a prolonged war and another protracted occupation of an Arab land. Again, Kosovo is instructive. The United States tolerated Milosevic staying in power in Serbia after the Kosovo war, and his own people ultimately held him accountable and drove him from office some time later. Qaddafi should ultimately be unseated, either by his own people or the international community after the war. But, as with the other occasion in which the United States "won ugly" by airpower and patient diplomacy, there are reasons to hope that the United States can accomplish some of these goals over time, without insisting on achieving all of them immediately and at gunpoint. Of course, a rapid military defeat of the mad dog of the Middle East would be preferable, but it may not be possible to secure at a reasonable cost right now.

Will Libya Become Obama's Iraq?

Meghan L. O'Sullivan

WASHINGTON POST, APRIL 1, 2011

In making his case this past week for the use of force in Libya, President Obama sought to assure the American people that this intervention is prudent and wise, and that it bears no resemblance to the controversial and costly war in Iraq. He even tried to preempt the comparison altogether, explaining why his administration will not attempt to overthrow Moammar Gaddafi by force: "To be blunt," Obama said, "we went down that road in Iraq."

Message: I am not Bush, and Benghazi is not Baghdad.

Given the most obvious differences between Iraq and Libya—no ground troops in Libya and no U.N. resolution in Iraq—few will take issue with Obama's protestation. Yet, Obama's road in Libya may prove more similar to President George W. Bush's than it now appears.

For those of us who were deeply engaged in the Iraq war, it is hard not to hear the echoes and recognize the potential pitfalls

MEGHAN L. O'SULLIVAN served as President George W. Bush's deputy national security adviser for Iraq and Afghanistan from 2005 to 2007. She is now the Jeane Kirkpatrick professor of the practice of international affairs at Harvard University's Kennedy School of Government and an adjunct senior fellow at the Council on Foreign Relations.

in America's new military intervention. Despite the different circumstances, the Iraq war, and the Afghan war as well, offer hard-won insights about the nature of coalitions, the limits of military force and the power of unintended consequences. Considering them now offers us a chance to avoid repeating past mistakes in Libya, particularly ones that proved so costly to us and the people we were trying to help.

To succeed, you need clear goals.

The Bush administration went into Iraq with a multitude of objectives, from finding and destroying weapons of mass destruction to building a new democratic country in the heart of the Middle East. But even at the highest levels, U.S. officials disagreed over how central the creation of a democratic Iraq was to American ambitions and interests. This ambiguity of purpose helped create a serious dilemma: The United States undertook a complicated, multifaceted occupation and nation-building project without the planning and resources required for it to succeed.

Yet, even after Obama's speech Monday at the National Defense University, it remains unclear what the president considers an acceptable outcome in Libya. Engaging in military action and claiming a desire for regime change, yet expressing unwillingness to use force to achieve that aim, even while providing support to those seeking to oust Gaddafi—this is a recipe for confusion, both within the administration and among the public. The president's lack of clarity could erode domestic support for the operation, particularly if it grows lengthy and messy. It could also slide the administration into a more ambitious mission than is in U.S. interests or lead to Arab disappointment over a more limited American role.

Don't sell the American public on a best-case scenario.

Bush's national security team was criticized for suggesting that the invasion of Iraq would be quick, cheap and simple.

This presentation turned out to be wrong, not because the costs and difficulties of ousting Saddam Hussein by military force were higher than expected, but because the administration failed to factor in the potential difficulties of a post-Hussein Iraq and the possibility of a protracted and complicated U.S. role in the country.

Obama could be setting himself up to make the same mistake. In his Monday speech, he focused on America's role in the military intervention and appeared confident that U.S. engagement could be significantly scaled back, even before that phase of the effort is complete. There was little suggestion that a future American role could depend on what happens in the aftermath of military action. Instead, Obama's decision to commit U.S. forces seems to have been based on a cost-benefit analysis focused on the military intervention, without consideration of the likely uncertainties of a post-Gaddafi Libya.

Should unintended consequences of military action require more extensive U.S. involvement in Libya—as they did in Iraq—Obama might wish that he had better prepared the American public for the possible downsides of this intervention.

Military force alone can achieve only so much.

Ask any American—military or civilian—his or her greatest takeaway from serving in Iraq or Afghanistan, and you are likely to hear some variant of this lesson. In both cases, overwhelming U.S. military superiority created quick initial victories but did little to secure medium- and long-term objectives. Washington needed to commit much greater political and economic resources to consolidate gains and fill the vacuums created by the removals of Hussein and the Taliban.

In Libya, while military force quickly gave rebel fighters a reprieve, the current situation is neither desirable nor sustainable. Whatever the outcome of the military operation—be it a divided country or the end of the Gaddafi regime—Libya will require significant infusions of political capital and financial resources, either to sustain the rebels in their enclave or to rebuild the nation.

Don't expect local authorities to do too much too quickly.

In Iraq and Afghanistan, the United States went in with plans for rapid transfers of political power once the bad guys were gone. In Afghanistan, the United Nations was immediately to take control of the country's political future; in Iraq, the initial plan was for a quick handoff of authority to Iraqis. But in both cases, the United States was unable to move to the sidelines and instead became embroiled in the intricacies of nation-building.

On Libya, Obama has already begun speaking of a handoff to international and Libyan authorities to create a legitimate government in a post-Gaddafi nation. "While the United States will do our part to help," he said Monday, "it will be a task for the international community and—more importantly—a task for the Libyan people themselves."

Regardless of the talents of the Libyan people, they will need substantial international help. Societies that have endured decades of oppression rarely flourish quickly once the dictator is gone. In Iraq, the traumas and international isolation of the Hussein era have permeated efforts to rebuild the country, making even seemingly straightforward activities, such as choosing a new flag, complicated and painful. Certainly, Libya's reconstruction might be smoother, but if it becomes harder or more expensive than expected, Obama's pledge of limited American involvement might ring hollow. The United States may struggle to disengage from a bickering, stalemated Libya without incurring sharp criticism from the Arab world, raising doubts about its credibility as a partner or encountering new security threats that come from a weak state or a civil war in North Africa.

Security, often provided by outsiders, is needed to build sustainable political institutions.

The Bush administration spent much of the early years in Iraq believing, mistakenly, that political progress would bring security. To its credit, it revised its thinking during the strategy review that led to the troop surge that Bush announced in early 2007; the new strategy was based on the premise that local and national leaders needed some modicum of security to make tough decisions about sharing power and resources. The extreme insecurity that Iraqi citizens had experienced was the single most important factor leading to rising sectarianism and the vicious civil conflict in 2006 and 2007.

Who will provide that security for the Libyans? A country such as Egypt may have security institutions that remain legitimate and workable after a revolution or regime change, but Egypt is the exception. People rejecting decades of dictatorial rule are unlikely to accept the security forces that were the primary instruments of oppression once they have overthrown the government. Gaddafi's army, having completely discredited itself in the eyes of most Libyans, will not offer a stabilizing force should the dictator fall. A neutral, outside peacekeeping force will be needed, at least in the interim, to provide security while Libyans construct their new political future.

Coalitions require constant care and attention.

The political benefits of a coalition (particularly one involving Arab countries) are enormous in an intervention such as the one in Libya. But maintaining a wartime coalition is incredibly difficult and requires continued American leadership, especially when the operation is managed by NATO. In Afghanistan, even though countries such as Canada, Denmark and Britain have made important contributions to the war effort, the United States remains far and away the dominant force; the "handing off" of Afghanistan to NATO in 2006 arguably proved more style than substance.

The Obama administration has made much of the handover of the Libya mission to NATO oversight. Given that European governments consider Libya more vital to their interests than Afghanistan, a NATO mission in Libya may command more political backing from Europe. However, such support is unlikely to translate into more economic or military resources, simply because European countries are cutting their already modest military and diplomatic budgets, not expanding them.

Quite apart from the question of resources is the issue of alignment. Coalitions are marvelous things as long as all the parties agree on strategy. When members disagree, as the United States and Britain fundamentally did over the approach toward narcotics in Afghanistan, valuable time is lost. In Libya, Obama's open embrace of regime change—which goes beyond the ambitions expressed by the Arab League and United Nations—probably already sits awkwardly with some U.S. allies.

Don't forget the neighborhood.

At least at the outset, the Bush administration did not appreciate how fundamentally the conflicts in Afghanistan and Iraq would reshape the regional balance of power. The removal of both the Taliban and Hussein—Iran's neighbors and greatest enemies—was a major boost to Tehran and its drive for regional dominance. In retrospect, actions against Hussein and the Taliban should have been accompanied by a broader regional strategy to deal with a predictably emboldened Iran.

What unintended consequences might come from military action in Libya? How will events there ricochet elsewhere in North Africa and the Middle East? The Obama administration certainly deserves sympathy for having to deal with such remarkable events in the region in such a short period. But the quick pace of history will be no excuse for a failure to forge a regional strategy that manages and capitalizes on the ripple effects of both the Libya intervention and more homegrown transformations in the region.

Small decisions today are magnified tomorrow.

The experiences in Iraq and Afghanistan clearly demonstrate that decisions made about Libya in the next weeks and months will disproportionately affect the course of the nation for years to come. For instance, the early choice to declare Iraq a federal country allowed the Kurdish north to thrive, but it also seeded current battles over who has the authority to develop Iraq's oil and gas. Similarly, early decisions to exclude certain groups from politics—senior Baath party members in Iraq or those associated with the Taliban in Afghanistan—determined who was invested in the new states, and who would fight their emergence and consolidation.

Libya, Tunisia and Egypt cannot escape this path dependency—the ability of one decision to force history down a particular avenue. But recognizing the importance of these early choices should encourage everyone involved—whether in Washington, Europe or the Middle East—to slow down and focus more on crafting a legitimate process for decision-making than on delivering specific outcomes at this early stage.

Prepared Statement Before the Committee on Foreign Relations

Richard N. Haass

UNITED STATES SENATE, FIRST SESSION, 112TH CONGRESS HEARING ON PERSPECTIVES ON THE CRISIS IN LIBYA, APRIL 6, 2011

Mr. Chairman: Thank you for asking me to appear before this committee to discuss recent U.S. policy toward Libya. Let me make two points at the outset. First, my statement and testimony reflect my personal views and not those of the Council on Foreign Relations, which as a matter of policy takes no institutional positions. Second, I will address today's topic from two perspectives: first, the lessons to be learned from recent U.S. policy toward Libya, and second, my recommendations for U.S. policy going forward.

Analysis must be rigorous. In two critical areas, however, I would suggest that what has been asserted as fact was in reality closer to assumption. First, it is not clear that a humanitarian catastrophe was imminent in the eastern Libyan city of Benghazi. There had been no reports of large-scale massacres in Libya up to that point, and Libyan society (unlike Rwanda, to cite the obvious influential precedent) is not divided along a

RICHARD N. HAASS, formerly director of policy planning in the U.S. State Department, is president of the Council on Foreign Relations.

single or defining fault line. Gaddafi saw the rebels as enemies for political reasons, not for their ethnic or tribal associations. To be sure, civilians would have been killed in an assault on the city—civil wars are by their nature violent and destructive—but there is no evidence of which I am aware that civilians per se would have been targeted on a large scale. Muammar Gaddafi's threat to show no mercy to the rebels might well have been just that: a threat within the context of a civil war to those who opposed him with arms or were considering doing so.

Armed intervention on humanitarian grounds can sometimes be justified. But before using military force to save lives, we need to be sure of the threat; the potential victims should request our help; the intervention should be supported by significant elements of the international community; the intervention should have high likelihood of success at a limited cost, including the cost to our other interests; and other policies should be judged to be inadequate. Not all of these conditions were satisfied in the Libyan case. Such an assessment is essential if we are asking our troops to put their lives at risk, if we are placing other important interests at risk, and if we are using economic and military resources that puts our future more at risk.

Second, it was (and is) not obvious that what happened or happens in Libya would or will have significant repercussions for what happens elsewhere in the region. Libya is not a particularly influential country; indeed, Gaddafi's isolation in no small part explains why it was possible to get Arab League and UN support for a resolution supporting armed intervention. The dynamics in Syria or Bahrain or Egypt, not to mention Iran, Iraq, and Saudi Arabia, will be determined mostly by local factors and forces and not by what happens in Libya.

American policymakers erred in calling explicitly early on in the crisis for Gaddafi's removal. Doing so made it far more difficult to employ diplomacy to help achieve U.S. humanitarian goals without resorting to military force. It removed the incentive Gaddafi might have had to stop attacking his opponents. The call for Gaddafi's ouster also put the United States at odds with much of the international community, which had only signed on to a humanitarian and not a political mission when voting for UN Security Council resolution 1973. It increased the odds the intervention would be seen as a failure so long as Gaddafi remained in power. And, as I shall discuss, requiring Gaddafi's removal actually makes it more difficult to effect the implemention of UN Security Council Resolution 1973 and stop the fighting.

Multilateralism is not a reason for doing something. Multilateralism is a mechanism, no more and no less, for distributing burdens. It can add to the legitimacy of an action; it can also complicate policy implementation. Such pros and cons need to be assessed. But multilateral support does not make a policy that is questionable on its merits any less so. To think otherwise is to confuse ends and means.

Inconsistency is unavoidable in foreign policy, and in and of itself is not a reason for rejecting doing something that makes sense or for undertaking something that does not. Some humanitarian interventions may be warranted. But inconsistency is not cost free, as it can confuse the American public and disappoint people in other countries, in the process opening us up to charges of hypocrisy and double standards.

It is acceptable in principle to intervene militarily on behalf of interests deemed less than vital, but in such cases—what I would deem "wars of choice"—it must be shown that the likely costs are commensurate with the interests involved and that other policies would not have done equally well or better in the way of costs and outcomes. Otherwise, a war of choice cannot be justified.

As I expect you have gathered from what I have said here today and both said and written previously, I did not support the decision to intervene with military force in Libya. But we are where we are. So what would I suggest the United States do in Libya going forward?

We must recognize that we face a familiar foreign policy conundrum, namely, that there is a large gap between our professed goals and the means we are prepared to devote to realizing them. The goals are ambitious: protecting the Libyan people and bringing about a successor regime judged to be preferable to what now exists. But the means are limited, as the president is clearly looking to our partners in NATO to assume the major military role and has ruled out the introduction of American ground forces.

Whenever there is such a gap between ends and means, a government has two choices: it can either reduce the ends or elevate the means. The Obama administration has up till now mostly emphasized the latter course. The no-fly zone was quickly augmented by additional air operations designed to degrade Libyan government forces. This proved insufficient to tilt the battlefield decisively in favor of regime opponents.

Now there is apparent interest in arming opposition forces. I would advise against taking this path. We cannot be confident of the agenda of the opposition towards either the Libyan people or various U.S. interests, including counter-terrorism. Nor can we be certain as to which opposition elements with which set of goals might in the end prove dominant. Arms once transferred can be used for any purpose. Bad situations can always get worse.

The only way to ensure the replacement of the current Libyan regime with something demonstrably better would be through the introduction of ground forces that were prepared to remain in place to maintain order and build capacities in the aftermath of ousting the government. As we have seen in Afghanistan and Iraq, the only thing certain about such a policy trajectory is its human, economic, and military cost.

U.S. interests in Libya simply do not warrant such an investment on our part. And it is obviously far from certain whether any other outside party has both the will and the capacity to introduce ground forces on a scale likely to make a decisive military difference.

There is little reason to conclude that the Libyan opposition will any time soon be able to defeat the Libyan government. It appears to lack the requisite cohesiveness and skill. The combination of a no-fly zone, bombing, and arming might, however, have the effect of leveling the playing field and prolonging the civil war, leading to more civilian casualties in the process. This would be an ironic result of an intervention designed to promote humanitarian ends. The Libyan government may implode, but we cannot base our policy on this hope.

This all argues for reducing the immediate aims of American foreign policy and giving priority to humanitarian as opposed to political goals. This would entail undertaking or supporting a diplomatic initiative to bring about the implementation of UN Security Council resolution 1973 and, most importantly, a cease-fire. A narrow cease-fire is probably unrealistic, though. What would also be required to gain the support of the opposition would be a set of political conditions, possibly including specified political reforms and a degree of autonomy for certain areas. Sanctions could be added or removed to affect acceptance and compliance. Gaddafi might remain in office, at least for the time being. The country might effectively be divided for some time. An international force could well be required on the ground to keep the peace.

Such an outcome would be derided by some. But it would stop the civil war and keep many people alive who would otherwise perish. It would create a window for political reform and possibly over time lead to a new government without Muammar Gaddafi. The United States could use this time to work with Libyans in the opposition and beyond to help build national institutions without the added weight of ongoing fighting.

A compromise, negotiated outcome would also be good for this country, as it would allow the United States to focus its resources—economic, diplomatic, military, and political—elsewhere. Far more important than Libya for U.S. interests in the region are Egypt, Syria, Bahrain, Saudi Arabia, Iraq, Jordan, and Iran. The United States also needs to reserve resources for other parts of the world (the Korean Peninsula comes to mind), for possible wars of necessity, for military modernization central to our position in the Pacific, and for deficit reduction.

Foreign policy must be about priorities. The United States cannot do everything everywhere. This consideration would have argued for avoiding military intervention in Libya; now it argues for limiting this intervention in what it seeks to accomplish and what it requires of the United States.

Thank you for this opportunity to appear before this committee. I look forward to your questions.

What It Means and What Comes Next

Demystifying the Arab Spring

Parsing the Differences Between Tunisia, Egypt, and Libya

Lisa Anderson

FOREIGN AFFAIRS, MAY/JUNE 2011

Egyptians rose in revolt as strikes across the country brought daily life to a halt and toppled the government. In Libya, provincial leaders worked feverishly to strengthen their newly independent republic.

It was 1919.

That year's events demonstrate that the global diffusion of information and expectations—so vividly on display in Tahrir Square this past winter—is not a result of the Internet and social media. The inspirational rhetoric of U.S. President Woodrow Wilson's Fourteen Points speech, which helped spark the 1919 upheavals, made its way around the world by telegraph. The uprisings of 1919 also suggest that the calculated spread of popular movements, seen across the Arab world last winter, is not a new phenomenon. The Egyptian Facebook campaigners are the modern incarnation of Arab nationalist networks whose broadsheets disseminated strategies for civil disobedience throughout the region in the years after World War I.

LISA ANDERSON is President of the American University in Cairo.

The important story about the 2011 Arab revolts in Tunisia, Egypt, and Libya is not how the globalization of the norms of civic engagement shaped the protesters' aspirations. Nor is it about how activists used technology to share ideas and tactics. Instead, the critical issue is how and why these ambitions and techniques resonated in their various local contexts. The patterns and demographics of the protests varied widely. The demonstrations in Tunisia spiraled toward the capital from the neglected rural areas, finding common cause with a once powerful but much repressed labor movement. In Egypt, by contrast, urbane and cosmopolitan young people in the major cities organized the uprisings. Meanwhile, in Libya, ragtag bands of armed rebels in the eastern provinces ignited the protests, revealing the tribal and regional cleavages that have beset the country for decades. Although they shared a common call for personal dignity and responsive government, the revolutions across these three countries reflected divergent economic grievances and social dynamics—legacies of their diverse encounters with modern Europe and decades under unique regimes.

As a result, Tunisia, Egypt, and Libya face vastly different challenges moving forward. Tunisians will need to grapple with the class divisions manifesting themselves in the country's continuing political unrest. Egyptians must redesign their institutions of government. And Libyans will need to recover from a bloody civil war. For the United States to fulfill its goals in the region, it will need to understand these distinctions and distance itself from the idea that the Tunisian, Egyptian, and Libyan uprisings constitute a cohesive Arab revolt.

BEN ALI'S TUNISIAN FIEFDOM

The profound differences between the Tunisian, Egyptian, and Libyan uprisings are not always apparent in the popular media. The timing of the popular revolts—so sudden and almost simultaneous—suggests that the similarities these autocracies shared, from their aging leaders and corrupt and ineffectual governments to their educated, unemployed, and disaffected youth, were sufficient to explain the wave of revolutions. Yet the authorities that these young protesters confronted were unique in each nation—as will be the difficulties they face in the future.

Former Tunisian President Zine el-Abidine Ben Ali—the first Arab dictator to fall to mass protests—initially seemed an unlikely victim. Tunisia has long enjoyed the Arab world's best educational system, largest middle class, and strongest organized labor movement. Yet behind those achievements, Ben Ali's government tightly restricted free expression and political parties. In an almost Orwellian way, he cultivated and manipulated the country's international image as a modern, technocratic regime and a tourist-friendly travel destination. Beyond the cosmopolitan façade frequented by tourists lay bleak, dusty roads and miserable prospects. It is small wonder that the Islamists' claim that the government was prostituting the country for foreign exchange resonated in Tunisia.

Ben Ali's family was also unusually personalist and predatory in its corruption. As the whistleblower Web site WikiLeaks recently revealed, the U.S. ambassador to Tunisia reported in 2006 that more than half of Tunisia's commercial elites were personally related to Ben Ali through his three adult children, seven siblings, and second wife's ten brothers and sisters. This network became known in Tunisia as "the Family."

That said, although the scale of corruption at the top was breathtaking, Ben Ali's administration did not depend on the kind of accumulation of small bribes that subverted bureaucracies elsewhere, including in Libya and, to a lesser extent, Egypt. This means that Tunisia's government institutions were relatively healthy, raising the prospects for a clean, efficient, and technocratic government to replace Ben Ali.

Tunisia's military also played a less significant role in the country's revolt than the armed forces in the other nations experiencing unrest. Unlike militaries elsewhere in the Arab world, such as Egypt, the Tunisian army has never experienced combat and does not dominate the domestic economy. Under Ben Ali, it existed in the shadow of the country's domestic security services, from which Ben Ali, a former military police officer, hailed. Although its refusal to support Ben Ali's regime contributed to the country's revolution, the military has not participated meaningfully in managing the transition period and is unlikely to shape the ultimate outcome in any significant way.

Since Tunisia's protests initiated the wave of unrest in the Arab world, they were more spontaneous and less well organized than subsequent campaigns in other nations. Yet they demonstrated the power of the country's labor movement, as repeated strikes fueled protests both before Ben Ali fled and as the first short-lived successor government—soon replaced by a second one more amenable to the major unions—attempted to contain the damage to what remained of his regime.

The protests also revealed a sharp generational divide among the opposition. The quick-fire demonstrations filled with angry youth made the generation of regime dissidents from the 1980s, primarily union activists and Islamist militants then led by Rachid al-Ghannouchi, appear elderly and outmoded. Images of an enfeebled Ghannouchi returning to Tunisia after 20 years in exile in the wake of Ben Ali's ouster reflected the radical changes in the agenda of Tunisia's protest movement. Tunisians may once again prove receptive to Ghannouchi's brand of political Islam, but only if his Islamists can capture the imagination of Tunisia's young people, who are principally concerned with receiving what they see as their fair share of the country's wealth and employment opportunities. Tunisia's new leadership must therefore incorporate a generation of young people with only theoretical exposure to freedom of belief, expression, and assembly into a system that fosters open political debate and contestation. And it must respond to some of the demands, especially of the labor movement, that will feature prominently in those debates.

EGYPT'S ARMY MAKES ITS MOVE

In Egypt, Hosni Mubarak's fumbling end epitomized the protracted decline of his regime's efficacy. The government's deteriorating ability to provide basic services and seeming indifference to widespread unemployment and poverty alienated tens of millions of Egyptians, a feeling that was exacerbated by growing conspicuous consumption among a business elite connected to Mubarak's son Gamal. Yet the army's carefully calibrated intervention in the uprising indicated the continuing power of a military establishment honed by equal parts patronage and patriotism. And the protesters' political and tactical sophistication came about as a result of Mubarak's reluctant but real tolerance of a raucous and unruly press.

As it assumed control of Egypt after Mubarak's downfall, the army revealed its enormous influence in Egyptian society. The military is run by generals who earned their stripes in the 1967 and 1973 wars with Israel and who have cooperated closely with the United States since Cairo's 1979 peace treaty with Jerusalem. In contrast to the other Arab militaries that have grappled with unrest this year, the Egyptian army is widely respected by the general populace. It is also deeply interwoven into the domestic economy. As a result, the military leadership remains largely hostile to economic liberalization and private-sector growth, views that carry considerable weight within the provisional government. Thus, as in Tunisia (although for different reasons), the pace of privatization and economic reform will likely be slow, and so the emphasis of reforms will be on democratization.

Repairing decades of public-sector corrosion may also prove problematic. Everything in Egypt—from obtaining a driver's license to getting an education—is formally very cheap but in practice very expensive, since most transactions, official and unofficial, are accompanied by off-the-books payments. The government pays schoolteachers a pittance, so public education is poor and teachers supplement their salaries by providing private lessons that are essential preparation for school exams. The national police were widely reviled long before their brutal crackdowns at the inception of the January 25 revolt because they represented, in essence, a nationwide protection racket. Ordinary citizens had to bribe police officers all too ready to confiscate licenses and invent violations. The disappearance of the police during the height of the protests—considered by many Egyptians a deliberate attempt to destabilize the country—only deepened that animosity. The process of applying democratic rule of law must begin with the police themselves, meaning that the Interior Ministry will need to reestablish trust between the police and the people.

But the remarkable discipline demonstrated by Egypt's protesters and their subsequent wide-ranging debates about how to reshape their country speak to the unusually high tolerance for free expression in Egypt (by regional standards) prior to the revolution. The campaign to honor Khaled Said, the blogger killed by Egyptian police and whose death initiated the uprising, for example, would have been unimaginable in Tunisia. Egyptians were relatively well prepared to engage in serious and sustained conversations about the composition of their future government, even as they understood that, whatever the outcome, the military would not allow its institutional prerogatives to be substantially eroded.

This latent political wisdom reflects the changes that transformed Egyptian society over the last 15 years, even while the country's aging and ineffectual autocracy remained in place. As Tahrir's protesters were at pains to demonstrate, Egypt has a culture of deep communal bonds and trust, which manifested itself in the demonstrators' incredible discipline: their sustained nonviolence, their refusal to be provoked by thugs and saboteurs, their capacity to police themselves and coordinate their demands, and their ability to organize without any centralized leadership. Perhaps the finest example of this egalitarian spirit was the appearance, in communities rich and poor, of spontaneous citizen mobilizations to maintain order once the police had disengaged. All these developments should give one cause for optimism today about the new Egypt's potential to build and sustain an open society.

THE WRECKAGE OF LIBYA

Whereas demonstrators in Tunis and Cairo successfully ousted their former rulers, Tripoli collapsed into a protracted civil war. Its sustained fighting resulted from Libyan leader Muammar al-Qaddafi's four-decade-long effort to consolidate his power and rule by patronage to kin and clan. Years of artificially induced scarcity in everything from simple consumer goods to basic medical care generated widespread corruption. And the capricious cruelty of Qaddafi's regime produced widespread and deep-seated suspicion. Libyans' trust in their government, and in one another, eroded, and they took refuge in the solace of tribe and family. Libyan society has been fractured, and every national institution, including the military, is divided by the cleavages of kinship and region. As opposed to Tunisia and Egypt, Libya has no system of political alliances, network of economic associations, or national organizations of any kind. Thus, what seemed to begin as nonviolent protests similar to those staged in Tunisia and Egypt soon became an all-out secession—or multiple separate secessions—from a failed state.

Libya under Qaddafi has borne traces of the Italian fascism that ruled the country in its colonial days: extravagance, dogmatism, and brutality. In the name of his "permanent revolution," Qaddafi also prohibited private ownership and retail trade, banned a free press, and subverted the civil service and the military leadership. In the absence of any public-sector bureaucracy, including a reliable police force, kin networks have provided safety and security as well as access to goods and services. It was along such networks that Libyan society fractured when the regime's capacity to divide and rule began to unravel at the beginning of the protests. Meanwhile, Qaddafi had distributed his armed forces across a deliberately confusing and uncoordinated array of units. Some forces joined the opposition quickly but were prevented from organizing effectively or deploying sophisticated military equipment.

This lack of social and governmental cohesion will hamper any prospective transition to democracy. Libya must first restore security and introduce the law and order missing for decades under Qaddafi's regime. As daunting as that task may seem, further difficulties lie on the horizon: reviving trust across clans and provinces; reconstructing public administration; strengthening civil society through political parties, open media, and nongovernmental organizations. Libya's decades of international isolation have left the generation in its 30s and 40s—the one likely to assume leadership in a new Libya—poorly educated and ill equipped to manage the country. Others have been co-opted by the regime and stand to lose should Qaddafi fall. The challenge for Libya is both simpler and more vexing than those facing Tunisia and Egypt: Libya confronts the complexity not of democratization but of state formation. It will need to construct a coherent national identity and public administration out of Qaddafi's shambles.

THE CHALLENGES AHEAD

The young activists in each country have been sharing ideas, tactics, and moral support, but they are confronting different opponents and operating within different contexts. The critical distinctions between Tunisia, Egypt, and Libya will shape the outcomes of their respective movements. While Tunisia and Egypt grapple in their own ways with building political institutions—constitutions, political parties, and electoral systems—Libya will need to begin by constructing the rudiments of a civil society. While Egypt struggles with the long shadow of military rule, Tunisia and Libya will need to redefine the relationship between their privileged capital cities and their sullen hinterlands. Tempting as it is to treat the Arab uprisings as a single movement, their causes and future missions demonstrate the many variations between them.

These distinctions will matter for the United States and its allies. In June 2009, little more than 90 years after Woodrow Wilson's ringing endorsement of self-determination, U.S. President Barack Obama invigorated the Muslim world with his historic speech in Cairo. There, he declared that he has

> an unyielding belief that all people yearn for certain things: the ability to speak your mind and have a say in how you are governed; confidence in the rule of law and the equal administration of justice; government that is transparent and doesn't steal from the people; the freedom to live as you choose. These are not just American ideas; they are human rights. And that is why we will support them everywhere.

His proclamation did not produce this year's democratic upheavals in the Arab world, but it set expectations for how the United States would respond to them. If Washington hopes to fulfill its promise to support these rights, it will need to acquire a nuanced understanding of the historic circumstances of the uprisings. The Obama administration must encourage and rein in various constituencies and institutions in each country, from championing the labor movement in Tunisia to curtailing the military in Egypt. In each case, the United States cannot pursue the goals so eloquently identified by Obama without discarding the notion of a singular Arab revolt and grappling with the conditions of the countries themselves.

Understanding the Revolutions of 2011

Weakness and Resilience in Middle Eastern Autocracies

Jack A. Goldstone

FOREIGN AFFAIRS, MAY/JUNE 2011

The wave of revolutions sweeping the Middle East bears a striking resemblance to previous political earthquakes. As in Europe in 1848, rising food prices and high unemployment have fueled popular protests from Morocco to Oman. As in Eastern Europe and the Soviet Union in 1989, frustration with closed, corrupt, and unresponsive political systems has led to defections among elites and the fall of once powerful regimes in Tunisia, Egypt, and perhaps Libya. Yet 1848 and 1989 are not the right analogies for this past winter's events. The revolutions of 1848 sought to overturn traditional monarchies, and those in 1989 were aimed at toppling communist governments. The revolutions of 2011 are fighting something quite different: "sultanistic" dictatorships. Although such regimes often appear unshakable, they are actually highly vulnerable, because the very strategies they use to stay in power make them brittle, not

JACK A. GOLDSTONE is Virginia E. and John T. Hazel, Jr., Professor at George Mason University's School of Public Policy.

resilient. It is no coincidence that although popular protests have shaken much of the Middle East, the only revolutions to succeed so far—those in Tunisia and Egypt—have been against modern sultans.

For a revolution to succeed, a number of factors have to come together. The government must appear so irremediably unjust or inept that it is widely viewed as a threat to the country's future; elites (especially in the military) must be alienated from the state and no longer willing to defend it; a broad-based section of the population, spanning ethnic and religious groups and socioeconomic classes, must mobilize; and international powers must either refuse to step in to defend the government or constrain it from using maximum force to defend itself.

Revolutions rarely triumph because these conditions rarely coincide. This is especially the case in traditional monarchies and one-party states, whose leaders often manage to maintain popular support by making appeals to respect for royal tradition or nationalism. Elites, who are often enriched by such governments, will only forsake them if their circumstances or the ideology of the rulers changes drastically. And in almost all cases, broad-based popular mobilization is difficult to achieve because it requires bridging the disparate interests of the urban and rural poor, the middle class, students, professionals, and different ethnic or religious groups. History is replete with student movements, workers' strikes, and peasant uprisings that were readily put down because they remained a revolt of one group, rather than of broad coalitions. Finally, other countries have often intervened to prop up embattled rulers in order to stabilize the international system.

Yet there is another kind of dictatorship that often proves much more vulnerable, rarely retaining power for more than a generation: the sultanistic regime. Such governments arise when a national leader expands his personal power at the expense of formal institutions. Sultanistic dictators appeal to no ideology and have no purpose other than maintaining their personal authority. They may preserve some of the formal aspects of democracy—elections, political parties, a national assembly, or a constitution—but they rule above them by installing compliant supporters in key positions and sometimes by declaring states of emergency, which they justify by appealing to fears of external (or internal) enemies.

Behind the scenes, such dictators generally amass great wealth, which they use to buy the loyalty of supporters and punish opponents. Because they need resources to fuel their patronage machine, they typically promote economic development, through industrialization, commodity exports, and education. They also seek relationships with foreign countries, promising stability in exchange for aid and investment. However wealth comes into the country, most of it is funneled to the sultan and his cronies.

The new sultans control their countries' military elites by keeping them divided. Typically, the security forces are separated into several commands (army, air force, police, intelligence)—each of which reports directly to the leader. The leader monopolizes contact between the commands, between the military and civilians, and with foreign governments, a practice that makes sultans essential for both coordinating the security forces and channeling foreign aid and investment. To reinforce fears that foreign aid and political coordination would disappear in their absence, sultans typically avoid appointing possible successors.

To keep the masses depoliticized and unorganized, sultans control elections and political parties and pay their populations off; with subsidies for key goods, such as electricity, gasoline, and foodstuffs. When combined with surveillance, media control, and intimidation, these efforts generally ensure that citizens stay disconnected and passive.

By following this pattern, politically adept sultans around the world have managed to accumulate vast wealth and high concentrations of power. Among the most famous in recent history were Mexico's Porfirio Díaz, Iran's Mohammad Reza Shah Pahlavi, Nicaragua's Somoza dynasty, Haiti's Duvalier dynasty, the Philippines' Ferdinand Marcos, and Indonesia's Suharto.

But as those sultans all learned, and as the new generation of sultans in the Middle East—including Bashar al-Assad in Syria, Omar al-Bashir in Sudan, Zine el-Abidine Ben Ali in Tunisia, Hosni Mubarak in Egypt, Muammar al-Qaddafi in Libya, and Ali Abdullah Saleh in Yemen—has discovered, power that is too concentrated can be difficult to hold on to.

PAPER TIGERS

For all their attempts to prop themselves up, sultanistic dictatorships have inherent vulnerabilities that only increase over time. Sultans must strike a careful balance between self-enrichment and rewarding the elite: if the ruler rewards himself and neglects the elite, a key incentive for the elite to support the regime is removed. But as sultans come to feel more entrenched and indispensable, their corruption frequently becomes more brazen and concentrated among a small inner circle. As the sultan monopolizes foreign aid and investment or gets too close to unpopular foreign governments, he may alienate elite and popular groups even further.

Meanwhile, as the economy grows and education expands under a sultanistic dictator, the number of people with higher aspirations and a keener sensitivity to the intrusions of police surveillance and abuse increases. And if the entire population grows rapidly while the lion's share of economic gains is hoarded by the elite, inequality and unemployment surge as well. As the costs of subsidies and other programs the regime uses to appease citizens rise, keeping the masses depoliticized places even more stress on the regime. If protests start, sultans may offer reforms or expand patronage benefits—as Marcos did in the Philippines in 1984 to head off escalating public anger. Yet as Marcos learned in 1986, these sops are generally ineffective once people have begun to clamor for ending the sultan's rule.

The weaknesses of sultanistic regimes are magnified as the leader ages and the question of succession becomes more acute. Sultanistic rulers have sometimes been able to hand over leadership to younger family members. This is only possible when the government has been operating effectively and has maintained elite support (as in Syria in 2000, when President Hafez al-Assad handed power to his son Bashar) or if another country backs the regime (as in Iran in 1941, when Western governments promoted the succession from Reza Shah to his son Mohammad Reza Pahlavi). If the regime's corruption has already alienated the country's elites, they may turn on it and try to block a dynastic succession, seeking to regain control of the state (which is what happened in Indonesia in the late 1990s, when the Asian financial crisis dealt a blow to Suharto's patronage machine).

The very indispensability of the sultan also works against a smooth transfer of power. Most of the ministers and other high officials are too deeply identified with the chief executive to survive his fall from power. For example, the shah's 1978 attempt to avoid revolution by substituting his prime minister, Shahpur Bakhtiar, for himself as head of government did not work; the entire regime fell the next year. Ultimately, such moves satisfy neither the demands of the mobilized masses seeking major economic and political change nor the aspirations of the urban and professional class that has taken to the streets to demand inclusion in the control of the state.

Then there are the security forces. By dividing their command structure, the sultan may reduce the threat they pose.

But this strategy also makes the security forces more prone to defections in the event of mass protests. Lack of unity leads to splits within the security services; meanwhile, the fact that the regime is not backed by any appealing ideology or by independent institutions ensures that the military has less motivation to put down protests. Much of the military may decide that the country's interests are better served by regime change. If part of the armed forces defects—as happened under Díaz, the shah of Iran, Marcos, and Suharto—the government can unravel with astonishing rapidity. In the end, the befuddled ruler, still convinced of his indispensability and invulnerability, suddenly finds himself isolated and powerless.

The degree of a sultan's weakness is often visible only in retrospect. Although it is easy to identify states with high levels of corruption, unemployment, and personalist rule, the extent to which elites oppose the regime and the likelihood that the military will defect often become apparent only once large-scale protests have begun. After all, the elite and military officers have every reason to hide their true feelings until a crucial moment arises, and it is impossible to know which provocation will lead to mass, rather than local, mobilization. The rapid unraveling of sultanistic regimes thus often comes as a shock.

In some cases, of course, the military does not immediately defect in the face of rebellion. In Nicaragua in the early 1970s, for example, Anastasio Somoza Debayle was able to use loyal troops in Nicaragua's National Guard to put down the rebellion against him. But even when the regime can draw on loyal sectors of the military, it rarely manages to survive. It simply breaks down at a slower pace, with significant bloodshed or even civil war resulting along the way. Somoza's success in 1975 was short-lived; his increasing brutality and corruption brought about an even larger rebellion in the years that followed. After some pitched battles, even formerly loyal troops began to desert, and Somoza fled the country in 1979.

International pressure can also turn the tide. The final blow to Marcos' rule was the complete withdrawal of U.S. support after Marcos dubiously claimed victory in the presidential election held in 1986. When the United States turned away from the regime, his remaining supporters folded, and the nonviolent People Power Revolution forced him into exile.

ROCK THE CASBAH

The revolutions unfolding across the Middle East represent the breakdown of increasingly corrupt sultanistic regimes. Although economies across the region have grown in recent years, the gains have bypassed the majority of the population, being amassed instead by a wealthy few. Mubarak and his family reportedly built up a fortune of between $40 billion and $70 billion, and 39 officials and businessmen close to Mubarak's son Gamal are alleged to have made fortunes averaging more than $1 billion each. In Tunisia, a 2008 U.S. diplomatic cable released by the whistleblower Web site WikiLeaks noted a spike in corruption, warning that Ben Ali's family was becoming so predatory that new investment and job creation were being stifled and that his family's ostentation was provoking widespread outrage.

Fast-growing and urbanizing populations in the Middle East have been hurt by low wages and by food prices that rose by 32 percent in the last year alone, according to the United Nations' Food and Agriculture Organization. But it is not simply such rising prices, or a lack of growth, that fuels revolutions; it is the persistence of widespread and unrelieved poverty amid increasingly extravagant wealth.

Discontent has also been stoked by high unemployment, which has stemmed in part from the surge in the Arab world's young population. The percentage of young adults—those aged 15–29 as a fraction of all those over 15—ranges from 38 percent in Bahrain and Tunisia to over 50 percent in Yemen (compared to 26 percent in the United States). Not only is the proportion of young people in the Middle East extraordinarily high, but their numbers have grown quickly over a short period of time. Since 1990, youth population aged 15–29 has grown by 50 percent in Libya and Tunisia, 65 percent in Egypt, and 125 percent in Yemen.

Thanks to the modernization policies of their sultanistic governments, many of these young people have been able to go to university, especially in recent years. Indeed, college enrollment has soared across the region in recent decades, more than tripling in Tunisia, quadrupling in Egypt, and expanding tenfold in Libya.

It would be difficult, if not impossible, for any government to create enough jobs to keep pace. For the sultanistic regimes, the problem has been especially difficult to manage. As part of their patronage strategies, Ben Ali and Mubarak had long provided state subsidies to workers and families through such programs as Tunisia's National Employment Fund—which trained workers, created jobs, and issued loans—and Egypt's policy of guaranteeing job placement for college graduates. But these safety nets were phased out in the last decade to reduce expenditures. Vocational training, moreover, was weak, and access to public and many private jobs was tightly controlled by those connected to the regime. This led to incredibly high youth unemployment across the Middle East: the figure for the region hit 23 percent, or twice the global average, in 2009. Unemployment among the educated, moreover, has been even worse: in Egypt, college graduates are ten times as likely to have no job as those with only an elementary school education.

In many developing economies, the informal sector provides an outlet for the unemployed. Yet the sultans in the Middle East made even those activities difficult. After all, the protests were sparked by the self-immolation of Mohamed Bouazizi, a 26-year-old Tunisian man who was unable to find formal work and whose fruit cart was confiscated by the police. Educated youth and workers in Tunisia and Egypt have been carrying out local protests and strikes for years to call attention to high unemployment, low wages, police harassment, and state corruption. This time, their protests combined and spread to other demographics.

These regimes' concentration of wealth and brazen corruption increasingly offended their militaries. Ben Ali and Mubarak both came from the professional military; indeed, Egypt had been ruled by former officers since 1952. Yet in both countries, the military had seen its status eclipsed. Egypt's military leaders controlled some local businesses, but they fiercely resented Gamal Mubarak, who was Hosni Mubarak's heir apparent. As a banker, he preferred to build his influence through business and political cronies rather than through the military, and those connected to him gained huge profits from government monopolies and deals with foreign investors. In Tunisia, Ben Ali kept the military at arm's length to ensure that it would not harbor political ambitions. Yet he let his wife and her relatives shake down Tunisian businessmen and build seaside mansions. In both countries, military resentments made the military less likely to crack down on mass protests; officers and soldiers would not kill their countrymen just to keep the Ben Ali and Mubarak families and their favorites in power.

A similar defection among factions of the Libyan military led to Qaddafi's rapid loss of large territories. As of this writing, however, Qaddafi's use of mercenaries and exploitation of tribal loyalties have prevented his fall. And in Yemen, Saleh has been kept afloat, if barely, by U.S. aid given in support of his opposition to Islamist terrorists and by the tribal and regional divisions among his opponents. Still, if the opposition unites, as it seems to be doing, and the United States becomes reluctant to back his increasingly repressive regime, Saleh could be the next sultan to topple.

THE REVOLUTIONS' LIMITS

As of this writing, Sudan and Syria, the other sultanistic regions in the region, have not seen major popular protests. Yet Bashir's corruption and the concentration of wealth in Khartoum have become brazen. One of the historic rationales for his regime—keeping the whole of Sudan under northern control—recently disappeared with southern Sudan's January 2011 vote in favor of independence. In Syria, Assad has so far retained nationalist support because of his hard-line policies toward Israel and Lebanon. He still maintains the massive state employment programs that have kept Syrians passive for decades, but he has no mass base of support and is dependent on a tiny elite, whose corruption is increasingly notorious. Although it is hard to say how staunch the elite and military support for Bashir and Assad is, both regimes are probably even weaker than they appear and could quickly crumble in the face of broad-based protests.

The region's monarchies are more likely to retain power. This is not because they face no calls for change. In fact, Morocco, Jordan, Oman, and the Persian Gulf kingdoms face the same demographic, educational, and economic challenges that the sultanistic regimes do, and they must reform to meet them. But the monarchies have one big advantage: their political structures are flexible. Modern monarchies can retain considerable executive power while ceding legislative power to elected parliaments. In times of unrest, crowds are more likely to protest for legislative change than for abandonment of the monarchy. This gives monarchs more room to maneuver to pacify the people. Facing protests in 1848, the monarchies in Germany and Italy, for example, extended their constitutions, reduced the absolute power of the king, and accepted elected legislatures as the price of avoiding further efforts at revolution.

In monarchies, moreover, succession can result in change and reform, rather than the destruction of the entire system. A dynastic succession is legitimate and may thus be welcomed rather than feared, as in a typical sultanistic state. For example, in Morocco in 1999, the public greeted King Mohammed VI's ascension to the throne with great hopes for change. And in fact, Mohammed VI has investigated some of the regime's previous legal abuses and worked to somewhat strengthen women's rights. He has calmed recent protests in Morocco by promising major constitutional reforms. In Bahrain, Jordan, Kuwait, Morocco, Oman, and Saudi Arabia, rulers will likely to be able to stay in office if they are willing to share their power with elected officials or hand the reins to a younger family member who heralds significant reforms.

The regime most likely to avoid significant change in the near term is Iran. Although Iran has been called a sultanistic regime, it is different in several respects: unlike any other regime in the region, the ayatollahs espouse an ideology of anti-Western Shiism and Persian nationalism that draws considerable support from ordinary people. This makes it more like a party-state with a mass base of support. Iran is also led by a combination of several strong leaders, not just one: Supreme Leader Ali Khamenei, President Mahmoud Ahmadinejad, and Parliamentary Chair Ali Larijani. So there is no one corrupt or inefficient sultan on which to focus dissent. Finally, the Iranian regime enjoys the support of the Basij, an ideologically committed militia, and the Revolutionary Guards, which are deeply intertwined with the government. There is little chance that these forces will defect in the face of mass protests.

AFTER THE REVOLUTIONS

Those hoping for Tunisia and Egypt to make the transition to stable democracy quickly will likely be disappointed. Revolutions are just the beginning of a long process. Even after a peaceful revolution, it generally takes half a decade for any type of stable regime to consolidate. If a civil war or a counterrevolution arises (as appears to be happening in Libya), the reconstruction of the state takes still longer.

In general, after the post-revolutionary honeymoon period ends, divisions within the opposition start to surface. Although holding new elections is a straightforward step, election campaigns and then decisions taken by new legislatures will open debates over taxation and state spending, corruption, foreign policy, the role of the military, the powers of the president, official policy on religious law and practice, minority rights, and so on. As conservatives, populists, Islamists, and modernizing reformers fiercely vie for power in Tunisia, Egypt, and perhaps Libya, those countries will likely face lengthy periods of abrupt government turnovers and policy reversals—similar to what occurred in the Philippines and many Eastern European countries after their revolutions.

Some Western governments, having long supported Ben Ali and Mubarak as bulwarks against a rising tide of radical Islam, now fear that Islamist groups are poised to take over. The Muslim Brotherhood in Egypt is the best organized of the opposition groups there, and so stands to gain in open elections, particularly if elections are held soon, before other parties are organized. Yet the historical record of revolutions in sultanistic regimes should somewhat alleviate such concerns. Not a single sultan overthrown in the last 30 years—including in Haiti, the Philippines, Romania, Zaire, Indonesia, Georgia, and Kyrgyzstan—has been succeeded by an ideologically driven or radical government. Rather, in every case, the end product has been a flawed democracy—often corrupt and prone to authoritarian tendencies, but not aggressive or extremist.

This marks a significant shift in world history. Between 1949 and 1979, every revolution against a sultanistic regime—in China, Cuba, Vietnam, Cambodia, Iran, and Nicaragua—resulted in a communist or an Islamist government. At the time, most intellectuals in the developing world favored the communist model of revolution against capitalist states. And in Iran, the desire to avoid both capitalism and communism and the increasing popularity of traditional Shiite clerical authority resulted in a push for an Islamist government. Yet since the 1980s, neither the communist nor the Islamist model has had much appeal. Both are widely perceived as failures at producing economic growth and popular accountability—the two chief goals of all recent anti-sultanistic revolutions.

Noting that high unemployment spurred regime change, some in the United States have called for a Marshall Plan for the Middle East to stabilize the region. But in 1945, Europe had a history of prior democratic regimes and a devastated physical infrastructure that needed rebuilding. Tunisia and Egypt have intact economies with excellent recent growth records, but they need to build new democratic institutions. Pouring money into these countries before they have created accountable governments would only fuel corruption and undermine their progress toward democracy.

What is more, the United States and other Western nations have little credibility in the Middle East given their long support for sultanistic dictators. Any efforts to use aid to back certain groups or influence electoral outcomes are likely to arouse suspicion. What the revolutionaries need from outsiders is vocal support for the process of democracy, a willingness to accept all groups that play by democratic rules, and a positive response to any requests for technical assistance in institution building.

The greatest risk that Tunisia and Egypt now face is an attempt at counterrevolution by military conservatives, a group that has often sought to claim power after a sultan has been removed. This occurred in Mexico after Díaz was overthrown, in Haiti after Jean-Claude Duvalier's departure, and in the Philippines after Marcos' fall. And after Suharto was forced from power in Indonesia, the military exerted its strength by cracking down on independence movements in East Timor, which Indonesia had occupied since 1975.

In the last few decades, attempted counterrevolutions (such as those in the Philippines in 1987–88 and Haiti in 2004) have largely fizzled out. They have not reversed democratic gains or driven post-sultanistic regimes into the arms of extremists—religious or otherwise.

However, such attempts weaken new democracies and distract them from undertaking much-needed reforms. They can also provoke a radical reaction. If Tunisia's or Egypt's military attempts to claim power or block Islamists from participating in the new regime, or the region's monarchies seek to keep their regimes closed through repression rather than open them up via reforms, radical forces will only be strengthened. As one example, the opposition in Bahrain, which had been seeking constitutional reforms, has reacted to Saudi action to repress its protests by calling for the overthrow of Bahrain's monarchy instead of its reform. Inclusiveness should be the order of the day.

The other main threat to democracies in the Middle East is war. Historically, revolutionary regimes have hardened and become more radical in response to international conflict. It was not the fall of the Bastille but war with Austria that gave the radical Jacobins power during the French Revolution. Similarly, it was Iran's war with Iraq that gave Ayotallah Ruhollah Khomeini the opportunity to drive out Iran's secular moderates. In fact, the one event that may cause radicals to hijack the

Middle Eastern revolutions is if Israeli anxiety or Palestinian provocations escalate hostility between Egypt and Israel, leading to renewed war.

That said, there is still reason for optimism. Prior to 2011, the Middle East stood out on the map as the sole remaining region in the world virtually devoid of democracy. The Jasmine and Nile Revolutions look set to change all that. Whatever the final outcome, this much can be said: the rule of the sultans is coming to an end.

The Heirs of Nasser

Who Will Benefit From the Second Arab Revolution?

Michael Scott Doran

FOREIGN AFFAIRS, MAY/JUNE 2011

After a long absence, a strategic player has returned to the Middle Eastern stage: the people. In Tunisia, Algeria, Jordan, Yemen, Saudi Arabia, Egypt, Syria, Bahrain, Iran, and Libya, protesters are demanding either comprehensive reform or total revolution. Only once before in modern history has a populist wave of this magnitude swept the region.

Half a century ago, a series of Arab nationalist movements shook the ground beneath the feet of Arab rulers. The immediate catalyst for that revolutionary shock was the Suez crisis. Throughout 1955, Gamal Abdel Nasser, Egypt's charismatic leader, championed pan-Arabism, challenged Israel militarily, and mounted a regionwide campaign against the lingering influence of British and French imperialism. By the end of the year, he had aligned Egypt with the Soviet Union, which provided him with arms. After Nasser nationalized the Suez Canal in July 1956, the European powers, in collusion with

MICHAEL SCOTT DORAN is a Visiting Professor at the Robert F. Wagner Graduate School of Public Service at New York University. He is a former Senior Director for the Middle East at the National Security Council and a former U.S. Deputy Assistant Secretary of Defense.

Israel, invaded Egypt to topple him. They failed, and Nasser emerged triumphant.

Much like the ouster of Zine el-Abidine Ben Ali from Tunisia in January, the Suez crisis generated a revolutionary spark. Nasser's victory demonstrated that imperialism was a spent force and, by extension, that the Arab regimes created by the imperialists were living on borrowed time. Egyptian propaganda, including Cairo's Voice of the Arabs radio station, drove this point home relentlessly, depicting Nasser's rivals as puppets of the West whose days were numbered. Nasser was the first revolutionary leader in the region to appeal effectively to the man in the street, right under the noses of kings and presidents. Before Nasser's rivals even felt the ground shifting, they found themselves sitting atop volcanoes.

In the 18 months that followed Nasser's victory, the region underwent what can only be described as an eruption. Egypt's defeat of the French was a boon to the National Liberation Front in Algeria, which had launched a war of independence from France—with Nasser's support—even before the Suez crisis had erupted. In Jordan, popular protests, along with a Nasser-inspired movement in the military, threatened King Hussein. He managed to save his crown only by carrying out a "royal coup"—dismissing parliament, outlawing political parties, and ruling by martial law. Meanwhile, the Syrian elite splintered into numerous factions, each with its own external patron. In the summer of 1957, Turkey attempted to pull Syria away from Egypt by, among other things, massing troops on its border with Syria. Fearing a loss of influence, Nasser took drastic action: in early 1958, he unified Egypt and Syria, establishing the United Arab Republic. The sudden union roiled Syria's neighbors. In Lebanon, violence erupted between groups that favored joining the UAR, such as the Sunnis, and those that favored an independent Lebanon, such as the Maronites. Then, in July 1958, the most consequential event of all took place:

the Iraqi revolution. A Nasser-style military putsch toppled the Hashemite regime and removed Iraq from the Western camp in the Cold War.

Regimes fell and rose, countries united and fragmented, and armed conflicts erupted. Today's turmoil, then, is not unique; rather, it represents the second Arab revolution.

NASSER'S GHOSTS

Although the pan-Arab fervor of Nasser's time and the political unrest of today are similar, there are at least two obvious differences. First, the dominant ideology of Nasser's revolution, pan-Arabism, focused on external threats: gaining independence from imperialism and confronting Israel. In contrast, today's revolutionary wave is driven by domestic demands: for jobs and political representation. Second, the political upheaval of the 1950s had a leader, Nasser, who guided—or appeared to guide—events, whereas today's unrest has so far been an exercise in synchronized anarchy.

Yet the underlying ethos in both revolutions is very similar. Then, as now, the people in the street believed that the existing order was dominated by corrupt cliques that exploited the power of the state to serve their own interests. In the 1950s, popular imagination understood the unrepresentative nature of the system as an outgrowth of imperialism. Today, however, people see the problem as homegrown.

Nasser's authority was not as great as his myth might lead one to believe. In retrospect, his greatest achievement was creating an informal coalition against imperialism, which he did by aiding and abetting anti-status-quo forces that operated independently of him. Nasser quickly learned that tearing down regimes was one thing, but building a new order was another altogether. His pan-Arab movement dissolved once it had achieved its immediate aim of ousting the imperialists.

Even Syria, the one country that Nasser had managed to control directly, chafed under his domination. Before the UAR had reached its fourth anniversary, Syria withdrew and denounced Nasser's authoritarianism. For the next decade, Arab politics were more chaotic than at any point in modern history. Nasser's revolution promised unity—but it delivered fragmentation and discord.

The underlying anarchic nature of Arab politics remains a constant, as does the difficulty of finding a distinction between "domestic" and "foreign" in Arab states, particularly in revolutionary moments. Such constants suggest that today's revolution will also usher in a period of prolonged turmoil.

The balance of power between state and society is shifting. As popular participation in politics expands—and as the power of the police state recedes—two interconnected dynamics will accelerate: one, the number of politically significant actors within each state will increase; two, some of these actors will establish relationships across international boundaries. Malign and disruptive forces will benefit from this change. Transnational movements hostile to the interests of the United States—such as al Qaeda and the Muslim Brotherhood—will find fertile new fields to plow. Even more worrisome, the porousness of Arab politics will give states greater opportunities to meddle in the affairs of their neighbors. This will take many forms: indirect cultivation of constituencies located across frontiers, the formation of loose networks of direct association, overt construction of proxies (on the model of Iran and Hezbollah), and covert sponsorship of terrorism. Considerable friction will result. Years will pass before a stable order emerges.

VIVE LA RÉSISTANCE BLOC

In navigating the Arab world's ongoing turmoil, the United States must determine the central principles that will guide the building of a stable, new order. One perspective sees the enlargement of political participation as the key step, arguing, therefore, that democracy promotion should become the touchstone of the United States' regional strategy. Another eschews overarching principles entirely, instead pointing to the complexity of the region and advocating a pragmatic, country-by-country approach. Yet a third view sees Arab-Israeli peace as the essential first step to revitalizing the U.S.-led order in the region.

As it considers these competing paradigms, the Obama administration should remember that it is not the only actor attempting to shape the turmoil. Although there is no one personality like Nasser towering above the revolutionary events, there is one state seeking to reprise Egypt's historic role: Iran. Under Nasser, Egypt opposed British and French imperialism, which it associated with Israel. Iran is taking a similar stand today against the United Kingdom's "imperial successor": the United States. And like Nasser, Iran has created an anti-status-quo coalition—made up of itself, Syria, and their proxies, Hezbollah and Hamas. The DNA of Nasserism is certainly recognizable in the "resistance bloc" of Iran and its allies; Nasserist genes may have commingled with pan-Islamism, but the resemblance is nevertheless unmistakable. Iran, of course, is neither Arab nor Sunni. One might expect its Persian and Shiite identity to prevent it from emulating Nasser, especially in a region where Sunni Arabs predominate and where identity politics remains significant. Tehran, however, has managed to surmount this disability, thanks in part to the fact that each member of the resistance bloc represents a different ethnoreligious identity, which allows it to present a distinctive and familiar face to radically different constituencies.

The insurgency in Iraq, which reached its height in 2006, provides an instructive example of how Tehran and Damascus divide their labor along ethnoreligious lines. In Iraq, they manipulated Sunni and Shiite Islamist networks—groups that, if left to their own devices, would never have cooperated with each other. Yet the resistance bloc turned them into synchronized fists attached to a single body. Damascus constructed a covert pipeline of foreign fighters, pushing al Qaeda suicide bombers into the Sunni regions of Iraq, where they provided the human ammunition in a sectarian war. Al Qaeda's attacks pushed the Shiite Iraqis toward the patronage of Shiite Iran. Meanwhile, Tehran used the Iranian Quds Force (and, perhaps, Hezbollah) to provide Shiite militias with lethal assistance, including the training and material necessary to deploy the explosively formed penetrator, an armor-piercing, remote-activated roadside bomb that killed more U.S. soldiers than any other weapon in Iraq.

With this one-two, Sunni-Shiite punch, the resistance bloc pummeled the United States and the new Iraq. Of course, Tehran and Damascus never proclaimed this strategy publicly. On the contrary, they denied the accusations of their cooperating with al Qaeda and manipulating Iraqi politics. Even as they visited carnage on their Iraqi neighbor, their propaganda was blaming the bloodshed on the United States, which, they claimed, was using democracy promotion as a cover for slaughtering Muslims.

Beneath the surface, the seemingly random violence in Iraq was a shadow war between two alliances: the status quo system, led by the United States, which seeks to stabilize the region under its hegemony by building more consensual political systems, and the anti-status-quo alliance, led by Iran, which seeks to wear down this U.S.-led effort. The struggle between the two is asymmetric. Iran, regardless of its propaganda, does not think it can compete with the United States—but it does believe that it can exhaust it.

Iran's exhaustion strategy relies on the inherent anarchy of the Middle East. The shadow war in Iraq was thus a prelude to an impending regional contest. As the revolutionary wave expands political participation, the resistance bloc will insinuate itself into the politics of many different Arab states. In countries divided along ethnic, tribal, or sectarian lines, such as Iraq, it will use terrorism and will search for partners on the ground that are willing to make direct alliances. In more homogeneous and stable countries, such as Egypt, it will resort to more subtle and insidious means—for example, inciting violence against Israel.

ALL ROADS RUN THROUGH JERUSALEM

Over the years, Iran has injected itself into the Arab-Israeli conflict as a way of projecting its power and influence into Arab societies and, importantly, as a way of undermining American prestige. As such, hostility to Israel has become the bread and butter of Iran and its allies in the resistance bloc.

To understand the role of the Israeli question in Iran's asymmetric regional contest with the United States, it is useful to borrow a word from Arabic: *tawreet*, which translates as "embroiling." You embroil someone by goading him to take actions against a third party that will result in political effects beneficial to you.

Nasser was a master of *tawreet*. For example, in the mid-1950s, Egypt, without the knowledge of King Hussein and his government, launched terrorist attacks from Jordanian territory against Israel. The goal of these strikes was not to tip the balance against Israel; instead, Nasser sought to drive a wedge between Jordan and the United Kingdom, Egypt's primary strategic rival. At the time, the United Kingdom subsidized the Jordanian army, whose officer corps, led by Sir John Bagot Glubb, was staffed primarily by British soldiers. Israel responded with massive retaliation, countering the terrorism with brutal reprisal raids. With each Israeli operation, Jordanian public opinion grew increasingly agitated—precisely the result Nasser had hoped to achieve. Meanwhile, his Voice of the Arabs radio station stirred the pot, accusing King Hussein of being a puppet of the United Kingdom, the supposed ally of Israel. What good, the Egyptian broadcasts asked, was a British-led military if it protected the Israelis and divided the Arabs? Before long, Jordanian public opinion became so inflamed that King Hussein had no choice but to dismiss the British officers and terminate the special relationship. The blow to the United Kingdom's prestige was enormous: if Jordan, a client state, could expel the British, bag and baggage, then they were truly finished in the region. Egypt had won a major strategic victory.

In those days, it was the United Kingdom that guaranteed the security of Arab countries. Today, it is the United States—and the conditions are once again ripe for *tawreet*, especially in Egypt. The resistance bloc is clearly thinking along similar lines. Consider, for example, the Hezbollah plot foiled by Egypt's security services in 2009. Hezbollah had constructed a clandestine network in the Sinai and planned to attack Israeli targets on Egyptian soil. Given the organic connection between Hezbollah and the Iranian Quds Force, the plot should be read as part of an Iranian regional strategy.

The resistance bloc's behavior during Israel's war with Hezbollah in 2006 and its invasion of Gaza in December 2008 demonstrates how the bloc will exploit the next round of violence. In these past conflicts, it ridiculed the Arab leaders aligned with the United States. For example, in a famous speech in August 2006, Syrian President Bashar al-Assad called the rulers of Egypt, Jordan, and Saudi Arabia "half men" for failing to support Hezbollah out of their supposedly servile attitude toward the United States and Israel. Meanwhile, during both conflicts, Arab media outlets under the control or influence of the resistance bloc inflamed public opinion by broadcasting gruesome scenes of suffering women and children. During

Israel's incursion into Gaza, the bloc heaped special vitriol on Egyptian President Hosni Mubarak, who tacitly supported Israel's actions, not least of all by refusing to open the border crossing to Egypt. Although the bloc depicted him as a puppet of the Jews, he stood firm.

Faced with the accountability of the democratic process, Egypt's new rulers will not feel nearly as free as Mubarak did to side with Washington and Jerusalem when the next round of conflicts involving Israel erupts. In the post-Mubarak era, the resistance bloc has a new weapon: the Egyptian crowd, which is now freer than before to organize on its own. Renewed violence will undoubtedly spark massive street demonstrations, not only in Egypt but also in Iraq, Jordan, and Saudi Arabia. But it is in Egypt where the bloc will concentrate its energies, providing the Muslim Brotherhood and similar groups with a pretext for organizing the mob and casting themselves as the conscience of the Egyptian people. They will demand that the military sever all ties with Israel and the United States—and it is far from certain whether Egypt's insecure army officers will have the mettle to withstand the campaign.

Tehran and Damascus view post-Mubarak Egypt as a chunk of the United States' security architecture that has broken loose from key moorings. With a little effort, they believe, it can now be severed entirely. Arab-Israeli violence would help—either by undermining the Egyptian-Israeli peace treaty, by complicating U.S.-Egyptian cooperation, or simply by increasing the power of the Muslim Brotherhood and like-minded groups in Egypt.

EMBROILING POINT

In navigating the crosscurrents of Middle Eastern politics, policymakers in Washington must remember the fundamental interests of the United States: ensuring the uninterrupted flow of oil at stable and reasonable prices; blocking the proliferation of weapons of mass destruction; protecting key allies, especially Egypt, Israel, and Saudi Arabia; countering terrorism and political violence; and promoting democratic reform in a way that bolsters the U.S.-led order in the region.

The resistance bloc opposes Washington on almost every item. It has built an alliance that advocates expelling the United States from the Middle East and undermining U.S. allies across the region. Iran and Syria are two of the most egregious state sponsors of terrorism: Tehran provides weaponry to the Taliban, and Damascus has covertly given al Qaeda use of its territory, from which it conducted a terror campaign in Iraq. Both regimes openly support Hamas. In defiance of the international community, they have built up Hezbollah's military capability to such an extent that it now possesses a missile arsenal and a covert operations capability that rival those of most states in the region. Beyond all this, Iran is universally assumed to be developing a nuclear weapons program in defiance of numerous UN Security Council resolutions. Collectively, then, the bloc represents the single greatest threat to U.S. interests in the Middle East. Therefore, one might expect Washington to adopt a containment strategy, as it did with respect to the Soviet Union during the Cold War. Such an approach would entail, among other things, renouncing engagement of Iran and Syria and seeking to build an international coalition against them. In addition, it would call for subordinating all other major regional initiatives to the overarching goal of containment.

Yet the Obama administration has rejected this strategy. Why? For one, the immediate danger does not appear to justify such an elevated effort. Both Iran and Syria at times have the appearance of sclerotic regimes, deeply vulnerable to the democratic revolution sweeping the region. Unlike the Soviet Union, the resistance bloc hardly constitutes a serious conventional threat. It does not endanger the supply of oil, and it certainly does not threaten the West with global war. In addition, the bloc is less cohesive than the Soviet Union and its allies were. Tehran's influence over Syria, Hezbollah, and Hamas does not resemble the iron grip with which Moscow controlled its satellites. To treat them as components of a cohesive unit assumes that the divisions between the members of the bloc are less important than the ties that bind them. Containing Iran, the White House argues, would actually force allies of Tehran deeper into its embrace. With a more nuanced policy, Washington could entice them away.

To this end, the Obama administration has made the Arab-Israeli peace process the organizing principle of its Middle East policy. In June 2009 in Cairo, when President Barack Obama delivered his most important statement on U.S. Middle East policy to date, he envisioned the United States as an honest broker, mediating between the Arabs and Muslims and the Israelis. "I have come here to seek a new beginning between the United States and Muslims around the world," he said. A major cause of tension between the two, he explained, was "the situation between Israelis, Palestinians, and the Arab world." Obama, clearly, was seeking to demonstrate American goodwill. As a result, the peace process grew into something much bigger than just a practical tool for normalizing relations between Israel and its neighbors. It became a litmus test of the United States' intentions toward Arabs and Muslims around the world. Of course, it would certainly be desirable if the peace process delivered tangible results. But the White House has created an environment in which the peace process cannot be abandoned. Even if it fails, it must continue to exist in order to demonstrate the United States' goodwill.

From the outset, the Obama administration has believed in the importance of pursuing a "comprehensive" settlement—meaning a peace treaty that includes not just the Palestinians but, in addition, all the Arab states, especially Syria. As the administration has failed to make any headway in

Israeli-Palestinian negotiations, the Syrian track has grown in importance. Consequently, Washington has chosen to treat Syria not as an adversary deserving containment but rather as a partner in the negotiations deserving of engagement. In fact, the Obama administration sees the peace process as an instrument for wooing Syria away from Iran. At the very least, Washington believes that by bringing Damascus to the negotiating table, it can give the Syrians an incentive to tamp down Arab-Israeli violence. But such a strategy fails to acknowledge that the Syrians understand the thinking in Washington all too well—they recognize the United States' fervent desire for negotiations and see in it an opportunity to bargain. Damascus seeks to trade participation in diplomatic processes, which costs it nothing, for tangible benefits from Washington, including a relaxation of U.S. hostility. In short, the Syrians believe that they can have it both ways, reaping the rewards of *tawreet* without being held to account. And why would they think otherwise? After all, nobody held them responsible for similar double-dealing in Iraq, where they were accomplices to the murder of Americans.

THE RETURN OF THE MEN WITH GUNS

As the United States seeks to build a new order in the Middle East, it is worth remembering what happened in the course of the last Arab revolution. Like Obama, U.S. President Dwight Eisenhower came to power intent on solving the Arab-Israeli conflict in order to line up the Arab world with the United States. Together with the United Kingdom, Eisenhower focused on brokering an Egyptian-Israeli agreement. Nasser, like Damascus today, played along, while simultaneously turning up the heat on the Israelis, working to oust the British, and sparking a regionwide revolution. By 1958, the United States' position had grown so tenuous that Eisenhower felt compelled to send U.S. troops to Lebanon, lest one of the last overtly pro-U.S. regimes in the region fall to Nasser-inspired forces.

This is not to say that the resistance bloc is poised to mimic Nasser's achievements in every respect. The comparison is not entirely symmetrical. In some countries, the United States faces a perfect Nasserist storm. In Bahrain, for instance, a Shiite majority—which the Bahraini authorities claim is influenced by Tehran—threatens an unrepresentative, pro-U.S. regime that provides Washington with a valuable strategic asset, basing rights for the Fifth Fleet. In Bahrain, Iran wins no matter what: If the state violently represses the Shiite majority, as it has, Tehran can plausibly claim that it did so at the behest of the United States. And if the protesters topple the regime, Iran can work to shape the new order. But in other countries, such as Egypt, Libya, and Tunisia, Iran has little or no influence over events, which are clearly spinning on their own independent axis.

Although the resistance bloc may not be as influential as Nasser was, it is nevertheless poised to pounce, jackal-like, on the wounded states of the region. Moreover, it has already proved itself capable of mounting an effective asymmetric challenge that should not be underestimated. Over the last five years, it has defied the United States on a number of critical fronts. Despite eight years of effort by Washington and its allies, Tehran continues to move toward a nuclear weapons capability. In addition, it has developed a credible deterrent to any conventional attack against its nuclear infrastructure, thanks to a diverse set of covert and overt capabilities in Lebanon, Gaza, Iraq, the Persian Gulf, and Afghanistan. In Lebanon, Hezbollah recently took effective control of the government, and the resistance bloc depicted this development, correctly, as a defeat for U.S. policy. In Iraq, the combined covert efforts of Iran and Syria prolonged the war and cost both Washington and Baghdad considerable blood and treasure. Finally, in the last half decade, both Hamas and Hezbollah have ignited major conflicts with Israel that have complicated relations between the United States and its Arab allies. The resistance bloc will certainly continue this effort, working to shape the emerging regional order to its benefit and to the detriment of the United States. And it will do so with a deceptiveness, a ruthlessness, and an intensity of focus that the United States—a distracted Gulliver—cannot match.

The most important arena in the months and years ahead, therefore, is the struggle for regional hegemony. Many U.S. interests will be threatened by conflicts that, at first glance, will appear unrelated to the future of the United States' position in the region. If Washington is to minimize the pain of the transition to a new order, it must remain focused, amid all the turmoil, on the sophisticated asymmetric threat that the resistance bloc presents. Yet the United States must remember that this hegemonic struggle is not the central force behind the unrest coursing its way through the region. The second Arab revolution may not have a charismatic leader, like Nasser, but it does have a representative figure who expresses the core aspirations of the revolutionaries: Mohamed Bouazizi, the 26-year-old Tunisian fruit vendor who set himself on fire out of despair and frustration with the state's corruption and caprice. The widespread influence of Bouazizi's desperate cry for justice and dignity should stand as a sharp reminder for Washington: for all that the struggle with the resistance bloc is about power politics, the emphasis must be on politics as much as on power. However vital the struggle for regional hegemony is to Washington, it is certainly not the central concern to the people who are protesting in the streets.

A call for justice and dignity also drove the first Arab revolution. The fact that a military man—Nasser—symbolized those aspirations in the 1950s speaks volumes about the pan-Arab movement, which, in the end, was hijacked by men with guns.

In Bouazizi, the second revolution has chosen as its representative an entirely different kind of personality. His selection, too, speaks volumes, but the precise meaning of the message is ambiguous. As a humble fruit vendor who wanted nothing more than a fair shake in life, Bouazizi could symbolize the triumph of the human spirit. On the other hand, Bouazizi died a broken man. The men with guns are only hiding in the shadows, and they may yet play a decisive role in fashioning the new Middle East.

The Rise of the Islamists

How Islamists Will Change Politics, and Vice Versa

Shadi Hamid

FOREIGN AFFAIRS, MAY/JUNE 2011

For decades, U.S. policy toward the Middle East has been paralyzed by "the Islamist dilemma"—how can the United States promote democracy in the region without risking bringing Islamists to power? Now, it seems, the United States no longer has a choice. Popular revolutions have swept U.S.-backed authoritarian regimes from power in Tunisia and Egypt and put Libya's on notice. If truly democratic governments form in their wake, they are likely to include significant representation of mainstream Islamist groups. Like it or not, the United States will have to learn to live with political Islam.

Washington tends to question whether Islamists' religious commitments can coexist with respect for democracy, pluralism, and women's rights. But what the United States really fears are the kinds of foreign policies such groups might pursue. Unlike the Middle East's pro-Western autocracies, Islamists have a distinctive, albeit vague, conception of an Arab world that is confident, independent, and willing to project influence beyond its borders.

SHADI HAMID is Director of Research at the Brookings Doha Center and a Fellow at the Saban Center for Middle East Policy at the Brookings Institution.

There is no question that democracy will make the region more unpredictable and some governments there less amenable to U.S. security interests. At their core, however, mainstream Islamist organizations, such as the Muslim Brotherhood in Egypt and Jordan and al Nahda in Tunisia, have strong pragmatic tendencies. When their survival has required it, they have proved willing to compromise their ideology and make difficult choices.

To guide the new, rapidly evolving Middle East in a favorable direction, the United States should play to these instincts by entering into a strategic dialogue with the region's Islamist groups and parties. Through engagement, the United States can encourage these Islamists to respect key Western interests, including advancing the Arab-Israeli peace process, countering Iran, and combating terrorism. It will be better to develop such ties with opposition groups now, while the United States still has leverage, rather than later, after they are already in power.

SMART POLITICS

The Middle East's mainstream Islamist movements, most of which are branches or descendants of the Egyptian Muslim Brotherhood, began as single-issue parties, preoccupied with proselytizing and instituting sharia law. Beginning in the 1990s, however, for various reasons in each case, they increasingly focused on democratic reform, publicly committing themselves to the alternation of power, popular sovereignty, and judicial independence. That said, Islamists are not, and will not become, liberals. They remain staunch social conservatives and invariably hold views that most Americans would find distasteful, including that women's rights should be limited and the sexes segregated. Given the chance, they will certainly try to pursue socially conservative legislation.

Yet to the consternation of their own conservative bases, the region's mainstream Islamist groups have also shown considerable flexibility on core ideological concerns. Despite popular support in the Arab world for the implementation of sharia, for example, many Islamist groups, including the Egyptian Muslim Brotherhood, have gradually stripped their political platforms of explicitly Islamist content. In the past few years, instead of calling for an "Islamic state," for example, the Muslim Brotherhood began calling for a "civil, democratic state with an Islamic reference," suggesting a newfound commitment to the separation of mosque and state (although not of religion and politics). This move seems to have been deliberately aimed, at least in part, at alleviating international fears; with the goal of improving its image, moreover, the group launched an internal initiative in 2005 called Reintroducing the Brotherhood to the West.

When it comes to foreign policy, mainstream Islamists have rhetorically retained much of the Muslim Brotherhood's original Arab nationalism and anti-Israel politics. Today's Egyptian and Libyan Muslim Brotherhoods and Tunisia's al Nahda refuse to recognize Israel's right to exist and call for the liberation of all of historic Palestine. They also view Hamas not as a terrorist group but as a legitimate force of resistance.

Still, Islamist groups did not create the anti-Israel sentiment that exists in Arab societies; they simply reflect and amplify it. In a 2005 Pew Global Attitudes poll, 100 percent of Jordanians polled were found to hold unfavorable views of Jews. In Morocco, home to the Arab world's largest Jewish community, the figure was 88 percent. The Middle East provides such fertile ground for public posturing against Israel that many groups—not only Islamists but also leftists and nationalists—seek to outdo one another in demonstrating their dislike for Israel.

A country's physical proximity to the Israeli-Palestinian conflict informs how aggressive such posturing is. It is no accident that Jordan's Islamic Action Front—the political arm of the Jordanian Muslim Brotherhood—is one of the more vehemently anti-Israel Islamist groups in the Arab world, given that a majority of the Jordanian population is of Palestinian origin. Unlike many of its counterparts, the IAF still uses religious language to frame the conflict; in its 2007 electoral platform, the party affirmed that the conflict between the Israelis and the Palestinians is "theological and civilizational," and not one of borders or territories, as many groups now frame it. The IAF's so-called hawks, who tend to be of Palestinian origin, advocate even closer ties with Hamas. In Algeria and Tunisia, by contrast, Palestine ranks much lower as a priority for local Islamists.

FROM SHADOW TO STAGE

Although most Islamist groups share a broadly similar ideology, their expression of it has differed depending on their unique domestic and regional constraints and whether the group happens to be included in government. When a group is not included in government, and the ruling elite is unpopular and generally pro-Western, Islamists are more likely to define themselves in opposition to the government's policies to garner support.

Taking a hard line against Israel, for example, has been an effective way for Islamists in opposition to criticize regimes that they see as beholden to Western interests and antidemocratic. For example, before Jordan's 2007 parliamentary elections, the IAF released a statement arguing that freedoms in Jordan had diminished after Amman signed a peace treaty with Israel in 1994. Their attempt to connect pro-Israel policy with a loss of freedom was convincing, because it happened to be true. In 1989, before the treaty, Jordan had held free elections for the first time in decades, and Islamists and nationalists won a majority of the seats. But with peace with Israel on the horizon in the early 1990s, the king grew increasingly more autocratic, dismissing the parliament and enacting a new electoral law designed to limit Islamists' power at the polls.

As political systems across the Middle East open up, Islamist groups such as the Egyptian Muslim Brotherhood and al Nahda will likely try to move from the opposition into coalition or unity governments. During the euphoria of the democratic transition, new political parties—perhaps including Salafi groups that are more hard-line than the older Islamist organizations—will proliferate. As the parties compete for votes, the incentives for Islamists to indulge in anti-American posturing to win the votes of the faithful may be greater.

Once actually in government, however, a new set of constraints and incentives will prevail. Rather than ruling, Islamists will likely be partners in coalition or national unity governments. Indeed, none of the Islamist groups in question even plans to run a full electoral slate; the Egyptian Muslim Brotherhood, for example, has explicitly stated that it will not seek a parliamentary majority. Islamists will be satisfied with dominating narrower parts of the government. They are likely to try to gain influence in ministries such as health and justice, while avoiding more sensitive portfolios, such as defense and foreign affairs.

Notably, the Middle East's generally secular security establishments have been hesitant in the past to hand over control of defense and foreign affairs to Islamists. Consider, for example, Necmettin Erbakan, the former leader of Turkey's Welfare Party, who was elected prime minister in 1996, making him the first-ever democratically elected Islamist head of government anywhere. Before coming to power, Erbakan had routinely denounced Israel and pledged to revisit existing military arrangements with the Jewish state. Yet once in office and faced with a powerful secular military and judicial establishment, he reversed course. During his one year in office, Erbakan presided over a deepening of relations with Israel and signed military agreements that allowed Israeli pilots to train in Turkish airspace. His government also set up joint naval drills with Israel in the Mediterranean.

Moreover, mainstream Islamist groups are surprisingly sensitive to international opinion. They remember the outcry that followed Islamist electoral victories in Algeria in 1991 and the Palestinian territories in 2006 and know that a great deal is at stake—hundreds of millions of dollars of Western assistance, loans from international financial institutions, and trade and investment. Islamists are well aware that getting tied up in controversial foreign policy efforts would cause the international community to withdraw support from the new democracies, thus undermining the prospects for a successful transition.

That is why, for example, in 2003, although Turkey's staunchly secular Republican People's Party overwhelmingly voted against supporting the U.S.-led war in Iraq, most of the ruling Islamist-leaning Justice and Development Party voted for it: the Bush administration exerted heavy pressure and offered billions of dollars in aid. And even Hamas—still regarded as the most radical of the mainstream Islamist groups—tempered its policies toward Israel after its 2006 electoral victory, saying it would accept the 1967 borders between Israel and the Palestinian territories.

For similar reasons, even before coming to power, some officials in the Egyptian and Jordanian Muslim Brotherhoods have explicitly stated that they would respect their countries' peace treaties with Israel (although others have threatened to leave the organization if it ever recognizes Israel). Despite the recent alarm, if Islamists join a coalition government in Egypt, moderation will likely prevail, and the country's 1979 Camp David peace agreement with Israel will be accepted, however reluctantly, as a fact of life.

ACCIDENTALLY ALIGNED

Islamist and U.S. interests can come together almost incidentally as well. The Syrian Muslim Brotherhood—brutally repressed by President Hafez al-Assad in the 1980s—has long shared U.S. fears of a powerful Iranian-Syrian-Hezbollah axis. Its opposition to the Syrian regime is well documented; the government made mere membership in the Brotherhood punishable by death. Like the United States, the group has often criticized Iran as a dangerous sectarian regime intent on projecting Shiite influence across the Arab world. Defying public opinion, Syrian Muslim Brotherhood figures even criticized Hezbollah for provoking Israel to attack Lebanon in 2006.

Similarly, the Lebanese Muslim Brotherhood, known as al-Gama'a al-Islamiyya, has opposed Syria and Hezbollah's role in Lebanon and allied itself with the pro-U.S. March 14 alliance. Elsewhere, mainstream Sunni Islamists, while applauding Iran's support of Palestinian resistance, have been careful to maintain their distance from the Shiite clerical regime, which they see as a deviation from traditional Islamic governance.

This is not to say that the United States has nothing to be concerned about. Democratic governments reflect popular sentiment, and in the Middle East, this sentiment is firmly against Israel and U.S. hegemony in the region. If the Arab-Israeli conflict persists or, worse, war breaks out, Middle Eastern governments—Islamist or not—will come under pressure to take a strong stand in support of Palestinian rights.

In mature and young democracies alike, such pressure can be difficult to resist. The case of Jordan in the early 1990s is worth considering. In 1991, the Muslim Brotherhood, which had won a plurality of the vote in the 1989 elections, gained control of five ministries, including education, health, justice, religious affairs, and social development, as part of a short-lived coalition government. (This marked the first time—and one of the only times—the Brotherhood has held executive power anywhere in the world.) When, in late 1990, the United States began preparing to take military action against Saddam Hussein in response to his invasion of Kuwait, Jordan's parliament condemned the Western aggression and intensified its pressure on King Hussein to oppose the U.S. intervention—which he did, despite the obvious international consequences. For its part, the Muslim Brotherhood—a staunch opponent of Saddam's secular regime—at first spoke out against the Iraqi aggression and expressed full support for Kuwait. But as Jordanians took to the streets to protest the war, the Brotherhood reversed course, riding the wave of anti-Americanism to even greater popularity.

THE ISLAMIST EXPERIMENT

So what does all of this mean for Tunisia, Egypt, and other countries facing popular upheaval? Like many others, Muslim Brotherhood activists in Egypt's Tahrir Square broke into applause when, on February 1, U.S. President Barack Obama called for a meaningful and immediate transition to genuine democracy in Egypt. Numerous Muslim Brotherhood members even said they wished the Obama administration would more forcefully push for Hosni Mubarak's ouster. Meanwhile, Sobhi Saleh, the only Brotherhood member on the country's newly established constitutional committee, told *The Wall Street Journal* that his organization was "much closer to the Turkish example," suggesting that the Brotherhood would evolve in a more pragmatic, moderate direction.

For their part, the Western media have tended to idealize the revolutions sweeping the Middle East. Tahrir Square was portrayed as a postideological utopia and Egyptians as pro-American liberals in the making. True, Egyptians (and Tunisians and Libyans) have wanted democracy for decades and showed during their revolution a knack for protest, peaceful expression, and self-governance.

But for all the changes of the past months, the United States remains a status quo power in a region undergoing radical change. Arabs across the region have been protesting an authoritarian order that the United States was, in their view, central in propagating. At their core, the revolutions sweeping the Middle East are about dignity and self-determination. For the protesters, dignity will mean playing a more active and independent role in the region. The moment of apparent convergence between Islamists and the United States during the revolutions does not mean that they will—or should—agree on all foreign policy questions in the future.

During the uprisings, the protesters have sensed that U.S. pressure on the autocratic regimes would prove critical to their success. Like any political group, Islamists are more cautious when they are vulnerable. But once Islamist groups solidify their position, they will have less patience for U.S. hectoring on Israel or the peace process. Already, they have started speaking more openly about their regional ambitions. On February 17, Mohammed Badie, the Egyptian Muslim Brotherhood's "general guide," stated that the revolution "must be a starting point for Egypt to take up its place in the world again, through recognizing the importance of our responsibilities toward our nations and defending them and their legitimate demands." Meanwhile, Hammam Said, the hard-line leader of the Jordanian Muslim Brotherhood put it more bluntly: "America must think seriously about changing its policy in the region, for people will no longer remain submissive to its dictates."

It will take a while for the new governments in Tunisia and Egypt to form cogent foreign policies, but Washington should start thinking ahead to mitigate the long-term risks. In the transition phase, the introduction of constitutional and institutional reforms to devolve power will be critical. Proportional electoral systems that encourage the formation of coalition governments may be better than majoritarian systems because they would make foreign policy formulation a process of negotiation among many parties, necessarily moderating the result. Already, most mainstream Islamists have significant overlapping interests with the United States, such as seeing al Qaeda dismantled, policing terrorism, improving living standards and economic conditions across the Arab world, and consolidating democratic governance.

By initiating regular, substantive dialogue with Islamist groups to work on areas of agreement and discuss key foreign policy concerns, the United States might discover more convergence of interests than it expects. Indeed, one of the few low-level dialogues the United States has had with an Islamist group—that with Morocco's Justice and Development Party—has been successful, leading the party to be relatively restrained in its criticism of the United States. At any rate, the revolutions have made the shortsightedness of current U.S. policy—studiously avoiding formal contacts with the Muslim Brotherhood and like-minded groups—clear. The West knows much less about Egypt's most powerful opposition force than it should, and could.

The United States can take precautions—and it should—but this does not alter an unavoidable reality. Anti-Israel public opinion will remain a feature of Middle Eastern politics until a final and equitable peace treaty is struck. Whether that happens anytime soon will depend in part on Hamas. If Hamas finally joins a national unity government in the Palestinian territories that then negotiates an accommodation with Israel, this will effectively resolve other Islamist groups' Israel problem. Emboldened by the revolutions, however, Hamas is unlikely to be so cooperative.

For decades, Islamists postponed the difficult question of what they would do in power for a simple reason: the prospect of power seemed so remote. But the democratic wave sweeping the region has brought Islamists to the fore. What comes next may be the Arab world's first sustained experiment in Islamist integration. Fortunately, for all their anti-Americanism, mainstream Islamists have a strong pragmatic streak. If they have not already, they will need to come to terms with regional realities. And, for its part, the United States—and the rest of the international community—will need to finally come to terms with Islamists.

Terrorism After the Revolutions

How Secular Uprisings Could Help (or Hurt) Jihadists

Daniel Byman

FOREIGN AFFAIRS, MAY/JUNE 2011

On December 17, Mohamed Bouazizi, a Tunisian street vendor, set himself on fire to protest police harassment. His death incited unrest throughout Tunisia; less than a month later, protests toppled Tunisian President Zine el-Abidine Ben Ali. Egypt, the most populous and influential country in the Arab world, soon followed suit. Al Qaeda met both these dramatic events with near silence. Only in mid-February did Osama bin Laden's Egyptian deputy, Ayman al-Zawahiri, offer comments. But even then, he did not directly address the revolutions or explain how jihadists should respond. Instead, he claimed that the Tunisian revolution occurred "against the agent of America and France," gamely trying to transform Tunisians' fight against corruption and repression into a victory for anti-Western jihadists. On Egypt, Zawahiri offered a rambling history

DANIEL BYMAN is a Professor in the Security Studies Program at the School of Foreign Service at Georgetown University and Research Director at the Saban Center for Middle East Policy at the Brookings Institution. He is the author of *A High Price: The Triumphs and Failures of Israeli Counterterrorism*.

lesson, ranging from Napoleon to the tyranny of the Mubarak government. He released his statement on Egypt on February 18, a week after Hosni Mubarak resigned, and offered little guidance to potential followers on how they should view the revolution or react to it.

U.S. politicians are moving quickly to claim the revolutions and al Qaeda's muted response as victories in the struggle against terrorism. "This revolution is a repudiation of al Qaeda," declared Senator John McCain during a visit to Cairo on February 27. And indeed, looking out from bin Laden's cave, the Arab world looks less promising than it did only a few months ago. Although bin Laden and al Qaeda have been attempting to overthrow Arab governments for more than 20 years, the toppling of the seemingly solid dictatorships in Tunisia and Egypt caught them flat-footed and undermined their message of violent jihad.

Nevertheless, al Qaeda and its allies could ultimately benefit from the unrest. For now, al Qaeda has greater operational freedom of action, and bin Laden and his allies will seek to exploit any further unrest in the months and years to come.

OFF MESSAGE

Al Qaeda is dangerous not only because it has hundreds of skilled fighters under arms but also because tens of thousands of Muslims have found its calls for violent change appealing. When dictators reigned supreme in Arab lands, al Qaeda could score points by denouncing despotism—Zawahiri even wrote a book condemning the crimes of Mubarak. When dictators such as Mubarak fall due to pressure from pro-democracy protesters, however, al Qaeda loses one of its best recruiting pitches: the repression Arab governments inflict on their citizens. The rise of less repressive leaders would deprive al Qaeda propagandists of this valuable argument.

Genuine democracy would be a particular blow to bin Laden and his followers. "If you have freedom, al Qaeda will go away," claims Osama Rushdi, a former spokesperson for al-Gama'a al-Islamiyya, once Egypt's most important jihadist group. Rushdi may be too optimistic, but the possible movement toward a free press, free elections, and civil liberties throughout the Middle East would highlight the least appealing part of al Qaeda's dogma: its hostility toward democracy.

Although the word "democracy" means different things to different audiences, polls suggest that the generic concept is quite popular in the Arab world, as befits a region that knows firsthand how brutal autocracy can be. A 2010 Zogby poll found that a majority of Egyptians favored democracy, and a 2006 survey by the scholars John Esposito and Dalia Mogahed found that 93 percent of Egyptians favored a constitution that guaranteed freedom of speech. At the same time, however, Esposito and Mogahed found that a majority wanted Islamic law to be the only source of legislation. In contrast, al Qaeda believes that democracy is blasphemous, arguing that it places man's word above God's. So if Tunisia's emerging democratic movement does not soon hand power over to clerics that implement an Islamic state, then—according to al Qaeda in the Islamic Maghreb (AQIM)—"the duty upon Muslims in Tunisia is to be ready and not lay down their weapons." Al Qaeda's message is clear: secular democracy is as abhorrent as secular dictatorship.

Even more ominous for al Qaeda is the way in which Ben Ali and Mubarak fell. Al Qaeda leaders insist that violence carried out in the name of God is the only way to force change. Zawahiri had long demanded that Egyptian youths either take up arms against the Mubarak government or, if that proved impossible, "go forth to the open arenas of Jihad like Somalia, Iraq, Algeria and Afghanistan." Youths in Tunisia and Egypt did not heed his call; the protesters were peaceful and largely secular in their demands. As U.S. Secretary of State Hillary Clinton said of al Qaeda's leaders, "I hope they were watching on television as Egyptian young people proved them wrong." A number of prominent jihadist scholars, such as Abu Basir al-Tartusi and Hamid al-Ali, echoed her, praising the protesters' courage and endorsing the revolutions despite their largely secular demands.

Even more distressing to al Qaeda, change occurred in the Arab world without an initial blow being struck against the United States. Al Qaeda has long insisted that Muslims must first destroy the region's supposed puppet master in Washington before change will come to Tunis or Cairo.

Finally, the fact that the young are leading the revolution is bad news for bin Laden. Young people, especially young men, are al Qaeda's key demographic—the ones al Qaeda propagandists expect to take up arms. For over a decade, al Qaeda has portrayed its young fighters as the most audacious and honorable defenders of Muslim lands in the face of Western aggression. Now, youths in the Arab world are afire with very different ideas—of freedom and nonviolent action. Recent events have shown idealistic young Arabs who dream of a new political order in the Middle East that they need not travel to Afghanistan or Iraq to engage in jihad; they can accomplish more by remaining in their own countries and marching peacefully against their authoritarian rulers.

THE CHAINS COME OFF

U.S. counterterrorism officials have long praised countries such as Tunisia and Egypt for their aggressive efforts against terrorism and their cooperation with the United States. Since 9/11, the United States has tried to work with Algeria, Mali, Mauritania, and Morocco as well to improve regional counterterrorism cooperation against AQIM. Even Libyan leader Muammar al-Qaddafi—long derided as "the mad dog of the Middle East"—has been valued as a partner against al Qaeda since 9/11. In the face of unrest in Libya, following on the heels of the revolution in Egypt, Qaddafi even declared that al Qaeda was behind the protests, warning Libyans, "Do not be swayed by bin Laden"—most likely in an effort to gain legitimacy for his crackdown against the demonstrators.

Arab tyranny has often served U.S. purposes. U.S. counterterrorism officials have worked well with authoritarian leaders because their regimes have generally had a low bar for imprisonment and detention. The United States could send a suspect captured in Europe to Egypt and be assured that he would be kept in jail. This low bar also meant that many minor players and innocents were swept up in security-service roundups. The Egyptian regime was even willing to threaten the families of jihadists, putting tremendous pressure on militants to inform, surrender, or otherwise abandon the fight. Assuming that a truly democratic government comes to Egypt, the easy incarceration of dissidents and ruthless threats against militants and their families will disappear.

Indeed, one measure of how much progress the Arab regimes are making toward democracy will be how much their security services are purged. The same security services that have fought al Qaeda and its affiliates have also imprisoned peaceful bloggers, beaten up Islamist organizers to intimidate them, and censored pro-democracy newspapers.

Those who replace the current security forces will not necessarily be friendly to Washington, and the governments they report to may also seek an arm's-length relationship with the United States. If new governments take popular opinion into account, as democratic leaders do, cooperation will not be as close as it once was. Many of the new political players, particularly the Islamists, see the United States as a repressive power that aids Israel and other enemies. Indeed, it is hard to imagine an Egyptian government that includes the Muslim Brotherhood instructing its security services to work as closely with the CIA as Mubarak's forces did.

Regional cooperation—vital because al Qaeda and its affiliates cross state boundaries—was fitful at best before the recent unrest. Now, it will become even harder, as old regimes and new leaders greet one another with suspicion.

AL QAEDA'S PATH FORWARD

Despite the challenge that the secular revolutions have posed to al Qaeda's narrative, there is a chance that the organization could rebound and become even stronger operationally.

Dictatorships have crumbled, but nothing solid has yet replaced them. During the recent unrest, some jails in Egypt and Libya were emptied, putting experienced jihadists back on the street. In both countries, many of the jailed jihadists had turned away from violence in the last decade, arguing—quite publicly—that the jihadists' struggle represented a misunderstanding of Islam, killed innocents, and had ultimately failed. This renunciation of jihad produced bitter polemics against al Qaeda (which were met by even more vitriolic responses from al Qaeda). Nevertheless, among those released, there are some unrepentant extremists who are willing to wreak havoc on their enemies. These ex-prisoners threaten U.S. interests at a time when Arab governments are least willing or able to monitor and constrain them.

And in countries where autocrats still cling to power, the security services will probably become less effective against jihadists. The services of Algeria, Morocco, and Yemen are now likely to make democratic dissenters their top priority, rather than suspected terrorists. Dictators such as Yemen's Ali Abdullah Saleh have a long history of quietly working with jihadists against mutual enemies, as Saleh did when he employed jihadists to fight on his side against rebellious southerners in Yemen's 1994 civil war. Saleh and al Qaeda in the Arabian Peninsula are both hostile to those demonstrating for democracy, and they may cooperate, or at least not disrupt each other's efforts.

Meanwhile, new democratic governments may be unlikely to target the recruiters, fundraisers, propagandists, and other less visible elements of the jihadist movement. These individuals are often far more important to the movement's overall health than the actual bombers and assassins, but they can more easily cloak their work as legitimate political action. Freedom of speech may protect some activities, and many Arabs see the jihadist struggles in Afghanistan, Iraq, and elsewhere as legitimate. Jihadists are media savvy and will try to exploit any new freedoms to expand their propaganda efforts.

A particularly tricky issue is the role of Islamist parties such as Egypt's Muslim Brotherhood. From a counterterrorism point of view, a greater role for Islamists could be good news. Although Brotherhood theologians such as Sayyid Qutb helped inspire the modern jihadist movement, and many important al Qaeda members were Brotherhood members before joining bin Laden, there is bad blood between the two organizations.

In his book *The Bitter Harvest*, Zawahiri angrily criticized Brotherhood leaders for rejecting violence and participating in politics. Hamas, a Brotherhood spinoff, has quarreled bitterly with al Qaeda. Zawahiri has blasted Hamas for adhering to cease-fires with Israel, not implementing Islamic law in Gaza, and deviating from the pure faith of jihadism. To prevent these ideas from gaining currency and eroding its support, Hamas has harshly repressed al Qaeda–inspired jihadists in the Gaza Strip. If the Brotherhood gains influence in a new Egyptian government, as seems likely, the organization will carry this feud with it. And because many jihadists grew out of its ranks, the Brotherhood knows the jihadist community well and can effectively weed out the most dangerous figures.

When the Muslim Brotherhood had little chance of gaining power, ignoring it and other Islamist movements seemed prudent to both Republican and Democratic administrations. Now, the tables have turned, and the United States needs to catch up. In particular, Washington should clarify that it does not want these movements excluded from government but rather wants them to participate. Inevitably, this will lead to tension as Islamist groups seek policies that do not jibe with U.S. preferences.

But excluding the Brotherhood from power would be worse, for it would endanger the U.S. campaign against al Qaeda. In 1992, the Algerian government nullified elections that Islamists had won, provoking a bloody civil war. This war, in turn, radicalized the country's Islamist movement. *Takfiri* Islamists—those who believe other Muslims are apostates—dragged Algeria into a frenzy of gratuitous violence that alienated other jihadists and even bin Laden, due to the *takfiris*' horrific attacks on fellow Muslims. (Bin Laden worked with a less extreme faction of Algeria's jihadists, which later became the core of AQIM.) Although such an extreme scenario seems unlikely in Tunisia or Egypt, suppressing the Brotherhood's political aspirations would alienate younger, less patient Islamists. They, in turn, may find bin Laden's message attractive, believing that the new government is inherently anti-Islamic.

Here, perhaps, the goal of counterterrorism clashes with other U.S. interests. Although the Brotherhood is mouthing all the right slogans, its commitment to true democracy is uncertain. In any event, it is likely to seek restrictions on the rights of women and minorities in Egypt's political life. Islamist organizations in general are highly critical of U.S. military intervention in the Middle East, skeptical of cooperation with the CIA, and strongly opposed to anything that smacks of normal relations with Israel. Supporting a strong Islamist role in government risks creating a regime less friendly to the United States;

excluding the Islamists risks radicalizing the movement and reinvigorating al Qaeda.

Opportunities for al Qaeda will also arise if unrest turns to civil war, as has happened in Libya. In Afghanistan, Chechnya, Iraq, Somalia, and Yemen, civil wars began largely for local reasons, with little jihadist involvement. Over time, however, al Qaeda and like-minded groups moved in. First, they posed as supporters of the opposition. Then, they spread their vitriol, using their superior resources to attract new recruits, while the surrounding violence helped radicalize the opposition. Al Qaeda now has a strong presence in all these countries. Already, AQIM—the regional al Qaeda affiliates geographically closest to Libya—is issuing statements in support of the anti-Qaddafi fighters.

In Libya, it is possible that the United States and local jihadist fighters will end up fighting the same enemy. This happened in the Balkans in the 1990s, when Washington was helping the Bosnian Muslims just as Arab jihadists were seeking to assist the Muslims against the Serbs and turn Bosnia into a new Afghanistan.

AFTER THE REVOLUTION

The Obama administration must prevent al Qaeda from exploiting its increased freedom of movement in the Arab world and at the same time take advantage of the fact that its narrative has been discredited. U.S. public diplomacy efforts should relentlessly highlight al Qaeda's criticisms of democracy and emphasize the now credible idea that reform can come through peaceful change. The message should be spread by television and radio, as always, but particular attention should be paid to the Internet, given the importance of reaching young people.

The United States must also continue to use drone strikes and other means to put pressure on al Qaeda's senior leadership in Pakistan, even though these at times decrease support for the United States there. Part of the explanation for al Qaeda's slow response may be the fact that responding to such momentous change requires extensive consultations among leaders. Holding an open meeting, however, could invite a deluge of Hellfire missiles from U.S. drones.

Al Qaeda will presumably get its act together eventually and develop a coherent message regarding how jihadists should respond to the revolutions. Drone attacks remain vital to keeping al Qaeda behind the pace of events and preventing it from coordinating operations far from its base in Pakistan. Keeping al Qaeda's response slow and incoherent by inhibiting communication will make the organization appear irrelevant.

The United States must also recognize the risks for counterterrorism in the civil wars that break out as autocrats resist democratization. The danger is that al Qaeda will exploit such conflicts, so the United States must make clear to opposition figures early on that the United States will consider aid, recognition, and other assistance, but that this aid is contingent on jihadists' being kept out of the rebels' ranks. When jihadists set up shop in the Balkans in the 1990s, U.S. pressure helped convince Bosnia's mainstream Muslim leadership to purge them. Al Qaeda cannot compete with the United States and its allies when it comes to resources or bestowing international legitimacy, so the choice between Washington and al Qaeda should be easy for opposition groups. A failure to help the oppositionists, however, may lead desperate ones to seek help from whatever quarter they can.

Al Qaeda, of course, will try to have it both ways. When the United States does not intervene to stop authoritarian regimes from attacking their citizens, it will blast the United States as being a friend of tyranny. And when the United States does intervene, al Qaeda will try to drum up anti-U.S. sentiment among the locals, calling for attacks on U.S. forces while portraying the intervention as part of the United States' master plan to conquer the Middle East. The United States should counter this by emphasizing the support it has from the local Muslim community and Arab states; even so, the image of a U.S. soldier in full battle gear may still alienate many Muslims.

More quietly, the United States should develop efforts to train the intelligence and security forces of the new regimes that emerge. The first step is simply to gain their trust, as new leaders are likely to see their U.S. counterparts as bulwarks of the old order and a possible source of counterrevolution. Many of the new security-service leaders will be new to counterterrorism. Even more important, they will be unaccustomed to the difficult task of balancing civil liberties and aggressive efforts against terrorism. Here, the FBI and other Western domestic intelligence services have much to offer. Developing such cooperation will take time and patience, but the United States should make this a priority.

For now, there is reason to hope that the revolutions in the Arab world will benefit U.S. counterterrorism efforts. But this hope should be balanced with the recognition that in the short term al Qaeda will gain operational freedom and that the United States and its allies need to recast their message, maintain pressure on al Qaeda's core, prepare to counter al Qaeda's attempts to exploit civil wars, and renew their intelligence cooperation in the region if they are to prevent al Qaeda from reaping long-term benefits from the upheavals.

Remarks by President Barack Obama on a New Beginning

CAIRO UNIVERSITY, EGYPT, JUNE 4, 2009

PRESIDENT OBAMA: Thank you very much. Good afternoon. I am honored to be in the timeless city of Cairo, and to be hosted by two remarkable institutions. For over a thousand years, Al-Azhar has stood as a beacon of Islamic learning; and for over a century, Cairo University has been a source of Egypt's advancement. And together, you represent the harmony between tradition and progress. I'm grateful for your hospitality, and the hospitality of the people of Egypt; And I'm also proud to carry with me the goodwill of the American people, and a greeting of peace from Muslim communities in my country: *Assalaamu alaykum*.

We meet at a time of great tension between the United States and Muslims around the world—tension rooted in historical forces that go beyond any current policy debate. The relationship between Islam and the West includes centuries of coexistence and cooperation, but also conflict and religious wars. More recently, tension has been fed by colonialism that denied rights and opportunities to many Muslims, and a Cold War in which Muslim-majority countries were too often treated as proxies without regard to their own aspirations. Moreover, the sweeping change brought by modernity and globalization led many Muslims to view the West as hostile to the traditions of Islam.

Violent extremists have exploited these tensions in a small but potent minority of Muslims. The attacks of September 11, 2001, and the continued efforts of these extremists to engage in violence against civilians has led some in my country to view Islam as inevitably hostile not only to America and Western countries, but also to human rights. All this has bred more fear and more mistrust.

So long as our relationship is defined by our differences, we will empower those who sow hatred rather than peace, those who promote conflict rather than the cooperation that can help all of our people achieve justice and prosperity. And this cycle of suspicion and discord must end.

I've come here to Cairo to seek a new beginning between the United States and Muslims around the world, one based on mutual interest and mutual respect, and one based upon the truth that America and Islam are not exclusive and need not be in competition. Instead, they overlap, and share common principles—principles of justice and progress; tolerance and the dignity of all human beings.

I do so recognizing that change cannot happen overnight. I know there's been a lot of publicity about this speech, but no single speech can eradicate years of mistrust, nor can I answer in the time that I have this afternoon all the complex questions that brought us to this point. But I am convinced that in order to move forward, we must say openly to each other the things we hold in our hearts and that too often are said only behind closed doors. There must be a sustained effort to listen to each other; to learn from each other; to respect one another; and to seek common ground. As the Holy Koran tells us, "Be conscious of God and speak always the truth." That is what I will try to do today—to speak the truth as best I can, humbled by the task before us, and firm in my belief that the interests we share as human beings are far more powerful than the forces that drive us apart.

Now part of this conviction is rooted in my own experience. I'm a Christian, but my father came from a Kenyan family that includes generations of Muslims. As a boy, I spent several years in Indonesia and heard the call of the *azaan* at the break of dawn and at the fall of dusk. As a young man, I worked in Chicago communities where many found dignity and peace in their Muslim faith.

As a student of history, I also know civilization's debt to Islam. It was Islam—at places like Al-Azhar—that carried the light of learning through so many centuries, paving the way for Europe's Renaissance and Enlightenment. It was innovation in Muslim communities that developed the order of algebra; our magnetic compass and tools of navigation; our mastery of pens and printing; our understanding of how disease spreads and how it can be healed. Islamic culture has given us majestic arches and soaring spires; timeless poetry and cherished music; elegant calligraphy and places of peaceful contemplation. And throughout history, Islam has demonstrated through words and deeds the possibilities of religious tolerance and racial equality.

I also know that Islam has always been a part of America's story. The first nation to recognize my country was Morocco. In signing the Treaty of Tripoli in 1796, our second president, John Adams, wrote, "The United States has in itself no character of enmity against the laws, religion or tranquility of Muslims." And since our founding, American Muslims have enriched the United States. They have fought in our wars, they have served in our government, they have stood for civil rights, they have started businesses, they have taught at our universities, they've excelled in our sports arenas, they've won Nobel Prizes, built our tallest building, and lit the Olympic Torch. And when the first Muslim American was recently elected to Congress, he took the oath to defend our Constitution using the same Holy Koran that one of our Founding Fathers—Thomas Jefferson—kept in his personal library.

So I have known Islam on three continents before coming to the region where it was first revealed. That experience guides my conviction that partnership between America and Islam must be based on what Islam is, not what it isn't. And I consider it part of my responsibility as president of the United States to fight against negative stereotypes of Islam wherever they appear.

But that same principle must apply to Muslim perceptions of America. Just as Muslims do not fit a crude stereotype, America is not the crude stereotype of a self-interested empire. The United States has been one of the greatest sources of progress that the world has ever known. We were born out of revolution against an empire. We were founded upon the ideal that all are created equal, and we have shed blood and struggled for centuries to give meaning to those words—within our borders, and around the world. We are shaped by every culture, drawn from every end of the Earth, and dedicated to a simple concept: *E pluribus unum*—"Out of many, one."

Now, much has been made of the fact that an African American with the name Barack Hussein Obama could be elected president. But my personal story is not so unique. The dream of opportunity for all people has not come true for everyone in America, but its promise exists for all who come to our shores—and that includes nearly 7 million American Muslims in our country today who, by the way, enjoy incomes and educational levels that are higher than the American average.

Moreover, freedom in America is indivisible from the freedom to practice one's religion. That is why there is a mosque in every state in our union, and over twelve hundred mosques within our borders. That's why the United States government has gone to court to protect the right of women and girls to wear the hijab and to punish those who would deny it.

So let there be no doubt: Islam is a part of America. And I believe that America holds within her the truth that regardless of race, religion, or station in life, all of us share common aspirations—to live in peace and security; to get an education and to work with dignity; to love our families, our communities, and our God. These things we share. This is the hope of all humanity.

Of course, recognizing our common humanity is only the beginning of our task. Words alone cannot meet the needs of our people. These needs will be met only if we act boldly in the years ahead; and if we understand that the challenges we face are shared, and our failure to meet them will hurt us all.

For we have learned from recent experience that when a financial system weakens in one country, prosperity is hurt everywhere. When a new flu infects one human being, all are at risk. When one nation pursues a nuclear weapon, the risk of nuclear attack rises for all nations. When violent extremists operate in one stretch of mountains, people are endangered across an ocean. When innocents in Bosnia and Darfur are slaughtered, that is a stain on our collective conscience. That is what it means to share this world in the twenty-first century. That is the responsibility we have to one another as human beings.

And this is a difficult responsibility to embrace. For human history has often been a record of nations and tribes—and, yes, religions—subjugating one another in pursuit of their own interests. Yet in this new age, such attitudes are self-defeating. Given our interdependence, any world order that elevates one nation or group of people over another will inevitably fail. So whatever we think of the past, we must not be prisoners to it. Our problems must be dealt with through partnership; our progress must be shared.

Now, that does not mean we should ignore sources of tension. Indeed, it suggests the opposite: We must face these tensions squarely. And so in that spirit, let me speak as clearly and as plainly as I can about some specific issues that I believe we must finally confront together.

The first issue that we have to confront is violent extremism in all of its forms.

In Ankara, I made clear that America is not—and never will be—at war with Islam. We will, however, relentlessly confront violent extremists who pose a grave threat to our security—because we reject the same thing that people of all faiths reject: the killing of innocent men, women, and children. And it is my first duty as president to protect the American people.

The situation in Afghanistan demonstrates America's goals, and our need to work together. Over seven years ago, the United States pursued al-Qaeda and the Taliban with broad international support. We did not go by choice; we went because of necessity. I'm aware that there's still some who would question or even justify the events of 9/11. But let us be clear: Al-Qaeda killed nearly three thousand people on that day. The victims were innocent men, women, and children from America and many other nations who had done nothing to harm anybody. And yet al Qaeda chose to ruthlessly murder these people, claimed credit for the attack, and even now states their determination to kill on a massive scale. They have affiliates in many countries and are trying to expand their reach. These are not opinions to be debated; these are facts to be dealt with.

Now, make no mistake: We do not want to keep our troops in Afghanistan. We see no military—we seek no military bases there. It is agonizing for America to lose our young men and women. It is costly and politically difficult to continue this conflict. We would gladly bring every single one of our troops home if we could be confident that there were not violent extremists in Afghanistan and now Pakistan determined to kill as many Americans as they possibly can. But that is not yet the case.

And that's why we're partnering with a coalition of forty-six countries. And despite the costs involved, America's commitment will not weaken. Indeed, none of us should tolerate these extremists. They have killed in many countries. They have killed people of different faiths—but more than any other, they have killed Muslims. Their actions are irreconcilable with the rights of human beings, the progress of nations, and with Islam. The Holy Koran teaches that whoever kills an innocent is as—it is as if he has killed all mankind. And the Holy Koran also says whoever saves a person, it is as if he has saved all mankind. The enduring faith of over a billion people is so much bigger than the narrow hatred of a few. Islam is not part of the problem in combating violent extremism—it is an important part of promoting peace.

Now, we also know that military power alone is not going to solve the problems in Afghanistan and Pakistan. That's why we plan to invest $1.5 billion each year over the next five years to partner with Pakistanis to build schools and hospitals, roads and businesses, and hundreds of millions to help those who've been displaced. That's why we are providing more than $2.8 billion to help Afghans develop their economy and deliver services that people depend on.

Let me also address the issue of Iraq. Unlike Afghanistan, Iraq was a war of choice that provoked strong differences in my country and around the world. Although I believe that the Iraqi people are ultimately better off without the tyranny of Saddam Hussein, I also believe that events in Iraq have reminded America of the need to use diplomacy and build international consensus to resolve our problems whenever possible. Indeed, we can recall the words of Thomas Jefferson, who said: "I hope that our wisdom will grow with our power, and teach us that the less we use our power the greater it will be."

Today, America has a dual responsibility: to help Iraq forge a better future—and to leave Iraq to Iraqis. And I have made it clear to the Iraqi people that we pursue no bases, and no claim on their territory or resources. Iraq's sovereignty is its own. And that's why I ordered the removal of our combat brigades by next August. That is why we will honor our agreement with Iraq's democratically elected government to remove combat troops from Iraqi cities by July, and to remove all of our troops from Iraq by 2012. We will help Iraq train its security forces and develop its economy. But we will support a secure and united Iraq as a partner, and never as a patron.

And finally, just as America can never tolerate violence by extremists, we must never alter or forget our principles. Nine-eleven was an enormous trauma to our country. The fear and anger that it provoked was understandable, but in some cases, it led us to act contrary to our traditions and our ideals. We are taking concrete actions to change course. I have unequivocally prohibited the use of torture by the United States, and I have ordered the prison at Guantánamo Bay closed by early next year.

So America will defend itself, respectful of the sovereignty of nations and the rule of law. And we will do so in partnership with Muslim communities which are also threatened. The sooner the extremists are isolated and unwelcome in Muslim communities, the sooner we will all be safer.

The second major source of tension that we need to discuss is the situation between Israelis, Palestinians, and the Arab world.

America's strong bonds with Israel are well known. This bond is unbreakable. It is based upon cultural and historical ties, and the recognition that the aspiration for a Jewish homeland is rooted in a tragic history that cannot be denied.

Around the world, the Jewish people were persecuted for centuries, and anti-Semitism in Europe culminated in an unprecedented Holocaust. Tomorrow, I will visit Buchenwald, which was part of a network of camps where Jews were enslaved, tortured, shot, and gassed to death by the Third Reich. Six million Jews were killed—more than the entire Jewish population of Israel today. Denying that fact is baseless, it is ignorant, and it is hateful. Threatening Israel with destruction—or repeating vile stereotypes about Jews—is deeply wrong, and only serves to evoke in the minds of Israelis this most painful of memories while preventing the peace that the people of this region deserve.

On the other hand, it is also undeniable that the Palestinian people—Muslims and Christians—have suffered in pursuit of a homeland. For more than sixty years they've endured the pain of dislocation. Many wait in refugee camps in the West Bank, Gaza, and neighboring lands for a life of peace and security that they have never been able to lead. They endure the daily humiliations—large and small—that come with occupation. So let there be no doubt: The situation for the Palestinian people is intolerable. And America will not turn our backs on the legitimate Palestinian aspiration for dignity, opportunity, and a state of their own.

For decades then, there has been a stalemate: two peoples with legitimate aspirations, each with a painful history that makes compromise elusive. It's easy to point fingers—for Palestinians to point to the displacement brought about by Israel's founding, and for Israelis to point to the constant hostility and attacks throughout its history from within its borders as well as beyond. But if we see this conflict only from one side or the other, then we will be blind to the truth: The only resolution is for the aspirations of both sides to be met through two states, where Israelis and Palestinians each live in peace and security.

That is in Israel's interest, Palestine's interest, America's interest, and the world's interest. And that is why I intend to personally pursue this outcome with all the patience and dedication that the task requires. The obligations—the obligations that the parties have agreed to under the road map are clear. For peace to come, it is time for them—and all of us—to live up to our responsibilities.

Palestinians must abandon violence. Resistance through violence and killing is wrong and it does not succeed. For centuries, black people in America suffered the lash of the whip as slaves and the humiliation of segregation. But it was not violence that won full and equal rights. It was a peaceful and determined insistence upon the ideals at the center of America's founding. This same story can be told by people from South Africa to South Asia; from Eastern Europe to Indonesia. It's a story with a simple truth: that violence is a dead end. It is a sign neither of courage nor power to shoot rockets at sleeping children, or to blow up old women on a bus. That's not how moral authority is claimed; that's how it is surrendered.

Now is the time for Palestinians to focus on what they can build. The Palestinian Authority must develop its capacity to govern, with institutions that serve the needs of its people. Hamas does have support among some Palestinians, but they also have to recognize they have responsibilities. To play a role in fulfilling Palestinian aspirations, to unify the Palestinian people, Hamas must put an end to violence, recognize past agreements, recognize Israel's right to exist.

At the same time, Israelis must acknowledge that just as Israel's right to exist cannot be denied, neither can Palestine's. The United States does not accept the legitimacy of continued Israeli settlements. This construction violates previous agreements and undermines efforts to achieve peace. It is time for these settlements to stop.

And Israel must also live up to its obligation to ensure that Palestinians can live and work and develop their society. Just as it devastates Palestinian families, the continuing humanitarian crisis in Gaza does not serve Israel's security; neither does the continuing lack of opportunity in the West Bank. Progress in the daily lives of the Palestinian people must be a critical part of a road to peace, and Israel must take concrete steps to enable such progress.

And finally, the Arab states must recognize that the Arab Peace Initiative was an important beginning, but not the end of their responsibilities. The Arab-Israeli conflict should no longer be used to distract the people of Arab nations from other problems. Instead, it must be a cause for action to help the Palestinian people develop the institutions that will sustain their state, to recognize Israel's legitimacy, and to choose progress over a self-defeating focus on the past.

America will align our policies with those who pursue peace, and we will say in public what we say in private to Israelis and Palestinians and Arabs. We cannot impose peace. But privately, many Muslims recognize that Israel will not go away. Likewise, many Israelis recognize the need for a Palestinian state. It is time for us to act on what everyone knows to be true.

Too many tears have been shed. Too much blood has been shed. All of us have a responsibility to work for the day when the mothers of Israelis and Palestinians can see their children grow up without fear; when the Holy Land of the three great faiths is the place of peace that God intended it to be; when Jerusalem is a secure and lasting home for Jews and Christians and Muslims, and a place for all of the children of Abraham to mingle peacefully together as in the story of Isra, when Moses, Jesus, and Mohammed, peace be upon them, joined in prayer.

The third source of tension is our shared interest in the rights and responsibilities of nations on nuclear weapons.

This issue has been a source of tension between the United States and the Islamic Republic of Iran. For many years, Iran has defined itself in part by its opposition to my country, and there is in fact a tumultuous history between us. In the middle of the Cold War, the United States played a role in the overthrow of a democratically elected Iranian government. Since the Islamic Revolution, Iran has played a role in acts of hostage-taking and violence against U.S. troops and civilians. This history is well known. Rather than remain trapped in the past, I've made it clear to Iran's leaders and people that my country is prepared to move forward. The question now is not what Iran is against, but rather what future it wants to build.

I recognize it will be hard to overcome decades of mistrust, but we will proceed with courage, rectitude, and resolve. There will be many issues to discuss between our two countries, and we are willing to move forward without preconditions on the basis of mutual respect. But it is clear to all concerned that when it comes to nuclear weapons, we have reached a decisive point. This is not simply about America's interests. It's about preventing a nuclear arms race in the Middle East that could lead this region and the world down a hugely dangerous path.

I understand those who protest that some countries have weapons that others do not. No single nation should pick and choose which nation holds nuclear weapons. And that's why I strongly reaffirmed America's commitment to seek a world in which no nations hold nuclear weapons. And any nation—including Iran—should have the right to access peaceful nuclear power if it complies with its responsibilities under the Nuclear Nonproliferation Treaty. That commitment is at the core of the treaty, and it must be kept for all who fully abide by it. And I'm hopeful that all countries in the region can share in this goal.

The fourth issue that I will address is democracy.

I know—I know there has been controversy about the promotion of democracy in recent years, and much of this controversy is connected to the war in Iraq. So let me be clear: No system of government can or should be imposed by one nation by any other.

That does not lessen my commitment, however, to governments that reflect the will of the people. Each nation gives life to this principle in its own way, grounded in the traditions of its own people. America does not presume to know what is best for everyone, just as we would not presume to pick the outcome of a peaceful election. But I do have an unyielding belief that all people yearn for certain things: the ability to speak your mind and have a say in how you are governed; confidence in the rule of law and the equal administration of justice; government that is transparent and doesn't steal from the people; the freedom to live as you choose. These are not just American ideas; they are human rights. And that is why we will support them everywhere.

Now, there is no straight line to realize this promise. But this much is clear: Governments that protect these rights are ultimately more stable, successful and secure. Suppressing ideas never succeeds in making them go away. America respects the right of all peaceful and law-abiding voices to be heard around the world, even if we disagree with them. And we will welcome all elected, peaceful governments—provided they govern with respect for all their people.

This last point is important because there are some who advocate for democracy only when they're out of power; once in power, they are ruthless in suppressing the rights of others. So no matter where it takes hold, government of the people and by the people sets a single standard for all who would hold power: You must maintain your power through consent, not coercion; you must respect the rights of minorities, and participate with a spirit of tolerance and compromise; you must place the interests of your people and the legitimate workings of the political process above your party. Without these ingredients, elections alone do not make true democracy.

The fifth issue that we must address together is religious freedom. Islam has a proud tradition of tolerance. We see it in the history of Andalusia and Cordoba during the Inquisition. I saw it firsthand as a child in Indonesia, where devout Christians worshiped freely in an overwhelmingly Muslim country. That is the spirit we need today. People in every country should be free to choose and live their faith based upon the persuasion of the mind and the heart and the soul. This tolerance is essential for religion to thrive, but it's being challenged in many different ways.

Among some Muslims, there's a disturbing tendency to measure one's own faith by the rejection of somebody else's faith.

The richness of religious diversity must be upheld—whether it is for Maronites in Lebanon or the Copts in Egypt. And if we are being honest, fault lines must be closed among Muslims, as well, as the divisions between Sunni and Shia have led to tragic violence, particularly in Iraq.

Freedom of religion is central to the ability of peoples to live together. We must always examine the ways in which we protect it. For instance, in the United States, rules on charitable giving have made it harder for Muslims to fulfill their religious obligation. That's why I'm committed to working with American Muslims to ensure that they can fulfill *zakat*.

Likewise, it is important for Western countries to avoid impeding Muslim citizens from practicing religion as they see fit—for instance, by dictating what clothes a Muslim woman should wear. We can't disguise hostility towards any religion behind the pretence of liberalism.

In fact, faith should bring us together. And that's why we're forging service projects in America to bring together Christians, Muslims, and Jews. That's why we welcome efforts like Saudi Arabian King Abdullah's interfaith dialogue and Turkey's leadership in the Alliance of Civilizations. Around the world, we can turn dialogue into interfaith service, so bridges between peoples lead to action—whether it is combating malaria in Africa, or providing relief after a natural disaster.

The sixth issue that I want to address is women's rights. I know—and you can tell from this audience—that there is a healthy debate about this issue. I reject the view of some in the West that a woman who chooses to cover her hair is somehow less equal, but I do believe that a woman who is denied an education is denied equality. And it is no coincidence that countries where women are well educated are far more likely to be prosperous.

Now, let me be clear: Issues of women's equality are by no means simply an issue for Islam. In Turkey, Pakistan,

Bangladesh, Indonesia, we've seen Muslim-majority countries elect a woman to lead. Meanwhile, the struggle for women's equality continues in many aspects of American life, and in countries around the world.

I am convinced that our daughters can contribute just as much to society as our sons. Our common prosperity will be advanced by allowing all humanity—men and women—to reach their full potential. I do not believe that women must make the same choices as men in order to be equal, and I respect those women who choose to live their lives in traditional roles. But it should be their choice. And that is why the United States will partner with any Muslim-majority country to support expanded literacy for girls, and to help young women pursue employment through micro-financing that helps people live their dreams.

Finally, I want to discuss economic development and opportunity.

I know that for many, the face of globalization is contradictory. The Internet and television can bring knowledge and information, but also offensive sexuality and mindless violence into the home. Trade can bring new wealth and opportunities, but also huge disruptions and change in communities. In all nations—including America—this change can bring fear. Fear that because of modernity we lose control over our economic choices, our politics, and most importantly our identities—those things we most cherish about our communities, our families, our traditions, and our faith.

But I also know that human progress cannot be denied. There need not be contradictions between development and tradition. Countries like Japan and South Korea grew their economies enormously while maintaining distinct cultures. The same is true for the astonishing progress within Muslim-majority countries from Kuala Lumpur to Dubai. In ancient times and in our times, Muslim communities have been at the forefront of innovation and education.

And this is important because no development strategy can be based only upon what comes out of the ground, nor can it be sustained while young people are out of work. Many Gulf states have enjoyed great wealth as a consequence of oil, and some are beginning to focus it on broader development. But all of us must recognize that education and innovation will be the currency of the twenty-first century, and in too many Muslim communities there remains underinvestment in these areas. I'm emphasizing such investment within my own country. And while America in the past has focused on oil and gas when it comes to this part of the world, we now seek a broader engagement.

On education, we will expand exchange programs, and increase scholarships, like the one that brought my father to America. At the same time, we will encourage more Americans to study in Muslim communities. And we will match promising Muslim students with internships in America; invest in online learning for teachers and children around the world; and create a new online network, so a young person in Kansas can communicate instantly with a young person in Cairo.

On economic development, we will create a new corps of business volunteers to partner with counterparts in Muslim-majority countries. And I will host a Summit on Entrepreneurship this year to identify how we can deepen ties between business leaders, foundations and social entrepreneurs in the United States and Muslim communities around the world.

On science and technology, we will launch a new fund to support technological development in Muslim-majority countries, and to help transfer ideas to the marketplace so they can create more jobs. We'll open centers of scientific excellence in Africa, the Middle East and Southeast Asia, and appoint new science envoys to collaborate on programs that develop new sources of energy, create green jobs, digitize records, clean water, grow new crops. Today I'm announcing a new global effort with the

Organization of the Islamic Conference to eradicate polio. And we will also expand partnerships with Muslim communities to promote child and maternal health.

All these things must be done in partnership. Americans are ready to join with citizens and governments; community organizations, religious leaders, and businesses in Muslim communities around the world to help our people pursue a better life.

The issues that I have described will not be easy to address. But we have a responsibility to join together on behalf of the world that we seek—a world where extremists no longer threaten our people, and American troops have come home; a world where Israelis and Palestinians are each secure in a state of their own, and nuclear energy is used for peaceful purposes; a world where governments serve their citizens, and the rights of all God's children are respected. Those are mutual interests. That is the world we seek. But we can only achieve it together.

I know there are many—Muslim and non-Muslim—who question whether we can forge this new beginning. Some are eager to stoke the flames of division, and to stand in the way of progress. Some suggest that it isn't worth the effort—that we are fated to disagree, and civilizations are doomed to clash. Many more are simply skeptical that real change can occur. There's so much fear, so much mistrust that has built up over the years. But if we choose to be bound by the past, we will never move forward. And I want to particularly say this to young people of every faith, in every country—you, more than anyone, have the ability to reimagine the world, to remake this world.

All of us share this world for but a brief moment in time. The question is whether we spend that time focused on what pushes us apart, or whether we commit ourselves to an effort—a sustained effort—to find common ground, to focus on the future we seek for our children, and to respect the dignity of all human beings.

It's easier to start wars than to end them. It's easier to blame others than to look inward. It's easier to see what is different about someone than to find the things we share. But we should choose the right path, not just the easy path. There's one rule that lies at the heart of every religion—that we do unto others as we would have them do unto us. This truth transcends nations and peoples—a belief that isn't new; that isn't black or white or brown; that isn't Christian or Muslim or Jew. It's a belief that pulsed in the cradle of civilization, and that still beats in the hearts of billions around the world. It's a faith in other people, and it's what brought me here today.

We have the power to make the world we seek, but only if we have the courage to make a new beginning, keeping in mind what has been written.

The Holy Koran tells us: "O mankind! We have created you male and a female; and we have made you into nations and tribes so that you may know one another."

The Talmud tells us: "The whole of the Torah is for the purpose of promoting peace."

The Holy Bible tells us: "Blessed are the peacemakers, for they shall be called sons of God."

The people of the world can live together in peace. We know that is God's vision. Now that must be our work here on Earth.

Thank you. And may God's peace be upon you. Thank you very much. Thank you.

Hillary Rodham Clinton's Remarks to the Forum for the Future

DOHA, QATAR, JANUARY 13, 2011

DAVID FOSTER: Good morning. Thank you very much for joining us here, at the seventh Forum for the Future. My name is David Foster, and I will be moderating this discussion involving our panelists here, and of course, a great many of you out here, as well.

For the past five years, it's been my privilege to work here in Qatar for al-Jazeera English. And one of our mottos has always been, "Every angle, every side," which is, effectively, what this is about. It's about dialogue [inaudible]. And we will work our way from this side.

First of all, may I ask, Madam Secretary, Hillary Clinton, Secretary of State of the United States of America [inaudible].

SECRETARY HILLARY CLINTON: Thank you very much, David. I am honored to be here again at the Forum for the Future, especially with so many friends and colleagues from the G8 and from the Middle East.

I am delighted to join with Sheikh Khalid, who is a great colleague of mine in the foreign ministry, and I look forward to hearing from Slaheddine Jourchi, whose work on human rights and democracy in Tunisia I admire—and, of course, it is especially timely today—and Mohamed El-Masry, president of the Federation of Egyptian Chambers of Commerce.

This is the last stop on a trip that has brought me from Abu Dhabi and Dubai to Yemen, Oman, and now to Doha. On this short, but intense journey, I saw many signs of the potential for a new and innovative Middle East: a solar-powered city rising from the sands of the UAE; civil society leaders in Oman partnering with their government to improve education and create economic opportunities; a young Yemeni woman and a young Yemeni man, both of whom studied abroad and then returned to work for progress in Yemen. And of course, here in Qatar, the home of the 2022 World Cup, we see many examples of a commitment to innovation. Last year I visited Education City, which is connecting Qatar's young people to the global economy.

So, wherever I go, in my conversations with people from all walks of life—from officials at the highest levels of government to university students, religious leaders, and engaged citizens, one message has consistently emerged: People are deeply proud of this region and what it has accomplished, but they are also profoundly concerned about the trends in many parts of the broader Middle East, and what the future holds.

We all know this region faces serious challenges, even beyond the conflicts that dominate the headlines of the day. And we have a lot of work to do. This forum was designed to be not just an annual meeting where we talk with and at each other, but a launching pad for some of the institutional changes that will deal with the challenges that we all know are present.

For example, a growing majority of this region is under the age of thirty. In fact, it is predicted that in just one country, Yemen, the population will double in thirty years. These young people have a hard time finding work. In many places, there are simply not enough jobs. Across the region, one in five young people is unemployed. And in some places, the percentage is far more. While some countries have made great strides in governance, in many others people have grown tired of corrupt institutions and a stagnant political order. They are demanding reform to make their governments more effective, more responsive, and more open. And all this is taking place against a backdrop of depleting resources: water tables are dropping, oil reserves are running out, and too few countries have adopted long-term plans for addressing these problems.

Each country, of course, has its own distinct challenges, and each its own achievements. But in too many places, in too many ways, the region's foundations are sinking into the sand. The new and dynamic Middle East that I have seen needs firmer ground if it is to take root and grow everywhere. And that goal brings us to this Forum.

I believe that the leaders of this region, in partnership with their people, have the capacity to build that stronger foundation. There are enough models and examples in the region to point to, to make the economic and social reforms that will create jobs, respect the right of diversity to exist, create more economic opportunity, encourage entrepreneurship, give citizens the skills they need to succeed, to make the political reforms that will create the space young people are demanding, to participate in public affairs and have a meaningful role in the decisions that shape their lives.

So to my friends, the leaders of these countries, I would say: You can help build a future that your young people will believe in, stay for, and defend. Some of you are already demonstrating that. But for others it will take new visions, new strategies and new commitments. It is time to see civil society not as a threat, but as a partner. And it is time for the elites in every society to invest in the futures of their own countries.

Those who cling to the status quo may be able to hold back the full impact of their countries' problems for a little while, but not forever. If leaders don't offer a positive vision and give young people meaningful ways to contribute, others will fill the vacuum. Extremist elements, terrorist groups, and others who would prey on desperation and poverty are already out there, appealing for allegiance and competing for influence. So this is a critical moment, and this is a test of leadership for all of us.

I am here to pledge my country's support for those who step up to solve the problems that we and you face. We want to build stronger partnerships with societies that are on the path to long-term stability and progress—business, government and civil society, as represented on this panel, must work together, as in our new regional initiative called Partners for a New Beginning. We know that what happens in this region will have implications far beyond.

Now, America cannot solve these problems. And I know you understand that. But it bears repeating. What we need is a real vision for that future that comes from each of you, from governments that must deliver on their promises, from civil society and business leaders who must build their people up, and of course, from the people themselves.

The Middle East is brimming with talent. It is blessed with resources, enriched by strong traditions of faith and family. This rising generation of young people has the potential to achieve so much, and we need to give them the chance to do so.

So, here at the Forum for the Future, let us face honestly that future. Let us discuss openly what needs to be done. Let us use this time to move beyond rhetoric, to put away plans that are timid and gradual, and make a commitment to keep this region moving in the right direction. People are looking for real leadership in the twenty-first century, and I think it can be provided, and I know that this is the moment to do so.

Thank you very much.

The Last Official Address by Tunisian President Zine el-Abidine Ben Ali

JANUARY 13, 2011

People of Tunisia:

I am speaking to you today, everyone, both inside and outside Tunisia. I speak to you in the language of Tunisians. I am speaking to you now because the situation demands deep change. Yes, deep and comprehensive change.

I have understood you. Yes, I have understood you. I have understood everyone: the unemployed, the needy, the politician, and those demanding more freedoms. I have understood you. I have understood you all. However, the events currently taking place in our country are not part of us. Vandalism is not part of the customs of Tunisians—civilized Tunisians, tolerant Tunisians.

Violence is not part of us, nor is it part of our conduct. This trend must stop, with the concerted efforts of everyone: political parties, national organizations, civil society, intellectuals and citizens. Hand in hand, for the sake of our country. Hand in hand for the sake of all our children's security.

The change I am announcing now is in response to your demands, to which we have reacted. We have felt deep pain at what has occurred.

Translation by Tony Badran.

My sadness and pain are great, for I have spent more than fifty years of my life in the service of Tunisia, in different positions: from the National Army to various other responsibilities, and twenty-three years as head of state. Every day of my life has been and continues to be in the service of the country. I have offered sacrifices, which I do not like to recount as you all know them, and I have never accepted, and do not accept still, the shedding of a single drop of Tunisian blood.

We felt pain for the victims who fell and the persons who suffered damage, and I refuse to see more fall as a result of the continuation of violence and looting.

Our children today have stayed home and did not go to school. This is a shame and a disgrace, because we have become fearful for them from the violence perpetrated by gangs who have robbed and looted and assaulted people. This is a crime, not protest. This is abhorrent. The citizens, all citizens, must stand up to them. We have issued instructions, and we rely on everyone's cooperation, to distinguish between these gangs and groups of deviants who are taking advantage of the circumstances, and peaceful, legitimate protests, to which we do not object.

My sadness is very great and very deep. Very profound. Enough with violence! Enough with violence!

I have also issued instructions to the interior minister, and I have repeated, and today I confirm: do not use live ammunition. Live ammunition is not acceptable. It is not justified, unless, God forbid, someone tries to disarm you or attacks you with a firearm, or the like, and forces you to defend yourself.

I ask that the independent commission—I repeat, the independent commission, which will investigate the incidents and the abuses and the regrettable deaths—to delineate the responsibilities of all sides, without exception, in all fairness, integrity and objectivity.

We expect every Tunisian, those who support us and those who do not, to support the efforts to restore calm and to abandon violence, vandalism, and depravation. Reform requires calm. The incidents that we have witnessed were at the outset protests against social conditions, which we had made great efforts to fix, but we still require greater efforts to redress shortcomings. We all have to give ourselves the chance and the time required for all our important measures to materialize.

In addition, I have tasked the government—I called the prime minister—to reduce the prices of basic commodities and foodstuffs—sugar, milk, bread, etc.

As for political demands. I told you that I have understood you. Yes, I told you that I have understood you. And I have decided on full freedom for the media, in all its forms, and not shutting down Internet sites, and rejecting any form of censorship on them, while ensuring the respect of our morals and the principles of the journalistic profession.

As for the commission that I announced two days ago to look into corruption, bribery, and the mistakes of officials, this commission will be independent—yes, independent—and we will ensure its fairness and integrity.

The field is open, from this day onward, for freedom of political expression, including peaceful demonstrations—organized and orderly peaceful demonstrations, civilized demonstrations. That is fine. If a party or an organization wishes to organize a peaceful demonstration, they are welcome. But they should notify [us] of it, set its time and place, and organize it, and cooperate with the responsible parties to preserve its peaceful character.

I would like to assure you that many things did not happen the way I would have liked them to. Especially in the areas of democracy and freedoms. Sometimes, some misled me, by hiding the truth from me, and they will be held accountable. Yes, they will be held accountable.

Therefore, I reiterate to you, in all clarity, that I will work to promote democracy and to put pluralism into effect. Yes, to promote democracy and to put pluralism into effect.

And I will work to preserve and respect the country's constitution. And I'd like to reiterate here, in contrast to what some have claimed, that I have pledged, on November 7, that there would be no presidency for life. No presidency for life. Therefore, I renew thanks to all who have urged me to renominate myself in 2014, but I refuse to violate the age condition for candidacy for the presidency of the republic.

We want to reach the year 2014 in a framework of genuine civil consensus, and an atmosphere of national dialogue, with the participation of all national parties in assuming responsibilities.

Tunisia is the country of all of us. The country of all Tunisians. We love Tunisia and all of her people love her. We must protect her.

Let the will of her people remain in its hands and in the faithful hands that it will choose to continue the journey that began since independence and that we have continued since 1987.

To that end, we will set up a national commission headed by an independent national personality, with credibility among all the social and political parties, in order to review the electoral code, the press code, and the law of associations, etc. The commission will suggest the necessary provisional ideas until the 2014 elections, including the possibility of separating legislative elections and presidential elections.

Tunisia belongs to us all. Let us all preserve her. Her future is in our hands. Let us all safeguard it. Each one of us is responsible, from their position, for restoring her security, her stability, and for healing her wounds, and for ushering her into a new era that would better enable her to have a brighter future.

Long live Tunisia. Long live her people. Long live the republic. May peace and God's grace be upon you.

The Last Official Address by Egyptian President Hosni Mubarak

FEBRUARY 10, 2011

Fellow citizens, sons, the young men and women of Egypt. Today I address Egypt's youth in Tahrir Square and all throughout Egypt, I am speaking to you all from the heart, as a father to his sons and daughters, and I tell you that I am proud of you as a symbol of a new Egyptian generation calling for change for the better, and holding on to change and dreaming of the future and fashioning it. I tell you, first off, that the blood of your martyrs and your wounded will not go to waste. I assure you that I will not compromise in punishing those responsible harshly and decisively. And I will hold to account those who have committed crimes against our youth to the fullest extent of the law.

I tell the families of those innocents victims that I felt strong pain for them just as you have, and my heart ached just as yours ached.

I tell you that my responding to your voice and your message and your demands is a commitment from which there is no turning back, and that I am determined to fulfill what I have promised in all seriousness and honesty, and that I am very keen on implementing all of it without hesitation or looking back.

Translation by Tony Badran.

This commitment stems from a sure conviction of the honesty and purity of your intentions and your movement, and that your demands are just and legitimate. Mistakes are possible in any political system and in any country, but what's important is admitting them and rectifying them swiftly and holding those who commit them accountable.

I tell you, as president of the republic, that I never find it embarrassing or objectionable to listen to my country's youth and be responsive to them. But what is exceedingly embarrassing and shameful, and what I have never and will never accept, is to listen to foreign dictates coming from abroad, wherever their source, and whatever their pretexts and justifications.

Sons, the youth of Egypt, fellow citizens, I have declared in unambiguous terms that I would not run in the next presidential elections, satisfied with what I have offered my country over sixty years in war and in peace. I have expressed my commitment to that, and I have declared a similar and equal commitment to proceed with bearing my responsibility in protecting the constitution and the interests of the people until power and responsibility are handed over to whomever the voters choose next September, in free, fair elections, whose freedom and fairness will be guaranteed. That is the oath that I took before God and country, and I will keep it until we carry Egypt and its people to safety.

I have proposed a specific vision to get out of the current crisis and achieve what the youth and citizens have called for in a way that respects constitutional legitimacy and does not undermine it, and in a way that achieves the stability of our society and the demands of its sons, while at the same time presenting an agreed framework for the peaceful transfer of power through a responsible dialogue between all the forces of society and with utmost sincerity and transparency.

I proposed this vision in keeping with my responsibility to carry the nation out of these critical times, and I continue to implement it as my foremost priority, hour by hour, looking forward to the support and assistance of all who care for Egypt and its people, in order to succeed in turning it into a tangible reality, according to a wide and broad-based national consensus, whose implementation our brave armed forces will guarantee.

We have indeed begun a constructive national dialogue that includes Egypt's youth, who have led the call for change, and all the political forces. This dialogue has resulted in a preliminary consensus in opinions and positions, which puts us on the right path to get out of the crisis, and it should be continued in order to move it from broad headlines of what was agreed upon to a clear road map with a specific timetable that would proceed day by day on the road to the peaceful transfer of power from now until September.

This national dialogue has converged on forming a constitutional commission to study the requested amendments to the constitution and the required legislative amendments. It has also converged on forming a follow-up commission to pursue the faithful implantation of what I have promised before the people.

I made sure that the two commissions would be made up of Egyptian personalities whose independence and impartiality were well attested, as well as constitutional law scholars and judges.

In addition, facing all those we have lost as martyrs from the sons of Egypt, in tragic events that have pained our hearts and shaken the nation's conscience, I have issued instructions to quickly conclude investigations into last week's events, and to immediately refer their outcome to the attorney general for him to take the necessary deterrent legal action.

Yesterday I received the first report on the primary constitutional amendments suggested by the commission, which I created from judges and constitutional law scholars in order to study the requested constitutional and legislative amendments.

In response to the proposals in the commission report, and in line with the powers granted to the president of the republic according to Article 189 of the constitution, I submitted a request today to amend six articles of the constitution, which are Articles 76, 77, 88, 93, and 189, in addition to the annulment of Article 179, while also confirming readiness to submit at a later time a request to amend the articles which the constitutional commission will suggest, based on its consideration of the reasons and justifications.

These primary amendments aim to facilitate conditions for nomination for the presidency of the republic, and to adopt a specific limit on presidential terms, in order to achieve transfer of power, and to enhance election monitoring in order to ensure their freedom and fairness. The amendments also affirm the sole competence of the judiciary in deciding the validity and membership of members of parliament, and to amend the conditions and procedures for requesting constitutional amendments.

The proposal to abolish Article 179 of the constitution aims at achieving the required balance between protecting the homeland from the dangers of terrorism and ensuring respect for civil rights and liberties of citizens, such as to open the door to cease operating by the emergency law, as soon as calm and stability are restored and the appropriate conditions for lifting the state of emergency are attained.

Fellow citizens, the priority now is to restore confidence among Egyptians, confidence in our economy and our international reputation, and confidence that there will be no hesitation in or turning back from the change and transformation which we have begun.

Egypt is going through difficult times that we should not allow to continue, as they would inflict further damage and losses on us and our economy, and the situation in Egypt would end up such that the youth who have called for change and reform would become the first to suffer.

The present moment is not about my person; it's not about Hosni Mubarak. Rather, it has become about Egypt in its present and the future of its sons.

All Egyptians are in the same trench now, and we have to continue the national dialogue that we have started with the spirit of a single team, not multiple ones, and away from dispute and rivalry, in order for Egypt to overcome its current crisis and to restore confidence in our economy, and security and tranquility to our citizens, and daily normal life to the Egyptian street.

I was a young man like the Egyptian youth of today when I learned the honor of the Egyptian military and loyalty to the homeland and sacrifice on its behalf. I have spent a lifetime defending its soil and its sovereignty. I have witnessed its wars, in defeats and in victories. I have lived the days of defeat and occupation, and the days of the crossing [the Suez], victory and liberation. The happiest day of my life was when I raised the flag of Egypt over the Sinai. I have faced death a number of times as a fighter pilot and in Adis Ababa and many times more. I have never succumbed to foreign pressures or diktats. I have maintained the peace. I have worked for the security of Egypt and its stability. I have worked hard for its revival. I have never sought after power or a fake popularity. I trust that the overwhelming majority of the people know who Hosni Mubarak is. And it pains me what I am experiencing today at the hands of some of my fellow countrymen.

In any case, as I am aware the danger of the current difficult crossroad, and based on my conviction that Egypt is going through a defining moment in its history that requires us to put the country's supreme interest and to place Egypt first over any and every other consideration, I have delegated presidential prerogatives to the vice president, in accordance with constitutional specifications.

I am certain that Egypt will overcome its crisis. The will of its people will not be broken. It will stand up on its feet again with the sincerity and loyalty of all its sons, and it will repel the plotters and the gloaters.

We Egyptians will prove our ability to achieve the demands of the people through civilized and sensible dialogue. We will prove that we are not followers of anyone and that we don't take instructions from anyone, and that no one makes decisions on our behalf except for the pulse of the street and the demands of our countrymen.

We will prove that with the spirit and determination of Egyptians and with the unity and cohesion of this people and with our adherence to Egypt's pride, dignity and unique and eternal identity, as it is the foundation and essence of our existence for more than seven thousand years.

This spirit will live in us as long as Egypt and its people live. It will live in every one of our peasants, workers, and intellectuals. It will remain in the hearts of our elders, youth, and children—Muslims and Copts—and in the minds and consciences of our unborn children.

I say again that I have lived for this country, safeguarding its responsibility and trust. Egypt will remain above individuals and above everyone.

Excerpts from Libyan Leader Muammar al-Qaddafi's Televised Address

FEBRUARY 22, 2011

Muammar Qaddafi has no official post so that he can pout and resign from it, like other presidents did. Muammar Qaddafi is not a president. He is a revolutionary leader. Revolution means perpetual sacrifice until death.

This is my country, the country of my forefathers and of your forefathers. We planted it and watered it with the blood of our forefathers. We are more worthy of Libya than those rats and hirelings. Who are those hirelings, paid for by foreign intelligence services?! God damn them! They brought shame to their children, their families, and their tribes, that is if they have children, families, and tribes.

But they don't have tribes, for Libyan tribes are honorable, fighter, and combatant tribes, and they are rallying around me during this month.

All the tribes . . . They are all shouting the same thing. They are all confronting. We have confronted America—with its might and power. We challenged the great nuclear states of the world and we came out victorious. They bowed their heads here. Italy kissed the hand of the son of the martyr, the sheikh

Translation by Tony Badran.

of all martyrs, Omar al-Mukhtar. This is a glory beyond all glories. Not just for Mnifa [Mukhtar's tribe] . . . but for all Libyans, Arabs, and Muslims.

This is the victory they want to tarnish.

Italy, the empire at the time, was smashed on Libyan soil along with its hordes.

I am greater than the positions held by presidents and notables. I am a fighter. A mujahid. A combatant. A revolutionary from the tent. From the desert. All cities, villages, and oases united with me in a historic revolution that brought glories to the Libyans, that they will enjoy for generation after generation. Libya will remain at the top, leading Africa and Latin America and Asia; indeed, the whole world.

This handful of alien hirelings cannot stop this triumphant course—these cats and mice that jump from street to street, alley to alley, in the dark.

I have paid the price of staying here. My grandfather, Abdul Salam Buminyar, was the first martyr to fall in al-Khums during the first battle in 1911. I cannot betray this great sacrifice. I cannot leave my grandfather's pure remains in al-Marqab. In the end, I will die pure as a martyr. The remains of my father are in al-Hani. He was mujahid, a hero among the heroes of al-Qardabiya and Tala. And my uncle, Sheikh al-Saadi, lies in the cemetery of Mnaydar. I will not leave these pure remains; these are mujahids. Bashir al-Saadawi said, "Freedom is a tree in whose shade no one can sit except the one who planted it with his hands and watered it with his blood." Libya is a tree in whose shade we sit, for it is we who planted it with our hands and watered it with our blood.

I am addressing you from this steadfast place. This house in Tripoli, which was raided by 170 planes led by the great nuclear states, America and Britain and NATO. Forty Boeing planes were assisting in refueling the campaign. They bypassed all the palaces and all the houses—all your houses, they left your houses behind—looking for the house of Muammar Qaddafi.

Why? Because he is president of the republic? If he were a president, they would have treated him like they have treated other heads of state. But Muammar Qaddafi is history, resistance, liberation, glory, and revolution. This is recognition from the greatest power in the world, that Muammar Qaddafi is not a president, or an average person we either kill with poison or start a protest against to topple him.

When bombs were falling here in this place, pounding my house and killing my children, where were you, you alien riffraff? Where were you, you who sport beards? . . . Where were you? You were with America, applauding your American masters, while Muammar Qaddafi and his family were in this place being bombed.

One hundred seventy planes bypassed kings, presidents, bypassed the palaces of all the Arab world and came to Muammar Qaddafi's tent and house. This is glory that should not be squandered by Libya or the Libyan people, or the Arab nation, or the Islamic nation, of Africa or Latin America, or all people who desire freedom and human dignity and who resist tyrannical might.

We resisted the tyrannical might of America, Britain, and the nuclear states. We resisted the tyrannical might of NATO. We did not surrender. We remained steadfast right here.

Now, a small group of young men, who were given pills, are raiding police stations here and there like rats. They raided barracks. They used relative safety and security that Libya had enjoyed, and they raided unwary barracks, because we are not in a state of wars for us to tighten security on our warehouses and forts. . . . They raided some forts and stations and burned the files that contained their criminal records, and attacked the courts that held their files and the police stations where their interrogation records were kept.

But these young men bear no fault. They are young—sixteen, seventeen, eighteen years old. They sometimes mimic what is happening in Tunisia and Egypt. This is normal. Sometimes they hear that in some city in Libya, a group of young men attacked a courthouse and they say: "Let us go and attack the courthouse in our city." It's mimicry. They say: "They got hold of weapons. Why don't we get hold of weapons?"

However, there is a small sick group, implanted in the cities, that is giving out pills, and sometimes money, to these young men, and thrusting them into these side battles.

Those who were killed were members of the police and armed forces as well as these young men, but not those who were manipulating them. Those are in their houses or abroad, enjoying safety, comfort, and leisure with their children, while manipulating your children and giving them pills, telling them: "Go, get weapons. Raid, burn, you heroes!" So that your children die and we start fighting each other.

. . .

Get out of your homes, go out to the streets, secure the streets, seize the rats, do not be afraid of them. We did not yet use force. And [armed] force is to support the Libyan people. If it reaches a point where we have to use force, then we will use it. According to the international law, and according to the Libyan constitution and Libyan laws. Starting tomorrow, by God, starting tonight even, you should go out. All the Libyan cities, towns, and oases that love Muammar Qaddafi—because Muammar Qaddafi is glory. If I had an official position, if I were president I would have thrown my resignation in your faces, and [in the faces of] these germs. But I don't hold an official position. I don't have anything from which to resign. I have my rifle. I will fight until the last drop of my blood. And the Libyan people are with me. I have lived my life not afraid of anything. You are facing a solid rock, against which America's fleets have crashed.

. . .

Pull your children from the streets. They took your children away from you and inebriated them in order to throw them into the fire so they would die. Your children are dying. For what reason? For what purpose? For nothing, but to burn Libya. Your children have died. But their children did not die. They are in America, and in Europe. What is this fear of these gangs? Gangs, like rats, they represent nothing. They do not represent one out of a million of the Libyan people. They are worth nothing. They are a handful of young men, imitating what was happening in Egypt and Tunisia, and who were given pills, and were given orders to burn and loot. Mimicry! Rats!

Starting tomorrow the police and the army will impose security. They will open roads and remove all barricades. All barricades should be removed. You remove them yourselves out of your cities. Go out after them. Chase them everywhere. Do you want Benghazi to be ruined? Cut off from electricity and water? Who will bring you water and electricity? These rats can reach the oil fields and blow it up. And you would return to darkness, to 1952. I built Benghazi myself, brick by brick, and we are proud of it and we are building it anew. And they are coming to destroy it, using your own children.

. . .

Three tanks were burned. Even the airport they tried to ransack. Civilian flights have stopped using the airport. Ships said we cannot dock in Benghazi port, because the rats will attack us when we arrive and loot the ships. Darnah has been ruined. . . . As of today, one of those who sport beards [is in charge] . . . and he told them to start bringing him donations, saying, "I am a Caliph. I am a follower of bin Laden and Zawahiri." . . . Do you want Americans to come and occupy you? To turn you into Afghanistan and Somalia and Pakistan and Iraq? This is what will happen to our country. Our country will become like Afghanistan. Do you like that? If not, go out to the streets and block them. Seize them and chase after them. Take away their arms. Arrest them and prosecute them. Hand them over to security. They are a tiny few. . . . They are a terrorist few. They are turning Libya into the emirates of Zawahiri and bin Laden. Is this the where we will end up? So that America can come in and say they have a new Afghanistan here in North Africa, and so bring us colonialism and drop bombs on our country?

All free officers have been distributed to all their areas and their tribes, so that they could lead these areas and tribes to secure and cleanse them from these rats. And arrest those who tricked our young children and bring them to trial. And that will be their punishment according to the law.

Listen to the chants in the streets: "Our souls and our blood we sacrifice for you, our leader."

Look at their crimes. This is the Libyan penal code from before the revolution. Anyone who bears arms against Libya shall be punished by death. Scheming with foreign countries to incite war against Libya. Anyone who does so is punishable by death. This is the penal code. Undermining the territorial sovereignty of the state and facilitating war against it is punishable by death. Anyone who facilitates the entry of enemies into the country, or hands over cities, or fortifications or installations or locations or ports to them. These kinds of acts will lead to the handing over of locations to America. . . . Entering military installations, if the enemy benefits from this, the punishment will be a death sentence. . . . They have committed all these crimes. . . . They have handed all our secrets to the enemy. This is not the fault of the children. . . . It is those who are behind them and who are tricking you, whose fate will be before tribunals, where they will cry and lift their hands and beg for forgiveness. But this time we will not forgive them. . . . Anyone who employs force, or any other means not allowed by law and the constitution, in order to change the constitution and the system of governance, is punishable by death. They are changing the rule of the people. Their punishment is death according to the law.

. . .

No, please stop to listen. You are all excited, but please stop chanting so that the people can hear what I have to say. This is very serious. This is a different matter than bullets. I haven't yet given the order to use bullets. When the order is given to use force, we will be ready. Then everything will be burned.

Usurping military command, like what happened in al-Bayda and Benghazi. Unlawfully usurping a military command and refusing to relinquish it is punishable by death. Any use of force against state authorities is punishable by death. Acts of sabotage, looting, and murder is punishable by death. All of their crimes that they have committed from that day until now are punishable by death according to Libyan law, the Libyan penal code written before the revolution. Civil war: anyone who perpetrates an act whose aim is to start a civil war in the country is punishable by death. These acts will lead to civil war. Like Sayf al-Islam told you, we are all armed tribes. No one tribe can rule over another. . . . This will lead to civil war, if you do not apprehend them right away.

. . .

Lastly, gentlemen, if these things are not fulfilled: handing over the weapons, the prisoners, the troublemakers who tricked our children, and the removal of all blockades and returning life to normal . . . if this not fulfilled, and if Libya's unity is endangered . . . if we see this happening, we will prevent it. Then we will declare the march. . . . We will declare the holy march. Oh yes. . . . We will issue a call to the millions, from the desert to the desert. And I and the millions will march in order to cleanse Libya, inch by inch, house by house, home by home, alley by alley, individual by individual, so that the country is purified from the unclean. We cannot allow for Libya to be lost from our hands without justification. . . . I have millions on my side. I have God on my side, who has made me victorious over the great powers.

Excerpts from the Sermon of Shaykh Yusuf al-Qaradawi

TAHRIR SQUARE, CAIRO, EGYPT, FEBRUARY 23, 2011

O brothers, O my sons and my daughters, O my brothers and my sisters, O my grandsons and my granddaughters, children of Egypt! The usage of preachers, for their sermons, is to say "O Muslims!" but me, I say in this square, "O Muslims and Copts! O children of Egypt!" This is the day of the children of Egypt all together. It is not the day of the Muslims alone. I am addressing them from this tribune (*minbar*), and from this square, Tahrir Square—or, rather, from this day onwards, it ought to be called the "Square of the Martyrs of the January 25 Revolution." O Brothers, I am addressing you from above this tribune and from the Square of the Martyrs of the January 25 Revolution, this revolution which has taught the world how revolutions should be. It was not an usual revolution but it was a revolution teaching something. The youth who have triumphed in this revolution did not triumph over Mubarak only. They triumphed over Mubarak, they triumphed over injustice, they triumphed over falsehood. They triumphed over robbery and they triumphed over plundering. They triumphed over egoism and they initiated a new life by this revolution.

Translation by Yahya M. Michot with the collaboration of Samy Metwally at the Hartford Seminary. The original is available from www.hartsem.edu/documents/Qardawi.pdf.

. . .

This is Egypt when it believes. This is why these youth from all regions in Egypt, from all social classes, rich and poor, educated and illiterate, workers and cultured—though the majority were cultured and educated people—we saw altruism increase among them. They became, they fused into, one melting pot: Muslims and Christians, radicals and conservatives, rightists and leftists, men and women, old and young, all of them became one, all of them acting for Egypt, in order to liberate Egypt from injustice (*zulm*) and tyranny (*tâghût*). It was inevitable that Egypt be liberated, because these youth willed it, and when the youth will, their will participates of the will of God.

. . .

I recommend to these youth to keep their spirit. The revolution has not ended. The revolution has just started producing fruits. Do not think that the revolution is over! Consider that the revolution is continuing, because we will participate in the construction, the construction of the new Egypt, which has learned many things from this revolution. Be patient with your revolution and preserve it! Beware lest someone steal it from you! Protect this revolution! Be on your guard against the hypocrites, who are ready to put on, every day, a new face, and to speak with a new tongue! "When they meet those who believe, they say: 'We believe'; and when they are alone with their devils, they say: 'Surely we are with you'" (Q. 2:14). Yesterday they were against the revolution and, today, with the revolution! Be on your guard against those! Say to the youth: "Protect your revolution! Be vigilant about this revolution, and continue to protect it!" This is what I demand from my children, the youth of the revolution: to continue their revolution and to preserve their unity. Beware lest someone enter among you who would corrupt this excellent relationship and this fraternity which has brought you together in this square. These are my words to the youth of the revolution.

. . .

Egypt, O brothers, has triumphed in this revolution and has triumphed over what has been called "sectarianism." There was something that they used to call "sectarianism," and that they themselves had produced. In this square, the Square of the Martyrs of January 25, the Christian stood with the Muslim, side by side. I remember that yesterday, while I was coming from Qatar, a young man came to me, saying: "I am So-and-so, son of So-and-so, from Egypt. I am a Christian. I am one of those who follow the program *The Sharî'a and Life* and your Friday sermons in Qatar. I am proud of you, you who are calling for the unity of the Umma, and you . . . and you . . ." I said: "Praise is due to God! . . ." In Tahrir Square, the Copt brothers were standing as guards of their [Muslim] brothers while they were praying. And today I invite them not to guard their brothers, but to prostrate with their Muslim brothers in thankfulness to God Most High. To prostrate is something that the Muslims and the Christians both do. In this square, this sectarianism has come to an end, this cursed sectarianism. Yesterday, Ahmad Ragab, the satirist writer, mentioned that he had visited Tahrir Square and found a young Muslim girl pouring water for a Muslim man for the ablution; he said: "Now, the revolution has succeeded!" As for me, my granddaughter was leading a group of young people washing and cleaning the squares, and painting various things in need of paint. A priest passed by them, a priest, who said to them: "Do you need some help? I, I can help you." They said: "Yes, please," thinking that he would work with them. He took out a hundred Egyptian pounds and said: "This is my help to you." They said "God is greater!" (*Allâhu akbar!*) and bought some brushes, paints, and other things. This is the Egyptian spirit, the spirit that encompasses all. I hope from the people (*sha'b*) of Egypt that it sticks to this unity, the unity of a line of people praying. Let there be no fanaticism! We are all believers. We have to believe in God and to deepen our faith. We are all Egyptians. We are all rising up against falseness (*bâtil*). We are all angry on behalf of the Truth. That spirit must persist, O my brothers and sisters, O my sons and daughters!

Some words now to the army of Egypt. Some words to the army of Egypt. I salute the army of Egypt. I salute this army, which is the armor of the people (*sha'b*), its support and its pride. Some of the brothers told me: "Don't overpraise the army! It might let you down and not help the revolution to win!" I said to them: "By God, they will not let me down!" When I preached my latest sermon, after the first communiqué that had been issued and many people had been struck by disappointment because of it, I said: "I believe that the army of Egypt will not be less patriotic than the army of Tunisia. The army of Tunisia helped the revolution of Tunisia to win, and the army of Egypt, which entered four wars for Egypt and for Palestine, it is not possible that this army betray its country, it is not possible that it sacrifice the youth for the sake of a single individual. This army is too reasonable and too noble to do that." And I swore that the army would join with the people (*sha'b*). The army joined with the people (*sha'b*), issued these decisions that we had seen, and announced from the first day that the right to express itself peacefully was guaranteed to the people (*sha'b*) as long as it remained peaceful. It also announced that it understood the demands of the people (*sha'b*) and that it would not intervene against it; and it did not and would not use force against the children of the people (*sha'b*), who are making the revolution and demonstrating peacefully. This army, which has announced that it is not an alternative to the legitimate order (*shar'iyya*) that the people (*sha'b*) want and that the youth of this square would be pleased with. It also announced that it is attached to freedom and democracy. It has set up this commission for revising the constitution—within ten days!—and it is in a hurry that life be changed into civilian life—this commission, which is chaired by this eminent man, the legal adviser, the jurist, the historian, the thinker, the moderate, the fair-minded, Târiq al-Bishrî. We want from this commission that it play its role as soon as possible.

And we demand from the Egyptian army that it liberate us from the government that Mubarak formed in his time, a time now over, annihilated. We want a new government, in which there are none of these faces that people cannot bear anymore. Every time people see them, they remember the injustice, they remember the killing, they remember the falseness, they remember the raid of the camels, the mules, and the horses, they remember the snipers who kill people, they remember the vehicle that is going right and left, back and forth, and is killing people, running people over! Twenty people were killed, run over by this vehicle! People do not want to see these faces. We demand from the army and from its command that it liberate us from this government and set up a government, form a civilian government from the children of Egypt—and how many they are, the noble children of Egypt who did not commit such crimes! We also demand, we demand from the army that it immediately set free the political detainees and the political prisoners whom the prisons are holding and who have lived long years under the vaults of the prisons after being judged by military tribunals or emergency tribunals that give no evidence and do not care about the truth. The traces of these tribunals must be erased. I do not want our brave and noble army to be charged with any sin. Every day that passes while those people are in prison, every day that they spend in prison, or even, every hour, all those who caused this injustice and are not correcting it are committing a sin. Inasmuch as we are able to correct this injustice, this injustice must cease.

Before I finish speaking, I want to turn to the children of Egypt. I know that the children of Egypt have suffered a lot of injustice. Various groups of workers, peasants, and employees, how long they have suffered injustice! However, God did not build this world in a day, nor in hours. He built it in six days, although He had the power to build it with a "'Be!' and it is,"in order to teach us perseverance. We inevitably must be patient, a little longer. I call on everyone who has stopped working, or is striking, or is sitting-in, to contribute to this revolution with his work. Egypt wants you to work. The Egyptian economy is underdeveloped and it is not permitted to us who have supported the revolution, it is not permitted to us to be a cause retarding the construction of Egypt, retarding the economy of Egypt. On the contrary, we must convince all our brothers who are striking and who are sitting-in to be patient a little longer. I am calling on the army to contact them, to reassure them, and to promise them that this is indeed what we want, so that Egypt moves along in its construction, in the phase of construction. All the children of Egypt are now ready to build. Everyone is ready to take a stone and to build something in this country. I call on all the children of the country to work for construction. We are in a new phase, a phase in which the truth triumphs and falseness is brought to naught. Surely, it is the right of all these Egyptians that they get their rights, that they obtain that which they deserve and that they be treated equitably, but it is also our duty to be patient with our brothers in the army, so that all hopes be achieved, one after the other. "And say to them: 'Act!' God will see your action, and so will His Messenger and the believers, and you will be brought back to the Knower of the invisible and the visible, and He will inform you about what you used to do" (Q. 9:105). Pray to God Most High and He will hear your prayer.

. . .

Before I conclude my speech and these invocations, I will say some words to the regimes ruling in the Arab countries. I will say to them: "Don't be arrogant! Don't delude yourselves! Don't stop history! Nobody will be able to fight the divine decrees, nor to delay the day when it rises. This world has changed and the world has evolved. The Arab world has changed from the inside. So, do not stand against the peoples (*sha'b*). Try to come to an understanding with them! Don't deceive them! Don't try to get them with empty words! It is not possible that peoples (*sha'b*) remain silent. Dialogue with them in a real dialogue, not to patch things up, but with constructive actions, constructive actions that put things in their places, respect the minds of people (*nâs*) and respect the minds of the peoples (*sha'b*)!" This is my message to the rulers of the Arabs.

Now, a message to our brothers in Palestine. Myself, I have the hope that God, Glorified and Exalted is He, just as He has cooled my eyes with the victory of Egypt, will cool my eyes with the opening (*fath*) of al-Aqsâ Mosque and will make it possible for me to preach in al-Aqsâ Mosque. O God, make it possible for us to preach in al-Aqsâ Mosque and to enter al-Aqsâ Mosque safely, without fear or dread! O God, make for us a reality of this manifest opening! O children of Palestine, be confident that you will be helped to win! The Rafah crossing will be open for you. I demand this from the Egyptian army, from the Supreme Council of the Armed Forces: "Open the Rafah crossing! Open that which stands between us and our brothers! Gaza is part of Egypt and Egypt is part of Gaza. Egypt must be a support, an armor, a fortress. For Egypt, which has fought four wars for Palestine, it is not proper to block the road. The crossings that are in our hands must necessarily be open, especially the Rafah crossing. We should open it to the convoys that used to be prevented from giving succour to our brothers." This is what I demand from our dear, brave, and noble army.

What Is the Revolution? What Is the Regime?

FROM *REVOLUTIONARY EGYPT*, VOLUME 2

Beginning on January 25th, the Egyptian masses were stirred awake to announce their revolution against the regime and the people's desire for its downfall. They succeeded in overthrowing the head of the regime by deposing President Mubarak. Likewise, Ahmad Shafiq's government fell, and they have now entered their battle against the security apparatus. We do not have to detract from those great achievements, just as we should not be misled by the talk of those who say that the regime fell completely merely due to Mubarak's removal along with some of the regime's symbols. However, we do need to understand what the regime was and what its role and nature was. The regime is not a unbiased entity, but rather the result of an incompatibility of the interests of the rulers and the ruled. The regime was created in order to impose the authority and interests of the ruling class over the suffering masses, the sons of this people. It is an instrument that allows those who hold the power and wealth to exploit the masses. If we look at the essence of this regime, it consisted of the armed apparatus—the police, State Security, and Central Security, in addition to the army. That whole apparatus was designed to deprive the people of their freedom and to protect only the regime. If we now were to take a look at the situation in Egypt, we would

Translation by Alina Muelhauser and review by Thomas Levi Thompson. Document acquired on March 7, 2011.

see the regime as it really is. Despite the fact that it sacrificed some of its figureheads, here it is trying to use all of its forces, ferociously, to protect its interests. These victories that we have realized are nothing but concessions that it was forced to make under the pressure of the masses.

Regarding revolution, it does not mean exchanging one ruler with another. Instead, it means a total and complete change in which the former regime is demolished and a substitute emerges from it in harmony with the revolution's principles. In this case, the regime changes and the ruling authority is replaced by an authority that expresses the public. A change in the distribution of wealth also occurs. In the light of the revolution, the remains of the ruling authority are fighting desperately to keep their power. Even if its repressive apparatus failed in its self-protection, they will try to use the media to spread their opinions. We see the old ruling class trying to convince the masses that the regime fell with Mubarak when he fell. However, this is not true, and the regime is trying once again to convince the masses that it is not possible to change again—as if the authority of this class is unending and as if it would not be possible to change the regime. The counterrevolution promotes these lies to protect the interests of its own class. In reality, the revolution does not happen simply because the majority changed their minds overnight. Rather, these thoughts changed on the level of the masses by way of their struggle. The thoughts changed during the struggle when the masses realized their ability to enact change. They also realized that the toiling classes, ground to bits, had a shared interest in facing off against their leaders. They also realized that the differences the ruling class tried to use to split them do not have any importance. There is no difference between women and men or Muslims and Christians. As an example of this, every day we see attempts to incite sectarian riots in Egypt, such as what happened in the Atfih church. These must be overcome. Once again, this ruling class is trying to create a security panic amongst the crowds of the masses in order to impose their authority—as if we could not live without them and their apparatus. However, the experience proved that we do not need to use this repressive apparatus to secure our neighborhoods. The role of that apparatus is to protect the ruling minority and to repress the masses. As far as the security of the neighborhoods and the organization of the traffic movement are concerned, we can create more democratic and efficient instruments, able to deal with their matters in a better way. The revolution is not an event that happens on a specific day but is a process of change. If we want now to continue our revolution in order to realize the goals we have not yet achieved, then we have to organize ourselves to face off against the organized enemies of the revolution, the old regime. Our martyrs who gave their lives during the revolution did not do so in order that another ruler could take Mubarak's place nor to paint the sidewalks. They gave their lives for real change in society—a society with real freedom, free of any kind of repression and oppression, in which wealth is redistributed in order to realize social justice.

Arab League Resolution 7360 on the Repercussions of the Current Events in Libya

MARCH 12, 2011

The resolution of the Council of the Arab League at the ministerial level in its irregular session on 3/12/2011 regarding the repercussions of the current events in Libya and the Arab position.

The Council of the League at the ministerial level in its irregular session, held on 3/12/2011 at the headquarter of the General Secretariat in Cairo,

- After deliberating where the dangerous situation in Libya has led to, and its repercussions, and the crimes and violations perpetrated by the Libyan authorities against the Libyan people, especially the use of warplanes, artillery and heavy weaponry against citizens,
- Taking note of the ongoing consultations and contacts at the Security Council, as well as the positions issued by the Cooperation Council for the Arab States of the Gulf and the European Union and the African Union,
- Taking into account the appointment by the Secretary General of the United Nations of a high-level envoy to follow up on the humanitarian problems in Libya,

Translation by Tony Badran.

- Reaffirming what was stated in its Resolution 7298 of 3/2/2011, as well as the statement issued by the Council of the League on 2/22/2011,
- Reaffirming the need to respect international humanitarian law and the demand to stop crimes against the Libyan people and to end the fighting, the withdrawal of the forces of the Libyan authorities from the cities and regions which they have entered forcibly, and to ensure the right of the Libyan people in achieving its demands and building its future and institutions in a democratic framework,
- Recalling its commitment to preserve the unity, integrity and political independence of Libyan territory as well as civil peace and ensuring the safety and security of Libyan citizens and the national unity of the Libyan people and its independence and sovereignty over its land, and its rejection of all forms of foreign intervention in Libya, and reaffirming that not taking the necessary measures to end this crisis will lead to foreign intervention in internal Libyan affairs,

Has resolved to,

1. Request that the Security Council shoulder its responsibility regarding the deterioration of the situation in Libya, and take the required measures to impose a no-fly zone over the movement of Libyan warplanes immediately, and to establish safe areas in the places subjected to shelling, such as preventative measures that would provide protection to the Libyan people as well as residents of Libya from various nationalities, while taking into account the sovereignty and territorial integrity of neighboring states.
2. Cooperate and communicate with the Libyan Transitional National Council and to provide urgent and continuing support to the Libyan people, and to provide it with the necessary protection against the gross violations and serious crimes

it is being subjected to by the Libyan authorities, which strips them of legitimacy.

3. Renew the call to member states and friendly states and international organizations and the Arab and international civil society bodies to offer urgent humanitarian assistance to the Libyan people and to support it in this critical period of its history through various channels and to offer thanks to the states and bodies that offer such emergency assistance, as well as to the states that contribute to the evacuation of Arab citizens who wish to leave Libya.
4. Continue coordination over the situation in Libya with the United Nations and the African Union and the Organization of the Islamic Conference as well as with the European Union.

UN Security Council Resolution 1973, Libya

MARCH 17, 2011

This UN Security Council resolution regarding Libya was passed on March 17, 2011.

"*The Security Council,*

"*Recalling* its resolution 1970 (2011) of 26 February 2011,

"*Deploring* the failure of the Libyan authorities to comply with resolution 1970 (2011),

"*Expressing* grave concern at the deteriorating situation, the escalation of violence, and the heavy civilian casualties,

"*Reiterating* the responsibility of the Libyan authorities to protect the Libyan population and *reaffirming* that parties to armed conflicts bear the primary responsibility to take all feasible steps to ensure the protection of civilians,

"*Condemning* the gross and systematic violation of human rights, including arbitrary detentions, enforced disappearances, torture and summary executions,

"*Further condemning* acts of violence and intimidation committed by the Libyan authorities against journalists, media professionals and associated personnel and *urging* these authorities to comply with their obligations under international humanitarian law as outlined in resolution 1738 (2006),

"*Considering* that the widespread and systematic attacks currently taking place in the Libyan Arab Jamahiriya against the civilian population may amount to crimes against humanity,

"*Recalling* paragraph 26 of resolution 1970 (2011) in which the Council expressed its readiness to consider taking additional appropriate measures, as necessary, to facilitate and support the return of humanitarian agencies and make available humanitarian and related assistance in the Libyan Arab Jamahiriya,

"*Expressing its determination* to ensure the protection of civilians and civilian populated areas and the rapid and unimpeded passage of humanitarian assistance and the safety of humanitarian personnel,

"*Recalling* the condemnation by the League of Arab States, the African Union and the Secretary-General of the Organization of the Islamic Conference of the serious violations of human rights and international humanitarian law that have been and are being committed in the Libyan Arab Jamahiriya,

"*Taking note* of the final communiqué of the Organization of the Islamic Conference of 8 March 2011, and the communiqué of the Peace and Security Council of the African Union of 10 March 2011 which established an ad hoc High-Level Committee on Libya,

"*Taking note also* of the decision of the Council of the League of Arab States of 12 March 2011 to call for the imposition of a no-fly zone on Libyan military aviation, and to establish safe areas in places exposed to shelling as a precautionary measure that allows the protection of the Libyan people and foreign nationals residing in the Libyan Arab Jamahiriya,

"*Taking note further* of the Secretary-General's call on 16 March 2011 for an immediate ceasefire,

"*Recalling* its decision to refer the situation in the Libyan Arab Jamahiriya since 15 February 2011 to the Prosecutor of the International Criminal Court, and *stressing* that those responsible for or complicit in attacks targeting the civilian population, including aerial and naval attacks, must be held to account,

"*Reiterating its concern* at the plight of refugees and foreign workers forced to flee the violence in the Libyan Arab Jamahiriya, *welcoming* the response of neighbouring States, in particular Tunisia and Egypt, to address the needs of those refugees and foreign workers, and *calling* on the international community to support those efforts,

"*Deploring* the continuing use of mercenaries by the Libyan authorities,

"*Considering* that the establishment of a ban on all flights in the airspace of the Libyan Arab Jamahiriya constitutes an important element for the protection of civilians as well as the safety of the delivery of humanitarian assistance and a decisive step for the cessation of hostilities in Libya,

"*Expressing concern* also for the safety of foreign nationals and their rights in the Libyan Arab Jamahiriya,

"*Welcoming* the appointment by the Secretary General of his Special Envoy to Libya, Mr. Abdul Ilah Mohamed Al-Khatib and supporting his efforts to find a sustainable and peaceful solution to the crisis in the Libyan Arab Jamahiriya,

"*Reaffirming* its strong commitment to the sovereignty, independence, territorial integrity and national unity of the Libyan Arab Jamahiriya,

"*Determining* that the situation in the Libyan Arab Jamahiriya continues to constitute a threat to international peace and security,

"*Acting* under Chapter VII of the Charter of the United Nations,

"1. *Demands* the immediate establishment of a ceasefire and a complete end to violence and all attacks against, and abuses of, civilians;

"2. *Stresses* the need to intensify efforts to find a solution to the crisis which responds to the legitimate demands of the Libyan people and notes the decisions of the Secretary-General to send his Special Envoy to Libya and of the Peace and Security Council of the African Union to send its ad hoc High-Level Committee to Libya with the aim of facilitating dialogue to lead to the political reforms necessary to find a peaceful and sustainable solution;

"3. *Demands* that the Libyan authorities comply with their obligations under international law, including international humanitarian law, human rights and refugee law and take all measures to protect civilians and meet their basic needs, and to ensure the rapid and unimpeded passage of humanitarian assistance;

"Protection of civilians

"4. *Authorizes* Member States that have notified the Secretary-General, acting nationally or through regional organizations or arrangements, and acting in cooperation with the Secretary-General, to take all necessary measures, notwithstanding paragraph 9 of resolution 1970 (2011), to protect civilians and civilian populated areas under threat of attack in the Libyan Arab Jamahiriya, including Benghazi, while excluding a foreign occupation force of any form on any part of Libyan territory, and *requests* the Member States concerned to inform the Secretary-General immediately of the measures they take pursuant to the authorization conferred by this paragraph which shall be immediately reported to the Security Council;

"5. *Recognizes* the important role of the League of Arab States in matters relating to the maintenance of international peace and security in the region, and bearing in mind Chapter VIII of the Charter of the United Nations, requests the Member States of the League of Arab States to cooperate with other Member States in the implementation of paragraph 4;

"No-fly zone

"6. *Decides* to establish a ban on all flights in the airspace of the Libyan Arab Jamahiriya in order to help protect civilians;

"7. *Decides further* that the ban imposed by paragraph 6 shall not apply to flights whose sole purpose is humanitarian, such as delivering or facilitating the delivery of assistance, including medical supplies, food, humanitarian workers and related assistance, or evacuating foreign nationals from the Libyan Arab Jamahiriya, nor shall it apply to flights authorised by paragraphs 4 or 8, nor other flights which are deemed necessary by States acting under the authorization conferred in paragraph 8 to be for the benefit of the Libyan people, and that these flights shall be coordinated with any mechanism established under paragraph 8;

"8. *Authorizes* Member States that have notified the Secretary-General and the Secretary-General of the League of Arab States, acting nationally or through regional organizations or arrangements, to take all necessary measures to enforce compliance with the ban on flights imposed by paragraph 6 above, as necessary, and *requests* the States concerned in cooperation with the League of Arab States to coordinate closely with the Secretary General on the measures they are taking to implement this ban, including by establishing an appropriate mechanism for implementing the provisions of paragraphs 6 and 7 above,

"9. *Calls upon* all Member States, acting nationally or through regional organizations or arrangements, to provide assistance, including any necessary overflight approvals, for the purposes of implementing paragraphs 4, 6, 7 and 8 above;

"10. *Requests* the Member States concerned to coordinate closely with each other and the Secretary-General on the measures they are taking to implement paragraphs 4, 6, 7 and 8 above, including practical measures for the monitoring and approval of authorised humanitarian or evacuation flights;

"11. *Decides* that the Member States concerned shall inform the Secretary-General and the Secretary-General of the League of Arab States immediately of measures taken in exercise of the authority conferred by paragraph 8 above, including to supply a concept of operations;

"12. *Requests* the Secretary-General to inform the Council immediately of any actions taken by the Member States concerned in exercise of the authority conferred by paragraph 8 above and to report to the Council within 7 days and every month thereafter on the implementation of this resolution, including information on any violations of the flight ban imposed by paragraph 6 above;

"Enforcement of the arms embargo

"13. *Decides that* paragraph 11 of resolution 1970 (2011) shall be replaced by the following paragraph: "Calls upon all Member States, in particular States of the region, acting nationally or through regional organisations or arrangements, in order to ensure strict implementation of the arms embargo established by paragraphs 9 and 10 of resolution 1970 (2011), to inspect in their territory, including seaports and airports, and on the high seas, vessels and aircraft bound to or from the Libyan Arab Jamahiriya, if the State concerned has information that provides reasonable grounds to believe that the cargo contains items the supply, sale, transfer or export of which is prohibited by paragraphs 9 or 10 of resolution 1970 (2011) as modified by this resolution, including the provision of armed mercenary personnel, *calls upon* all flag States of such vessels and aircraft to cooperate with such inspections and authorises Member States to use all measures commensurate to the specific circumstances to carry out such inspections";

"14. *Requests* Member States which are taking action under paragraph 13 above on the high seas to coordinate closely with each other and the Secretary-General and *further requests* the States concerned to inform the Secretary-General and the Committee established pursuant to paragraph 24 of resolution 1970 (2011) ("the Committee") immediately of measures taken in the exercise of the authority conferred by paragraph 13 above;

"15. *Requires* any Member State whether acting nationally or through regional organisations or arrangements, when it undertakes an inspection pursuant to paragraph 13 above, to submit promptly an initial written report to the Committee containing, in particular, explanation of the grounds for the inspection, the results of such inspection, and whether or not cooperation was provided, and, if prohibited items for transfer are found, further requires such Member States to submit to the Committee, at a later stage, a subsequent written report containing relevant details on the inspection, seizure, and disposal, and relevant details of the transfer, including a description of the items, their origin and intended destination, if this information is not in the initial report;

"16. *Deplores* the continuing flows of mercenaries into the Libyan Arab Jamahiriya and *calls upon* all Member States to comply strictly with their obligations under paragraph 9 of resolution 1970 (2011) to prevent the provision of armed mercenary personnel to the Libyan Arab Jamahiriya;

"Ban on flights

"17. *Decides* that all States shall deny permission to any aircraft registered in the Libyan Arab Jamahiriya or owned or operated by Libyan nationals or companies to take off from, land in or overfly their territory unless the particular flight has been approved in advance by the Committee, or in the case of an emergency landing;

"18. *Decides* that all States shall deny permission to any aircraft to take off from, land in or overfly their territory, if they have information that provides reasonable grounds to believe that the aircraft contains items the supply, sale, transfer, or export of which is prohibited by paragraphs 9 and 10 of resolution 1970 (2011) as modified by this resolution, including the provision of armed mercenary personnel, except in the case of an emergency landing;

"Asset freeze

"19. *Decides* that the asset freeze imposed by paragraph 17, 19, 20 and 21 of resolution 1970 (2011) shall apply to all funds, other financial assets and economic resources which are on their territories, which are owned or controlled, directly or indirectly, by the Libyan authorities, as designated by the Committee, or by individuals or entities acting on their behalf or at their direction, or by entities owned or controlled by them, as designated by the Committee, and *decides further* that all States shall ensure that any funds, financial assets or economic resources are prevented from being made available by their nationals or by any individuals or entities within their territories, to or for the benefit of the Libyan authorities, as designated by the Committee, or individuals or entities acting on their behalf or at their direction, or entities owned or controlled by them, as designated by the Committee, and directs the Committee to designate such Libyan authorities, individuals or entities within 30 days of the date of the adoption of this resolution and as appropriate thereafter;

"20. *Affirms* its determination to ensure that assets frozen pursuant to paragraph 17 of resolution 1970 (2011) shall, at a later stage, as soon as possible be made available to and for the benefit of the people of the Libyan Arab Jamahiriya;

"21. Decides that all States shall require their nationals, persons subject to their jurisdiction and firms incorporated in their territory or subject to their jurisdiction to exercise vigilance when doing business with entities incorporated in the Libyan Arab Jamahiriya or subject to its jurisdiction, and any individuals or entities acting on their behalf or at their direction, and entities owned or controlled by them, if the States have information that provides reasonable grounds to believe that such business could contribute to violence and use of force against civilians;

"Designations

"22. *Decides* that the individuals listed in Annex I shall be subject to the travel restrictions imposed in paragraphs 15 and 16 of resolution 1970 (2011), and *decides further* that the individuals and entities listed in Annex II shall be subject to the asset freeze imposed in paragraphs 17, 19, 20 and 21 of resolution 1970 (2011);

"23. *Decides* that the measures specified in paragraphs 15, 16, 17, 19, 20 and 21 of resolution 1970 (2011) shall apply also to individuals and entities determined by the Council or the Committee to have violated the provisions of resolution 1970 (2011), particularly paragraphs 9 and 10 thereof, or to have assisted others in doing so;

"Panel of Experts

"24. *Requests* the Secretary-General to create for an initial period of one year, in consultation with the Committee, a group of up to eight experts ("Panel of Experts"), under the direction of the Committee to carry out the following tasks:

(a) Assist the Committee in carrying out its mandate as specified in paragraph 24 of resolution 1970 (2011) and this resolution;

(b) Gather, examine and analyse information from States, relevant United Nations bodies, regional organisations and other interested parties regarding the implementation of the measures decided in resolution 1970 (2011) and this resolution, in particular incidents of non-compliance;

(c) Make recommendations on actions the Council, or the Committee or State, may consider to improve implementation of the relevant measures;

(d) Provide to the Council an interim report on its work no later than 90 days after the Panel's appointment, and a final report to the Council no later than 30 days prior to the termination of its mandate with its findings and recommendations;

"25. *Urges* all States, relevant United Nations bodies and other interested parties, to cooperate fully with the Committee and the Panel of Experts, in particular by supplying any information at their disposal on the implementation of the measures decided in resolution 1970 (2011) and this resolution, in particular incidents of non-compliance;

"26. *Decides* that the mandate of the Committee as set out in paragraph 24 of resolution 1970 (2011) shall also apply to the measures decided in this resolution;

"27. *Decides* that all States, including the Libyan Arab Jamahiriya, shall take the necessary measures to ensure that no claim shall lie at the instance of the Libyan authorities, or of any person or body in the Libyan Arab Jamahiriya, or of any person claiming through or for the benefit of any such person or body, in connection with any contract or other transaction where its performance was affected by reason of the measures taken by the Security Council in resolution 1970 (2011), this resolution and related resolutions;

"28. *Reaffirms* its intention to keep the actions of the Libyan authorities under continuous review and underlines its readiness to review at any time the measures imposed by this resolution and resolution 1970 (2011), including by strengthening, suspending or lifting those measures, as appropriate, based on compliance by the Libyan authorities with this resolution and resolution 1970 (2011);

"29. *Decides* to remain actively seized of the matter."

Remarks by President Barack Obama in Address to the Nation on Libya

WASHINGTON, DC, MARCH 28, 2011

THE PRESIDENT: Tonight, I'd like to update the American people on the international effort that we have led in Libya—what we've done, what we plan to do, and why this matters to us.

I want to begin by paying tribute to our men and women in uniform who, once again, have acted with courage, professionalism, and patriotism. They have moved with incredible speed and strength. Because of them and our dedicated diplomats, a coalition has been forged and countless lives have been saved.

Meanwhile, as we speak, our troops are supporting our ally Japan, leaving Iraq to its people, stopping the Taliban's momentum in Afghanistan, and going after al-Qaeda all across the globe. As commander in chief, I'm grateful to our soldiers, sailors, airmen, Marines, Coast Guardsmen, and to their families. And I know all Americans share in that sentiment.

For generations, the United States of America has played a unique role as an anchor of global security and as an advocate for human freedom. Mindful of the risks and costs of military action, we are naturally reluctant to use force to solve the world's many challenges. But when our interests and values are at stake, we have a responsibility to act. That's what happened in Libya over the course of these last six weeks.

Libya sits directly between Tunisia and Egypt—two nations that inspired the world when their people rose up to take control of their own destiny. For more than four decades, the Libyan people have been ruled by a tyrant—Muammar Qaddafi. He has denied his people freedom, exploited their wealth, murdered opponents at home and abroad, and terrorized innocent people around the world—including Americans who were killed by Libyan agents.

Last month, Qaddafi's grip of fear appeared to give way to the promise of freedom. In cities and towns across the country, Libyans took to the streets to claim their basic human rights. As one Libyan said, "For the first time we finally have hope that our nightmare of forty years will soon be over."

Faced with this opposition, Qaddafi began attacking his people. As president, my immediate concern was the safety of our citizens, so we evacuated our embassy and all Americans who sought our assistance. Then we took a series of swift steps in a matter of days to answer Qaddafi's aggression. We froze more than $33 billion of Qaddafi's regime's assets. Joining with other nations at the United Nations Security Council, we broadened our sanctions, imposed an arms embargo, and enabled Qaddafi and those around him to be held accountable for their crimes. I made it clear that Qaddafi had lost the confidence of his people and the legitimacy to lead, and I said that he needed to step down from power.

In the face of the world's condemnation, Qaddafi chose to escalate his attacks, launching a military campaign against the Libyan people. Innocent people were targeted for killing. Hospitals and ambulances were attacked. Journalists were arrested, sexually assaulted, and killed. Supplies of food and fuel were choked off. Water for hundreds of thousands of people in Misurata was shut off. Cities and towns were shelled, mosques were destroyed, and apartment buildings reduced to rubble. Military jets and helicopter gunships were unleashed upon people who had no means to defend themselves against assaults from the air.

Confronted by this brutal repression and a looming humanitarian crisis, I ordered warships into the Mediterranean. European allies declared their willingness to commit resources to stop the killing. The Libyan opposition and the Arab League appealed to the world to save lives in Libya. And so at my direction, America led an effort with our allies at the United Nations Security Council to pass a historic resolution that authorized a no-fly zone to stop the regime's attacks from the air, and further authorized all necessary measures to protect the Libyan people.

Ten days ago, having tried to end the violence without using force, the international community offered Qaddafi a final chance to stop his campaign of killing, or face the consequences. Rather than stand down, his forces continued their advance, bearing down on the city of Benghazi, home to nearly seven hundred thousand men, women, and children who sought their freedom from fear.

At this point, the United States and the world faced a choice. Qaddafi declared he would show "no mercy" to his own people. He compared them to rats, and threatened to go door to door to inflict punishment. In the past, we have seen him hang civilians in the streets, and kill over a thousand people in a single day. Now we saw regime forces on the outskirts of the city. We knew that if we wanted—if we waited one more day, Benghazi, a city nearly the size of Charlotte, could suffer a massacre that would have reverberated across the region and stained the conscience of the world.

It was not in our national interest to let that happen. I refused to let that happen. And so nine days ago, after consulting the bipartisan leadership of Congress, I authorized military action to stop the killing and enforce UN Security Council Resolution 1973.

We struck regime forces approaching Benghazi to save that city and the people within it. We hit Qaddafi's troops in neighboring Ajdabiya, allowing the opposition to drive them out. We hit Qaddafi's air defenses, which paved the way for a no-fly zone. We targeted tanks and military assets that had been choking off towns and cities, and we cut off much of their source of supply. And tonight, I can report that we have stopped Qaddafi's deadly advance.

In this effort, the United States has not acted alone. Instead, we have been joined by a strong and growing coalition. This includes our closest allies—nations like the United Kingdom, France, Canada, Denmark, Norway, Italy, Spain, Greece, and Turkey—all of whom have fought by our sides for decades. And it includes Arab partners like Qatar and the United Arab Emirates, who have chosen to meet their responsibilities to defend the Libyan people.

To summarize, then: In just one month, the United States has worked with our international partners to mobilize a broad coalition, secure an international mandate to protect civilians, stop an advancing army, prevent a massacre, and establish a no-fly zone with our allies and partners. To lend some perspective on how rapidly this military and diplomatic response came together, when people were being brutalized in Bosnia in the 1990s, it took the international community more than a year to intervene with air power to protect civilians. It took us 31 days.

Moreover, we've accomplished these objectives consistent with the pledge that I made to the American people at the outset of our military operations. I said that America's role would be limited; that we would not put ground troops into Libya; that we would focus our unique capabilities on the front end of the operation and that we would transfer responsibility to our allies and partners. Tonight, we are fulfilling that pledge.

Our most effective alliance, NATO, has taken command of the enforcement of the arms embargo and the no-fly zone. Last night, NATO decided to take on the additional responsibility of protecting Libyan civilians. This transfer from the United States to NATO will take place on Wednesday. Going forward, the lead in enforcing the no-fly zone and protecting civilians on the ground will transition to our allies and partners, and I am fully confident that our coalition will keep the pressure on Qaddafi's remaining forces.

In that effort, the United States will play a supporting role—including intelligence, logistical support, search and rescue assistance, and capabilities to jam regime communications. Because of this transition to a broader, NATO-based coalition, the risk and cost of this operation—to our military and to American taxpayers—will be reduced significantly.

So for those who doubted our capacity to carry out this operation, I want to be clear: The United States of America has done what we said we would do.

That's not to say that our work is complete. In addition to our NATO responsibilities, we will work with the international community to provide assistance to the people of Libya, who need food for the hungry and medical care for the wounded. We will safeguard the more than $33 billion that was frozen from the Qaddafi regime so that it's available to rebuild Libya. After all, the money doesn't belong to Qaddafi or to us—it belongs to the Libyan people. And we'll make sure they receive it.

Tomorrow, Secretary Clinton will go to London, where she will meet with the Libyan opposition and consult with more than thirty nations. These discussions will focus on what kind of political effort is necessary to pressure Qaddafi, while also supporting a transition to the future that the Libyan people deserve—because while our military mission is narrowly focused on saving lives, we continue to pursue the broader goal of a Libya that belongs not to a dictator, but to its people.

Now, despite the success of our efforts over the past week, I know that some Americans continue to have questions about our efforts in Libya. Qaddafi has not yet stepped down from power, and until he does, Libya will remain dangerous. Moreover, even after Qaddafi does leave power, forty years of tyranny has left Libya fractured and without strong civil institutions. The transition to a legitimate government that is responsive to the Libyan people will be a difficult task. And while the United States will do our part to help, it will be a task for the international community and—more importantly—a task for the Libyan people themselves.

In fact, much of the debate in Washington has put forward a false choice when it comes to Libya. On the one hand, some question why America should intervene at all—even in limited ways—in this distant land. They argue that there are many places in the world where innocent civilians face brutal violence at the hands of their government, and America should not be expected to police the world, particularly when we have so many pressing needs here at home.

It's true that America cannot use our military wherever repression occurs. And given the costs and risks of intervention, we must always measure our interests against the need for action. But that cannot be an argument for never acting on behalf of what's right. In this particular country—Libya—at this particular moment, we were faced with the prospect of violence on a horrific scale. We had a unique ability to stop that violence: an international mandate for action, a broad coalition prepared to join us, the support of Arab countries, and a plea for help from the Libyan people themselves. We also had the ability to stop Qaddafi's forces in their tracks without putting American troops on the ground.

To brush aside America's responsibility as a leader and—more profoundly—our responsibilities to our fellow human beings under such circumstances would have been a betrayal of who we are. Some nations may be able to turn a blind eye to atrocities in other countries. The United States of America is different. And as president, I refused to wait for the images of slaughter and mass graves before taking action.

Moreover, America has an important strategic interest in preventing Qaddafi from overrunning those who oppose him. A massacre would have driven thousands of additional refugees across Libya's borders, putting enormous strains on the peaceful—yet fragile—transitions in Egypt and Tunisia. The democratic impulses that are dawning across the region would be eclipsed by the darkest form of dictatorship, as repressive leaders concluded that violence is the best strategy to cling to power. The writ of the United Nations Security Council would have been shown to be little more than empty words, crippling that institution's future credibility to uphold global peace and security. So while I will never minimize the costs involved in military action, I am convinced that a failure to act in Libya would have carried a far greater price for America.

Now, just as there are those who have argued against intervention in Libya, there are others who have suggested that we broaden our military mission beyond the task of protecting the Libyan people, and do whatever it takes to bring down Qaddafi and usher in a new government.

Of course, there is no question that Libya—and the world—would be better off with Qaddafi out of power. I, along with many other world leaders, have embraced that goal, and will actively pursue it through nonmilitary means. But broadening our military mission to include regime change would be a mistake.

The task that I assigned our forces—to protect the Libyan people from immediate danger, and to establish a no-fly zone—carries with it a UN mandate and international support. It's also what the Libyan opposition asked us to do. If we tried to overthrow Qaddafi by force, our coalition would splinter. We would likely have to put U.S. troops on the ground to accomplish that mission, or risk killing many civilians from the air. The dangers faced by our men and women in uniform would be far greater. So would the costs and our share of the responsibility for what comes next.

To be blunt, we went down that road in Iraq. Thanks to the extraordinary sacrifices of our troops and the determination of our diplomats, we are hopeful about Iraq's future. But regime change there took eight years, thousands of American and Iraqi lives, and nearly a trillion dollars. That is not something we can afford to repeat in Libya.

As the bulk of our military effort ratchets down, what we can do—and will do—is support the aspirations of the Libyan people. We have intervened to stop a massacre, and we will work with our allies and partners to maintain the safety of civilians. We will deny the regime arms, cut off its supplies of cash, assist the opposition, and work with other nations to hasten the day when Qaddafi leaves power. It may not happen overnight, as a badly weakened Qaddafi tries desperately to hang on to power. But it should be clear to those around Qaddafi, and to every Libyan, that history is not on Qaddafi's side. With the time and space that we have provided for the Libyan people, they will be able to determine their own destiny, and that is how it should be.

Let me close by addressing what this action says about the use of America's military power, and America's broader leadership in the world, under my presidency.

As commander in chief, I have no greater responsibility than keeping this country safe. And no decision weighs on me more than when to deploy our men and women in uniform. I've made it clear that I will never hesitate to use our military swiftly, decisively, and unilaterally when necessary to defend our people, our homeland, our allies, and our core interests. That's why we're going after al-Qaeda wherever they seek a foothold. That is why we continue to fight in Afghanistan, even as we have ended our combat mission in Iraq and removed more than one hundred thousand troops from that country.

There will be times, though, when our safety is not directly threatened, but our interests and our values are. Sometimes, the course of history poses challenges that threaten our common humanity and our common security—responding to natural disasters, for example, or preventing genocide and keeping the peace, ensuring regional security, and maintaining the flow of commerce. These may not be America's problems alone, but they are important to us. They're problems worth solving. And in these circumstances, we know that the United States, as the world's most powerful nation, will often be called upon to help.

In such cases, we should not be afraid to act—but the burden of action should not be America's alone. As we have in Libya, our task is instead to mobilize the international community for collective action. Because contrary to the claims of some, American leadership is not simply a matter of going it alone and bearing all of the burden ourselves. Real leadership creates the conditions and coalitions for others to step up as well; to work with allies and partners so that they bear their share of the burden and pay their share of the costs; and to see that the principles of justice and human dignity are upheld by all.

That's the kind of leadership we've shown in Libya. Of course, even when we act as part of a coalition, the risks of any military action will be high. Those risks were realized when one of our planes malfunctioned over Libya. Yet when one of our airmen parachuted to the ground, in a country whose leader has so often demonized the United States—in a region that has such a difficult history with our country—this American did not find enemies. Instead, he was met by people who embraced him. One young Libyan who came to his aid said, "We are your friends. We are so grateful to those men who are protecting the skies."

This voice is just one of many in a region where a new generation is refusing to be denied their rights and opportunities any longer.

Yes, this change will make the world more complicated for a time. Progress will be uneven, and change will come differently to different countries. There are places, like Egypt, where this change will inspire us and raise our hopes. And then there will be places, like Iran, where change is fiercely suppressed. The dark forces of civil conflict and sectarian war will have to be averted, and difficult political and economic concerns will have to be addressed.

The United States will not be able to dictate the pace and scope of this change. Only the people of the region can do that. But we can make a difference.

I believe that this movement of change cannot be turned back, and that we must stand alongside those who believe in the same core principles that have guided us through many storms: our opposition to violence directed at one's own people; our support for a set of universal rights, including the freedom for people to express themselves and choose their leaders; our support for governments that are ultimately responsive to the aspirations of the people.

Born, as we are, out of a revolution by those who longed to be free, we welcome the fact that history is on the move in the Middle East and North Africa, and that young people are leading the way. Because wherever people long to be free, they will find a friend in the United States. Ultimately, it is that faith—those ideals—that are the true measure of American leadership.

My fellow Americans, I know that at a time of upheaval overseas—when the news is filled with conflict and change—it can be tempting to turn away from the world. And as I've said before, our strength abroad is anchored in our strength here at home. That must always be our North Star—the ability of our people to reach their potential, to make wise choices with our resources, to enlarge the prosperity that serves as a wellspring for our power, and to live the values that we hold so dear.

But let us also remember that for generations, we have done the hard work of protecting our own people, as well as millions around the globe. We have done so because we know that our own future is safer, our own future is brighter, if more of mankind can live with the bright light of freedom and dignity.

Tonight, let us give thanks for the Americans who are serving through these trying times, and the coalition that is carrying our effort forward. And let us look to the future with confidence and hope not only for our own country, but for all those yearning for freedom around the world.

Thank you. God bless you, and may God bless the United States of America. Thank you.

Joint Statement by Nicolas Sarkozy and David Cameron on Libya

MARCH 28, 2011

Tomorrow in London, the international community will come together to support a new beginning for Libya. A new beginning in which the people of Libya are free from violence and oppression, free to choose their own future.

The world has witnessed momentous events over the last ten days. Following an appeal by the Arab League to take action to protect the people of Libya, on 17 March the United Nations Security Council passed an historic resolution to protect civilians from the violence unleashed by Qadhafi's war machine.

Two days later, the Paris Summit emphasized the determination of the participants to act collectively and resolutely to give full effect to UNSCR 1973.

The same day, a coalition of countries took action to help break the siege of Benghazi and drive back Qaddafi's forces. Hundreds of thousands of people have been rescued from the brink of humanitarian disaster.

Our countries are resolved to continue to enforce UNSCR 1973 to protect the people of Libya. More countries from Europe and the Arab world are joining us. It is only when the civilian population are safe and secure from the threat of attack and the objectives of UNSCR 1973 are met that military operations will come to an end.

We emphasize that we do not envisage any military occupation of Libya, which would be contrary to the terms of the resolution. We reaffirm our strong commitment to the sovereignty, independence, territorial integrity, and national unity of Libya.

Military action is not an objective as such. A lasting solution can only be a political one that belongs to the Libyan people. That is why the political process that will begin tomorrow in London is so important. The London conference will bring the international community together to support Libya's transition from violent dictatorship and to help create the conditions where the people of Libya can choose their own future.

In the words of the Arab League resolution, the current regime has completely lost its legitimacy. Qaddafi must therefore go immediately. We call on all his followers to leave him before it is too late. We call on all Libyans who believe that Qaddafi is leading Libya into a disaster to take the initiative now to organize a transition process.

In our view, this could include the Interim National Transitional Council, the pioneering role of which we recognize, the civil society leaders as well as all those prepared to join the process of transition to democracy. We encourage them to begin a national political dialogue, leading to a representative process of transition, constitutional reform and preparation for free and fair elections.

To help Libya make this transition, we are today also calling on all the participants at the London conference to give their strong support.

We have averted a humanitarian disaster but Libya still faces a humanitarian crisis. In London, our countries will come together with the United Nations, the European Union, the African Union, NATO, and the Arab League to consider how we can bring urgent relief now, and how we can support the needs of the people of Libya in the future.

In the last few weeks, the Libyan people have demonstrated their courage and their determination. Like all other peoples, they have the right freely to choose their leaders.

We must unite to help them make a new beginning.

Excerpts from Syrian President Bashar al-Assad's Speech Before the Syrian People's Assembly

DAMASCUS, SYRIA, MARCH 30, 2011

I speak to you at an extraordinary moment when events and developments seem to pose a test to our unity and altruism. It is a test which, as circumstances would have it, recurs every so often due to the continuous conspiracies against this country. And it is our will and solidarity, and God's will, that, when facing it, we pass it every time with flying colors, which only enhances our strength and immunity.

. . .

I know full well that the Syrian people have been waiting for this speech since last week. I deliberately delayed giving it until the picture became clear in my mind, or at least some of the main headlines of this picture. This way, today's speech would stay clear from emotional rhetoric, which comforts people but does not alter or impact anything, at the time when our enemies are working every day, in an organized and scientific way, in order to strike at Syria's stability. Of course, we acknowledge

Translation by Tony Badran.

their cunning in selecting highly advanced methods in what they have done, but we also acknowledge their stupidity in selecting the wrong country and people, where this type of conspiracy does not succeed.

We tell them, you have no choice but to continue to learn from your failure. As for the Syrian people, it has no choice other than to continue to learn from its successes.

Brothers, you are aware of the major changes taking place in our region over the past few months. They are major and important changes that will have repercussions on the entire region without exception; on the Arab states but maybe even beyond. This concerns Syria, as it is part of these states.

However, if we wished to look at what concerns us, as Syria, in what has happened so far in this great Arab arena, we can say that what has happened vindicates the Syrian perspective from a very important angle. What has happened expresses a popular consensus. When there is a popular consensus we should be assured, whether we agree or disagree on many points. What does this mean? It means that the Arab popular condition, which was marginalized for decades . . . has now returned to the center of events in our region. This Arab condition had not changed. They tried to domesticate it but it didn't succumb, and this will have much impact.

As far as we are concerned, you recall how in my previous speeches, I used to always speak about the Arab street, and the street's compass; about the opinion of the citizen. Many in the press used to sometimes ridicule this. And foreign politicians used to reject this and smile, especially during our meetings when Syria was under severe pressure. They used to propose to us proposals that went counter to and in contradiction with our interests, and which included conspiring against the resistance and against other Arabs. When the pressure used to mount I used to tell them, even if I were to accept these proposals, the people would not accept it. And if the people did not accept it, they will reject me, and that would mean political suicide. Of course, they used to smile incredulously. Today after these [popular] movements, there have been several meetings where I repeated the same talk, and they agreed with me.

. . .

The other side has to do with the directions of the Arab peoples toward the central causes, at the forefront of which is the Palestinian cause. We believe and hope that our belief is correct, that these changes will lead to a change in the course of the Palestinian cause, on which it has been for the last two or three decades. A change from the course of compromises to the course of adhering to rights.

. . .

Syria is not isolated from what is happening in the Arab world. We are part of this region. We interact. We influence and we are influenced. At the same time, however, we are not a copy of other countries. No one country resembles the other. We in Syria have characteristics that may be different in the domestic as well as in the foreign realms.

Domestically, our policy was built on development and openness; on direct communication between me and the people and citizens . . . regardless of what was and what was not achieved. In terms of general principles, these are the principles of domestic policy.

Our foreign policy has been based on adhering to national and pan-Arab rights, rights to independence, and support of Arab resistance where there is occupation. The link between domestic and foreign policies has always been the same thing I noted earlier, that the compass for us in everything we do is the citizen.

. . .

At any rate, the outcome of these two policies has been an unprecedented state of national unity in Syria. This national condition has been the reason, or the energy, or the true protector of Syria in the previous few years when pressures against Syria began. . . . Through [our national unity] we managed to maintain Syria's central role.

. . .

Increasing or maintaining this role, with its principles that are rejected by others, will push enemies to work to weaken it through other means. . . . You are aware that Syria today is being subjected to a major conspiracy, with strings extending to countries near and far, and with some strings inside the country. This conspiracy is relying—in its timing, not its form—on what is taking places in Arab countries.

Today there is a new fad, which they consider to be revolutions, but we don't call them that, because they are mostly a popular condition. But for them, if something is going on, it provides cover for action in Syria. There's revolution there and a revolution here. There's reform there and reform here. The tools are all the same, slogans of freedom. So if there are truly those who call for reform, and I believe we are all calling for reform, we will proceed with them without knowing what is truly happening. So they cunningly mixed three elements . . . sedition, reform, and daily needs. Most Syrians call for reform, and you are all reformers. Most Syrians have needs that have not been met, and we had our disagreements, our discussions, and our criticisms because we have not met the needs of many citizens. However, sedition has joined the fray and has begun to lead the other two factors, and hide behind them. That is why it was easy to trick many of the people who came out to the streets at first with good intentions. We cannot say that everyone who came out were conspirators. That is not true. We want to be realistic and clear.

Conspirators are always few in number. That is obvious. Even we in government did not know the truth. Like everyone else, we did not understand what was happening, until acts of sabotage clarified things. What is the relationship between reform and sabotage? What is the relationship between reform and killing? Some satellite TV stations say, "They're always thinking of conspiracies." There is no conspiracy theory. Conspiracy exists in the world. Conspiracy is part of human nature. In some satellite TV stations they announced the sabotage of specific public buildings a full hour before they were attacked. How did they know?

. . .

When things became clearer, it was difficult for us at first to fight this matter, since people would confuse our combatting sedition with fighting reform. We are for reform. We are for meeting needs. This is the duty of the state. However, we can never be for sedition. And when the Syrian people revealed, through its popular and national awareness, what was going on, things became simpler. The response followed, and it came from the citizens more so than the state. As you noticed, the state took a back seat and left the response to the citizens, which is what achieved a sound, safe, level, and patriotic treatment, and quickly restored national unity to Syria.

What we are seeing now is one stage out of many that we do not yet know. Is it the first stage? Are they advanced stages? But we care about one thing, and that is the final stage, which is the weakening and fragmentation of Syria. For Syria to fall and for the last obstacle facing the Israeli plan to be removed.

. . .

They first started with incitement. Incitement began weeks before the disturbances in Syria. They began incitement on satellite TV stations and on the Internet, and they did not achieve anything. Then, during sedition, they moved to falsehoods. They falsified information, sounds, images, everything. They then adopted the sectarian angle. This angle relied on the use of cell phone short text messages to tell one sect, "Be careful, the other sect will attack you," while telling the same to the other sect. . . . However, we were able, through meetings with influential notables, to prevent sedition. That's when they interfered with weapons and began randomly killing people in order for there to be blood.

. . .

We have not yet uncovered the whole structure—only a part of the structure has been revealed, but it is an organized structure. There are support groups with people in more than one province and abroad. There are media groups, there are falsification groups, and there are groups for eyewitnesses. They are previously organized groups.

. . .

They began in the province of Deraa. . . . Deraa is the frontline province with the Israeli enemy. The frontline defends the rear lines. . . . It cannot be that the same person who defends the nation is simultaneously conspiring against it or harming it. This kind of talk is impossible and unacceptable. Consequently, the people of Deraa do not bear any responsibility for what has happened. But they share responsibility with us in burying sedition. We are with Deraa as are all Syrians.

. . .

They then moved the plan to other cities, and as you know, it moved to Lattakia and other cities, using the same tools: murder, intimidation, incitement, and so forth. We gave specific instructions not to injure any Syrian citizen. Unfortunately, when things descend to the street and the conversation takes place in the street, outside institutions, then things naturally descend into chaos and reactive measures prevail, and what we call mistakes of the moment become prevalent, and blood is shed, and that is what happened.

. . .

Part of what is happening today resembles what happened in 2005. It's a virtual war, and I said at the time that they want us to sign an unconditional surrender for free, through a virtual war in the media and on the Internet. . . . Today, the same principle is at play: a planned virtual defeat of Syria, but using something different. There is chaos in the country for various reasons, essentially operating under the headline of reform. This chaos and the headlines of reform will lead to sects. Anxious sects. Sects at odds and at war with each other, and thus achieving Syria's virtual defeat.

. . .

There remains a central question. We talk about the changes that happened in the region on the premise that they are a wave. Every time we ask someone they tell us there is a wave and you must bend. Fine. Regardless of what we analyzed earlier about the positive aspects of this wave, should the wave lead us or should we lead it? When this wave enters Syria, it concerns Syrians. If it comes it is an energy force but this energy must be guided according to our interests. We are proactive, not reactive.

. . .

What I want to get at from all this is one thing only. When I started by asking how should we deal with this matter, what I wanted to say was that reform is not a seasonal fad. When it is merely a reflection of a wave being experienced by the region, then it is destructive, regardless of its content. That is what I said in my talk with the *Wall Street Journal* two months ago, when things began to deteriorate in Egypt and they asked me about reform, "What about Syria? Do you want to reform?" I told him, if you have not already begun, and did not already have the intention and the plan to reform, then you are already too late. If we did not already have this intention and vision, it would all be over; no need to waste our time. No, we and all the people and the government have this intention. And I wish to confirm another point, as it is my custom to be honest with you. This question was asked of me by more than one foreign official who passed by Syria recently. They wanted to know for sure if the president was a reformist but those around him were holding him back. I would tell them, on the contrary. They are the ones who are strongly pushing me forward. The point I want to make is that there are no obstacles. There is a delay. But there is nobody who objects to reform, and those who object are those with special interests and the corrupt, and you know who they are. It was a minority that no longer exists. A limited minority you know by name. But now there are no real obstacles. And I think that the challenge now is what kind of reform do we want to achieve. Therefore, we have to avoid subjecting the reform process to these momentary circumstances, which could be passing, in order not to harvest counterproductive results.

. . .

Some have asked me to announce a timetable now in the People's Assembly. But announcing a timetable for any subject matter is a technical issue. I may announce a timetable that is far less than what is necessary for this condition, and the resulting pressure would affect quality. I think it is our duty to present the best to the Syrian people, and not the quickest. We want to move quickly, but not to be hasty.

In any case, there will be those today who will say on satellite TV stations that this is not enough. We tell them, we do not have what is enough to destroy our country. On this occasion, do not be angry at what some satellite TV stations have done, because they always fall in the same trap. They try to impinge on us and on the Syrian people. In truth, they adopt the principle of "lie until you believe your lie."

. . .

Burying sedition is a national, moral, and religious duty. Anyone who can contribute to burying it and does not do so is complicit in it. Sedition is worse than killing, as the Holy Quran says. Anyone who is involved in it, willfully or not, is working to kill his country. Therefore, there is no place for anyone to stand in the middle. What is at stake is not the government, but the homeland. The conspiracy is great, and we do not seek battles. The Syrian people are a peaceful, gentle people. However, we have never hesitated to defend our causes, our interests, and our principles. If the battle is imposed on us today, we welcome it.

Hillary Rodham Clinton's Remarks at the Gala Dinner Celebrating the U.S.-Islamic World Forum

BROOKINGS INSTITUTION, WASHINGTON, DC, APRIL 12, 2011

Good evening, everyone. And let me thank you, Strobe, for that introduction and for your many years of friendship. It is such a pleasure for me to join you at this first U.S.-Islamic World Forum held in America. His Highness the Amir and the people of Qatar have generously hosted the Forum for years. And as Strobe said, I was honored to be a guest in Doha last year. And now I am delighted to welcome you to Washington. I want to thank Martin Indyk, Ken Pollack, and the Saban Center at the Brookings Institution for keeping this event going and growing. And I want to acknowledge all my colleagues in the diplomatic corps who are here tonight, including the minister of state for foreign affairs of Qatar, the foreign minister of Jordan, and the secretary general of the organization of the Islamic conference.

Over the years, the U.S.-Islamic World Forum has offered the chance to celebrate the diverse achievements of Muslims around the world. From Qatar—which is pioneering innovative energy solutions and preparing to host the World Cup—to countries as varied as Turkey, Senegal, Indonesia, and Malaysia, each offering its own model for prosperity and progress.

This forum also offers a chance to discuss the equally diverse set of challenges we face together—the need to confront violent extremism, the urgency of achieving a two-state solution between Israel and the Palestinians, the importance of embracing tolerance and universal human rights in all of our communities.

And I am especially proud that this year the forum is recognizing the contributions of the millions of American Muslims who do so much to make our country strong. As President Obama said in Cairo, "Islam has always been a part of American history," and every day Americans Muslims are helping to write our story.

I do not need to tell this distinguished audience that we are meeting at an historic time for one region in particular: the Middle East and North Africa. Today, the long Arab winter has begun to thaw. For the first time in decades, there is a real opportunity for lasting change, a real opportunity for people to have their voices heard and their priorities addressed.

Now, this raises significant questions for us all:

Will the people and leaders of the Middle East and North Africa pursue a new, more inclusive approach to solving the region's persistent political, economic, and social challenges? Will they consolidate the progress of recent weeks and address long-denied aspirations for dignity and opportunity? Or, when we meet again at this forum in one year or five years or ten, will we have seen the prospects for reform fade and remember this moment as just a mirage in the desert?

Now, these questions can only be answered by the people and leaders of the Middle East and North Africa themselves. The United States certainly does not have all the answers. In fact, here in Washington we're struggling to thrash out answers to our own difficult political and economic questions. But America is committed to working as a partner to help unlock the region's potential and to help realize its hopes for change.

Now, much has been accomplished already. Uprisings across the region have exposed myths that for too long were used to justify a stagnant status quo. You know the myth that governments can hold on to power without responding to their people's aspirations or respecting their rights; the myth that the only way to produce change in the region is through violence and conflict; and, most pernicious of all, the myth that Arabs do not share universal human aspirations for freedom, dignity, and opportunity.

Today's new generation of young people rejects these false narratives. And as we know and as we have seen, they will not accept the status quo. Despite the best efforts of the censors, they are connecting to the wider world in ways that their parents and grandparents could never imagine. They now see alternatives, on satellite news, on Twitter and Facebook, in Cairo and Tunis. They know a better life can be within reach—and they are now willing to reach for it.

But these young people have inherited a region that in many ways is unprepared to meet their growing expectations. Its challenges have been well documented in a series of landmark Arab Human Development Reports, independently authored and published by the United Nations Development Program. These reports represent the cumulative knowledge of leading Arab scholars and intellectuals. Answering these challenges will help determine if this historic moment lives up to its promise. That is why this January in Doha, just weeks after a desperate, young, Tunisian street vendor set fire to himself in public protest, I talked with the leaders of the region about the need to move faster to meet their people's needs and aspirations.

In the twenty-first century, the material conditions of people's lives have greater impact on national stability and security than ever before. It is not possible for people not to know what is happening beyond their own small village. And the balance of power is no longer measured by counting tanks or missiles alone. Now strategists must factor in the growing influence of citizens themselves—connected, organized, and often frustrated.

There was a time when those of us who championed civil society or worked with marginalized minorities or on behalf of women, or were focused on young people and technology, were told that our concerns were noble but not urgent. That is another false narrative that has been washed away. Because these issues—among others—are at the heart of smart power—and they have to be at the center of any discussion attempting to answer the region's most pressing questions.

First, can the leaders and citizens of the region reform economies that are now overly dependent on oil exports and stunted by corruption? Overall, Arab countries were less industrialized in 2007 than they were in 1970. Unemployment often runs more than double the worldwide average, and even worse for women and young people. While a growing number of Arabs live in poverty, crowded into slums without sanitation, safe water, or reliable electricity, a small elite has increasingly concentrated control of the region's land and wealth in their hands. The 2009 Arab Development Report found that these trends—and I quote—"result in the ominous dynamics of marginalization."

Reversing this dynamic means grappling with a second question: How to match economic reform with political and social change? According to the 2009 *Global Integrity Report*, Arab countries, almost without exception, have some of the weakest anti-corruption systems in the world. Citizens have spent decades under martial law or emergency rule. Political parties and civil society groups are subject to repression and restriction. Judicial systems are far from either free or independent. And elections, when they are held, are often rigged.

And this leads to a third and often-overlooked question: Will the door to full citizenship and participation finally open to women and minorities? The first Arab Human Development

Report in 2002 found that Arab women's political and economic participation was the lowest in the world. Successive reports have shown little progress. The 2005 report called women's empowerment—and I quote again—a "prerequisite for an Arab renaissance, inseparably and causally linked to the fate of the Arab world."

Now, this is not a matter of the role of religion in women's lives. Muslim women have long enjoyed greater rights and opportunities in places like Bangladesh or Indonesia. Or consider the family law in Morocco or the personal status code in Tunisia. Communities from Egypt to Jordan to Senegal are beginning to take on entrenched practices like child marriage, honor crimes, and female cutting. All over the world we see living proof that Islam and women's rights are compatible. But unfortunately, there are some who are actually working to undermine this progress and export a virulently anti-woman ideology to other Muslim communities.

Now, all of these challenges—from deep unemployment to widespread corruption to the lack of respect and opportunities for women—have fueled frustration among the region's young people. And changing leaders alone will not be enough to satisfy them—not if cronyism and closed economies continue to choke off opportunity and participation, or if citizens can't rely on police and the courts to protect their rights. The region's powerbrokers, both inside and outside of government, need to step up and work with the people to craft a positive vision for the future. Generals and imams, business leaders and bureaucrats, everyone who has benefited from and reinforced the status quo, has a role to play. They also have a lot to lose if the vision vacuum is filled by extremists and rejectionists.

So a fourth crucial question is how Egypt and Tunisia should consolidate the progress that has been achieved in recent months.

Former protesters are asking: How can we stay organized and involved? Well, it will take forming political parties and advocacy coalitions. It will take focusing on working together to solve the real big problems facing both countries. In Cairo last month, I met with young activists who were passionate about their principles but still sorting out how to be practical about their politics. One veteran Egyptian journalist and dissident, Hisham Kassem, expressed concerns this week that a reluctance to move from protests to politics would, in his words, "endanger the revolution's gains." So he urged young people to translate their passion into a positive agenda and to use political participation to achieve it.

As the people of Egypt and Tunisia embrace the full responsibilities of citizenship, we look to transitional authorities to guarantee fundamental rights such as free assembly and expression, to provide basic security on the streets, to be transparent and inclusive.

Unfortunately, this year we have seen too many violent attacks, from Egypt to Iraq to Pakistan, that have killed dozens of religious and ethnic minorities, part of a troubling worldwide trend documented by the State Department's Annual Human Rights Report released this past Friday. Communities around the world are struggling to strike the right balance between freedom of expression and tolerance of unpopular views. Each of us has a responsibility to defend the universal human rights of people of all faiths and creeds. And I want to applaud the Organization of the Islamic Conference for its leadership in securing the recent resolution by the United Nations Human Rights Council that takes a strong stand against discrimination and violence based upon religion or belief, but does not limit freedom of expression or worship.

In both Egypt and Tunisia, we have also seen troubling signs regarding the rights and opportunities of women. So far women have been excluded from key transitional decision-making processes. When women marched alongside men through Tahrir Square in the early days of the revolution, they were part of making the change that Egypt was seeking. When they recently walked again through the square to celebrate International Women's Day in their new democracy, they were met by harassment and abuse. You cannot have a claim to a democracy if half the population is left out.

And we know from long experience that building a successful democracy is a never-ending task. More than two hundred years after our own revolution, we are still working on it. Because real change takes time, hard work, and patience—but it is well worth the effort. As one Egyptian women's rights activist said recently, "We will have to fight for our rights. . . . It will be tough, and require lobbying, but that's what democracy is all about."

In a democracy, you have to persuade your fellow citizens, men and women alike, to go along the path that you wish to take. And we know that democracy cannot be transplanted wholesale from one country to another. People have the right and responsibility to devise their own government. But there are universal rights that apply to everyone and universal values that undergird vibrant democracies everywhere.

One lesson learned by transitions to democracy around the world is that it can be tempting to fight the old battles over and over again, rather than to focus on ensuring justice and accountability in the future. I will always remember watching Nelson Mandela at the luncheon he hosted after his inauguration as president welcome three of his former jailors. Because to him, they were as important as any king or president or prime minister who was there, because when he was powerless, when he was imprisoned, they treated him with dignity. They looked upon him as a fellow human being. It helped him to move beyond what he had suffered. He never looked back in anger, but always forward in hope.

The United States is committed to standing with the people of Egypt, Tunisia, and the region to help build sustainable democracies that will deliver real results for people who deserve them. We want to support the aspirations that are so important. On this our values and interests converge. History has shown that democracies do tend to be more stable, more peaceful, and ultimately, more prosperous. But the challenge is how we get from where we are to where we want to be.

So the fifth question for us as Americans is: How can America be an effective partner to the people of the region? How can we work together to build not just short-term stability, but long-term sustainability?

With this goal in mind, the Obama administration began to reorient U.S. foreign policy in the region and around the world from our first days in office. We put partnerships with people, not just governments, at the center of our efforts. The administration moved quickly to respond to recent events and to affirm the principles that guide our approach. The president and I have spoken about this on a number of occasions, most recently just late afternoon today. And I know that the president will be speaking in greater detail about America's policy in the Middle East and North Africa in the coming weeks.

And we start from the understanding that America's core interests and values have not changed, including our commitment to promote human rights, resolve longstanding conflicts, counter Iran's threats, and defeat al-Qaeda and its extremist allies. This includes renewed pursuit of comprehensive Arab-Israeli peace. The status quo between Palestinians and Israelis is no more sustainable than the political systems that have crumbled in recent months. Neither Israel's future as a Jewish democratic state nor the legitimate aspirations of Palestinians can be secured without a negotiated two-state solution. And while it is a truism that only the parties themselves can make the hard choices necessary for peace, there is no substitute for continued active American leadership. And the president and I are committed to that.

We believe our concerns are shared by the people of the region. And we will continue working closely with our trusted partners—including many in this room tonight—to advance those mutual interests.

We understand that a one-sized-fits-all approach doesn't make sense in such a diverse region at such a fluid time. As I have said before, the United States has specific relationships with countries in the region. We have a decades-long friendship with Bahrain that we expect to continue long into the future. But we have made clear that security alone cannot resolve the challenges facing them. Violence is not and cannot be the answer. A political process is—one that advances the rights and aspirations of all the citizens of Bahrain. And we have raised our concerns publicly and directly with Bahraini officials and we will continue to do so.

The United States also strongly supports the people of Yemen in their quest for greater opportunity, their pursuit of political and economic reform that will meet their aspirations. President Saleh needs to resolve the political impasse with the opposition so that meaningful political change can take place in the near term in an orderly, peaceful manner.

And as President Obama has said, we strongly condemn the violence committed against peaceful protesters by the Syrian government over the past few weeks. President Assad and the Syrian government must respect the rights of the Syrian people, who are demanding the freedoms that they have long been denied.

Going forward, the United States will be guided by careful consideration of all the circumstances on the ground and by our consistent values and interests, but also by something else: We believe in this region. We see no reason that it cannot be among the most progressive, prosperous, peaceful, successful regions in the world. When we look at other regions in the world that have undergone change—sometimes violent, sometimes difficult—we see no reason why this region cannot succeed.

And wherever we can, we will accelerate our work to develop stronger bonds with the people themselves—with civil society, business leaders, religious communities, women, and minorities. We are rethinking the way we do business on the ground with citizens, and we want the citizens themselves to help set the priorities. For example, as we invest in Egypt's new democracy and promote sustainable development, we are soliciting grant proposals from a wide range of local organizations. We want new partners. We want to invest in new ideas. We are exploring new ways to use connection technologies to expand dialogue and open lines of communication.

As we map out a strategy for supporting transitions already underway, we know that the people of the region have not put their lives on the line just to vote once in an election. They expect democracy to deliver jobs, sweep out corruption, extend opportunities that will help them and their children take full advantage of the global economy. So the United States will be working with people and leaders to create more open, dynamic, and diverse economies where there can be more inclusive prosperity.

In the short run, the United States will provide immediate economic assistance to help transitional democracies overcome the early challenges—including $150 million for Egypt alone.

In the medium term, as Egypt and Tunisia continue building their democracies, we will work with our partners to support an ambitious blueprint for sustainable growth, job creation, investment, and trade. The U.S. Overseas Private Investment Corporation will provide up to $2 billion to encourage private sector investments across the Middle East and North Africa—especially for small and medium-sized enterprises. And we look forward to working with Congress to establish enterprise funds for Egypt and Tunisia that will support competitive markets, provide small and medium-sized businesses with access to critical low-cost capital. Our Global Entrepreneurship Program is seeking out new partners and opportunities. And we want to improve and expand the Qualified Investment Zones, which allow Egyptian companies to send exports to the United States duty-free.

To spur private sector investment, we are working with Partners for a New Beginning, an organization led by former secretary Madeleine Albright, Muhtar Kent of Coca-Cola, and Walter Isaacson of the Aspen Institute. It was formed after President Obama's Cairo speech and includes the CEOs of companies like Intel, Cisco, and Morgan Stanley. These leaders will convene a summit at the end of May to connect American investors with partners in the region's transitional democracies, with an eye to creating more jobs and boosting trade.

Under the auspices of Partners for a New Beginning, the U.S.-North Africa Partnership for Economic Opportunity is building a network of public and private partners and programs to deepen economic integration among the countries in North Africa. This past December in Algiers, the Partnership convened more than four hundred young entrepreneurs, business leaders, venture capitalists, and Diaspora leaders from the United States and North Africa. These people-to-people contacts have already helped lay the groundwork for cross-border initiatives to create jobs, train youth, and support start-ups. And there will be a follow-up meeting later this year in Morocco.

For the long term, we are discussing ways to encourage closer economic integration across the region, as well as with the United States, Europe, and the rest of the world. The Middle East and North Africa are home to rich nations with excess capital as well as poorer countries hungry for investments. Forging deeper trade and economic relationships between neighbors could create many, many new jobs. And across the Mediterranean, Europe also represents enormous potential for greater trade and investment. If we were to reduce trade barriers in North Africa alone, just that one act could boost GDP levels by as much as 7 or 8 percent in Tunisia and Morocco, and it could lead to hundreds of millions of dollars in new wealth across the region every year.

The people of the Middle East and North Africa have the talent, they have the drive, to build vibrant economies and sustainable democracies—just as citizens have already done so in regions long held back by closed political and economic systems, from Southeast Asia to Eastern Europe to Latin America.

Now, it won't be easy. There are many, many obstacles. And unfortunately, Iran provides a powerful cautionary tale for the transitions underway. The democratic aspirations of 1979 were subverted by a new and brutal dictatorship. Iran's leaders have consistently pursued policies of violence abroad and tyranny at home. In Tehran, security forces have beaten, detained, and in several recent cases killed peaceful protesters, even as Iran's president has made a show of denouncing the violence against civilians in Libya and other places. And he is not alone in his hypocrisy. Al-Qaeda's propagandists have tried to yoke the region's peaceful popular movements to their murderous ideology. Their claims to speak for the dispossessed and downtrodden have never rung so hollow. Their arguments that the only way is violent change have never been so fully discredited.

Last month we witnessed a development that stood out, even in this extraordinary season. Colonel Qadhafi's troops turned their guns on their own people. His military jets and helicopter gunships had unleashed a reign of terror against people who had no means to defend themselves against the assault from the air. Benghazi's hundreds of thousands of citizens were in the crosshairs.

Now, in the past, when confronted with such a crisis, all too often the leaders of North Africa and the Middle East averted their eyes or closed ranks. But not this time. Not in this new era. The OIC, the GCC issued strong statements. The Arab League convened in Cairo, in the midst of all of the commotion of Egypt's democratic transition to condemn the violence and suspend Libya from the organization, even though Colonel Qadhafi held the league's rotating presidency. The Arab League went on to call for a no-fly zone. And I want to thank Qatar, the UAE, and Jordan for contributing planes to help enforce it.

But that's not all. The Arab League affirmed—and again I quote—"the right of the Libyan people to fulfill their demands and build their own future and institutions in a democratic framework." That is a remarkable statement. And that is a reason to hope.

All the signs of progress we have seen in recent months will only be meaningful if more leaders in more places move faster and further to embrace this spirit of reform, if they work with their people to answer the region's most pressing challenges—to diversify their economies, open their political systems, crack down on corruption, respect the rights of all of their citizens, including women and minorities.

Those are the questions that will determine whether the people of the region make the most of this historic moment or fall back into stagnation.

The United States will be there as a partner, working for progress. We are committed to the future of this region and we believe in the potential of its people. We look forward to the day when all the citizens of the Middle East and North Africa—in fact, all around the world—have the freedom to pursue their own God-given potential. That is the future that all of us should be striving and working toward.

Thank you all very much.

Acknowledgments

Providing serious intellectual context for world-historical upheavals in real time is a heroic challenge—and quickly pulling the highlights together into a book such as this adds still other layers of difficulty. The authors who appear in these pages did a wonderful job and made us proud to be able to showcase their work. But bylines are only part of the story, and they also serve who edit and publish. None of this would have emerged without the stellar efforts of the following: at CFR Publishing, Patricia Lee Dorff, Elias J. Primoff, and Lia C. Norton; at *Foreign Affairs* Editorial, Jonathan Tepperman, Stephanie Giry, Stuart Reid, Joshua Yaffa, Kathryn Allawala, Jordan Hirsch, Ann Tappert, Belinda Lanks, Sarah Foster, and Elira Coja; at CFR.org, Robert McMahon, Deborah Jerome, Bernard Gwertzman, Hagit Bachrach, Jayshree Bajoria, Toni Johnson, Jonathan Masters, Aimee Rawlins, Jeremy Sherlick, and Roya Wolverson; at *Foreign Affairs* Publishing, David Kellogg, Lynda Hammes, Edward W. Walsh, Emilie Harkin, Carolina Aguilar, Jonathan Chung, Christine Leonard, and Michael Pasuit; and at CFR Web Management and Development, Tom Davey, Cree Frappier, Thomas Katavic, and Carl Strolle. Richard N. Haass, CFR's president, was a crucial overseer of the project from start to finish and leads an extraordinary institution dedicated to generating precisely this sort of insight into American foreign policy and world affairs.

Gideon Rose
Editor, *Foreign Affairs*
April 2011

Made in the USA
Charleston, SC
14 July 2011